Celestial Music?

Some Masterpieces of European Religious Music

Celestial Music?

Some Masterpieces of European Religious Music

WILFRID MELLERS

THE BOYDELL PRESS

First published 2002
The Boydell Press, Woodbridge

ISBN 0 85115 844 7

The Boydell Press is an imprint of Boydell & Brewer Ltd
PO Box 9, Woodbridge, Suffolk IP12 3DF, UK
and of Boydell & Brewer Inc.
PO Box 41026, Rochester, NY 14604–4126, USA
website: www.boydell.co.uk

A catalogue record for this book is available
from the British Library

Library of Congress Cataloging-in-Publication Data
Mellers, Wilfrid Howard, 1914–
 Celestial music: some masterpieces of European religious music / Wilfrid
Mellers.
  p. cm.
 Includes bibliographical references (p.) and index.
 ISBN 0–85115–844–7 (alk. paper)
  1. Music – Religious aspects – Christianity.   2. Sacred vocal music –
Europe – Analysis, appreciation.   I. Title.
ML3865.M45   2002
781.71′0094–dc21   2001052557

Typeset by Joshua Associates Ltd, Oxford
Printed in Great Britain by
St Edmundsbury Press Ltd, Bury St Edmunds, Suffolk

Contents

To my priest-friend
Peter Hamilton,
in admiration and in gratitude
for many conversations about the nature of God,
knowable or unknowable

Foreword

This book, written in my eighty-seventh year and therefore likely to be my last, is a retrospect of material produced over a writing life of sixty or more years. It even borrows bits from my first book which, though published in 1945, was embarked on seven years previously, when I was still a student at Cambridge. More substantial material comes from my two volumes of a history of music called *Man and his Music*, published by Barrie & Rockliff in 1957, and several times reprinted in hardback and paperback. It was widely used as a text in schools, colleges, and universities over half a century, but is now out of print and unlikely to be salvaged. The chapter on Messiaen is adapted from one of my contributions to Faber's *Messiaen Companion*, while the section on Poulenc is adapted from my small book on this composer in Oxford University Press's Studies of Composers series. The section on Vaughan Williams is adapted from my book *Vaughan Williams and the Vision of Albion*, first published by Faber, but taken over by the Albion Press (the Vaughan Williams Trust). The chapter on Copland was first published, in a slightly different form, in the music-periodical *Tempo*. I am grateful to the various publishers for permission to use this material; and owe a special debt to the editors of *Choir and Organ* who initiated the project in commissioning the original versions of the pieces on Hildegard, Pérotin, Machaut, Dunstable, Dufay, Cornyshe, Tallis, Monteverdi, Bach, Berlioz, Beethoven, and Stravinsky.

J.S. Bach assembled his High and Solemn Mass, now usually inaccurately known as the Mass in B minor, from material he had composed in a variety of contexts over his productive working life. This book is an 'assemblage' in rather the same sense: which I hesitate to say since it makes my book seem a descent from the sublime into the ridiculous!

Note on the Musical Examples

Like many of my books, this one aims to describe in verbal terms the effects of musical events: a notoriously difficult assignment that involves problems both for authors and for readers, especially those who can 'read' music imperfectly, or not at all. Verbiage, however, may seem obfuscating if it has *no* musical documentation: so I have included a number of musical examples that he who runs may read. In the case of well-known works, such as Bach's B minor Mass, Handel's *Messiah*, and the Requiems of Mozart, Brahms, Verdi and Fauré, which most people likely to read the book will be familiar with, I have restricted these examples to a minimum, though it'll be helpful if the text is read with a score to hand, as a boost for memory. When dealing with what is now called Early Music, or with works of the twentieth century, I've been slightly more generous; but in all cases, familiar or unfamiliar, the book entails close relationships between the words of my text and the sounds of the music; so I hope that all readers, musically literate or not, will listen to the music in recorded form, in close contiguity with their reading of the book.

Prologue: What is religious music?

As I have said, the genesis of this book was in a commission I received to write five essays on 'Great Masterpieces of European Music' for the periodical *Choir and Organ*. The earliest piece I discussed was Monteverdi's *Vespers and Magnificat* of 1610: the others being Bach's Mass in B minor (1747), Beethoven's *Missa Solemnis* (1819–22), Berlioz's *Grande Messe des Morts* (1837), and Stravinsky's *Symphony of Psalms* (1930). Given the time at which I was writing (the 1990s) it wasn't, perhaps, surprising that none of the works I wrote of was created during the great ages of Christian faith; none the less, brooding over this matter, I decided to write a complementary series of essays dealing with the Christian era in its heyday, and the present book expands that notion to make a survey of religious music from around the first millennium to the beginning of the second. This led me to ask myself what religious music *is*, and, for that matter, what is religion?

Etymologically, religion is about *binding*, being initially a social construct and contract that binds people together in support of whatever authority may lead them. It can do this because it has another, complementary motivation: which is to provide not a rational but an emotionally assuaging answer to unanswered and probably unanswerable questions about the 'purpose' of life, the 'necessity' of evil, and the 'fact' of death. Palpably, religion's two aims are contradictory, for in binding ourselves to authority we are trying to console ourselves in being, or seeming to be, one with our neighbour: whereas those unanswered questions leave us ultimately alone, as we are at the moments of birth and death.

Music is often said to be the closest of the arts to religion since what we call its 'language' cannot be intellectually articulate; indeed, its very lack of articulacy may put us in touch with the numinous, and therefore presumably with the divine, or at least with the forces we call 'spiritual'. Although I am not myself a 'believer', I seem to be partial to religious music, I suspect because it asks, though it cannot answer, those eternally Unanswered Questions. For me, Bach and Beethoven are the two greatest of European composers since they are, in their different and even contradictory ways, religious: Bach in testifying to a faith that takes cognizance of both life and death and of good and evil; Beethoven in bravely asking the questions that are *beyond* answers – which is not quite the same as saying that they are unanswerable. Handel and Mozart – in my view the next 'greatest' duo in the hierarchy of European composers – are the supreme humanists of music: which is a fine thing to be since human beings are the 'highest' form of life we can know anything about at first hand. Still, there is a distinction; and Bach, who explored and affirmed a faith, and perhaps still more Beethoven, who discovered within himself an alternative to faith, are the composers I'd most hopefully turn to in need. Artists who are aware of the numinous, even if they don't know what it is, live on a plane of consciousness beyond the merely human; and since consciousness is what makes us human, it's even possible that numinous composers might be more humane than humanist composers!

Purists are apt to say that the only music that can be validly called religious is that which helps to activate devotional acts. Gregorian chant is the supreme Christian instance, and it is probably not fortuitous that it is usually anonymous, banning the intrusive ego. Byzantine, Greek, and Russian Orthodox Church musics likewise qualify in being usually anonymous and always religiously functional. But clearly it was not the intention of the editors of *Choir and Organ* that my essays should be confined to music that was in the strictest sense liturgical; rather they wanted, as did I as an author, an enquiry into some pieces of religious music that, over the centuries, have become immensely famous, bolstered by an enquiry into what their celebrity depends on. Is the 'religious' dimension crucial? Or is all music religious in that religiousness in music (I evade the word religiosity) simply means that the music is *good* because it embraces the heights and depths of human consciousness in ways that non-religious music doesn't? Clearly, not all religious music has any connection with a church (as the examples of Bach's *Art of Fugue* and Beethoven's late piano sonatas and string quartets prove). Nor is all music performed in churches necessarily religious in this fundamental sense; a few indubitably great works, such as the Requiems of Mozart and Verdi, are cases in point.

In arranging these essays more or less, though not quite, in chronological sequence I've inevitably presented the story as a process, or even progress, moving from Faith to Doubt. In moving from medieval monody and polyphony to Renaissance polyphony and homophony it's not so much a shift from faith to doubt as a transformation from a faith in 'spirit' to a celebration of flesh along with spirit, though the harmonically orientated polyphony of Byrd's later works does seem to me to involve a radical mutation which I call 'Shakespearean'. It's this dimension that leads, in Baroque works such as Monteverdi's *Vespers* and Schütz's *Matthew Passion*, Bach's B minor Mass, and perhaps Handel's *Messiah*, to an infiltration, and possibly a fusion, of the overtly dichotomous elements of Sacred and Profane. Although dichotomy need not obliterate faith, the nature of the faith is changing, since that of Handel's *Messiah*, and still more that of his

Old Testament oratorios, is ethically humane rather than religious. When Haydn's Roman Masses, and still more his quasi-Masonic oratorios, embrace ethical enlightenment unambiguously they cease to be devotional, at least in the sense promulgated in this book. Even Mozart's *Requiem* may be more a Masonic testament than a Roman rite; and Beethoven's *Missa Solemnis* – as I think the highest musical peak of religious transcendence – is, as a religions testament, unique. The masses of Schubert and Bruckner equivocate between faith and doubt in ways related to their technical equivocations between the old counterpoint and the new sonata: a compromise that for Schubert seems to have been regretfully nostalgic, though for Bruckner it was ultimately triumphal. Both Berlioz and Fauré were agnostics, yet the Requiems of both contain numinous music of vintage quality. The Requiems of Verdi and Brahms skirt numinosity in being testaments by human beings of opposed cultural backgrounds, faced with the fact of death, yet unafraid of its grisliness.

I'm not sure that Verdi's *Requiem*, great work though it is, ought to be in a book about religious music, though I feel no dubiety about Elgar's *The Dream of Gerontius*, which is more riddled by doubt than irradiated by faith; and I make out a case for considering Delius's *A Mass of Life*, made by a professed and vituperative atheist, as a *more* religious piece than Elgar's questing *Dream*. The ambiguities of Holst's *Hymn of Jesus*, Vaughan Williams's *Sancta Civitas*, and Howells's *Hymnus Paradisi* are basic to their Christian testaments, 'globally' theological in Holst, mystical–political in Vaughan Williams, Anglican and intimately personal in Howells. Britten's *War Requiem* sets the seal on this fusion of mystical, social, political, and personal issues, testifying simultaneously to Church and State and to the inner lives of individual human creatures, including himself, the poet Wilfred Owen, and you and me. That is why its place in history is crucial.

I call the last part of this book the Ancient Law and the Modern Mind because it is preoccupied with the ways in which very ancient religious lores and laws have been re-experienced, and sometimes re-created, in the light and dark of modern minds. In Janáček's awesome *Glagolitic Mass* we find a 'primitive' sacrament re-enacted, in an obsolete (ancient Czech) language, with an energy that makes it urgently 'contemporary' music; while in Messiaen we find a totally committed man of the Old Roman Faith who expands traditional liturgy in a pluralistic global context that mates Rome with ancient India, and even with Latin American Equador and Peru. Two radically different White Russian composers – Rachmaninov and Stravinsky – indicate how ancient liturgical ritual and modern concert music may find a *rapprochement*: Rachmaninov because he, an eclectic art-composer in late nineteenth-century Romantic tradition, found a spontaneous outlet – at the time when he was migrating from his native land, and even from Europe, to the New World – in a very old liturgy that he loved but did not believe in; and Stravinsky because in his concert music he increasingly called on liturgical conventions and serial techniques in seeking an aloofness from the lacerations of personal experience such as the 'human machine' of his music wished to bypass. One might almost say that ultimately Stravinsky identified Art *with* Religion.

The penultimate chapter, on Arvo Pärt's St John Passion, reverses this Stravinskian process in identifying Religion with Art, since the piece unequivocally reinstates ecclesiastical ritual, formalized with allegorical exactitude, in place of the concert hall, believing that a church is more likely to foster a future for music than a secular institution. This may be true for those who belong to a church but not for the multitudes who don't; and Pärt doesn't prohibit the performance of even his most 'doctrinal' works in concert conditions, any more than does John Tavener, our own holy minimalist who over the last ten years has, somewhat to his own astonishment, achieved a success of fabulous proportions.

Even so, the fact that this book seems at its end to have returned to its starting-point doesn't mean that history is circular, and that the whole process is happening over again. The existence of Jewry within the European context makes a difference, and this book was intended to incorporate a sixth part dealing with the Maximalism of Schoenberg (in *Verklärte Nacht*, *Erwartung* and *Moses und Aron*), and his search for a renewed synthesis of Word and Flesh; and with the Minimalism of Steve Reich, who sought the same end by an opposite path. Since, however, these two essays have recently been published in another book of mine called *Singing in the Wilderness**, I've decided that this book should proceed, from the point at which it appears to have returned to its starting-point, to a final chapter: the point of which is to indicate that, although phenomena like the musics of Pärt and Tavener are a not discountable strand in the story of music today, they are not its *central* tradition. The composer featured in this final chapter is not a Viennese Jew, like Schoenberg, nor an American Jew of Russian extraction like Reich, but Aaron Copland: another American Jew of Russian extraction who, almost single-handed, *invented* an American musical vernacular. Although Copland composed only one quite small work – the choral *In the Beginning* – that might be called religious in having a biblical text, he did, at the height of his powers in 1950, make a plainly American cycle of settings of poems by Emily Dickinson with themes that, touching on life and death, time and eternity, are almost independent of specific social and religious context. Between them, a hermetic private poet of nineteenth-century New England and a twentieth-century composer of metropolitan, multi-ethnic New York reveal the *bare bones* of what had happened to faith and doubt over the twentieth century. Copland's Emily Dickinson songs bring us home to common humanity in a New World that evolved from an Old World, speaking to us in intimately personal terms

---

* University of Illinois Press, 2000.

perhaps deeper, and certainly wider, than those overtly linked to Church and State. That feels to me 'on the mark', as I type this Prologue on 1 December 2000, in the ancient city of York.

Part I:
The Ages of Christian Faith

1

The Meanings of Monody

Oneness in Hildegard of Bingen's
Symphonia armonie celestium revelationum

For most people the origin of life is a sound: it was God's hum, croak, gibber, laugh or chuckle that stirred creation within the void. Why primitive peoples should believe this may be latent in the cry of the new-born babe who, separated from the mother as it struggles into an alien world, yells to be again part of Nature, mother of all creation. Physical factors are linked to mathematical laws in that the mathematical principles on which sound operates are a microcosm of those that control the universe: music springs simultaneously from our emotional instincts and from the extra-sensory harmony that we are all subject to, since, in Sir Thomas Browne's phrase, it 'Intellectually sounds in the Ears of God'.

With the great oriental cultures – Indian, Asian, Chinese – the purpose of most music is religious in that it seems to release people from the burden of consciousness and from the contagion of the world. Christian Europe in its heyday accepted this musical legacy, though in the West a dichotomy emerged between music for worship and the act of dance. Of course, medieval Christians danced, like every other people; but they regarded dance as suspect in being, like life itself, ephemeral. This mistrust became patent when Western man tried to preserve his artefacts in notation. 'Worldly' dance music was seldom thus perpetuated: whereas 'heavenly' ecclesiastical chant became a somewhat inadequately written, as well as aurally transmitted, law, springing from the sacred word. In the mono-phonic chants of Greek and Roman antiquity, in those of ancient oriental civilizations, in the cantillations of the Coptic, Greek, Russian, Byzantine, Roman and Anglican churches the participants renew themselves in con-sciously thanking God for the gift of consciousness. The word *incantare* means to enchant; and in Christian Europe no less than in distant Tibet the chant was sung in a hieratic language, remote from ordinary usage but appropriate to the mysteries of Church, Law, and State. Moreover, in that language pre-articulate vocables – *Alleluya, Selah, Hosanna*, and so on – persist along with the language of consciousness. The seventeenth-century theologian Jacob Boehme called them 'the sensual speech': a music of the vowels in which, at the Second Coming, all creatures would speak with one accord.

The magical character of religious cantillation is inseparable from its purely melodic and rhythmic nature. A single melodic line tends to be independent of metrical stress, moving in irregular rhythms that come as the wind listeth, often associated with the declaimed word. The monody of Byzantine chant, in descent from Greek monody, absorbed elements of oriental cantillation by way of Judaic synagogue music. In Gregorian chant itself the heart of the line is the modal patterns that, almost as 'natural' as breathing, become, like the *raga* of classical Indian music, a fount of creation. To compose is to embellish the formulae with ornament, culminating in 'jubilations' that are instances of Boehme's sensual speech. For the medieval monk, dedicated to his Christianized *rāg*, to sing was to free the spirit as the line, moving mainly by step, the pentatonic minor third, and the godly intervals of fifth and fourth, effaced metrical time and the no more than latent pull of harmonic tensions, the 'superhuman' effect being enhanced by the nasal vocal production and by the vaulted church's echoes. So, by derationalizing the words and by evading temporal progression and overtly expressive accents, the ritualized chant became the Voice of God, perhaps.

As an example of medieval Christian monody I choose, however, not an excerpt from Gregorian liturgy, but a rare example from a woman composer with a defined identity, moulded by the matriarchal cultures that preceded our much-vaunted patriarchy. The Abbess Hildegard of Bingen has only comparatively recently been restored to her once-fabulous fame, partly through the advance of feminism and partly by way of the popularity of New Age mythologies such as have burgeoned in reaction to the crass materialism of industrial technocracy. Born in Rheinhessen in 1098, she was by the mid-twelfth century internationally celebrated as visionary, naturalist, healer, playwright, poet, and composer; in her own time she was known as 'the Sybil of the Rhine', and acted as adviser to several popes. Her formidable charisma must have been dependent on her extraordinary talents; and although, through the ages, a few niggardly men have tried to discredit the purity of her Latin and the rigour of her science, her vindication lies in her published works, which she herself assembled in the monumental *Symphonia armonie celestium revelationum*. The title stresses the significance of her arts as revelation, rather than as expression and communication, though she is Orphic in the multifariousness of her gifts, embracing most that was then known of the visible and invisible world, versified in Latin which, if occasionally 'incorrect', is true poetry, drawing on traditional sacred texts while being imbued with personal identity. These verses she alchemized into music simply by singing them, probably at first without notated form: which later became an aid to memory, albeit incomplete and often inaccurate. In the convoluting flow of this monody, passion is sublimated into air-borne melody wherein power and pathos co-exist: not so much elevating the human to the divine as revealing the interdependence of physical and metaphysical worlds.

There is something deeply moving, and psychologically as well as theologically revelatory, in the fact that the visionary art of a woman – a creature regarded by monkish medieval man as ancillary to the devil – should thus sublimely consummate the melodic essence of the Middle Ages. It would seem that there was always both ambiguity and dubiety in the unblinking acceptance of male superiority: for the celibate Catholic priesthood woman was indeed flesh, sin, and damnation; yet in being a creature of instinct, woman was also an Orphic agent of the numinous and a gateway to the spiritual world. In a justly famous phrase Hildegard described herself as 'a feather on the breath of God'; as a magic angel and agent she plumbs the heart of the human paradox, prefiguring the New Birth that will become the Re-naissance.

Although Hildegard was and is so potent a presence, we have to face the fact that she lived a long time ago: so that we do not know a great deal about how her music was performed, and how it sounded when sung in her (male and female) monastery, operated under Benedictine rule, at Rupertsburg on the Rhine. The pitches can be accurately interpreted, but the rhythms must be guess-work; and it is in the rhythms that the quasi-divine afflatus is most perceptible. Given the current popularity of Hildegard's music among a surprisingly wide cross-section of people, there are now many recordings of her work available and, due to the inadequacy of our knowledge about performance-practice, it is inevitable that the recorded 'interpretations' should be startlingly disparate; I'll take examples from two of them which, although not necessarily the 'best', indicate how radically opposed readings may be equally impressive. The first CD comes from Sequentia, a group of (young or youngish) women singers directed on this recording by the late Barbara Thornton. The disc in question is called *Canticles of Ecstasy*, and centres around hymns, psalms, and antiphons addressed to the Virgin Mary, the Mother of God, as Hildegard was a goddess-mother to her flock. The voices are sometimes supported by drones played on a stringed instrument, signifying eternity, and occasionally by ritornelli, played monodically, also on strings. The instrumental intrusions are highly effective, though some scholars dispute their authenticity.

These versions, sung by youthful voices, stress the humanity of the chants and the sense of wonder generated by the verse, which presents the Virgin as *mediatrix* between God and us: as a *pulcher flos* which uses its phrygian (E) mode with sensitive awareness of its 'closed' minor second's ability to flower into ecstatic release; or as a *viridissima virgo* who shines in the 'open' mixolydian mode on G:

De - in - de fa - cta est e - sca ho - mi - ni - bus et gau - di - um

mag - num e - pu - lan - ti - um. Un - de o sua - vis Vir - go.

These performances genuinely induce rapture; while musically the rhapsodic style of Hildegard's verse sometimes impels her – though she had no pretensions to being a radical – to subvert conventional modal practice, as favoured by the Cistercians. The precise disposition of the tones and semitones in the church modes conditions their effect in an act that is at once divine (because presumed to be within prescribed Law) and human (because the Law may be modified in the ardency of the moment). This equilibrium between law and instinct is typical of these Sequentia performances which will appeal, I suspect, to youngish New Age types who are searching for, and here finding, spiritual rejuvenation.

My other example is a recording by Marcel Pérès Ensemble Organum of the *Laudes* of St Ursula, a possibly legendary saint whom Hildegard identified with, making many cantillations to her honour. Ursula's dolorous story tickled the popular imagination when bones were discovered, during the twelfth century, in a burial ground in Cologne. These remains were believed to be those of a nobly-born adolescent girl, murdered with ten other playmates. The tale so haunted the popular imagination that, over the years, the number of martyred maidens swelled from 11 to 11,000! Assaulted by the barbarous Huns, the girls died defending their chastity, the sacred invulnerability of which was a necessary step towards Christian purgation of the savagery of the Dark Ages – though they are called dark mostly because we know so little about them.

Marcel Pérès is a scholar who has made some of the most convincing resuscitations of very early music that we have; and here he presents – makes present – Hildegard's music within the aesthetic and liturgical context of twelfth-century Rhineland. It seems that he doesn't think that twelfth-century Rhineland was much like Barbara Thornton's view of it: for the 'green-ness' of Thornton's reading is remote from the austere blackness of Pérès's – and he offers some historical evidence for the use of chest registers and other brown or black rather than green sonorities. Yet both versions seem to me to contain a truth about this marvel-making music: Thornton's versions reanimate the sounds of a New Birth, which was surely the main miracle the work was about; while Pérès's version gives us a probably more accurate notion of how the music sounded and functioned, in Hildegard's ancient abbey, stressing the grim tale's tragic dimension. Do we trust the wisdom of the Sybil of the Rhine, or the presumptive innocence of many of her young charges? Both, surely, are trust*worthy*; and I quote the antiphon *Deus enim rorem*: in which we may note Hildegard's use of contrasted registers, initially launched by God's perfect fifth, soaring from its phrygian E to the upper octave, countered by the second clause's declension through the minor second, only to be radiantly released in the fifth clause's flight to high G. The tragic dimension lies in the final clause's descent through the minor second, F to E: which sounds lower, heavier, more remorseless, after the previous winged ascent.

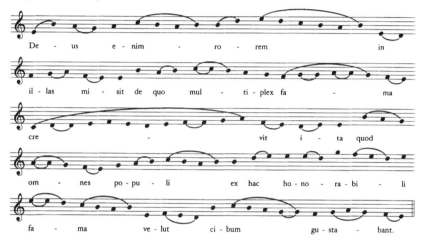

Paradoxically, the very difference between Thornton's and Pérès's 'interpretations' of similar texts helps us to understand why the music, after so many centuries, still seems meaningful to us. Thornton's verdantly flowing *melismata* reawaken ecstasy and the promise of spring, restoring the healing power that the Abbess believed her therapeutic music possessed; Pérès's darker tones and severely liturgical formulation emphasize the discipline of suffering which is the pre-condition of renewal. The two experiences, however disparate, are complementary, and equally 'true'. This is why the rediscovery of Hildegard's music has revealed that it is in no way alien to us, and not even very remote from us.

Note: The two recordings referred to are:
Hildegard of Bingen: *Canticles of Ecstasy*, performed by Sequentia, directed by Barbara Thornton, Harmonic Mundi 05472 773207; Hildegard of Bingen: *Laudes de Sainte Ursule*, performed by Ensemble Organum, directed by Marcel Pérès, Harmonia Mundi 290893. The scores are published by Hildegard Publishing Co., Bryn Mawr, Pennsylvania, USA.
The scores as quoted here give only the pitch of the notes, with no

indication of rhythmic contours: so the performers, like Hildegard herself, have to allow the melodies to grow and flow from the words, expanding the *melismata* as instinct suggests. A contemporary chronicler reports that she was deeply moved by overhearing the Abbess singing her verse into audible life, as she wandered in the cloisters.

2

The Meanings of Polyphony

Many-in-oneness in Pérotin's *Viderunt omnes* and *Sederunt principes*

In the first chapter I explored the 'meanings' of medieval monody as exemplified in the *Symphonia armonie celestium revelationum* of Hildegard of Bingen. The main meaning lies in the fact that there is only one melodic line, springing from formulae inherent in Nature's acoustics and especially in the human voice: which means that melody germinates from pentatonic patterns, modified by effects of pitch distortion, vibrato and portamento, along with conscious embellishments, all introducing a quasi-oriental awe, and perhaps exoticism, into Christian holiness. Yet paradox is rampant, since 'consciousness' brings duality even into ostensibly monophonic music: as is patent when medieval monks (or nuns) cantillate not in pure monody but in monody that soars over drones that, representing eternity, serve as backcloth to our brief lives. As it floats above the 'everlasting' drone, the single line inevitably creates alternating degrees of tension between the intervals formed by the melody line and the drone, thereby making incipient harmony wherein two different pitches coincide in differing vibration ratios. Such accidents must have occurred in both 'primitive' and in ancient oriental chant: the difference being that whereas those musicians were undisturbed by such harmonic fortuities – Peter Crossley-Holland, on the evidence of chants surviving in remote Tibet, has suggested that the musicians didn't even notice them! – European Christians found them fascinating to the point of obsession.

The reasons for this are psychological and theological as well as musical. Christianity, being a religion that stressed God's incarnation in man, and complementarily man's Fall from God, was potently responsive to *guilt*, and so needed the contrarieties of a music that carried harmonic dualities. Although the great oriental religions have always admitted to the dualities

9

of light–dark, hot–cold, good–evil, self–not self, they at the same time made the evasion of the moral implications of duality the heart of their philosophy and ritual. Fulfilment could not be through conflict, only through its relinquishment in a fusion of the Many in the One. Although 'primitive' peoples must have been aware of the simultaneous sounding of differing pitches, they were neither philosophically nor psychologically interested in exploiting them. The Christian God, however, in himself becoming Man, encouraged human beings to think of our earthly life as a pilgrimage from guilt to redemption and salvation. The Christian symbol of the Cross is itself a duality, opposing the vertical to the diagonally horizontal, as compared with the circular eternity-symbols of Eastern religions. The notion of a pilgrimage implies that Time matters whereas, to religions centred on eternity, time is illusory. This is why the first great revolution in European music – the transition from monody to polyphony – began, though its consequences were eventually harmonic, as rhythmic and mensural innovation.

Pérotin, the most illustrious composer associated with this revolution (which happened only in the occident, not the orient), is usually bracketed with Léonin, who may have been his teacher. Between them, they are said to have invented, or at least evolved, polyphony around the turn from the twelfth into the thirteenth century. They are often referred to, along with other mainly anonymous composers, as the 'School of Notre Dame', though there is no firm evidence that they ever officiated at the great cathedral, only that the *Magnus Liber* of chants compiled by Léonin was for some time in the cathedral's keeping. Although the book does not survive, we have a fair idea of its contents, which consisted of notated plainchants, many with an added, composed, part appropriately known as a *duplum*. This was in one or another of the church modes, each of which – as noted in the previous chapter – had a different disposition of the tones and semitones contained within the octave: and therefore had, unlike our equal-tempered major and minor scales, a distinct emotional and acoustical character. The modes were basically diatonic, though they admitted the occasional chromatic note – most commonly B flat or F sharp, to 'correct' the imperfection of the devilish tritone, F to B natural.

There were two main types of the new polyphony. One, called *organum*, presented the plain chant in relatively long notes, so that its verbal message, if sung, was barely comprehensible, though this didn't matter since its function was talismatic, signifying sacred import beyond any humanly ephemeral intelligibility. Over and through the Firm Song of the plain chant, the *duplum* ranged freely, often with an independent, especially composed text that was also unlikely to be intelligible, since it made no attempt at synchronicity with the cantus firmus. The other style, called *conductus* because it was originally processional, was sung by two or three singers 'in process'. Their parts, if they were to keep together, had to be mensurated, usually note for note; and the metrical patterns of this mensuration were highly stylized and even allegorized, being grouped in (trinitarian?) triplet figurations in what came to be called rhythmic 'modes', comprising the sundry possible arrangements of longs and shorts, notably dactyls, iambics, anapests and spondees. Together, the linear and metrical modes served functions similar to those of the *rāg* and *tāl* in classical Indian music, being not so much a linear scale or a metrical formula as a continuum within which, or even a group of religions and/or social postulates according to which, we may conduct our lives.

Léonin, who compiled the *Magnus Liber*, was a shadowy figure whom some doubting Thomases have even dubbed 'legendary'. But Pérotin, who indubitably revised, extended, and in some cases curtailed, the *Liber* was honoured by scribes – especially the Malmesbury monk known as Anonymous IV – who fêted him for his inspirational musical accomplishments. It was Pérotin who, in adding a *triplum* to the *duplum*, dazzlingly enhanced the excitement of polyphonic enterprise. The lilting triple pulse – which in addition to trinitarian associations has a more basically physical source in the spontaneous in–hold–out process of breathing and therefore staying alive – functions corporeally, since what we might call a $\frac{3}{8}$ 'unit' may be heard as two measures making $\frac{6}{8}$, or four measures making $\frac{12}{8}$, with an engagingly lilting lollop. This accentual feeling has as yet no harmonic implications. The only 'real' harmonies are God's 'absolute' consonances of fifth and fourth, such literally 'passing' dissonances as occur being arbitrary consequences of the linear flow and its melismatic embellishments. Despite his physical pulse, Pérotin mutates bodily energy into spiritual levitation, perhaps with even more elevating effect, given its corporeal dimensions, than that displayed by Hildegard when she 'takes off' in her monodic cantillation. Modern theory tells us that we can *know* nothing about *their* responses to an art-work *then and there*, as compared with our responses *here and now*; even so, human beings retain, over vast reaches of time and place, elements in common, and even if we can't finally know, we may feel and think, to the best of our abilities. From some such exercise I come up feeling and thinking that whereas Hildegard's poetry and music involve and/or create an aspiration towards Godhead that is singularly pure and embraces the tragic sense, Pérotin's lilting polyphony involves and/or creates the purity of a child-like innocence that one might think of as paradisal.

As one might expect, this paradisal quality is especially evident in the whirligig tropes on vocables like Alleluya. A fascinating example is the 'Alleluya nativitatis', which has an anonymous Latin text that charmingly pays homage to the Virgin who, by way of an Easter-Egg, a Christ-Fish, and some Bread-Life, steers us to salvation through the manifest contagions of World, Flesh, and Devil. Unsurprisingly, the journey proves tricky, for the *duplum* and *triplum* are nervously skittish and often syncopated; and

11

syncopation, of its nature, *plays tricks* with the temporal dimension we live in. It also here emulates the 'Fire' which the Virgin is said to have lit: so the passing dissonances make for a music that corybantically over-rides, rather than ex-presses, our individual identities:

Here the fortuitous dissonances – especially the tritonal Fs to B natural that flicker around the lowest part's cantus firmus – let in the 'dirt' as do the pitch distortions in classical Indian music, and startlingly anticipate effects in improvised African-American jazz, especially in its 1950s and 1960s manifestations when artists such as John Coltrane and Ornette Coleman mated African with Indian polymodalities and polymetres. It's also interesting that Steve Reich, father of today's minimalists, counts Pérotin as an influence on his work, along with the multi-modal and multi-metrical musics of Africa, Asia, India, and Bali, in most of which cultures he has lived, studying their musics 'in the field'. Another early minimalist, Terry Riley, who found fame in the early 1960s with his still-enduring *In C*, has attained, during the 1980s and 1990s, in mainly improvised piano music, a comparably Pérotin-like festive exuberance, seeking identification with both God and Tribe, who and which are greater than our puny selves. I noted in the previous chapter how Hildegard's monodies found a ready response in New Age 'seekers'; the parallels I've drawn between, on the one hand, Pérotin and on the other hand Reich and Riley, suggest that thirteenth-century polyphony is also seen or rather heard as vividly relevant to those today who think that the Western obsession with Will, Ego and Progress has gone too far. I hope, however, that we'll never get to the point of claiming that Europe would be *better* without Shakespeare and Beethoven! If Pérotin's polyphony may validly be allied to the notion of paradise, it also reminds us that paradise was a place, or a condition, from which we had to *fall*.

Pérotin's masterpieces are usually reckoned to be his biggest works – the two four-part pieces, *Viderunt omnes* and *Sederunt principes* – and homage is due to what are probably the first four-part compositions ever created. The description is, however, a shade generous, since the active parts are three – the plainchant base, a *duplum* and *triplum* composed in a sanctioned mode both linear and metrical, usually to a different if doctrinally related text: while the fourth part is intermittent, sometimes moving metrically, but more commonly fragmented or drone-like. In any case each part is an entity that could be sung alone as a monody, though as an extra adornment of the cantus firmus's Word it creates an excitation that unwittingly promises a new dawn: that of the Renaissance, which was indeed a spiritual, and in some cases a physical, rebirth.

Viderunt omnes is a Gradual interlacing solo verses with choric responses, on the old analogy of Priest and Choir; the brief text simply announces that since God has arrived in all corners of the earth, salvation will follow, and justice be briskly administered. The words don't ask for any evidence of this, and the music blithely bounces in its jolly racket, with voices chanting and limbs cavorting in triplet convolutions. Listen to this in the performance by the Hilliard Ensemble, who have devoted much scholarly research to matters of performance practice, especially the arcane problems of *musica ficta*, tuning, and intonation, all of which are not merely technical, but also 'philosophical' or at least theological, problems. Equal temperament is alien to this music; the Hilliards favour various compromises between Pythagorean and mean-tone tunings, and explain the principles they followed in the booklet that goes with the CD they recorded in 1996 for their *Hilliard Live* series.* Their performance is austere in that they admit no instrumental intrusions, even in the drones, which some think should be sustained on a stringed instrument or portative organ, rather than by 'staggered' voices. But their approach to the bouncing rhythms, open sonorities, and passing dissonances is dizzily audacious, especially when they relish the incipient canons that occur (again perhaps fortuitously) when a beat's silence disrupts the on-going patterns. Normally, that the patterns continue 'regardless' is the point, for they bear us through the many calamities (oddly known as Acts of God) likely to assail a medieval community – though the diurnal calamities that threaten *us* on the roads and streets, not to mention the calamities accruing from such other modern threats as nuclear fission, excel quantitatively, if not qualitatively, those characteristic of the medieval world.

A notated score cannot reveal much; but here's a passage that suggests how this music's merry hubbub resembles a tintinnabulation of bells, with their clashing overtones, rather than a music that is harmonically 'functional' in the modern sense:

---

* *Hilliard Live I: Pérotin and Ars Antiqua* HL 101. It is pertinent to note that the first (anonymous) chant on this CD, 'Vetus abit littera', celebrates the fact that 'the Old Law passes away, the rites of the Ancients have gone, a Virgin in childbirth gives us a New Son'.

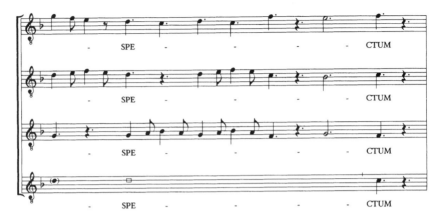

When we reach the chapter of this book on Arvo Pärt's *Passio Domini nostri Jesu Christi secumdum Joannem* we'll see that he, in 1982, reintroduced a technique similar to Pérotin's, and, interestingly, named it 'tintinnabulation'. Possibly the effect of pealing bells was intended by the Church to simulate the eternal moments of Paradise, with no before or after; if so, this may explain why pealing bells induce in many folk (including me) an indefinable melancholy! Fallen creatures find it difficult to encompass a return to Eden.

The other four-part piece, *Sederunt principes*, is still more expansive and ecstatic, though (or perhaps because) the text is still briefer, merely asking God to save us, and to 'cast down' anyone who might 'deal wickedly' with us. But if the music is more exalted, it is also more agitated, more wobbly in its *musica ficta* (which sports some unusual E flats), and more jazzy in its rhythms, as in this tipsy passage at the end, wherein the regularity of the plainchant *cantus firmus* in the lowest voice seems only to stimulate the vivacity of the upper parts:

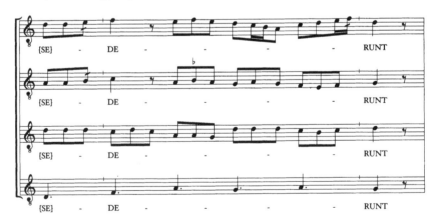

14

Here the Hilliard's tuning enhances the zany, even manic, effect, though of course we cannot be sure that that is how Pérotin's congregation heard the sounds, any more than we can know for certain whether Hildegard of Bingen's cantillation sounded seraphically sweet (like Sequentia) or alarmingly super-natural (like Ensemble Organum). On the whole, I find the Hilliard's performance of Pérotin convincing as well as impressive. In some ways their 'interpretation' is highly sophisticated; in other ways it generates a naïvety almost as wide-eyed and open-eared as is some Third World African polyphony of the present day, some 800 years after Pérotin. This makes sense, for there are genuine parallels between Pérotin's Ars Antiqua, 'invented' at that most crucial of transitions between an Age of Faith and an Age of Reason and Science, and some of the musics now being forged on the brink of our electronic age in the New Millennium. It wouldn't, after all, be surprising if we experienced frissons of fright, mingled with hazardous hope, in ways not entirely dissimilar from those experienced by medieval folk as they desperately danced, or fearfully tottered, into the bewildering re-birth of the Renaissance, which eventually produced *us*. Indeed, Pérotin's *Sederunt principes* sounds as though it is currently *being born*, in the light and heat of the moment: as in a sense it is, since sundry extant notations, by partly improvising solo performers, offer several alternative versions. The idea of a 'given' score was still embryonic: which may be why we find the music so enlivening, as incorrigibly simple-minded as it is single-hearted.

3

The Antique and the Novel in Ars Antiqua and Ars Nova

Machaut's *Messe de Notre Dame* and *Le Lai de la Fontaine*

It wasn't all that long before the art of Pérotin, that radical innovator, was designated as Ars Antiqua, to distinguish it from the Ars Nova that had evolved from an attempt to face up to the implications of polyphony – the several-(if not many)-voiced, music now viewed 'vertically' in harmonic, as well as 'horizontally' in linear and mensural, terms. Looking back, we may say that Pérotin's or whomever's invention of polyphony was an accident comparable, in musical terms, with the Christian notion of a Fall from grace – grace being the musical equivalent to 'just', as distinguished from 'tempered', intonation. We'll understand what this means if we reflect on two fortuitous events that we will all have experienced when indulging in 'community singing'.

The first of these is that, while everyone thinks that he or she is singing at the same pitch, some singers adapt the melody to a pitch convenient to their own voices by singing a fifth above or a fourth below the main body of singers without realizing – so 'absolute' is the hold of the consonances of the fourth and fifth – that they are not singing at the same pitch. Such parallel consonances of fifth and fourth are unconscious examples of *organum*: which probably began fortuitously among 'primitive' peoples and in the early medieval church, but was later deliberately exploited, since the sound was awe-ful. Once the duplication of tones at different pitches had been accepted, it was only a matter of time – a *crucial* factor – before the parts would sometimes move, at first by chance, later by design, in contrary as well as parallel motion: so that intervals more acoustically complicated than fourths and fifths would become familiar, and a compositional principle

16

based on alternating degrees of harmonic tension and relaxation would be feasible, if not immediately necessary.

Another accident that occurs in primitive community singing reinforces this awareness of dualism: the singers, intending to utter the same tone simultaneously, may not succeed; and their 'wrong' notes will then create fortuitous harmonies as likely, or more likely, to be dissonant as consonant. Before long, however, such 'heterophonic' effects (on the analogy of the word 'heterogeneous') will be used to artistic purpose, the more skilful singers being encouraged to improvise embellishments around the melody as chanted by the main group. Medieval polyphony, as practised by Pérotin, evolved from these two principles of organum and heterophony, both devices being intended not as a denial, but as an enrichment, of monodic principle. Pérotin's music still flourished in a state somewhere between improvisation and a notated text – which explains why his music generates so lively a sense of the *process* of birth. But the more potently the techniques of polyphony – the notion of several distinct parts sung simultaneously – intruded, the more complicated the problems of mensuration became, and the more essential were relatively sophisticated types of notation. At the end of the Middle Ages we may detect this change in the work of Guillaume de Machaut, who lived from around 1300 to 1377, and was simultaneously a priest–composer of the Church at Rheims Cathedral, a troubadour–poet of the Court, and a diplomat–warrior of the State. It is significant that, whereas we know nothing about Pérotin apart from his music, Machaut has an impressive identity as an ecclesiastical, social, and political superman appropriate to, if not all that familiar in, the authoritarian establishments of the late Middle Ages and of the early Renaissance.

None of these roles has, as yet, much to do with our post-Renaissance notion of art as expression and communication. There is no 'I' attempting to contact a You or a Them; the artist is still a medium through whom or which an act of revelation may occur. The difference lies in the fact that Machaut was a much celebrated poet as well as a composer; words were his trade, and although the words he employed were stylized and ritualized, they had communicable meanings which, in his secular as distinct from his sacred work, increasingly affected his music. We can see this if we compare his most illustrious 'sacred' work, the *Messe de Notre Dame*, with almost any of his secular poems-with-music, especially *Le Lai de la Fontaine*, which is explicitly 'about' the metaphysical sanction of the physical. In the *Messe de Notre Dame*, however, Machaut as musician still has little concern with evolution, let alone development, in time; supremely a functionalist, he would lose the self rather than find it, and repetition is a means towards this relinquishment. The verbal content of the Mass has been effaced by centuries of repetition; repetition involves counting, and the permutations of number have magical associations. This was evident in the sophisticated oriental cultures; in classical Indian music *rāga* are not scales but pre-ordained pitch relationships which, in accord with the emotive properties of intervals, stemmed from the behaviour of the human voice. Similarly, *tāla* are pre-ordained metrical patterns that are permutations of mathematical law; and both *rāga* and *tāla* were believed to have cosmological significance.

Comparable notions underlie ancient Chinese and Arabian musics, whose practitioners were often noted for their mathematical skills. Similarly, ancient Greek music was inseparable from the Pythagorean science of numbers, the mathematical laws of harmony being themselves an aspect of a total cosmology. Something of this survived into Christian Europe, the metrical 'modes' of troubadour song being possibly related (by way of the Crusades) to Arabian permutation-theories, as well as to Greek and Latin prosody. According to Pythagoras, 'there is a mysterious connection between gods and numbers, on which the science of Arithmacy is based'. Only those tones which are numerically determined according to the harmonic series are music, the others being noise. Moreover, the harmonic spectrum parallels the movements of astral bodies: in which sense the Pythagorean aphorism that 'all is number' came to imply the Platonic doctrine of transcendent Ideas, and was so interpreted by the Church Fathers from Aquinas to Duns Scotus.

Given the putative link between mathematics, astronomy, and theology, it is logical that the structure of a Machaut motet should be related not so much to verbal meaning, as to the architecture of a Gothic cathedral. The main structure of such a building is a feat of mathematical engineering, however intuitively arrived at: to which individual craftsmen add their individualized contributions. Similarly, a medieval motet is built on the Rock of the plainsong *cantus firmus*, the other parts being added separately, each as an independent entity meaningful in itself, but more meaningful in relation to the whole. The linear–mathematical principles of Machaut's formidable *Messe de Notre Dame* have affinities with the Indian technique of the *rāg*, while its device of isochronous rhythm – whereby a metrical sequence remains constant throughout though the pitches change – is comparable with the Indian *tāl*, especially since the metrical patterns are usually complex and asymmetrical, and often have religious import. Harmonic contrarieties sometimes occur, but harmonic progression is never 'functional' in the post-Renaissance sense.

We may rather compare the dissonant effects that occasionally happen to those of the gargoyles in a Gothic cathedral. Since we now know that Machaut's Mass was intended for the Feast of Purification of the Virgin Mary and for the dedication, in 1364, of a new lady-chapel in Rheims Cathedral, we can have little doubt as to its potentially beneficent effects as an agent for the defusing of sexuality. Yet at the same time as those arbitrary dissonances assailed the ears and those gargoyles leered down from the walls, reminding people of human folly, sin, and damnation, so, simultaneously, were folk encouraged to transcend such horrors as eyes were lifted heavenwards by the building's soaring contours, and as ears were purged by the god-like reiteration of the absolute consonances of fifth and fourth, by the austere sonorities, and probably by the supernal reverberation of bells – that heaven-derived and possibly heaven-directed 'tintinnabulation'. The almost painfully severe effect of the recurrent 'Landini' cadences – named after the blind composer who did not invent them but rejoiced in them – emphasizes this fusion of holy awe with human fortitude, as both tonic and dominant are approached from the sharpened seventh and fourth below:

If, as some authorities maintain, the lines were played on or doubled by instruments, and sometimes supported by instrumental drones, the Byzantine splendour of this music would be intensified. Current scholarship, however, discredits the use of instruments: as is evident on the alternative recordings cited. The performance by Ensemble Organum, although instrumentless, confesses to a measure of terror (the 'Gothic desperation'), while the Hilliard's version, if less alarming, is stark rather than affirmative.* In Pérotin's day both gargoyles and things of beauty – angels, saints, mothers-with-child – were distractions that must be sublimated into a holy whole. By Machaut's day, sublimation has become more difficult, the gargoyles more sinisterly insidious, the things of beauty (especially those mothers-with-child) more deceptively alluring. This may be why the jittery metrical patterns in Machaut's Mass sometimes seem to our ears grotesque, especially when they're dislocated by the technique known as *hoquet* (meaning hiccup), whereby tones in a preordained sequence may drop out, leaving a gap like a gargoyle's missing tooth. Here's an example from, significantly, the Sanctus, which celebrates the Holy of Holies:

---

* Guillaume de Machaut: *Messe de Notre Dame*; *Le Lai de la Fontaine*: the Hilliard Ensemble, directed by Paul Hilliard. Hyperion CDA66358.

Guillaume de Machaut: *Messe de Notre Dame*: Ensemble Organum, directed by Marcel Pérès. Harmonia Mundi HMX 290891.

In the monodic section of *Le Lai de la Fontaine* the score is notated in the alto clef, sounding a seventh lower; in the polyphonic canon the score is notated in the soprano clef, sounding a minor third lower.

In late Gothic polyphony metrical intricacy was sometimes carried to such extravagant lengths that one scarcely knows whether the concourse of voices is held together by mathematical science or theological dogma, or by black magic rather than white.

Similar effects occur even in the narrative sections of the Credo which, in telling a story, veers slightly towards Renaissance expressivity. The metaphysical (divine?) dimension is audible in a seraphic passage in which the Virgin's Sacred Name is intoned in hugely slow concords, 'larger than life', outside Time – though according to Pérès's version these concords were intensified by a variety of scary wobbles, quaverings, and distonations (the Hilliards sing these concords 'straight', so one may take one's choice):

The physical (human) dimension is, on the other hand, painfully potent in the concatenations of arbitrary dissonances that understandably clash on the word 'Crucifixus':

Such musical events hint that the Middle Ages were on their way out; and it is indicative of Machaut's 'late' date that his secular far exceeds his sacred work in quantity.

Indeed, we may think of him not only as a cleric–composer but also as the last court–troubadour whose formidably severe Mass is, after all, dedicated to the Virgin Queen whose presence irradiated poetry, painting and music throughout the late Middle Ages and the early Renaissance. In his secular poetry and music Machaut specifically alchemized God's Mother into the troubadour's Eternal Beloved, as he sought a new principle of order in which mothers, saints, angels, and peasant-gargoyles were admitted on equal terms. The troubadour's beloved was a human woman, but outside marriage since that is a terrestrial institution. Throughout the long tradition of troubadour poetry one is seldom sure whether the woman is real or visionary; but even if she be the dark goddess of Gnosticism rather than the light-irradiating Virgin Queen, she is unattainable on either count, and so provokes a death-wish, tingeing the melodies' ecstasy with melancholy. The troubadour sang of an eternal longing in which the Renaissance was already latent.

Machaut left one work that epitomizes this transition from medievalism into something approaching the modern world: his *Le Lai de la Fontaine*, for which the words, as with almost all his secular songs, are his own. The *lai* was a near-obsolete, fastidiously stylized poetic genre deriving from medieval chivalry; and Machaut opens in the traditional vein of the Wailing Lover, admonishing his terrestrial love for the conventional 'cruelty' she displays towards him – probably as a bitter fruit of Eve's fall, and therefore all her fault! He reminds her that, lacking charity, she deprives herself and him of the greatest of the Christian virtues, and contrasts her with the Virgin Mary, an eternal beloved whose charity never fails. So what had seemed a secular love-song turns into abstract theological doctrine as he explains how the fountain (the Son), the stream feeding it (the Father), and the stream's eternal source (the Holy Ghost) are a trinity which is three in one, projecting the sweet, as distinct from the bitter, fruit of life into the Virgin's empty womb. Machaut's poem, in the French vernacular rather than hieratic Latin, is in twelve intricate stanzas, six of which are sung monodically, like a troubadour love-song, while the other six are given harmonic flesh in being sung polyphonically in, of course, three Trinitarian parts.

So the fearsome, and possibly fear-ful, austerity of the *Messe de Notre Dame* is transmogrified into the tender grace, at once physical and metaphysical, with which the late Middle Ages imbued the Virgin Mother, atemporal eternal beloved of all-too-temporal humankind. The liquidity of the ambiguously sensual–ethereal sanctity sounds, to our ears, a shade wistful, perhaps even regretful, rather in the same way as late, relatively naturalistic medieval stained glass seems to us, when compared with the previous century's more lustrous colours – which seem to accord well with the bouncing, jazzily syncopated polyphony of Pérotin. This seems an appropriate point to leave Machaut on the threshold of the Renaissance, with two quotations from the end of his *Le Lai de la Fontaine*: first, in a monody that addresses the 'Fountain of Harmony' as though it were a divine lover, but also the human source of mercy that may dispel sin:

He! fon - tein - ne de con - cor - de, la duis de mi - se - ri - cor - de,

And secondly in a 'canon three in one', in which the Virgin Queen of Light and of the Angels annuls the dreaded day of Judgment to lead us into 'la joie qu'est entierre', for ever and ever, as in the fairy-tale:

In that canon luminously 'abideth these Three – consubstantial and co-existent, neither confounding the Persons, nor dividing the Substance. And in this Trinity none is afore, or after other; none is greater or less than another; Unity is Trinity and Trinity is Unity.' In Machaut's verse and song music is theologized, and theology becomes music.

4

From the 'Gothic Desperation' to Harmonic Congruence

Dunstable's *Veni Sancte Spiritus* and Dufay's *Ave Regina Celorum*

In the last chapter I discussed the shift from 'theocratic' medieval values towards the 'humanistic' values of the Renaissance, as manifest in two works of Guillaume de Machaut: the liturgical *Messe de Notre Dame* and the courtly *Le Lai de la Fontaine*. This transition signified a *crucial* revolution in European history as well as in Europe's music. As the God-praising tintinnabulations of religiously ecclesiastical *cloches* were effaced by the mechanical ticking of civic and computing *clocks*, so the forms of music became associated with the swing of the pendulum and the alternations of harmonic tension that could accrue from it. For the basic technique of the *suspension* involved, in Renaissance music, a 'strong' beat on which a dissonance is 'prepared' in suspension, followed by a 'weak' beat on which it is resolved: a notion inconceivable except in relation to chronometric time. The suspended dissonance, through its variously complex vibration-ratios, to varying degrees excites, and *hurts*: so that the acceptance of time implies not only an awareness of beginnings, middles, and ends (which we call history), but also a conscious awareness of passion and of pain (which we call drama). If this is latent in the fourteenth-century polyphony of Machaut, it is patent in the fifteenth-century polyphony of Dunstable (whose name, we are now told, should be spelt Dunstaple); while it reaches fruition in the polyphony of his Burgundian successor, Guillaume Dufay. Perhaps it was a 'sign of the times' that commercial links between Britain and the Low Countries had cultural consequences. Two quite short pieces powerfully demonstrate this process of cultural infiltration: Dunstable's motet, *Veni Sancte Spiritus*, which became famous throughout Europe, turning up in widely scattered manuscripts; and Dufay's *Ave Regina Celorum*, which unwittingly marked, technically, a turning-point in history.

Having been nurtured, over around six centuries, on Europe's time-obsessed harmonic music, we may be tempted to think (or feel) that Dunstable's late medieval *Veni Sancte Spiritus*, though dreamily 'beautiful', seems to go on too long, implying for us a traditional dichotomy between content and form. Such a judgment is strictly irrelevant, for although Dunstable was in one sense a man of the Renaissance, his approach to composition remained basically medieval. He was not concerned with his own emotional response, which could only seek incarnation in time, but was rather, like Machaut, concerned to create, through his music, an 'atmosphere' in which an act of revelation might occur. He did not know when, or even if, it would happen, but he did his best to create the conditions in which it might. Just as an Indian vina player would perform for hours or even, with a few necessary intermissions, all day or all night while his audience of 'participants' came and went, so the ritual music in a medieval cathedral might resound for hours, while the congregation fluctuated.

In his own day – coming up for a hundred years later than Machaut – Dunstable was as celebrated for his skills as mathematician, astronomer, and astrologer as he was for his music; early Renaissance people, as well as those of the late Middle Ages, still found in the science of Number the heart of a music that had cosmological implications. A puzzle-piece such as Machaut's *Ma fin est mon commencement* (recorded as a fill-up on the Hilliard's CD of *Le Lai de la Fontaine*) marks a high point of mathematical ingenuity that is also theological and musical dialectic. The tenor part accompanies the alto with the same melody moving backwards, while the counter-tenor proceeds to its middle point and then inverts itself. The music *enacts*, as it were 'doctrinally', the words of T.S. Eliot in his *Burnt Norton*:

> Time past and time future
> What might have been and what has been
> Point to one end, which is always present . . .
>
> . . . . . .
> Only through time time is conquered

or

> Only by the form, the pattern,
> Can words or music reach
> The stillness, as a Chinese jar still
> Moves perpetually in its stillness.
> Not the stillness of the violin, while the note lasts,
> Not that only, but the co-existence,
> Or say that the end precedes the beginning,

And the end and the beginning were always there
Before the beginning and after the end.
And all is always now.

Even so, although theological and philosophical 'doctrine' is the essence of Machaut's motet, humanity seems to flower – in the piece's smooth lines and mellifluous harmony – through the acceptance of (God's?) mathematical law; and one finds an exactly comparable effect in Dunstable's most famous piece, the motet *Veni Sancte Spiritus*. Here the harmony is consistently triadic, built on the blissful euphony of the 'common' major or minor chord, in the sensuousness, or even the sensuality, of High Renaissance music. Yet this sensuality is passive, directionless; and the motet's structure is austerely linear and mathematical, and to that extent medieval in concept. The plainchant *cantus firmus* is repeated three times in notational values that decrease by Trinitarian thirds; the metrical structure is isochronous; three different liturgical texts are sung simultaneously, so that their doctrinally related meanings cannot be apprehensible in the hearing. Thus a Christian-ized version of the Indian *rāg* and *tāl* is still evident; and the rhythms of the ornate lines dissolve any sense of progression since the complex metrical proportions are independent of an earthily temporal 'beat'. So although the sonorities themselves glow in their thirds and sixths, being fruits of the Renaissance's enhanced sensuality, the effect is to a degree countered by the music's strictly mathematical and numerical discipline. There's a precarious equilibrium between inherited metaphysical faith and immediately physical exploration: as we can note in the opening of the motet, in which the initial melodic figure is an arpeggiated *major triad* in the alto part: while as the treble (*motetus*) part grows melismatically free, so it is balanced by the intrusion of the *cantus firmus*, now transferred from the ('held') tenor part to the bass, where its relatively long-sustained notes are a Rock that may hopefully support us. If the *cantus firmus* is played instrumentally, on trombone or organ, its rocky properties will, of course, be palpable.

Despite the strong medieval heritage in the motet's structure, its total effect is 'progressive' rather than regressive. The 'Dark' Ages are irradiated with light; and the music's physical effect is also dependent on its being composed in four, rather than in the traditionally Trinitarian three, parts (Dunstable made a three-part version too, but it was the more sonorous four-part version that became famous throughout the 'civilized' world).

Although this music entails awareness of the flesh, flesh did not bring the Devil with it. The harmony is much influenced by the early Renaissance style known as faux-bourdon, wherein chains of $_3^6$ chords, floating without before or after, hypnotize us in sensory bliss, like a cat lying on his back, paws wafting, as he purrs in the sun. Some think, on no very decisive evidence, that Dunstable 'invented' faux-bourdon; he and other English composers certainly relished *both* its independence of the Will and its *lack* of dramatic intentionality. None the less, that triadic harmony became familiar through the pop-music-like status of faux-bourdon meant that sooner rather than later the dramatic potentiality of triadic harmony would be recognized. We can almost date a moment in history at which this happened.

In 1472, as one of his last compositions, Guillaume Dufay – a canon of Cambrai Cathedral in charge of the music for liturgical offices and also a court composer of songs in troubadour tradition – made a Hymn to the Virgin to the favoured Latin text of *Ave Regina Celorum*: which views the Virgin Queen as an Eternal Beloved who was also an angel (and agent) of redemption. Two years later, he requested that this piece should be sung at his funeral, and interpolated into the text an appeal to God that he should have pity on his dying Dufay (*Misere tui labentis Dufay*). This unmedieval intrusion of the personal – parallel to the portraits of artists and even donors that were creeping into Renaissance paintings – brings with it a 'modern' harmonic technique. Up to this point the four-voiced texture has absorbed its triadic euphonies into the continuous flow of melody; but with the *miserere* that introduces Dufay's name the liquid major-third sonorities are abruptly contradicted by a *minor* triad; and the dramatic effect – which later came to be accurately termed *false relation* – is inseparable from the fact that it involves contradiction, and therefore dualism, rather than monism. Because it is a *shock*, we are conscious of *when it happens*; momentarily, the music no longer carries us outside time, but freezes us within it, in an agonizing awareness that the sands of Time – our time, for we are dying – are running out:

Of course it wouldn't be true to say that 'expressive' dissonance had not been used before in European music: we noted how, even in Machaut's severe Mass, a reference to the Crucifixion provoked a virulent coruscation of (admittedly arbitrary) dissonances. But a case might be made that dissonance *dramatically* conceived, in reference to our *awareness* of temporality and the place of our suffering self within it, had not previously been employed; certainly, the essence of late Renaissance (sixteenth century) polyphonic technique is here latent. In Dufay's music, monism, the principle of Oneness, still survives in the use of *cantus firmus* technique; harmonically, he remains partial, no less than Machaut, to the almost painful gravity of the 'Landini cadence', with its doubled leading-notes to both tonic and fifth; and one might say that the imitative process itself – whereby each part, freely flowing in an act of worship, *emulates* its predecessor – is an attempt to cling to unity during a time of disintegration. For this music is no longer an act of worship only: its polyphonic rather than monophonic principle makes it a social as well as a religious act, and the sought-for harmonic order, now based on the triad rather than the fifth and fourth, is a search for a humanly (rather than mathematically) imposed 'togetherness'. Monody is a matter between man and God. Polyphony may start from the man–God relationship, but involves social contracts also since several persons, attempting to make order out of their separateness, must modify their identities accordingly. Climacterically, the dissonant *contrast* in Dufay's setting of the word 'miserere' presents Separateness itself: for as soon as we centre our experience on our individual identities existing in time, we have to face the fact that these identities are not only multifarious, but are also conflicting and even contradictory. The Oneness of God is presumed to be eternal and unalterable; but the oneness that man seeks in his social institutions (and in his polyphony) must be fallible, because dependent on the vagaries of personal passions. It's worth remembering that in medieval polyphony (that of Pérotin and to a degree of Machaut) strict imitation was not an imperative necessity as an aid to union between man and God. Various numerical devices testified to the oneness of God's creation – which was none the less 'beyond' man's arbitration. But once the principle of 'functional' harmony had been admitted, polyphonic composers developed a fanatical obsession with canonic imitation as a bastion against both the 'Gothic desperation' and the horror of duality which the 'new' harmony had unwittingly revealed. We may note that the consummatory effect of this piece's close depends equally on triadic sonority and on expanded canonic imitation, rising scalewise through an octave:

Dufay stands midway between the Middle Ages and the High Renaissance, reconciling the various types of Ars Nova as practised in France, Italy, and England. This is evident if we compare Machaut's *Messe de Notre Dame* with Dufay's Mass *Se la face ay pale*. We noted that, for all the modern-sounding elements in Machaut's polyphony, his *Messe de Notre Dame* remains medieval in concept, with scarcely a trace of personal expressivity to disturb the logic of the Pythagorean science of numbers; something of the awe-ful grandeur of the old Byzantine Godhead survives in Machaut's attempts to recapture the Age of Chivalry. But although Dufay's Mass *Se la face ay pale* still displays the medieval respect for authority in the shape of a Firm Song or Cantus Firmus, for the traditional plain-chant Dufay substitutes a popular song, and a love song at that. Even in the invocatory Kyrie the tune is recognizable for what it is, while its harmony, influenced by Dunstable and the English school, is serenely triadic, as contemplation of the divine merges into delight in the senses:

A Dufay mass has often been compared to a painting of Van Eyck wherein the Celestial Queen becomes a human mother without ceasing to be divine; the transparency of the colours parallels the 'aural luminosity' of Dufay's sonorities. We may recall the increasingly human and humane angels in fifteenth-century Flemish painting in general: from being Essences, they turn into choirboys, some of them holy in church, but others mischievous, animated at once by a sense of wonder and a sense of the ridiculous! Humour no doubt received a fillip when art increasingly observed our vulnerably human follies.

A recent, superb recording of Dufay's *Mass for St James the Greater* brings home how Dufay may be the essential composer to reveal the moment when the Christian Age of Faith was in full bloom, yet at the same time at the turning-point into a disintegration that proffered a wonder-ful, if also fear-ful, promise.* The heart of the work is where it ought to be, in the Offertorium that initiates Communion: the music of which culminates in an extraordinary sequence of interlocking triads that seem not to depict, but to be, an identifying of Flesh and Spirit.

This ritualized fulfilment is capped by the jubilations of the Sanctus which, taking off from the earth, attain a ripeness of sonority and a luxuriance of ornament barely credible from such slender resources. None the less, credit it we do: which makes it a testament to belief if not in God, then in the possibility of human renewal in the face of desperate odds. Dufay's paradoxical gift of Praise that is also divinely ribald Mirth (in the medieval as well as the modern sense) culminates in AMENS to the Gloria and the Credo that are miraculously compound of holy reverence and of human (choirboy-like) irreverence. They make Dufay an aspect of our distant past who vividly illuminates our present and future, as only major composers can.

---

* Guillaume Dufay, *Mass for St James the Greater and other works.* The Binchois Consort, directed by Andrew Kirkman: Hyperion, CDA66997.

5

Sacred and Profane in the music of the William Cornyshes, father and son

The father's *Magnificat* and the son's *Adieu mes amours, Ah, Robin,* and *Woefully arrayed*

Comparatively little of the music of William Cornyshe has survived: which makes it tricky to decide whether his stature as a composer is on a par with the other musicians discussed in this book. A further dubiety lies in Cornyshe's dual identity, for there were two William Cornyshes: the father, a lay-clerk who composed ecclesiastical music to Latin texts, and died in 1503; and his son, a courtier under Henry VIII, a poet, dramatist, and composer who devised entertainments for court banquets, masques, and other official ceremonies, and who, being a person of some consequence, frequently visited France, and was present at the Field of the Cloth of Gold in 1520. We don't know his date of birth; he died in 1523.

The two Cornyshes offer fascinating evidence as to the shift from the old-style, mathematically and philosophically ecclesiastical composers of the Burgundian court and of their English contemporaries (notably John Dunstable), to the progressive composers of the first Elizabethan age, who steered church music towards madrigalian secularity and sometimes overt drama. While it isn't proven that all Cornyshe-composed church music with Latin texts is by the elder William, it seems reasonable to attribute the famously ornate *Magnificat* ascribed to William Cornyshe to the father, since it is a piece of considerable artistic maturity as well as technical ingenuity. I'll consider this work as an example of the 'old' manner, and will then examine three pieces probably by the younger Cornyshe, two of them love-songs and the third a passionate lament that turns out to be about the Passion of Christ. Together, the four works illuminate the transition, between the fifteenth and the sixteenth centuries, from Sacred to Profane, as well as from Gilded Chapel to Village Green or Street.

The Magnificat is a canticle of praise reputedly sung to God by the Virgin Mary, in gratitude for her divinely allotted role as intermediary between God and Man. We would expect a music thus inspired to sound God-like, and therefore to be related to the plain chant in which, over several centuries, Christians had addressed God in Latin, a hermetic language. Cornyshe's *Magnificat* derives its thematic material direct from plainsong's Sacred Word, the traditional liturgical intonations being sung to introduce each section. But plainsong is the everyday utterance of prayer; if we are avowedly celebrating God's glory in song, one would expect that the newly composed chant would, while respecting the 'natural' vocal intervals, be freer in rhythms, more expansive in lyrical contours, than plainsong itself. Such is the case: as we can see in the opening of Cornyshe's setting which, after the preludial intonation, flows in five parts, in the mixolydian mode. The manner in which the number of parts accepted as a norm increased between the fourteenth and sixteenth centuries, from (trinitarian) three to four to five, is fairly obvious testimony to a strengthening human and humane orientation; yet even so, the weightier the harmonic texture becomes, the more the rhythms, oblivious of bar-lines, float in airy and aqueous liquidity, even hinting at god-like levitation.

In the music of the Eton Choirbook, especially in the work of Cornyshe or the Cornyshes and of John Browne, an increase in harmonic density usually parallels an increase in polyphonic intricacy. In the earliest kind of medieval polyphony (that associated with Pérotin) the acoustical fact of the triad added 'depth' to the music's rhythmic vivacity: whereas in the late fifteenth century the composers of the Eton Choirbook seem to be attempting, perhaps consciously, to *purify* their cantillations of the theological Fall. For although the singing parts soar upwards in *ecstasis*, the harmonic textures are prevailingly consonant, making little effort to express, let alone 'illustrate', the words. One wouldn't expect God to fuss overmuch about our follies and foibles: which may be why, trying to invent what may pass as His music, we opt for grace, light, and concord, out of which may be generated a rapture that sounds, if only momentarily, out of this world's vale of tears. This occurs in the dazzling doxology to this Magnificat which might, at least in moments of confused consciousness, be heard as the Voice of God Himself. The *effect* of this music, though not its harmonic technique, reminds us of the jubilations of Pérotin at Notre Dame, during the heyday of the Middle Ages. When, in his secular music, one of the Cornyshes – more probably the son than the father – explored the humaner aspects of early Renaissance feeling, we may detect a kinship with the courtly secular style of Machaut. A four-part *chanson* like *Adieu mes amours* may be love music, but troubadour tradition still insists that merely human love must end certainly in disillusion, probably in disaster. Cornyshe's *chanson*, in courtly French, is, though exquisitely 'beautiful', inducive of spiritual fortitude rather than of passionate *désir*. Each line moves tranquilly by step, sometimes fluttering into ornamental passage-work, sometimes sharpening the seventh degree of the scale, thereby hinting at *false* relation. Only at the end, when the poet–lover admits that his love has been not only agonizing, but also bootless, does the music's sobriety erupt in *melismata*. That the mood seems assertive rather than wistful derives not only from the vigorous passage-work, but also from the translation of the mode from mixolydian G to ionian C – identical with our diatonic C major scale.

An eternity of consonantly plashing harps, such as is evoked in the elder Williams's *Magnificat*, might seem to most of us wondrously beautiful yet, in human terms, too good to be true. On the other hand, the wistful abnegation of a love-renouncing song like *Adieu mes amours* may seem, despite the slight show of spunk in the final bars, too true to be good. But William the son moves into a potential future in a secular song that proves to be as subtle as it is simple. The part-song *Ah, Robin* sets for three male voices a quasi-love poem that mysteriously equivocates between the human body and its presumptively divine spirit: for the words concern 'doubleness' without admitting, as does *Adieu mes amours*, to the vanity of human wishes. The young man who asks 'gentle Robin' for news of his leman (lover), wondering why she displays a doubleness that hurts, may be trying to cheer himself up, for he admits that women *may* be true, and in so doing adds a rare dimension to troubadour tradition. The music is as mysterious as the words, being 'mathematically' canonic while also having the haunting plangency and timeless repetitiveness of a modern, if exceptionally gentle, pop-song. The initial apostrophe to Robin, moving by step or pentatonic minor third or perfect fourth, is presented in canon by three voices. At the conclusion of the canons the two upper voices repeat the refrain, while the third voice expounds the case about love's dubiety. But at this point the lowest voice drops out, and another voice enters to answer it, though there are never more than three voices sounding simultaneously. It's the new voice that asserts faith in the leman's constancy, though the faith is not much less wavery than the doubt:

I suspect that the heart-rending effect of this little song has something to do with its hinting, however faintly, at the possibility of a humanly fulfilled love, after the long centuries of medieval sublimation and abnegation. The first phrase is at once open and frail in its gently drooping third, while harmonic pathos accrues from ambivalence between the aeolian mode (with flat sixth) and the dorian mode (with sharp sixth). When the second voice enters the theme is inverted, the falling minor third being translated into a rising fourth (bar 9). This imparts a slight sense of wonder, even of quest and questioning, as compared with the passively sighing declining third. Pathos

32

deepens when, at the end of the stanza, the first voice resolves on the major instead of the minor third (bar 13). Although this is not a 'dramatic' use of false relation such as we commented on in Dufay's *Ave Regina Celorum*, it is emotive, for the ambiguous third mirrors the poem's uncertainty about love, whether it be sacred or profane. When the new (narrative) voice is added to the two refrain-voices (bar 13), the trance-like reiteration is even more insidious, like a sophisticated pop-song; it seems that uncertainty, though a fact of life, need not be totally irremediable. So this apparently slight song is pregnant with human possibility: even though hope will probably be, once again, dis-illusioned. The strange *potentiality* of the piece hints at personal identity; and the 'anonymous' words may, I suspect, be by the younger William, who was esteemed as a poet.

This is even more likely in the case of another song which, if perhaps not as memorable as *Ah, Robin*, must count as Cornyshe's 'greatest' piece, *Woefully arrayed*. This too is structured as a series of 'verses' with narrative texts, introduced by a 'burden' and interspersed by a 'refrain' on the words 'Woefully arrayed'. The powerful but anonymous words, presumed to be uttered by Christ, alternate between verse sections and lyric refrain; in the narrative verses Christ describes his physical suffering on the Cross, and the emotional and mental assaults made on him by traitorous Judas and the Jews. The corporeality and the emotionalism of the words condition the music's impact, which is at once spiritual in being modally free and rhythmically fluid, yet also harmonically humane and theatrically direct. This is immediately evident in the monodic invocation, in which the tenor chants 'woefully arrayed' on repeated Ds, oscillating at the end between D and E flat. It sounds – at least in the recorded performance – microtonally dissonant, and is ambivalent since at this point one doesn't know whether the mode is dorian or aeolian on G, or phrygian on D. The ambiguity has something to do with the disturbing effect the song has on us; and John Stevens, who edited the piece for *Musica Britannica*, thinks that problems of *musica ficta* are here even more than usually tricky. He introduces numerous E flat accidentals, thereby evading many false relations that would accrue. It might be argued that a plethora of false relations would be apposite to so painful a subject: though Stevens's E flats make the music insidiously seductive (and easier to sing), whilst they 'point' the severity of the false relations when they occur.

The 'burden' is freely canonic between tenor and bass; but when the treble and alto have entered to sing the refrain to a more emotionally expansive phrase with rising sixth, quicker-rhythmed motifs assert that Christ's blood (his sacrifice) 'may not be nayed'. A false related E natural in the treble, on the word 'blood', shines seraphically; and the burden ends with a cadence shifting from the leading note (F sharp) to a godly bare fifth of G to D, with an undulating E flat quaveringly clashing with the D natural.

In the three verses Christ recounts his sufferings in increasingly violent

33

language, with active internal rhymes and assonances: 'With *pains* my *veins* con*strained* to crake, thus *tuggéd* to and fro, thus *wrappéd* all in *woe*'. Later, the scourging of Christ and the grimacing of his persecutors are presented almost naturalistically, so that each verse grows more metrically complicated and rhythmically distraught. Thus verse 1 opens with a rising minor third in canon and in stretto at a crotchet's distance, but soon coruscates in lissom triplet figurations, expressive of the body's agony rather than of potential bliss. As in the burden, treble and alto delay their entries and are not strictly imitative, though they follow the theme's contours. The 'sharp chords' of the persecutors make a Judas-like pun as cadentially sharpened sevenths are combined with dissonant suspensions:

In the second verse harmonic shock reinforces metrical enterprise, for although the theme returns to the repeated notes of the original invocation, there is a painful diminished fourth in bar 73: which also involves a false relation between the melodic F natural and the sharpened F in the cadence. The verse ends on a mixolydian G major triad, decorated with an undulating sixth here sung as E natural, not E flat, and therefore sounding slightly 'smoochy', like the 'added sixths' once favoured by jazzy cocktail-lounge pianists.

Although the third verse begins by recalling the austerity of the canonic burden, it reflects, in being at once fragmented and wide in compass, the 'painéd, strainéd, rueful and red' nervosity of the words, as well as the crudely corporeal 'bobbing' and 'robbing' that Christ complains of. The latent ferocity is enhanced when Christ reminds us that his suffering is on our behalf, and invites us to join him – presumably in death. Whatever the invitation purports, the end of the song is strictly speaking 'transcendental': for the increasingly broken phrases, spilling into intricate *melismata*, ultimately cadence on a major triad not of G, but of D, elevated one step up the cycle of fifths, and approached, moreover, by another suspended 'added sixth'.

The effect is plangent, as though the Godhead were indeed 'woefully arrayed' in human flesh; and it's this directness and particularity that makes the younger Cornyshe – certainly as composer and probably as poet – a harbinger of the great Elizabethans, including the master, William Byrd. *He* sometimes wrote madrigals, or ayres for a solo voice with instruments, that are tentatively operatic; and we shouldn't forget that Byrd was Shakespeare's exact contemporary. Cornyshe hadn't quite attained this Shake-spearean status: which is why, after that dramatically elevated D major cadence, he has to return to the opening invocation and burden, thereby re-establishing a quasi-religious ritual to succour us through the sufferings that are bound to assail us sons of the Son of God.

6

The Tudors and the Church Re-formed

'False relation' in Tallis's
Lamentations of Jeremiah

The Church of England, being a Reformed Church that broke from the Universal Church of Rome, was unstably founded on intellectual and spiritual bifurcation. God as absolutist, with the King as his earthly lieutenant and the New Man as a Pro-testant testifying on his own behalf, redefined the relationship between Church and State. The English Prayer Book, which although not subversive, redefined the relationship between Church and State, offered a vernacular liturgy for 'all sorts and conditions of men': being no more than the tip of an iceberg which effected, below the waters of the conscious mind, a mutation at once exhilarating and catastrophic.

For the Catholic and Universal Church was undermined as man substituted individualized human power for what had been thought of as the Will of God. Henry VIII quarrelled with the Pope because the King's royal but mundanely sexual and pecuniary greed came to a head over the matter of his divorce. Although it was indubitable that the Church harboured abuses that called for reform, Henry's motivations, being personal, were suspect; and when once the immense wealth of the Church had been plundered by disputatious men, power went to their heads. Spiritual motivations could no longer withstand the seductions of the vast material profit that Reform brought to the Reformers.

This was not merely an insular state of affairs but also a European phenomenon, given its most pungent expression by Montaigne when he pointed out that 'it is not possible for a man to rise above himself and his humanity . . . We are, I know not how, double in ourselves, and what we believe we disbelieve, and cannot rid ourselves of what we condemn.' None the less, the most crucial manifestation of this bifurcation was at the heart of the Anglican Establishment; and is exemplified with peculiar force in the life and art of Thomas Tallis who, according to a funeral tribute, 'as he dyd live, so dyd he dy, in myld and quyet Sort (O happy MAN)'. The word 'man' appeared thus capitalized, originally, perhaps testifying to a contemporary hunch that whatever tranquillity of mind Tallis attained to was due more to human stoicism than to divine intervention in terrestrial affairs. Muddled and hazardous those affairs certainly were for Renaissance man who, trying to be responsible for himself, found that he was, in the words of Sir John Davies in his *Nosce Teipsum* of 1599, 'a proud, and yet a wretched, Things'. Tallis, surviving a long time by contemporary standards (c. 1505–1585), and serving under four monarchs with shifting creeds, was a seismograph to the century's turbulence, however unruffled the surface of his almost exclusively liturgical music may seem.

During his early years at Canterbury Cathedral and at Waltham Abbey Tallis made music within the Roman rite and in the vocally polyphonic idiom inseparable from it. The traditional music of the Universal Church remained the essence, for the lines move, as in plainchant, smoothly by step or through the primary consonances of fifth and fourth and the pentatonic minor third, as described in the last few chapters. The euphony of the voices is stabilized on the triad, to which any passing dissonance is no more than a momentary disturbance. Similarly the pulse of time, the dimension in which we mortals exist, is no more than latent; a swing of the pendulum is necessary if the parts are to keep together, yet a 'beat' is effaceable in so far as there are few metrical accents, and no aggressive ones.

Yet at the same time Tallis's early music demonstrates how English composers of the mid-sixteenth century unconsciously modified ecclesiastical practice because they worked for a church that was re-forming Roman hegemony. Beneath the outward calm of Tallis's liturgical music we may detect evidence of the religious and political dissensions he weathered. In his earliest four-part setting of the Latin Mass, dating from before 1540, he opens monophonically with the traditional plainchant intonation that preserves the old order unsullied; yet the 'new music' of the Kyrie that succeeds the intonation substitutes for monody four-part (SATB) homophony for voices moving note for note in rhythms following the spoken inflexions of the words. The human import is thus more readily apprehensible than it is in the mazes of Catholic counterpoint such as is evident in Cornyshe's *Magnificat*. It is easy to understand why Reformed composers favoured a simple, homophonic style when they set vernacular texts: for man, *here* on this earth, is becoming the centre of what we may appositely think of as the stage, whilst God is up *there*, in his Heaven. Punningly, we may speak of a transition from plainchant's *mono*-phony (representing the *monos* of the One God); to *poly*-phony (a socially harmonizing concourse of 'many voices' acting in togetherness, whilst each voice individually seeks a plainsong-like spirituality); to the *homo*-phony of a communal solidarity (wherein homogeneous men and women sing in consort, on the earth, with their fellow creatures). It is significant that this homophonic 'community' singing latently, if not patently, involves dance as well as song since (as noted in the previous chapter) the bases of sixteenth-century choral technique involved a 'strong' and a 'weak' beat on which dissonances could be 'prepared' and 'resolved'. English homophonic anthems were usually brief, as though fearful of too protracted a stay in measured temporality; even so, in the second half of the sixteenth century, they resonated diurnally in parish churches throughout the land, being acts of devotion whose more significant function was to affirm fellowship and the durability of tradition.

Transitions between the old Roman dispensation and the newly Reformed dispensations were initially neither substantial nor abrupt. Roger Bowers tells us that 'the number, character, and disposition of the singers intended for the reformed liturgy in, say, 1564, was virtually identical to that deemed suitable for the Latin rite in 1540'.* What mattered was the reduction in the number of services, and the use to which the resources were put; and although simplification often entailed artistic impoverishment, this did not mean that music of complexity and subtlety was totally expunged. We have no date for one of Tallis's finest, and most technically consummate, works, the *Lamentations of Jeremiah*; but music of such technical sophistication is unlikely to predate Henry VIII's dissolution of the monasteries; and the use of a Latin text and of polyphonic intricacy may be outweighed by the fashionable five-part texture, sonorously weighted to the bass. In total effect the music's richness depends on its allying of 'old' allegorical techniques with 'new' harmonic expressivity: thus each section is introduced by plainchant-like intonations on letters of the Hebraic alphabet, 'magically' invoking the Old Testament, but alternating with harmonic–polyphonic settings of passages from the Book of Jeremiah, as Tallis calls fallen and bifurcated man to Christian repentance – in Old Testament words, but in the humane spirit of the New Testament. Although Tallis's lamentations refer to the general condition of fallen man, they apply specifically to then current religious and political dichotomy.

Part I opens with an intonation in the archaically severe phrygian mode, canonically, yet with many repeated notes that spring from liturgical declamation whilst distantly prophesying operatic recitative:

* Roger Bowers, *English Church Polyphony: Singers and Sources from the 14th to the 17th Century*. Aldershot: Ashgate, 1999: IV, 429.

The lamenting passages from Jeremiah are denser in texture than the Hebraic cantillations, and attain a climax of expressivity in the 'Plorans ploravit' section, centred on B flat, a devilish tritone away from the initially heavenly, if purgatorial, phrygian E. For the final appeal to 'Jerusalem' (fallen mankind) to 'convertere ad Dominum' the repeated notes of the opening clause return in more overtly dramatic guise. When D minor-major shifts to A minor, this prefaces a cadence not in, but on, the dominant triad of E major, reminding us of the key's and chord's celestial connotations. Though the music remains liturgical, the inner intensity is potentially theatrical, and the final triad, with its major third in the top (alto) part and the second bass on the deep low E, has an awesome sonority that sounds like a re-formation since that is what it is.

Part II also opens canonically, but with fewer 'speaking' repeated notes and more flowing part-writing in the dorian mode on G. The cantillations on letters of the Hebrew alphabet are longer and more ornate than in Part I, though they never reach the intricacy of the Eton Choirbook, and their relative richness rather serves to generate greater harmonic energy in the Jeremiah sections. In the 'Daleth' incantation arpeggiated triads overlap in bell-like, Trinitarian patterns:

This imbues with urgency the people's groans (*gementes*) and the clattering of the city's sundered gates in the next Lamentation, wherein the grinding dissonances accrue from the simultaneous or near-simultaneous sounding of major and minor thirds. We've previously noted how this phenomenon, which came to be called False Relation, sprang from the clash between the two worlds, medieval and Renaissance, that Tallis straddled. Voices nurtured on monadic plainchant (and on monodic folk song) naturally favoured the flat sevenths and thirds that are acoustically basic, while lively modern man also relished the sharpened *leading* notes and major thirds that *dominated* harmonically resolving cadences, marking the passage of Time. The two concepts could literally bump into one another, since two or three of the lower parts may define a cadence by way of the sharp leading note, while another part overlaps as it enters on a new phrase descending through the 'natural' flat seventh. A metaphysical and a physical view of the world thus meet in an equilibrium both precarious and painful, as on the words 'et ipsa oppressa amaritudine'.

This section, in the aeolian mode on G transposed down a fifth to C, ends in a cadence that supports a sensuous, even sensual, 'added sixth' comparable with that commented on in Cornyshe's 'Woefully arrayed'. It sounds the more poignant in Tallis's habitually severe context, and is reinforced by the final appeal to fallen man to 'convertere ad Dominum'. In the ultimate 'converteres' the top part is on one note (tonic G), in declamatory speech rhythm, while the other parts, in the aeolian mode on G, melismatically resolve in a blissful *tierce de Picardie*, prophetic of the state of blessedness that G major often signified for J.S. Bach.

Yet Tallis's anguish, though sometimes fierce, is never insupportable, for out of pain and conflict evolves the possibility of *growth*: which is why Tallis, despite his Anglican sobriety, is a 'modernist'. The repeated notes in the 'convertere' appeals do indeed con-vert, and do so, moreover, in the humanly reassuring, if priestly, accents of a speaking voice. The peace this music nourishes 'passes understanding' *because* it is aware of fallen man's anguish. In the thick of spiritual conflict, which also had political dimensions, Tallis makes music that, while rending the heart, remains serene.

Two other works of Tallis call for comment because they are very famous, if partly for adventitious reasons. One is the motet *Spem in alium* which we admire for its technical virtuosity, since it is in forty real parts, divided into overlapping groups of SATB choirs. Its effect is sublime – especially if sung in a Perpendicular building such as it was designed for, wherein the canonic choirs may evanesce in empty space. If, despite the contrapuntal ingenuity, it tends to sound like a common triad endlessly reiterated, that makes a point, since the 'togetherness' of harmonic euphony dissolves physicality into an eternity that seems meta-physical. This theological inversion may be the ultimate re-formation.

The other piece is famous not because of its technical virtuosity but because of its 'elemental' simplicity – which prompted Vaughan Williams to use it as basis for his deservedly much performed *Fantasia on a Theme of Thomas Tallis*. This Tallis piece is the third in a series of congregational hymns that Tallis contributed to the 1567 Psalter of Matthew Parker, first Anglican Archbishop of Canterbury, in which the togetherness of Tallis's four vocal parts is attuned to the reforming Archbishop's deliberately populist, end-stopped, internally rhyming metrics. The Psalter was 'published by John Day, dwelling over Aldersgate beneath St. Martin's'; and the homely description accords with the hymns' having easily memorable tunes for common men and women who used the wonder-ful New Book of Common Prayer. The tune's melodic nobility and harmonic potency (rich in false relations) must have appealed to Vaughan Williams, the more so since the hymn's words bear on his deepest concerns:

> Why fum'th in fight the Gentiles' spite, in fury raging stout?
> Why tak'th in hand the people fond, vain things to bring about?
> The Kings arise, the Lords devise, in counsels met thereto,
> Against the Lord with false accord, against his Christ they go.

The crudely populist verse reflects deep conflicts of material and spiritual, political and religious, values: which the music's verbal rhythms and abrupt harmonic tensions vigorously enhance. When 'the Kings arise' the tune lifts through a minor third with a lyrical effect the more potent because the mode is phrygian, with the flat seconds sounding cabinned, cribbed, and confined (Vaughan Williams makes magical play with that lift through a third). So the unearthly Music of the Spheres or *musica mundana* of Tallis's forty-part motet, and the toughly *mundane* music of his four-part hymn, are opposite but complementary poles of Tallis's art. Reared in the Old World. he was a prime maker of the New, an essential composer of Reformation. He was also the teacher of William Byrd, a man of the Old Faith who worked *for* the Reformed Faith and was honoured and esteemed for so doing. Byrd's 'doubleness', which we may think of as Shakespearean, inaugurates the Modern World.

7

Byrd as Roman–Anglican, Elizabethan–Jacobean, Double Man

His *Mass* in five voices (1588) and his
Psalm-Sonet, 'Lullaby, my swete litel baby'
(first version for solo voice and viols [1588],
second version for *a cappella* voices [1607])

In discussing Thomas Tallis we noted that the sixteenth century was a
period of transformation not only between the Old (Roman) and the
Reformed (Anglican) Faith but also in a general sense between concepts
of order and morality inherited from the Middle Ages, and a growing
concern with individual consciousness – with the humanist's belief in the
power of the human will to control its destiny. Men boldly explored the
furthest reaches of the physical universe, and plumbed the darkest depths
of the human mind: as is evident in the most vividly representative medium
of the time, Shakespearean theatre: for the conventions within which
Shakespeare's art flourished were not only the beginning of modern
theatrical techniques, but were also an evolution from medieval religious
drama.

British music reached an apex in these Shakespearean years – the last
two decades of the sixteenth century and the first two of the seventeenth.
This is manifest in the work of the composer William Byrd, which might be
claimed as 'Shakespearean' in range and depth of experience. Even at a
superficial level we may observe in Byrd's career a fusion of two distinct
worlds: for although he worked for and (for his exceptional talents) was
revered by a Protestant Queen, he was himself a Catholic recusant who at
the height of his powers composed three Latin masses, in three, four, and
five voices respectively, for the Catholic liturgy. Admittedly, these masses

42

were performed only in private Catholic chapels, while being in no way anachronistic in the context of Elizabethan vocal polyphony. This suggests that the Reformation was not a sharp fight between opposed creeds. The Reformatory conflicts of the sixteenth century, like the overt Civil War of the seventeenth, were merely external symbols of a change in consciousness that inevitably entailed changes in social structure. Rather than division, there was interpenetration between the two – as there was in the all-embracing art of Shakespeare.

This is evident in the most solemn moments of Byrd's strictly liturgical music. Consider the Agnus Dei of the five-voiced Mass. As we've noted, the Agnus Dei is always the most sacred moment of the Eucharistic rite; and Byrd approaches it not as a personal experience but as a sacrament, as did his predecessors. Its form is freely fugal, in the sixteenth-century sense, since it is an incarnation of Oneness. Indeed, a single theme pervades not only this movement, but the entire Mass. Thus the opening phrase of the Agnus Dei, invoking the Lamb of God, is identical with the Kyrie theme that opens the Mass. Almost without metrical stress or harmonic implication, it is a simple undulation below and above God's interval of the fifth: a suspiration as inevitable as breath or the heart-beat, seemingly equated with the source of life itself:

Initially, the theme is presented in canon at the fifth, in three Trinitarian voices; but with the words 'Qui tollis peccata mundi' the sins of the world distract us from contemplation of the Godhead towards our sinful selves. A chromatic note, contradicting the tranquil modality, creeps into the treble to consummate the cadence; and this sharp third conflicts with the natural third sung by the tenor, who has just entered with the theme. Another chroma-ticized cadence, C sharp to the tonic D, creates a sobbing chord of the augmented fifth when the alto undulates from E to F: as a consequence of which this opening clause, despite the timeless serenity of its elements, effects a gradual increase in tension. The slow rise of the melodies, increasingly dissonant in interrelationship, culminates in a cadence on the dominant of the dominant, the stressed suspended fourth being lingeringly, lovingly yet painfully, resolved. In this point of heightened consciousness the music seems to have 'got somewhere', in a way that the music thus far commented on had not even wanted to.

From here, however, the music declines: literally, in that the words 'miserere nobis' are set to a simple falling scale. Only it is not simple in effect, since the two drooping scales enter in canon, not simultaneously. Since one part is sustained while the other falls, passing dissonances of minor ninth and minor second pierce our nerves. The music has acquired, within its tranquillity, human pathos as, contemplating our fallibility, we appeal for God's helping hand.

The declining phrase stills the music in the relative major; and it is significant that we may speak of Byrd's key-sense in modern diatonic terms, as well as in terms of traditional modality. So far, the music has been scored for three voices in fugato. The same text is set twice more, first for four voices, then for five; each Trinitarian repetition describes the same arch, and creates a similar equilibrium of tensions, albeit in a more overtly emotional, because harmonically denser, form. Thus in the four-part setting the original undulation is extended both up and down: the 'qui tollis' is pointed by the bass's octave leap, while the scalewise 'miserere' is more tenderly sensuous since it warbles in parallel thirds or tenths. The protractedly chromaticized cadence now has a suspended seventh in the tenor, and this quasi-romantic dominant seventh almost melts with compassion. That this is not *self*-pity, but pity for human fallibility, is suggested by what follows the first appearance of that dominant seventh. An augmented version of the 'miserere' undulation in the bass clashes with the suspended F natural of the alto, hinting at a severity in the acceptance of suffering only partially annulled by the reappearance of the dominant seventh.

The three-voiced section had, with passion suppressed beneath the unruffled surface, modulated sharpwards. The four-voiced setting offers assuagement in modulating flatwards towards the subdominant, though the relaxation of the G major triad is only transitory. For the sharpened third is immediately cancelled by the minor third as the text leads into the five-voiced setting, in which for the first time the parts move note for note. The massive sonority entails a more dance-like lilt that also follows the natural declamation of the words, as the music mounts to a climax that may be called dramatic, even in music liturgically conceived. Then, with the words asking for God's peace, the steadying Fs of the bass restore the stepwise undulations of the contrapuntal style, to a degree obliterating the recently upsurging pulse of Time. But the appeal for peace cannot immediately efface the awareness of Christ's suffering, which carries *our* burden: so the slow arches of the melodies, quiet as breathing, create the most acutely dissonant passing notes in the piece, the suspended seconds of the final cadence being a stab of pain. Minor second resolves on to major second, and that on to the major triad which, in this context, approximates even more closely than do Tallis's cadences in his *Lamentations of Jeremiah* to the peace that passes understanding.

So we have in this Agnus music of religious sensibility, conceived as a devotional act. The modal nature of the vocal lines and the fluidity of the rhythms release us from the burden of selfhood, while at the same time the dissonances that the overlapping parts create render suffering 'incarnate'. Dissonance – indeed the technique of suspension itself – we have seen to be inseparable from an awareness of chronometric time. I described Byrd's teacher, Thomas Tallis, as a 'modernist', despite the austerity of his art; but Tallis's pupil Byrd was still more immediately apprehensive of man's mortality. His awareness of the fact that his own passions, however deeply felt, must be snuffed out like a candle, is still experienced in the light of eternity. It is thus justifiable to detect in this Agnus Dei a tragic pathos that may be called Shakespearean. One could not pay Byrd a higher compliment than to say that his achievement, in his three Masses, complements Shakespeare's achievement in his late plays, especially *The Winter's Tale* and *The Tempest*. Both deal with the grace man may wring from his joys and sorrows; both have the painful serenity of a faith not accepted, but attained. This is why Byrd is more 'modern' than any of the composers so far discussed in this book.

The probable date of the five-voiced Mass is 1588. In the same year he also published his *Lullaby, my swete litel baby*, originally for solo voice accompanied by four viols, but later transcribed for five unaccompanied voices. In both versions the piece is not liturgical music intended either for the Roman or the Anglican Church, but domestic music for the home. Its character is implicit not only in Byrd's inclusion of the five-voiced version in his preponderantly secular *Psalms, Sonets, and Songes* published in 1588, but also in its atmosphere and theme. It deals with the Nativity story which, even in the Middle Ages, had encouraged artists in all media to stress human tenderness and compassion, rather than an abstract mysticism. The cult of the Virgin Mary was not an exclusively Christian symbol but was rather everyman's search for the Mother image; although the Babe was the Godhead incarnate, he was also our futurity, a promise of life's renewal after the winter's dark.

The deeply moving quality of Byrd's *Lullaby* springs more from this seasonal significance than from traditionally Christian associations, though they are, as always, potent. We begin with the physical reality of movement in time – a rocking. Yet although the piece opens with imitative points, we don't listen to them contrapuntally but recognize, in the dotted duple rhythm of the drooping minor thirds, a declension that roots us to the earth, and has traditionally been associated with sleep, and by inference, with the final sleep which is death:

Against the rocking, the tenor at first sings long, almost motionless As in semibreves: which shift to a triple rhythm against the duple-pulsed swaying, as though they are trying to make the rocking cease. At this point the child would *fall* asleep, liberated from the pulse of time and the pull of the earth and, indeed, from death itself since, sleeping, he would no longer be *conscious* of mortality.

This is why the rocking isn't, after all, lethal, though the fall *is* a Fall. The tonality looks like D minor, which we have seen to be a key of uncertain human pilgrimage; but the frequently sharpened sixths shift the aeolian mode on D to the dorian mode, and thence into a plagal approach to the dominant A minor. This upward lift recalls the comparable effect in Cornyshe's *Ah, Robin*, almost a century earlier (see page 31); and here it exerts an effect on the re-established diatonic D minor, transmuting it to its relative, F major, as the singing mother croons to her 'sweet little baby'. The treble part establishes the new, pastorally positive key, cancelling the cadential C sharps with C naturals, though it then rises *up* the scale with *sharp* sevenths, attaining the new tonic in a fulfilled form of the 'sweet little baby' phrase, alchemizing the earth-rooted minor thirds into an exquisitely cantabile *smile*:

This phrase, rising through pentatonic minor thirds, to fall through a *major* third, complements the death-instinct of the initial lulling with the life-force of the baby's sweetness and the mother's caress. We are in the presence not only of the archetypal Babe and Mother, but also of a real baby and a real woman, possibly ourselves and *our* mother. The quicker, syncopated cross-rhythms on the words 'sweet little' (especially the alto's quaver tremor and the tenor's arabesque that mutates a minor third into a pentatonic cooing) literally enact the infant's stirring. Moreover, *because* the baby is humanly real, whatever else it may be, it is born, like us and William Byrd, to suffering and death. As the song evolves, we realize that the 'stirring' is not only evidence of the baby's corporeal presence, but is also an emotional unease beneath the surface: perhaps also a dis-ease, because the baby's wriggling is the beginning of his earthly pilgrimage that can end only in death.

The climax comes, with a disturbing octave leap, followed by a wistful *nota cambiata* cadence modulating to the 'going on' dominant, when the Mother asks the Child 'What meanest thou to cry?' She tries to soothe the infant's distress with a falling 'lulla' phrase, no longer drooping through minor thirds, but by a step down the scale, through the interval of a (godly?) fifth. The descending scalewise movement is a physical gesture, a smoothing of the brow of care, as though she were asking him to forget the pain of being human – a natural instinct in mothers. Yet although the texture becomes tenderly sensuous as the scales droop in parallel sixths and the tenors resume their long-sustained semibreve As, the child cannot escape his mortal humanity. Trance doesn't work, and the syncopations and cross-accents grow more obtrusive as the falling scales change back into falling minor arpeggios that extend the falling minor thirds of the original rocking.

The descending arpeggios sound a knell as dust returns to dust, earth to earth. Even so, the life-instinct of the mother–child relationship isn't obliterated. The resolution of the dominant of a D minor chord on to an F major triad reintroduces the 'sweet little baby' refrain, soaring above the knell, though the modulation to the relative major is soon contradicted by the tenor's sharpened B and a painful false relation between the tenor's C natural and the treble's ornamented C sharp. This C sharp also clashes with the first alto's passing D natural, so that in the penultimate bar A, B, C natural, C sharp, D, and E are sounded almost simultaneously. Following so uncompromising a statement of the paradox of human existence the final major triad sounds both poignant and frail:

So the First Part of the *Lullaby* presents us with the Mother and Child and evokes, but does not comment on, his disquiet. The Second Part goes on to offer reasons for the baby's distress, and in so doing becomes overtly dramatic. The triple movement is more animated than the First Part's duple movement (probably dotted minim = minim), and although the Mother appeals to her Child to 'be still', the music tells us that he cannot, or won't. The knell-like *stretti* intensify anxiety, swinging in regular periodicity often at odds with the bar-metre, with disruptive effect on the harmony. The music becomes physically descriptive; we feel the baby's struggle against his mother's body and sustaining arms, as the syncopations *enact* his squirming, introducing too another passing B natural that makes for the melting, weeping effect of an added sixth.

Even so, the point of this physical activity is not, given the significance of the Christian story, really negative: as has already been hinted in the fact that the tolling minor thirds in Part II no longer fall, but rise! This baby's fate concerns us all. The text of the beautiful, complex, and personal if anonymous poem tells us that the baby cannot sleep because the 'cruel king' has sworn to shed the blood of innocence. This cruel king, though specifically Herod, is also the burden of human guilt in that we all harbour a Herod within us. At this point the music garners greater energy: false relations between tenor and alto are reinforced by cross-accents like thrusting swords, with an expansion of the tessitura both up and down; blood is shed from a high A. Paradoxically, this gathering of momentum, provoking modulation, ultimately to A major, is positive in effect, since we know that this babe might be our redemption because Christ suffered and died in order that, hopefully, we might live. Climax comes when the text specifically relates the Two Kings, of Life and of Death, who are within us: 'a King is born which King this King would kill'. These words are set in resonant A major homophony, that key being indicative of youth, hope, and spring: so the original tolling minor thirds have become finally affirmative, alchemized from Death to Life, as is Hermione's 'statue', in *The Winter's Tale*, a play written around the time of the publication of Byrd's Carol.

But then we recall that the promise, for mankind, is not yet fulfilled because 'wretches' (the Herod within us) still 'have their will' over the holy babe that is within us too. So the final refrain turns the falling thirds once more into lament. The words 'When wretches have their will' are set to the same falling scale in dotted rhythm as the Mother had sung, in the First Part, to encourage forgetful oblivion. The false relations return, now thick and heavy, while the strained melodic interval of a diminished fourth in the treble produces, harmonically, a weeping augmented fourth. Only the major third in the final *tierce de Picardie* reminds us that this babe is blessed, and that we hope (expect?) to be blessed through him.

The story told, we return to the physical presence of the Virgin Mother who sings to her Child, repeating the First Part of the *Lullaby*. We hear it afresh, now we know why the babe stirs and cannot sleep. This piece is not liturgical ritual, but human experience dramatically enacted. Though it moves us deeply because of its religious implications, it is its humanly psychological truth that Byrd starts from. So the piece is a dramatic complement to the musical image of Incarnation that Byrd made nearly twenty years later, in his motet *Ave verum corpus* of 1607: a fact perhaps more patent in the original version of the *Lullaby* for solo voice with viols, since in this form the piece is identical in style with the songs that Byrd actually wrote for the Shakespearean theatre. There are many parallels between the techniques of the *Lullaby* and those of the motet *Ave verum corpus*: which is specifically about the Incarnation of holy spirit into human body, and which functions harmonically rather than contrapuntally in that the four voices, moving mostly note for note, generate emotive false relations, but finally resolve Christ's humanly finite suffering on the Cross into his divinely infinite beatitude. In 1607 Byrd made his 'mystically' abstract statement of the fundamental Christian doctrine which, in 1588, he had almost operatically dramatized in the two Parts of his *Lullaby*. The operatic implications latent in Byrd's *Lullaby* were soon to be patent in the work of an Italian composer who made the first opera that is still part of the repertory, and whose religious music fuses, on equal terms, song, dance, drama, and visual spectacle. He was Claudio Monteverdi, whose *Vespers and Magnificat* of 1610 is the subject of the next chapter.

Part II:
The Re-birth of a Re-birth:
from Renaissance to High Baroque

8

The Opera-house as Church

Monteverdi's *Vespers and Magnificat* (1610), as a Fare-well and as an Annunciation of the Renaissance

Claudio Monteverdi, although reared in the Old Faith as a Roman Catholic, is most celebrated as the inventor of opera, a sublimated imitation of human actions – or, if not for its invention, at least for the making of the first opera (based on the legend of the man-god Orpheus) to become, and remain, part of the mainstream of European culture. It would seem that from this time forth some, or even most, of Europe's supreme 'religious' musical creations have paid homage to Man in the Highest; or to his however foolhardy courage in affirming, or dreaming up, a faith that helped him to survive.

Interestingly enough, Monteverdi composed his major ecclesiastical work immediately after his trail-blazing Orphic opera of 1607. Given that he was a humanistic, secular, and theatrical composer, it makes sense that his biggest and best ecclesiastical work should be a setting of the Vespers service, long associated with the cult of the Virgin Mary who, over the centuries, had humanized and ameliorated the rigours of Christian orthodoxy. Even so, the history of Monteverdi's *Vespers* is obscure; there is no definitive score, and the Vespers settings, with the attendant Psalms and 'sacred concertos' that the composer published in Venice in 1610, would seem to be an anthology of specimens of his art and craft, possibly intended as self-advertisement. We don't know why Monteverdi assembled the collation, nor is there evidence that the work was ever performed, as a totality, during his lifetime; nor, indeed, that it was even intended to form a whole. Nowadays, it is established, along with Bach's *B minor Mass* and *St Matthew Passion*, and with Handel's *Messiah*, as a pinnacle among 'European religious master-pieces', and is performed almost as frequently as they are. The quality of the music justifies this celebrity; but doesn't solve the problems inherent in its dubious identity. We do not know whether it was intended for the panoply of soloists, choruses, and largish instrumental forces who now perform it, or for small bodies of virtuosi such as were available at courts. It seems improbable that the mass of material that Monteverdi published together was intended to be a totality, since the various sections are variously scored; and although the considerable variety of types of music that are, in Dr Johnson's phrase, 'yoked by violence together' reflects the swirl of contradictory impulses that were then coalescing to create the modern world, most of the problems of performance practice raised can be answered only by guess-work. Still, the work, however hazardously innovative, is now a part of the repertory. When, after having subsided underground for the best part of three hundred years, it was fortuitously rediscovered in the early 1930s, its revelatory genius was immediately recognized, and it was 'arranged' and performed by scholars who disputed as to whether it was liturgical or concert music. If the former, there were some numbers that didn't 'fit'; if the latter, it seemed to be *sui generis*. Coming at a turning-point in history, it was probably both: as Professor Denis Stevens, most fanatical among the liturgists, recognized when, in 1994, he produced a revised version of his original publication, incorporating all the material from Monteverdi's 'folio', more or less in the original order. These comments use Stevens's Novello edition as text.

Despite dubieties about the contents of the work, and the ordering of the numbers, the general plan is clear enough. The piece is 'traditional' in that it follows the Vespers liturgy, quoting each section of the medieval plainchant monodically, and following each clause with a big Psalm setting, not necessarily with Marian implications. The Psalm settings are for chorus or double chorus, reinforced, in Venetian style, by instrumental doubling or support, and by interludial ritornelli, scored for violins, viols, recorders, cornetti, and occasionally trombones. The style of these 'public' choruses compromises between the *prima prattica* of Palestrinian polyphony, and instrumental dance music mostly in forms favoured at princely courts. Operatic elements culled from what Monteverdi called the *seconda prattica* crop up intermittently, and sometimes alarmingly, scored for virtuosic solo voices accompanied by a continuo of chamber organ, harpsichord, and/or chitarrone. These recitative and arioso sections balance the chorus's public testaments with more private experience, manifest in 'sacred concertos' that are substituted for the traditional antiphons of plainsong liturgy.

As soon as the initiatory plainchant intonation has evaporated into the building's empty spaces, the Vespers startlingly begin by literally quoting the opening ceremonial fanfares from Monteverdi's *L'Orfeo*, currently immensely famous. It's as though the Sacred Word of the old Plainchant were being brusquely brushed away by the New Fanfares that proclaim worldly Glory, resonating on bouncily dancing cornetti and bright-glittering violins (as distinct from the more ethereal viols). 'For the time being', man's momentary splendour counts for more than his spiritual aspiration; proud monarchs think they need no more than the glamour that hopefully identifies them with gods (if not with God). This must be wish-fulfilment, since there is nothing 'to' the fanfares except colour and rhythm: no melody apart from the sharply shooting scales, no harmony except sonorously 'common' triads. The rest of the work will indicate how hollow, if momentarily enlivening, this glamour is; and will demonstrate how the complexity of our newly savoured human impulses is inherent in the infiltration of 'new' (*seconda prattica*) into 'old' (*prima prattica*) techniques.

This is immediately evident in the first of the Psalm settings – of Psalm 109, 'Dixit Dominus', in which the Lord indeed 'speaks' in parlando passages of recitative not far from plainsong intonation, but burgeoning into wide-flung, swinging polyphony in which stepwise movement is progressively energized in dotted rhythms. Despite the luxuriant scoring in six parts and the vigorous corporeal impetus, the music doesn't totally surrender its old-fashioned aeolian modality, first cadencing on a chord of God's bare fifth, with neither major nor minor third. Instrumental ritornelli, for strings or brass or both, reanimate the mundane festivities, until the Psalm ends with a grand Amen not in, but on, the dominant.

Although, as indicated, we cannot be certain about the order of the movements nor even about how many of them were meant to be performed when and where, we can see and hear that the Psalm settings make for public affirmation, fusing the age-old plainchant intonation with Renaissance polyphony as practised in the then present, and with operatic and terpsichorean techniques destined to dominate the future. Public junketing is then capped by the private experience of operatic arioso, sung by pyrotechnical soloists accompanied only by continuo. The words of the 'Nigra sum' from the Song of Songs, most sensually erotic of biblical books, are allotted to alto and tenor soloists, in a radiant G major, the lines adorned with tendrils of ornamentation. This *black* girl may hint at non-Christian cultures rampant in the commercialism of Venice; and a similar pattern is repeated in the collocation of the next (public) psalm setting (Psalm 112, 'Laudate pueri') with the next (private) arioso for solo voices, the 'pulchra es', which also has a text from the Song of Songs. An excess of secular energy may be indicated by the fact that the public music is here for *double* chorus employed antiphonally, while the arioso is scored for two intricately entwining sopranos, not one.

The next psalm setting (Psalm 121, 'Laetatus sum') further energizes secular humanism, being in elaborate six-part polyphony yet also corporeally metrical – almost a martial march. Lines take off into whirling roulades for solo voices; moreover, the burgeoning styles (perhaps taking a hint from 'Nigra sum') become ethnically pluralistic, for Denis Stevens plausibly suggests that the notorious procession of 'Lombard sobs' introducing the words 'Propter fratres' may be an emulation of Hungarian gypsy music heard by Monteverdi on a military campaign as regimental musician; they impart more than a hint of savagery to the hopefully civilized festivities:

Although probably written at Mantua, Monteverdi's Vespers are exuberantly Venetian in their potentially democratic eclecticism, embracing sundry life-styles from the hyper-refined to the aggressively barbaric. This may be why the next arioso section in Monteverdi's folio, the 'Duo Seraphim', is the most exotic thus far, rising to a thrilling climax when the duetting Seraphim, who are angels related to but larger than human life, are alchemized, by way of a mysterious passage of bare diatonic concords, into a Trinity of Father, Son, and Holy Ghost, incarnate in glottal trills ('nanny-goats') borrowed from Jewish synagogue music, and possibly from incantations of the Islamic Church:

Goats are notoriously Dionysiac and sexy creatures, while mercantile and sea-going Venice was a melting-pot of the nations wherein clashing cultures generated both heat and light.

No doubt because of its transcendental quality, the 'Duo Seraphim' is sometimes shifted by editors and/or conductors towards the work's end. Yet it makes (perhaps better) sense in Stevens's (and I suspect Monteverdi's) order, since the next collection of public psalm-settings and private ariosi continues, and enhances, the pattern previously established. The setting of Psalm 126 ('Nisi Dominus') for double chorus is the longest, most contrapuntally elaborate, and grandest thus far, its counterpoint being a many-in-oneness that allows for tonal licence and surprise, on the basis of an earthy F major. And the succeeding arioso, 'Audi coelum', stresses dichotomy between earth and heaven in being a dialogue in echo between two tenors, spatially distant from one another. The obsession of the seventeenth century with echoes is fascinating: for it's as though the physical were mirrored in the metaphysical, or it may be the other way round. Either way, Heaven, invented by us, can only be like us, but purer; the echo, if blissful, is a long way off. The words, from Isaiah, praise the Virgin Mother as intermediary between death and life; and guide the music into a triple-rhymed choral dance, ending on a D major triad that is dominant rather than tonic.

The next psalm-setting (Psalm 147, 'Lauda Jerusalem') is, after the plainchant intonation, scored for double chorus, with resplendent instrumental backing in the doxology. Monteverdi's flexible terminology means that it is seldom easy to be certain about the precise instrumentation he wanted; but we can have little doubt that after this vainglorious Psalm, he was making a special point by following it, not by arioso for soloing or duetting voices, but by a Hymn to the Virgin, based on her own incantation, 'Ave Maris Stella', which links her, as a Star of the Sea, with the unconscious waters from which 'consciousness' springs. At first Monteverdi treats the words in solemn antiphonal polyphony, half-way between traditionally Palestrinian 'old practice', and a masked masque such as the Duke of Mantua staged for the delectation of worldly lords and masters. This music is, however, mutated into a dance-song in lilting triple rhythm, with stimulating hemiola cross-rhythms between $\frac{6}{4}$ and $\frac{3}{2}$. The refrain remains majestic, yet sheds class-distinctions in becoming also tenderly humane, haunting as a love song, compulsive as an (unusually potent) pop number:

Here the divine finds *incarnation* in human feeling and in corporeal movement, irrespective of time or place. The Renaissance theory of dance was primarily a vision of a heaven-on-earth created by and for Top People; but it owed its force to its mating of secular and sexual satisfactions with a spiritual, or at least other-than-secular, link between the physically disposed Order achieved by dancing and prancing bodies, and the mathematical order inherent in the Pythagorean science of numbers. In the hands of a composer of genius, which Monteverdi pre-eminently was, this can imbue a social act with an extraordinary sense of the numinous: as it does here, making Monteverdi a prophetic Hero of Western Music, 'mistaking Earth for Heaven', as Dryden a little later put it. Philosophically, psychologically, and possibly religiously, this refrain might be considered the goal of Monteverdi's Vespers – and even of his music as a whole.

After it, there is no more to be said in terms of the liturgical Vespers: which is why Stevens – and I suspect Monteverdi – follow it with the mainly instrumental *Sonata sopra Sancta Maris*, wherein he calls on the old doctrinal device of *cantus firmus* not in order to assert the Word and Will of God, but to induce sensual excitation! Whereas in the Middle Ages the plainsong *cantus firmus* had been 'held' in long, often instrumentally sustained, notes, here the plainchant is *sung* by (probably female) sopranos and altos, as tribute to the Virgin Mary, while the proliferating counter-points are instrumental, scored in skittish dotted rhythms for violins, viols, cornetti, recorders, trombones, or shawms, bolstered by organ, creating not a synonym for divine many-in-oneness, but a simulation of men and women dancing together in metrically ebullient, blazingly coloured 'divisions'. Since the Fall, human beings have been divisive by nature; it is, however, just feasible that divisiveness might itself generate a tipsy *ecstasis* – nothing to do with the Pythagorean science of numbers but none the less an ultimate manifestation of Monteverdi's pluralistic democracy.

Whether or not this celebration of Man in the Highest be placed last in the Vespers cycle, it is not the last music we hear in performances today. For Monteverdi added to the Vespers sequence a setting of the Magnificat, most famous of all hymns of praise, reputed to have been sung to God by Mary, in gratitude for the honour he'd accorded her in choosing her as 'vessel' for his Son's birth. Sensible of the occasion, Monteverdi made *two* settings, one in six purely vocal parts, presumably for use on non-festive days, the other in seven parts both vocal and instrumental, this being the version usually heard today, when performances of the work are not only frequent, but usually Grand. Certainly, the seven-part setting seems designed to outdo the splendour even of the Vespers itself: for although the 'Et miserecordia' starts with pure plainchant and suavely Palestrinian 'Old Practice' poly-phony, the 'Fecit potentiam', taking its cue from the word 'potentia', garlands a plainsong *cantus firmus* with frisky, almost ribald, instrumental divisions. In the 'Deposuit' the voices again have the *cantus firmus*, while the cornetti and violins dialogue in dizzying echo. In the 'Esurientes' the voices, cooing in parallel thirds, sound simultaneously sensual and angelic; and although Monteverdi's directives are ambiguous about the instrumental forces involved, the words – which concern the blessedness of the meek – leave us in little doubt that cooing Renaissance flutes are more appropriate than blatant shawms. The doxological 'Gloria Patri' then takes us to the heart of the Counter-Reformation, since its baroque opulence is echoed in mystical etheriality, and one isn't sure which comes first.

As a High Renaissance humanist Monteverdi delighted in world, flesh, and devil; but delight tingled his nerves the more acutely because he still knew God. The Word become Flesh was the first miracle, whereby man, fearfully frail yet potentially divine, recognized himself as – in the words previously quoted from Sir John Davies's *Nosce Teipsum* of 1599 – 'a proud, and yet a wretched, Thinge'. But if the Word become flesh was the first miracle, maybe there is a second miracle whereby the flesh becomes Word, resounding in the gloriously overlapping canonic Amens with which this Magnificat leaves us, proud to be human, and satisfied in our pride. On the other hand, our pride may be self-conceit and self-deceit; and an epiphany is not the only possible end to Monteverdi's magnificent Magnificat. Some versions, notably that of Andrew Parrott, eschew final monumentality and return to declaimed liturgy, which views post-Renaissance man's self-glorification in the light of eternity. Glory turns into vainglory, flickering and fading in the Light of the Word which, whether we like it or not, remains as it was in the Beginning, is Now, and Ever shall be, World without End, AMEN. Some scholars, Parrott among them, believe that some of the most baroquely ostentatious sections of the work ought to be transposed a fourth down, which would dampen their glory, while perhaps allowing the still, small voice to speak more clearly. This suggests how technical problems of performance practice may mirror philosophical and theological issues of some profundity; at a crucial juncture in history Monteverdi's *Vespers and Magnificat* at once heralds a New Dawn and sings a threnody on a Lost World. Its ambiguity makes it a key-work in Europe's story.*

---

* Although the Monteverdi Vespers are now frequently performed, usually in a 'festive' form for large forces, scholarly disputation about their true nature still rages. I've written about the piece in the form(s) in which we usually hear it; but one may keep track of the current state of play by consulting the confrontational arguments about the work's nature and genesis between Jeffrey Kurtzman and Peter Holman, published in *The Musical Times* vol. 141 no. 1872, and vol. 142 no. 1877.

9

Reformation and Opera in Church

Crucifixion and Redemption in Schütz's
Passion according to St Matthew (*c.*1665)

The meanings of the word *passio* are multiple. Its root is in passive suffering, but its association with *pathos* relates it to pity and terror, while it has undertones of anger and overtones of sexual desire. The evolution of the *passio* as a musical–dramatic–liturgical convention harks back to a need, already latent in the Middle Ages, to humanize the mythological. Long before the Reformation, this had been a step towards popularization: the illiterate would more readily assimilate a lesson if it were presented lyrically, dramatically, and visually. So medieval liturgical drama emerged as the priest, speaking or intoning monodically, assumed several voices to impersonate different characters in the Gospel story; and no aspect of the story lent itself better to dramatization, or was more *crucial* in eschatological significance, than was the Crucifixion itself. By the late Middle Ages the liturgical passion was an accepted convention, the narration being presented in plainchant-like monody by a priest–evangelist, while Jesus and the lesser characters were presented by other voices. The music – as is evident in one of the earliest Renaissance Passion-settings, by Richard Davy, chaplain to Anne Boleyn's grandfather – makes no claim to dramatic fervour, and remains monodic and basically pentatonic, or at most modally heptatonic. Even when it includes a part for the crowd or *turba* it doesn't exploit the *turbulence* of harmony, but remains ritualistic. Even so, this ritual was dramatic and theatrical *in potentia*; and it was hardly fortuitous that war-ravaged seventeenth-century Germany battened on the convention's simultaneously theatrical and liturgical properties.

The flowering of German (Lutheran) Protestantism naturally concentrated on the story of Christ's life and death, though this did not necessarily entail a break with Roman doctrine. If the Tale was increasingly emphasized, that's because what Protestantism protested against was the substitution of frozen ritual for revealed truth. This is idolatry which, according to Protestantism, is recurrently a threat to the religious mind. There is no answer to Christ's question 'to whom shall you liken me that I am like?' except the story of his life; and that is why composers, especially in war-racked Germany, tried to tell the tale with all the dramatic force and musical cogency of which they were capable. The devastations made by Germany's Thirty Years War of religion were perhaps more appalling than those of any war before the presumptively enlightened twentieth century. But if a man is strong enough, belief may batten on distress, since he feels the psychic realities of his nature the more deeply the more the world seems to be passing them by. This was true of Heinrich Schütz, whose long life (from 1585 to 1672) and whose work offer evidence of the material and spiritual bifurcation between southern Catholicism and northern Protestantism that the war entailed.

Culturally, this was not all loss: it was to its enrichment that Schütz's religious music fused the Italianate flamboyance of southern autocratic Catholicism and the abnegatory fervour of northern, incipiently proletarian Protestantism. Musically, the Italianate elements meant operatic lyricism, harmonic luxuriance, and figurative elaboration; while the German elements involved old-fashioned contrapuntal science harking back to Netherlands polyphonists such as Ockeghem and Obrect, along with a harmonic ardency learned from the Italians, but rendered darker and gloomier.

Schütz himself, in youth, visited Italy to study with 'the sagacious Monteverdi', the sun-baked brilliance of whose music irradiated his early works and, through them, the chapels of German princelings. Yet Schütz's music preserved a mystical fervour that concentrated on Christ's suffering as God-become-Man, equating his suffering with ours; and in Schütz's day 'our' suffering was patent enough, since after the War Teutonic oases of humanism survived, precariously, over an abyss. This was sometimes literally true. Esterházy, later the home of Haydn's patron, was a fairy-tale Versailles erected by woefully oppressed serfs over a marshy morass, hopefully offering evidence that anything a Roi Soleil could do an Esterházy could do, if not better, than at least in the teeth of more inimical circumstances. In the face of such desperate vainglory it is hardly surprising that Schütz, surviving into old age, concentrated increasingly on Christ's Passion, incarnate in musical styles which, in comparison with his youthful flamboyance, grew gradually more austere, ending in a vernacular version of plainchant monody, without even a continuo instrument and with minimal choral interludes. Although this suited the penury of war-impoverished courts, the economic was less powerful than the spiritual motive.

The extreme economy and austerity of Schütz's Passions, while being a winnowing down of the resources he'd drawn on though a long life, give them uncommon potency as an expression of the heart of Protestantism. In Schütz's four Passion settings, written in his seventies and eighties, a narrator or Evangelist tells the tale in what the composer himself called 'German recitative'. It is closer to plainchant than to Monteverdian arioso: though it accords with Monteverdi's statement that recitative is the language of passion, and that there are three heroic passions, love, hate, and prayer. In particular, this Evangelist's monody suggests prayer, as it follows the inflexions of speech, eschewing harmonic support; and if the minor characters are granted snatches of pliantly expressive lyricism, and the *turba* is allowed moments of harmonic and rhythmic fervour that amount to action music, Christ himself is sometimes not characterized at all. In the *Resurrection History*, for instance, his divine attributes are indicated by setting his words for two or three voices rather than one, thereby symbolizing the relationship of Son to Father and Holy Ghost. Schütz's Passions are thus simultaneously drama and sacrament: an equilibrium preserved in the more wide-ranging and complex Passions of Bach. But although Schütz's Passions cannot compete with Bach's in range and scale, they have a powerful if embryonic rawness that springs from the shock of immediate conflict between the 'old' spirituality and the 'new' physicality. In this music the Re-formation seems literally a new start: wide-eyed in wonder, as well as in fear-and-trembling.

Schütz's *Passion According to St Matthew* was the last of his Passion settings and is, like the others, scored for vocal resources exclusively. As had by this time (the 1660s) become traditional, the Evangelist–narrator is a tenor, possibly because tenors may seem to override sexual differentiation; whereas Jesus is a 'manly' baritone whose lines sometimes attain the intensity of Monteverdian arioso. Judas – with cunning, and perhaps even wit – is cast as a counter-tenor, a falsetto voice befitting his falsity. The minor characters – Peter, Caiaphas, Pilate, his wife, and sundry soldiers, servants, and 'maidens' – are divided between SATB registers, and were sung by members of the *turba* choir. The tenuity of these forces does not lead to impoverishment; on the contrary, it imparts to the music a startling immediacy. Since the solo voices are independent of any continuo instrument, whether plucked (as with theorbo or harpsichord) or blown (as with chamber organ), they speak directly to us, as though they were in a play – which of course they are. The rhythms accord with those of vernacular German speech; the linear contours are those that naturally pertain to human voices, with a partiality for pentatonic figurations. All the words – significant in a sacred text – are audible and intelligible, their pace and variety of articulation being more 'realistic' than any form of continuo-backed recitative; and although the musical structure is subservient to the spoken and acted drama, the New Testament narrative is lively (and familiar) enough to lend momentum to the interaction of the characters, interpolating as occasion offers groups of priests and scribes, disciples, false witnesses, and soldiers, not to mention a mob of *hoi polloi*. Listening to this piece – assuming one has a reasonable acquaintance with the German language – is an experience that totally engages mind and senses.

The immediacy of the sung dialogue and narrated action is the more potent because it is presented in a context of ritual. The choral Introitus is in austere four-part harmony, mostly plain diatonic, with a few imitative 'points', though not in fugato. Acute dissonances occasionally remind us that the tale to be unfolded is more sorry than merry – climaxing in the painful suspension in the last bar, when the high E flat, clashing with the D a semitone below, is approached by a rising sixth:

From that invocation the Evangelist plunges *in medias res*, presenting Jesus and his disciples in an 'It came to pass'. The chief priests and scribes set the plot in motion by telling of Jesus's foreknowledge of his fate and of his enemies' intentions to 'take him by subtlety and kill him'. Brief contrapuntal points are used, not as a principle of order, but rather to promote dramatic urgency. The Evangelist, as narrator, has the most volatile lines, notated in a fashion recalling plainchant calligraphy. Jesus, a 'natural' human baritone, has a more committed arioso style, which his disciples tend to sing in canonic togetherness, in conversationally madrigalian fashion, creating a context within which the story unfolds. This is the disciples' normal function – except for Judas, who is by definition an outsider. The sinuosity of his recitative, as well as its 'false' tone-colour, makes a point: as when, in response to Jesus' enquiry about his betrayal, Judas asks, 'Master, is it I?' When Jesus initiates the Eucharistic rite of breaking bread and drinking wine, his line is simultaneously truthful and mysterious:

Jesus: Du sa - gest es, doch ich sa - ge euch, von nun an wird es ge - sche - hen, daß ihr se - hen wer - det des Men - schen Sohn sit - zen zur Rech - ten der Kraft

especially in contrast with his exchanges with the impetuous Peter about the trice-crowing cock. When the Evangelist speaks of Christ's heaviness of heart, his tone is veiled and his pitch wavering.* His drawing aside to pray occasions a weird wanness of tone on the word '*betet*', again revealing how a monophonic technique may have advantages denied to continuo-accompanied recitative. The holy awe of Jesus's praying leads, however, to Judas's traitorous kiss, and that to the animation of the 'arraignment', through which Jesus resolutely 'holds his peace'. The unbridgeable gulf between the almost comic gabble of the canonic False Witnesses and Jesus's calm vision of his coming 'in the clouds of heaven' underlines the contradictory physical and metaphysical dimensions of the story. There is no let-up in the scene of Peter's denial. Drama alarmingly mounts as Pilate offers the mob a choice between Jesus and barbarous Barabbas as sacrificial victim; and the mob's opting for Christ ('Let him be crucified') is energetically rhythmic and harmonically savage, anticipating the comparable effects in Bach's larger-scaled version of the same events.

The Evangelist's long recitative recounting the mob's mocking of and spitting at Jesus, leading to Golgotha and the Crucifixion, evolves from metrically aggressive fury to heart-rending and heart-easing lyricism, culminating harshly in the rending of his garments and the casting of lots. The 'motto' affixed to the Cross ('Diest ist Jesu der Juden König') is declaimed in one spine-chilling tone; and the choric interjections by priests, scribes and elders increase in energy and blatancy, evolving from homophony into theatrical, rather than musical, fugato. The climax of the Passion occurs, as it should, on Jesus's cry 'at the ninth hour', and with 'a loud voice', of the words 'Eli, Eli, la'ma sabach-tan'-ni?' in which arioso flowers into impassioned song. The cry is echoed by the Evangelist in vernacular German, and capped by the Soldiers' canonic question on the rising minor sixth. Here the style is madrigalian without ceasing to be appropriate to liturgy; but when Christ 'yields up the ghost' in an upward-drifting line pallid in tone, Word and flesh become one as Christ's paradoxically victorious death is consummated. The Soldiers' awed recognition that this man must, after all, be 'truly the Son of God' opens with melismata in canon at the godly fifth:

---

* Such effects will, of course, vary from performance to performance. The version to which I refer is the magisterial one of 1971 by Peter Pears, John Shirley-Quirk, and Roger Norrington's Heinrich Schütz Choir.

This prepares the way for the Evangelist's epilogic account of the Two Marys and the sealing of the empty sepulchre. This recitative is tranquilly beyond temporality, though the choric responses of priests and pharisees develop from madrigalian homophony into near-dramatic fugato. The concluding doxology on Kyrie eleison and the Gloria returns, however, to the ritualistic style of the Introitus, albeit in a manner more expansively sustained. Madrigalian part-writing is mutated into polyphonically rising sequences in which we (almost) seem to take off, along with the Lord, risen on the Third Day.

It isn't easy to think of another work that achieves, by way of such modest resources, so cumulative an effect. Compared with the cornucopia of Monteverdi's Vespers, recklessly spilling its fruits, Schütz's Lutheran reformation of Christian music-theatre is literally created out of penury. Oddly enough the two works – one a sacred concert, the other a play in music – are complementary, equal in both dramatic and liturgical potency.

10

The Glory of God and a Man's Glory

J.S. Bach's High and Solemn Mass (1747)

That Bach, a committed eighteenth-century Lutheran, should have composed a Roman High Mass is only superficially odd for, as the greatest of Christian composers, he was preoccupied with the heart of the Christian mystery, which is beyond denomination. Luther himself, who loved music (especially that of Josquin), had admitted the Kyrie and Gloria into Protestant liturgy; and Bach wrote four short masses, with Kyrie and Gloria only, for use in his Church's rites. In also completing a full-scale setting of the Ordinary of dimensions so huge that it was unlikely to be performed, his unconscious motivation may have been to make an absolute statement of faith comparable in grandeur with his Passions: which tell a human story in operatic terms, while revealing that that history is transhistorical. The B minor Mass enacts a rite in the ceremonial terms of the High Baroque, while revealing that the rite incorporates – gives body to – a human tale that is also divine.

Opera seria was the supreme medium of the classical baroque era since people who believed in Man in the Highest naturally thought that men's actions were worthy of emulation. Bach, who believed in God in the Highest, none the less employed, with exceptional richness, almost all the conventions of *opera seria* while adhering to the basic plan of Eucharistic ritual. Like a Catholic Mass, Bach's is divided into Kyrie, Gloria, Credo, Sanctus, Benedictus, and Agnus Dei; though its scope is vastly extended since most sections are subdivided into alterations of contrapuntal or polyphonic–harmonic choruses with operatic arias or ensemble numbers. Although Bach copied out the score, in his noble calligraphy, at the end of his life, between 1747 and 1748, he garnered its material from at least twenty-five of his sixty-five years. The Sanctus was composed in 1724, the Kyrie and Gloria in 1733, for specific occasions; throughout the work many movements were borrowed from already-written cantatas, usually to

German texts. None of these borrowings was prompted by lack of time consequent on a harried professional life. Bach chose from his prolific output precisely those pieces that were most appropriate, rewriting them subtly and extensively. One might even say that, since his musical language was consistent, his remoulding of earlier sources worked towards rather than against integration: so that the Mass became both a summation of Bach's life-work and also a, perhaps the, central musical manifestation of Christian faith.

Although usually referred to as the 'Mass in B minor', the piece is complementarily in B minor and in its relative, D major, with the latter slightly preponderant. D major was traditionally the key of baroque Glory (because it was the key of natural trumpets and of brilliantly open-stringed violins); B minor, as 'relative' to D major, acquired associations with the darker aspects of human experience – and with their potential transcendence. Unsurprisingly, B minor is a key favoured by Bach for much of his deepest music. A major, D major's dominant, tended to be youthfully buoyant, but also spiritually exalted; while G major, D's subdominant, was a key of peace and blessedness. Complementarily, F sharp minor, dominant of B minor, tended to add edge to B minor's pathos, while E minor, B minor's *sub*dominant, became Bach's key of ultimate suffering, epitomized in the Crucifixion. These tonal allegories were scrupulously adhered to by Bach, giving to baroque musical convention a defined theological dimension.

The first part of the rite – Kyrie-Christe-Kyrie – is a tripartite structure wherein a duet-aria for Christ is enclosed within two monumental choruses for us the people. It opens with an exhortation to the Godhead lasting a mere four bars yet creating, through its interlocked 'horizontal' (polyphonic) and 'vertical' (harmonic) axis, a sense at once of heroic aspiration and of tragic depth. After those hair-raising, spine-chilling bars the Kyrie opens as a five-voiced (SSATB) fugue in B minor, with a theme stalking in a stately $\frac{4}{4}$ pulse, beginning with four repeated notes in dotted rhythm, attesting to the Rock we might cling to. Yet from this affirmation the theme expands in wedge shape, creating as aural synonym for the Cross, culminating in a rising sixth painfully resolved in a Neapolitan cadence (dominant-tonic approached by way of the tightly flattened supertonic):

The texture, thickly scored, grows dense as well as tense, yet the pulse remains constant since the ravages of 'our' suffering, in the light of the *mysterium* of the crucified Christ we're about to celebrate, are an impetus to worship and a tower of strength. Significantly, the fugue subject always appears, throughout its five parts, in its original (*rectus*) form and in its original note-values (without augmentation or diminution), as unalterable as the Will of God. The immense length of this fugue – with Klemperer it could last an (inauthentic) 15 minutes – is an aspect of its godly majesty which remains as it was, is now, and ever shall be, notwithstanding the fact that the music embraces the total hierarchy of classical baroque tonality, generating both power and (sometimes painful) momentum.

The Christe complements the grandeur of the Kyrie by invoking Christ in a shift from monumental chorus to intimate aria. The key is D major, relative of 'suffering' B minor, for Christ brings salvation. That the number is in the form of an operatic aria stresses human intimacy as distinct from the chorus's monumentality, the more so because the textures are those of humanly gracious chamber music, albeit with a theological gloss in that the aria is scored not for a solo voice, but for two equal treble voices in harmonic concordance and often in canon 2 in 1, with an obbligato part for two violins in unison, symbolizing the identity of Father and Son. The opening figure is an inversion of a cliché of ecclesiastical polyphony (rising fourth followed by falling scale) that had been prevalent in the episodes of the Kyrie. Yet this is not a 'closed' *aria de capo* but one that is consequential: for the threat, which is also the promise, of Christ's crucifixion, steers the music, during the 'middle' section, through sighing appoggiaturas in Crucifixion's E minor, and so to a D major *da capo* that is brief but far from perfunctory. The second Kyrie, though much shorter than the first, intensifies it in being in F sharp minor, B minor's dominant, and in being even more acutely dissonant than the first. For after the emergence of the human-but-divine Christ in the 'Christe', Bach doesn't merely repeat the original Kyrie according to convention; he rather composes a *new* chorus which paradoxically is at once more humane – in its coruscating dissonances and in its surging corporeal momentum – and at the same time more 'doctrinally' severe – in its use of 'old-fashioned' *alla breve* notation and style. Although the parts move mainly stepwise, like a seventeenth-century *ricercar*, the textures compromise between old and new: indeed, some of the steps that sound like major seconds are in fact diminished thirds, so that at the climax the four-part counterpoint, harmonically screwed up, makes for an almost savage excitation.

That the second Kyrie is scored for four parts, whereas the first is for five, also makes a point. It would seem that Bach, even more than most of his contemporaries, was fascinated by the Pythagorean science of numbers: on the psychological implications of which Jung (in *Psychology* and *Alchemy*) has written perceptively. 'Four forms or frames the one', which is the Centre.

> By unfolding into four it acquires distinct characteristics, and can therefore be known . . . So long as a thing is in the unconscious it has no recognizable qualities and is therefore merged into the universal unknown, with what the Gnostics called 'a non-existent all-being'. But as soon as unconscious content enters into the sphere of consciousness it has already split into four; that is to say it can become an object of experience only by virtue of the four basic functions of consciousness. The splitting into four has the same significance as the division of the horizon into four quarters, or the year into four seasons. Through the act of becoming conscious the four basic aspects of a whole judgment (perception, recognition, distinction, and evaluation) are rendered visible.

The addition of the One (monad) to this fourfold consciousness is the inevitable next step; and the Hebrew word for 5, *chamesh*, means facultative comprehension, while the Greek word for 5, *pente*, is derived from Pan, who represents Nature and the All. Five is the mind of God that, brooding 'over the waters', brings what subsists in matter into *ex*istence.

Such arcane speculations may not have been present in the forefront of Bach's mind, but he was sufficiently impregnated with Pythagoreanism to have un- and half-wittingly associated *human* consciousness with the number 4, and the (divinely?) pantheistic All with 5. We may also observe that the three sections of the Kyrie-Christe-Kyrie stand in mediant relation to one another, being respectively in B minor, D major, and F sharp minor, so that together they define the stability of a triad that incorporates both a minor and a major third. In this context it is also not fortuitous that the fugal theme of the second Kyrie insinuates into the polyphony the B-A-C-H motif inverted. Bach introduces his own 'signature' into the apparently hieratic structure since he is proud to be the 'maker' of the work, as 'our' representative. In such minutiae the vastness and complexity of Bach's musical cosmology is encapsulated: God's preordained 'plan', humanity's burgeoning consciousness, and Bach's own individualized identity as com-poser who, through human consciousness, puts things together, may be said to create the Whole. The end of the second Kyrie sets the seal on this: for it concludes with the blazing light of an F sharp major triad – only for the light to be momently cancelled by a false relation when the key returns to D major for the Gloria.

The Kyrie and Christe thus start from God's almightiness, within which they embrace the humanity of Christ the saviour, so that the second Kyrie, although harmonically and rhythmically more 'humanized' than the first, also attains a higher degree of exaltation. Relatively, the Gloria seems to begin with an exuberant tribute to Earthly Powers, resonating on trumpets, wood-wind, violins, and drums, with fanfare-like arpeggiated themes such as might enliven the junketings of a supernal Sun-King. Although the chorus is in (God's or the All's) five parts, as was the first but not the second Kyrie, it is freely polyphonic though not strictly contrapuntal; indeed, its overlapping entries suggest a riotous round-dance, with agile leaps and proud prancings. When the words refer, however, to 'Et in terra pax' the parts move stepwise, in parallel $\frac{6}{3}$ chords, and the tonality sinks to blessed G major. So in this long, wild movement God 'in excelsis' displays *man*'s arpeggiated corporeal energy, while man, on his earth, has music traditionally associated with holy matters. The human and the godly musics are inextricably fused as the 'Et in terra pax' phrases are garlanded with virtuosic roulades ending, after sharpwards modulations, back in D major, sonorously jubilant on trumpets and drums.

Characteristically, this ostensibly mundane majesty is immediately succeeded by a treble aria with violin obbligato: music in 'youthful' A major, D major's dominant, in which the violin twitters like a lark ascending, promoting grace both physical and metaphysical as he soars aloft in demisemiquavers. The soprano's song of adoration twines with the violin–lark in chains of trills and lilting syncopations; but the middle section wafts around the 'suffering' keys of B, F sharp, and C sharp minors, hinting at sonata-style development. This does not, however, occur: for the music simply stops at its maximum point of tonal adventure (C sharp minor), as though the praise is blithe enough to conquer contradiction and flow into a *da capo* in which the lark wings to vertiginous heights for the rational eighteenth century:

The 'Laudamus Te' is a vision of bliss within the individual psyche. The next movement, 'Gratias agimus', starts the process of atonement, or at-one-ment – back in a D major employed in a style very different from the pomp and circumstance in which the Gloria had opened. The chorus returns to four basic parts, SATB, but again presents this 'human' formula in archaic *alla breve* notation, the theme being the simplest possible version of the motif of rising and falling fourths, with the interval now filled in by scalewise steps. Instead of the personal ecstasy of the 'Laudamus Te' we have corporate identity, embraced in smooth but often dissonant canonic *stretti*.

The impersonality of this grave music serves as preparation for the at once physical and metaphysical drama of Incarnation, approached in the next sequence of movements. The 'Domine Deus' and the 'Qui tollis' are Annunciation music in that the first prophecies the 'Et in unum Dominum' of the Credo, while the 'Qui tollis' annunciates its 'Et incarnatus', the keys (G major and B minor) being the same. The 'Domine Deus' is the first movement notated in benedictory G major: the words, invoking God as Father and as Son, foretell but do not enact His descent into human form. The duet-aria is scored for treble and alto voices, with flute obbligato and muted string ritornello wherein the first violin often functions as a second canonic part complementing the two voices, with the flute. The pulse is gentle, the texture limpid; but the piece doesn't behave like a formal *da capo* aria since its 'middle' modulates into the Crucifixion key of E minor; and an attempted *da capo* fails to re-establish G major. Indeed, the duet ends poignantly in B minor, dominant of E minor, and proceeds without break into a choral 'Qui tollis' that is dramatic, even operatic, as Word becomes flesh. Though not a fugue, this movement is 'in fugato', based on falling triads and painfully aspiring sixths, with softly sobbing quavers on strings and winging semiquavers on two flutes, emblematic of the Holy Ghost. The movement ends with a beginning – a new vista on the major triad of the dominant; but the time of fulfilment is not yet, and Bach follows this sublime moment with two arias that deliberately lower the emotional temperature. The text of the 'Qui tollis' had paid homage to Christ because he 'taketh away the sins of the world'; in this context the next two arias threaten to remove God the Father from us, since they are formally heroic, comparable to those made in tribute to mundane potentates: the formality of the 'Qui sedes' would seem to be triggered by the words' physical image of Christ 'sitting', enthroned at God's right hand. The key of B minor, rather than royal D major, is paradoxical, especially in association with the two love-oboes as obligato instruments: it's as though the aria were a 'thought up' idealization of the Man–God relationship, telling us that the salvation presaged in the 'Qui tollis' cannot be in this world, whatever a Louis XIV may have thought or hoped. The companion aria, scored for a royal *corno da caccia* and two woody bassoons, makes the same point, more boldly. The solo parts are tricky to perform, and although the words concern Deus altissimus up in his high heaven, what we *hear* is low, even grumpy. Is the celebration of God's separateness also a testament to Man's Fall?

Such conscious or unconscious equivocations are swept away by the Gloria's final chorus, back in triple-rhythmed D major with widely arpeggiated themes in free dialogue rather than polyphony, supported by pulsing heartbeats in the form of rather frantically thudding quavers. Chuckling demisemiquavers on stratospheric trumpets almost suggest a Rite of Spring, or even the Midsummer Day festivities that were banished from the Christian calendar. Jesus is mutated into Orpheus–Dionysus, with a hint of the Wrath of God that more scarily pervades Beethoven's *Missa Solemnis*. Despite its basis in baroque concerto grosso style there is no movement in Bach that sweeps on in such unbridled, and un-Protestant, force. For those who have ears to hear, voices to exult with, and limbs to cavort, Bach's 'Cum sancto' is a present excitation far more potent than anything our jaded world can offer – including Powerhouse music or Heavy Metal.

Bach treats the Credo, as an affirmation of belief, with appropriate severity, beginning in old-fashioned *alla breve* style, and in the five parts he deems appropriate to God, as distinct from humanity's four that 'square the circle'. The fugal theme is the original plainchant intonation, in long notes as in a traditional *cantus firmus* motet; and the tonality is ambiguously modal, in a mixolydian A major with two instead of three sharps. The scholasticism of the fugue is numerately theological as well as musical. Since in the figure alphabet CREDO equals 43, Bach makes 43 entries of the plainsong motif, representing God's law in a rigid metre that makes it seem infrangible, as Bach perhaps thought it was. In contrast with the orgiastic conclusion of the Gloria, this music sounds like a call to order; and seems the more so when we discover that there are 45 bars in the *cantus firmus* passage and 84 in the succeeding, more homophonic, 'Patrem omnipotentem'. The sum of those bars (45 + 84) amounts to 129, which is three (Trinitarian) times 43, the number representing CREDO in the figure alphabet! These numerical puzzles don't affect the *sound* of the music though they testify to the temper of Bach's mind and condition the music's architectural (and mathematical) proportions. They also prepare the way for the most 'crucial' turning point in the Eucharist, since at the word 'invisibilium' – referring to the things we cannot *know* – D major returns as home key, and shifts flatwards to G major for the duet 'Et in unum Dominum': an explicitly 'doctrinal' double canon for two treble voices at the unison, and for flute and violin. The 'mystery' of the two canons 2 in 1 aurally enacts the words, though in the middle section of the aria form both vocal and instrumental canons expand across the bar-lines, modulating to B minor and then E minor on the words 'Deum verum de Deo vero'. When the music returns to G major we seem to be embarking on an orthodox *da capo*; but G major unexpectedly darkens to G minor, this being only the second appearance of this key in the Mass, and a point on which the whole structure pivots, since it immediately precedes the Crucifixion and Resurrection.

Bach originally included the words 'Et incarnatus' within the 'Et in unum' aria; his decision to add a separate choral movement was an inspired afterthought. Covering 49 (seven times seven) holy bars, the 'Et incarnatus' mirrors the Gloria's 'Qui tollis' in its key (B minor), its swaying triple pulse, its bass beating in crotchets, and in its quavers sighing on muted strings. The vocal entries steal in, enhancing tension by way of *falling* triads; a German sixth effects a modulation to the 'enhanced' pain of F sharp minor. In the concluding bars the bass throbs in 'heaviness of soul', until it finds release in emulating the violins' weeping which is never whimpering. The voices' fugato fades in broken thirds and anguished appoggiaturas, yet from dissolution flowers the radiance of a *tierce de Picardi*. The passage induces awe-struck wonder; and paradoxically, that B minor triad proves to be no final resolution, but rather an initiator of the Mass's central crux, for it is alchemized into a dominant of E minor, and so leads to the Crucifixion itself.

The Crucifixion is depicted in a chorus in four parts rather than five, the first sopranos being omitted partly one suspects, because their bright sonorities would be inappropriate to the occasion, but also to underline the fact that the ultimate sacrificial act was that of a human being even though he also happened to be God. The $\frac{3}{2}$ metre is slightly more urgent than the $\frac{3}{4}$ of the 'Et incarnatus', though here both the bass and the vocal lines droop more oppressively, since they are chromaticized. At the same time any disintegrative tendency is resisted since the movement is a passacaglia, built over a ground bass that has illustrious parallels in musical history, notably in the Lament of Purcell's Dido. But Bach gives his chromatic bass Christian connotations, since he repeats his ostinato thirteen times, a number that 'stood for' Christ and his twelve disciples and, more fundamentally, was at once unlucky and lucky since God's fall into flesh, like Adam's and Eve's fall into sin, proves to be a *felix culpa*. The ostinato generates a sequence of enharmonic mysteries consummated when Bach abandons his source (a chorus from an early cantata, *Weinen, Klagen, Sorgen, Zagen*) to compose it anew, making a miracle manifest. The 'Crucifixus' motif is now syncopated on the second beat of the sarabande rhythm; and the sixth degree of the scale resolves on to the fifth not in a falling second, but by way of a diminished third. The strange harmonic progressions that ensue make the lines flow in contours that increasingly embrace the fourths that pervade the entire Mass, making – in context – for the most lyrically fulfilled music conceivable. God's death awakens our hearts in song: after which the ultimate, deepest possible cadence transmutes Crucifixion's E minor into G major bliss. There is no more magical instance of the physiological and psychological impact of tonality in European music. The 'Et resurrexit' returns to tonic D major and to celebratory music such as typified the big choruses of the Gloria, with themes bouncily arpeggiated in triple time, and with whirling semiquaver scales, sometimes speeded up to triplets; again the bass pulses in unflagging energy. Yet this corporeal resurrection is complemented by a pastoral aria for bass voice, with obbligato parts for twinned love-oboes, the key being A major – like that of the Gloria's ascending lark, but humanly tranquil rather than divinely ecstatic. Bach concludes his Credo with the orthodox 'confession' of belief which develops – as affirmations of faith perhaps shouldn't, and, except with composers who share Bach's rare if terrifying honesty, cannot – from attested doctrine into momently enacted drama. Initially, the sacredly five-part chorus is in *alla breve* style in diatonic F sharp minor with tonal rather than 'real' answers. An instrumental bass marches in remorseless crotchets, and a plainchant *cantus firmus*, as in the first Credo, offers the authority of the Law. Even so, the contrapuntal textures grow distraught, modulating with a freedom that hints that human sin might even undermine God's law. This seems to happen as interweaving polyphonies, praying 'in remissionem peccatorum', create painful suspensions and sobbing augmented fifths; and although the Law's *cantus firmus* hopefully re-enters in canon, personal apprehension seems to be momently stronger than doctrine. Frightened dismay creates a weird deliquescence in chromatic sequences, evaporating in a passage marked 'Adagio' wherein, over a throbbing bass reminiscent of that of the 'Crucifixus', the music wildly wanders through E flat and B flat minors.

Very slowly, on the word 'expecto', the line rises through a third, with an enharmonic shift from C natural to C sharp, leaving us marooned in time and space. Except for the 'Crucifixus' itself, this is the most awesome moment in the Mass, revealing again why Bach is the greatest, because the least evasive, of all religious composers. Living in an age of faith and composing for the glory of God he yet, faced with the prospect of the 'world to come' and the 'judgment of the quick and the dead', betrays this tremor of dubiety and fear: which dams the forward movement, slows the pulse, disintegrates harmony and tonality. Momently Bach the Lutheran Christian, within the liturgy of a Roman Catholic Mass, becomes not only a Protestant humanist, but also a post-Faustian man aligned, in fear and trembling, with Beethoven who, in composing *his* Solemn Mass, explored the dynamic conflicts of sonata in despite of the closed structures of the Classical Baroque.

Even so, Bach has the courage to end his Credo with music of breath-takingly innocent corporeality. The Power and the Glory are reinstated in startlingly physical images. The dead leap from their graves in almost frisky arpeggios: one can almost hear the rending of shrouds and the clatter of discarded coffins. The introversion of the previous section is banished by an extroversion as palpable as that displayed in the Resurrection paintings of Stanley Spencer and of the medieval artists who inspired him. All movement is upwards, in clear dominant-tonic harmony, culminating in *stretti* on the root interval of a fourth. Tipsy Amens scurry in pell-mell scales, sometimes springing to crazy heights.

The Gloria and Credo – the most substantial sections of the Eucharist – contain narrations of the Christian story from both Man's and God's point of view. In the consummatory Sanctus, Benedictus, and Agnus Dei, however, the rite is presently enacted in moments that, being transhistorical, 'place' the naïve naturalism of the Resurrection music as wish-fulfilment. The Sanctus exploits the panoply of heroic, indeed divine power, being scored for six-part chorus divisible into two trinities, with three trumpets, three oboes, strings and timpani. The expansion of God's five parts to six is fortuitous in the sense that the Sanctus was composed for a special occasion way back in 1724; but its concentration on threes and sixes, probably inspired by the six-fold wings of the Seraphim in Isaiah, exactly accords with Bach's present purposes, since it caps the allegory of Resurrection with a *Revelation* of Glory. Although the movement is physical, it doesn't have the driven volition of the Credo's end, but rather swings like an immense censer wafted by God over his cosmos, while the orchestra blazes like the suns that, in Isaiah, serve as haloes for the angels.

Compared with this Byzantine splendour or even terror, the janglingly resurrected skeletons in the Credo seem almost farcical; and it may be that Bach is unique in being able to proceed from that divinely comic vision to the *as it were* superhuman grandeur of his Sanctus, wherein canonic entries of falling octaves in the bass are ballasted by triplet-garlanded rising scales, tolling like gigantic bells. The six parts, divided into threes, remind us that for the Pythagoreans the soul was a double trinity of spirit and matter, and the number 6 represented perfection, peace, health, and harmony, and by analogy marriage. This is a further reason why the expansion to six parts, at this holiest of holy moments, is so potent.

Even so, the sublime chorus, being a man-made artefact subject to time, does end – with a crucial modulation to F sharp minor: from which, switching back abruptly to D major, the tempo changes from God's magisterial march to a perky $\frac{3}{8}$. In the 'Pleni sunt coeli', celebrating Nature's fecundity, we move from the Sanctus's heaven into a fast round-dance in fugato; the music is merrily mundane as we dance in our own palatial church which, like Leipzig's St Thomas's, is a meeting-place for the community as well as a House of God. Arpeggiated figures and brilliant roulades recall the Gloria music as we rejoice, in our own terms, at God's bounty. An enhancement of worldly jollification occurs because the most conspicuous interval is now the rising major sixth, even jauntier than the habitual fourths and fifths. This music preserves the six parts of the holy Sanctus, adapted to humanly skittish ends; but the climacteric Hosanna expands the six parts to eight, this number being thought of as twice four, forming a double SATB chorus, used homophonically and antiphonally. This, the most 'worldly' music in the piece, with its many-voiced coexistences of figurations and tempi, creates an effect as of milling crowds – the huzzaing of multitudes as Jesus makes his last entry into Jerusalem. Large stretches of the 'Pleni' and 'Hosanna' were appropriately borrowed by Bach from a secular cantata he'd written in earlier days, in praise of a worldly Lord; yet again, he does not define barriers between the sacred and the profane; and something like awe is induced by this crowd-music, with its whiff of danger in the long-trilling trumpets. Humanity, in the mass, tends to be frightening; yet in facing up to this Bach makes the *mysterium sacrum* of the heart of the Mass feasible.

This being so, it's interestingly paradoxical that the *ultimately* sacred moments of the 'Benedictus' and the Agnus Dei are conceived not in chorically grand terms, but in the intimacy of solo arias, presumably because mystical illumination can only be a private matter. In the 'Benedictus' blessedness and happiness are distilled for those who 'come in the name of the Lord': as we learn from a private meditation in the form of an intimate operatic aria for a high, quasi-androgynous tenor, neither in glorious D major nor in blessed G major, but in B minor, the key of suffering! The tenor sings in duo with an unspecified obbligato instrument, almost certainly an angelic flute: which, in a long prelude, establishes this as one of Bach's 'flight' arias, as the solo flute levitates from a slow, level bass through broken arpeggios, descends through a 'Neapolitan' sixth, and flows into liquid triplets. In both solo lines, vocal and instrumental, there's an equivocation between ecstasy and anguish; interlaced, they soaringly sing, yet generate pain through their linear angularity. When, in the middle section, they grow both more fragmented and more urgent, they chase one another in drooping phrases and aspiring arpeggios, often cut off in silence:

There is no vocal *da capo*, though the flute repeats its opening *ritornello*, its final painful descent through a major seventh being brushed aside by a repetition of the rumbustious Hosanna. Indeed, man attains seraphic blessedness *within* the tawdry hubbub of the world's milling crowds. The tenor's vocal lines, in their wide-ranging, long-leaping lyricism, seem to be seeking even as they are flying; the tenor *becomes* that 'still small voice' that heals through (B minor) suffering. In the context of the Christian sacrament, the tenor solo *is* Jesus Christ.

This is confirmed by the final aria, the Agnus Dei, which had been prophesied in the Credo's G minor end to the 'Et in unum Dominum'. The effect of purgation achieved by the appearance of G minor as home-key at this point cannot be explained by its being minor subdominant to glorious D major. Subconsciously, we recall its relation to the Mass's central mystery; moreover, despite the aria's intimacy, we respond to it as the consummation of the entire vast work. It's a rebirth of the first Kyrie, in that its melody fuses maximum lyrical expressivity with maximum harmonic tension; and it thereby fulfils Bach's equation between passion and Passion, making the divine sacrament quintessentially *human*. Bach directs that the obligato part be played not by a solo violin, but by all the violins in unison, thereby universalizing it as an ultimate threnody. The instruments begin low in register, more wearily broken than the Benedictus's flighting; yet at the same time the phrases' syncopation suggests ardent expectation as the melody, rising and falling, breathes like a human creature, each falling tritone being balanced by a rising tritone:

At first the alto voice doesn't sing the syncopated phrase, but muses on the words 'peccata mundi' and 'miserere', attaining an incandescent intensity in the middle section but breaking off, in a half close, at the thirty-third bar, in homage to Christ's reputed death at that age. The violin's postlude returns to the syncopated figure, riddled with those devilish tritones that have become the gateway to salvation; until the line's final Fall through a major seventh induces a rest the more 'perfect' because it doesn't deny pain. Its angularity recalls the postlude to the Benedictus, which also ceased on a declension through a major seventh. In both passages the agony of Incarnation and of Crucifixion has been dis-embodied. The Agnus distils *lacrimae rerum* into peace; and that Bach refurbished it from an earlier source demonstrates his recognition of the inevitable. This, he knew, was the consummation demanded by his greatest work; and around 250 years later we can still hear that he was right.

The Agnus Dei attains peace for the individual spirit and does so, as had Christ, through an extremity of suffering. The Mass ends, however, with a return to its public function, with a 'Dona nobis pacem' for which Bach uses the same music as he'd used for the 'Gratias agimus'. This has occasioned surprise, even dismay, as though Bach were skimping of effort. But the image of a giving that is also a receiving is ratified by Bach's use of the same music, and the fusion of two different texts into identical music is a representation of the hypostatic union of Christ with his Church. Because Jesus gave thanks when he broke bread, Christians called it the Holy Eucharist, 'our sacrifice of praise and thanksgiving'. They believe, or are supposed to believe, that in the act of communion God comes down to dwell in his communicants, effecting a union of the divine with the human. The idea that the Dona nobis pacem is a prayer *for* peace negates that efficacy: rather may it be considered a laudation of the peace(ful union) that passes understanding, not because sacrifice consists of praise and thanksgiving, but because it is offered with those ends in view. The use of the same music for the 'Gratias agimus' and the 'Dona nobis pacem' thus rounds off the Mass both musically and theologically. After those two tragically purgatorial arias, the Benedictus and the Agnus Dei, there could be no further progress, or even process; we leave the church to resume our daily lives, renewed in strength. To compose for the good of the work was to com-pose – to put things together – 'for the Glory of God and the Instruction of my Neighbour'. Bach believed that his work, well done, *perfectum ex perfecto*, could make people 'better'.

And it does.

11

A Rara Avis *at the Seat of Power*

François Couperin at the Chapelle Royale of
Versailles: his *Quatre Versets d'un Motet* (1703),
his *Motet de Ste Suzanne* (*c.*1705), and his
Troisième Leçon des Ténèbres
(between 1713 and 1717)

Few people have any doubt that J.S. Bach is the greatest of European
religious composers, and many think that he owes his crucial position to his
being a Protestant who, against a backcloth of the Old Faith, identified God
with a specific Man. Apart from Bach, church composers of the High
Baroque age paid homage to Man (rather than God) in the Highest,
taking their cue from a (mere) man called Louis XIV of France, who
imbued himself with deity as the Roi Soleil. Yet oddly enough the French
court was the only European centre of social gravity in the late seventeenth
and early eighteenth centuries wherein we find an ecclesiastical composer
(albeit working for the Palais de Versailles) who made music both highly and
deeply spiritual. This suggests that the panoply of material power wasn't
what made the court of Louis XIV 'great'; the composer in question,
François Couperin, was 'dit le Grand' because of the quality of his
unpretentious art, as well as to distinguish him from other members of his
large and illustrious musical family, exceeded in number and fame only by
the German Bachs.

Louis XIV had, of course, a State Composer imported from Italy,
where musicians were supposed to come from, to sing his praises and
record his military triumphs. He, Jean-Baptiste Lully, concentrated on
theatre music which, whether produced ritualistically at court or in Paris,
related the glamour of Louis's majesty to classical, mythical, and

legendary themes, so that opera dealt with how things might or ought to be, rather than with how they were. On occasion he also composed monumental choral works to mark state occasions, sometimes allowing God a part in the plot, sometimes dispensing with his services. Couperin, a younger man than Lully, born in 1668, made no attempt crudely to serve the State, and perhaps wasn't asked to; yet as a harpsichordist who wrote mostly short pieces for his instrument – offering portraits of particular though not always famous people, and describing rural or urban scenes and social institutions, including the myths of the popular theatre inherent in the commedia dell'arte – Couperin made a World and was grandly ennobled. It is slightly surprising that music as subtly discreet as Couperin's should have earned such fame; and there must be a connection with the fact that Couperin wrote church music that is not in the least pompous and circumstantial, but is cast modestly in the form of chamber music for solo voices and instruments, with supportive continuo. There were a few other composers, notably Marc-Antoine Charpentier, who created genuinely 'spiritual' music for the church; but Couperin was recognized as pre-eminent, even in a society apparently dedicated to complacent ostentation. Many people recognized that France was made truly great by unanalysable qualities such as 'pudeur' and 'l'honnêteté' – qualities that are detectable in most of Couperin's music, at whatever ostensible level. I'll comment on three religious pieces, two composed for the King's elegant Royal Chapel, the third commissioned by a near-by community of nuns.

Quatre Versets d'un Motet chanté à Versailles, 1703 sets words from the psalm 'Mirabilia testimonia tua' to music which marks the emergence of the authentic, possibly even unique, Couperin manner in Latin church music. The piece is modestly scored for two soprano voices, two flutes, and two violins, with chamber organ and string bass continuo; and opens with the ultimate modesty of two high soprano voices chanting canonically 'sans Basse-Continue ny aucun Instrument', in flexible, often elliptical rhythms. This does indeed sound like 'celestial music', with the voices' clashing overtones hinting at the super-natural: so that when the instruments enter, we realize how 'art' may make God socially amenable. The first aria is scored for the two sopranos in dialogue with duos of flutes and violins, the delicate theme beginning with a godly rising fifth followed by a tripping, maybe *falling*, scale-figure. The texture resembles that of Couperin's first major work, the organ masses he published in 1690, after serving as choirmaster at the church of St Gervais. The lightly fugal textures suggest French ballet music, though the vocal lines are more Italianate, with ornamental roulades prompted by the words:

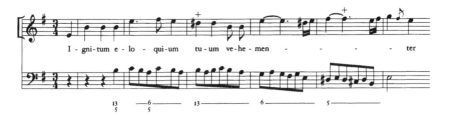

The next verse, 'Adolescentulus sum', shifts from purgatorial E minor to E major which – as often noted – was a key traditionally associated with heaven. This heaven would seem to imply innocence, for the limpid sonorities of soprano, flutes, and violins accord with the simple diatonicism of the lines, the caressing passing-notes, and the symmetrical rhythm. There's a link with the courtly tradition of the pastoral *brunette*; but in this guileless intertwining of soprano and flutes there's also a quality that harks back, from the sensual emotion of Carissimi in the *grand siècle*, to the linear purity of Renaissance composers like Dufay and Josquin; consider the liquidly dissolving effect of Couperin's passing notes:

This movement leads into a lightly dancing setting of 'Justitia tua', wherein the leap of a tenth imbues the soprano line with airiness, and there are piquant canonic entries that make for dissonant suspensions without impairing the lively delicacy. The final section, 'Qui dat nivem', is scored for the same euphonious consort as the 'Adolescentulus sum' and likewise generates, through passing notes and appoggiaturas in a gentle crotchet pulse, a silvery radiance: a texture that no-one but Couperin could have encompassed.

The second piece on which I'll comment, the *Motet de Ste Suzanne* written a few years later, is more Italianate in style, though this in no way affects Couperin's paradox of a synthesis of harmonic sensuality with a virginal spirituality of line. The opening recalls the youthful Handel in an apprentice-piece like *Dixit Dominus*, the somewhat immaterial 'material' being generated from a wriggling coloratura phrase on the word 'coronaberis', bandied between the haut-contre soloist and the two violins. In the minor episode

Couperin's seventh and ninth chords hint at introspection without affronting the music's playfulness. Indeed this smiling playfulness, being innocent, carries no suspicion of irreverence: as becomes evident in the succeeding duet, 'Date serta, date flores', a piece blossoming in the *tendresse* of soft suspensions anticipatory of those Couperin will use so cunningly in the two two-violin sonatas that offer 'Apotheosis' to French Lully and Italian Corelli as accredited masters of 'les deux goûts'. This delicious duet leads into what is called a 'Chorus' but was probably sung by the three soloists (SSB), who 'jubilate' and 'exult' in transparent sonorities on the words 'resonet coelum plausibus'.

The climacteric movement is a *sarabande grave* notated in $\frac{3}{2}$ time, the melody superbly moulded in Carissimi's or the early Handel's Italianate fashion. Its fusion of spiritually fragrant melody with tenderly voluptuous harmony is consummate:

and is strong enough to propel the music into more energetically duple-rhythmed fugato for the 'Voluit Dominus sacrificium'. After a repetition of the 'Jubilemus' chorus comes a duet for soprano and bass with continuo, in which the gentle rise of the voices in canon is balanced by the string bass's augmented descent. Suspended seconds and ninths imbue emotional warmth with naïve wonder.

Probably Couperin would have claimed no more for the *Ste Suzanne* motet than that it was simply a sensuous act of veneration for a saint who was also a pretty girl threatened by the contagion of the world. Yet in the candour of the sensuality a spiritual dimension is involved. The 'douceur' of the music touches an emotion which the priest Fenelon described as 'tranquille et désintéressé'. Far from being a matter of any 'inspiration extraordinaire', it amounted to a simplicity and honesty of response which, if achieved, will encourage God to reward us with his grace and peace. This quality elevates Couperin's church music beyond the range of Lully's – except possibly in the Florentine's great choral *Miserere* in which, momently, Lully discards the triumphs and tribulations of State to confront the common lot of us 'miserable offenders'. Couperin too could on occasion accept the tragedy of the human predicament undismayed; and did so between 1713 and 1715, when, in his early forties, he was invited to compose for a community of nuns at Longchamps a series of nine settings of that most solemnly sacred of rites, the *Leçons des Ténèbres*, traditionally performed around Good Friday. Only three works from the cycle survive;

and as we might expect two of them are scored for a solitary soprano voice without obbligato instruments and with a continuo of chamber organ and gamba or possibly cello. Even so, though the music preserves 'pudeur' and a civilized decorum, it also attains an intensity of passion that Couperin seldom assayed, as it fuses the tradition of the Old Testament with that of the New by harking back to a convention that, as we noted, had been used by Tallis around a 150 years previously. According to this convention the Latinized words of the prophet Jeremiah are interspersed with ritualistic Hebrew phrases set as *vocalises* of remarkable, sometimes almost levitatory, elaboration. Barriers are broken not only between Hebraic Old Testament and Gentile New Testament tradition, but also between Italian operatic techniques and vocal techniques of the French court. The *ports de voix* and *tremblements* of the latter lose their enervating nostalgia and reconcile fragility with strength; complementarily, Italian vocal lines reveal a quality of inwardness that isn't habitual to them. This explains how if not why Couperin's church music could preserve a 'religious' spirituality in a pervasively hedonistic society. I'll comment on the third of the surviving *Leçons*: which is usually considered to be the finest since, in being conceived for two voices rather than one, it offers opportunities to combine melismatic vocalise with polyphony, including formal canon.

This is evident in the opening vocalise in which the two sopranos soar after the manner of a two-violin sonata, in lines that move, winged and disembodied, mainly by conjunct motion, while passing through dissonant suspensions tersely reinforced by the harmonically conceived clashes of the continuo part. Spiritual ecstasy and corporeal drama are thus allied – a representative compromise between religious and theatrical conventions:

The first arioso incorporates Couperin's favourite modulation to the minor of the dominant; the second begins with a weird chromatic deliquescence, starting from 'tragic' B minor but rescued by trumpet-like vocal calls on the words 'Vide Domine'. The rondo-like reappearance of the vocalise hints at evolution, if not development, in that it is now more 'theatrically' ornamented and more 'spiritually' unified in being in canon. The 'O vos omnes' section also balances a speech-like freedom of line, along with acute dissonances from the continuo, against trumpet-like vocal summonses on the word 'Attendite'. The pace quickens on the words 'Quoniam vindemiavit me' until a climax occurs on a (for Couperin) unusual diminished seventh chord. The section concludes with an even more expansive version of the vocalise, while the succeeding arioso alarmingly invokes desolation through the Fall of a diminished octave!

de - so - la - tam, po - su - it me de - so - la-tam,

The following vocalise responds in pathetic, almost painfully introverted, false relations.

The 'Vigilavit jugum' arioso returns to homophonic *brunette* tradition, but only as preparation for the grandest final statement of the vocalise, canonically adapted to the Latin text of the 'Jerusalem convertere', a call for the people's repentance and a return to the True Faith. Over level crotchet movement the duet-aria evolves with architectural modulations to dominant and subdominant, in lines that combine acutely expressive intervals with traditional counterpoint – notably a rising fourth followed by a falling scale presented in canon, a tag that was common property among sixteenth-century polyphonists. When Stravinsky heard this music, late in his life, it bowled him over and possibly inspired his emulation in the *Requiem Canticles*. Certainly Couperin's *Leçons des Ténèbres* are tragically tenebrous while remaining inwardly radiant. We don't know whether Louis XIV bothered to hear them at the neighbouring convent, and we may suspect that he might have dismissed them as distractions from affairs of State. On the other hand, I suspect that their equivocations would have been relished by the grand ladies of the Versailles court who wrote, in impeccable French, those fairy-tales that reveal the ironically tangled myths that still mould our psyches. Performed as intended, by candlelight slowly extinguished, in liturgical conditions, by French 'petites voix' rather by Italian 'voix grandes', Couperin's *Leçons* make an effect the singing teacher Bacilly called 'douce, nette, et claire', yet also 'touchante' and 'brillante'. We are fortunate that we now have, presided over by the magical and magisterial Emma Kirkby, several sopranos of this character and quality, who may give us a notion of what Couperin's cantillating cousin Marguerite-Louise Couperin sounded like, as she simultaneously assailed heights and plumbed depths.

12

The Democratization of the High Baroque

God and the Common Man, from the youthful virtuosity of Handel's *Dixit Dominus* (1708), by way of the Old Testament morality of *Saul* (1739), to the democratic universality of *Messiah* (1742)

With Mozart, Handel is the supreme humanist of European music. Born in Germany, trained in Italy, and eventually launched in the prosperous Establishment of Augustan England, he was a citizen of Europe who sang Glory to Man in the Highest, celebrating human accomplishments at a peak point in civilization, with a fervour almost religious in potency, though it reveals no hint of the numinous. The sheer energy of the young Handel's genius has a touch of the miraculous: nowhere more than in the music he composed, ostensibly to praise God, during his apprentice years in Rome in the first decade of the eighteenth century.

In 1707–8, at the age of twenty-two, he made the most remarkable of these pieces: a setting of Psalm 110 (*Dixit Dominus*) for five soloists (two sopranos, alto, tenor, and bass), with five-part SSATB chorus, string orchestra, and continuo. The work was commissioned by one of the several cardinals who befriended him during his student days, perhaps believing that such exceptional talents could have been ignited only by a divine spark. Living in Rome, Handel set the imperious Latin text. Later he became familiar with the Anglican version. Both texts somewhat obscurely recount God's (or man's) unorthodox acceptance of Prince Simon the Manachee as both Supreme Governor and High Priest: a theme appealing to a young top-composer of the High Baroque since it identifies Church with State. Admittedly, Handel makes, in deference to the Roman Church and to his cardinal friends, use of the traditional plainsong intonations, presented in sturdy minims in the opening chorus and again in the Amen of the concluding chorus. Even so, his music is light years away from the spirit of the medieval Church, as one would expect of a brilliantly endowed young composer displaying his mastery of the most up-to-the-minute techniques and stylizations.

The very first two words – DIXIT DOMINUS – proclaim that the Lord has spoken, uttering the Law. He invites Man to sit at His right hand, promising to demote our enemies to footstools: behaviour more appropriate to a merely human tyrant than to God Himself. Unsurprisingly, the opening chorus is fierce, in a driving $\frac{4}{4}$ pulse and in tough G minor, a key associated by high baroque composers with harshness and severity, and incipiently with tragic experience such as was commented on in the sublime Agnus Dei of Bach's B minor Mass. First and second violins hurl arpeggios in furious descents, countered by immense upward leaps to prepare for the next declension; violas and cellos pad in level quavers, bolstered by the continuo. The five-voiced chorus bandies brief phrases in fugato though not in fugue, boldly reiterating the word DIXIT as God asserts his Law's remorselessness, perhaps ironically coincident with the quotation from the holy plainchant intonation. When the soloists enter the fray in wide-arpeggiated coloratura they are thanking God for inviting mere mortals to sit at his Right Hand. The Law, blazoned in minims as a *cantus firmus* by the sopranos, effaces the lower parts' dialogue in fragmented arpeggios. Momentum is enhanced by modulation to the relative B flat major, traditionally a power-key, and then to D minor, G minor's *dominant*. The sopranos exult in long high notes but also savour dissonant suspensions, in which our 'enemies' are deservedly 'abased'. Returned to tonic G minor, the strings round off the chorus with fanfare-like arpeggiated flourishes.

After this startling start we are offered momentary respite in two arias, first for alto, then for soprano. The words of the alto aria encourage us to 'send forth our mighty sceptre' and to rule 'in medio iniquicorum tuorum'. The music is severely matriarchal rather than overtly bellicose, though coloratura passages cockily assert our almightiness (with God's help), depicting our adversaries' defeat in lopsided Lombard syncopations. The soprano's complementary aria is less complacent because more rhythmically complex, and possibly because it has moved tonally from G minor to traditionally dynamic C minor. The soprano, probably a castrato, acts the Prince begotten by God expressly to fulfil his Will; and the aria admits, as the previous one had not, that obeying God's behests may be problematical. The deviousness of the Prince's path is suggested by the varying textures and recurrent hemiola rhythms that disturb the sequential patterns of the flowing quaver triplets, though we're left in no doubt that the Prince, being God's surrogate, must prevail.

The next chorus, 'Juravit Dominus', however, stresses the 'mysterious way' in which God must work his 'wonders', since the piece admits – in five-part homophony riddled with the operatic cliché of 'horrendous' diminished sevenths shifting chromatically – that God may be stupid enough never to change his mind. Predictably, this seems to scare the chorus (us), for the quick number they sing in response to God's *grave* admonishment is fragmented, nervily reiterating the word 'non'. God's further remonstrance bolsters our jitteriness, with long-held, lofty tones from the two solo sopranos. Yet recovery is no more than temporary, and the texture peters out pianissimo, so marked.

After that subsidence we the people need to gird our loins, and do so in a chorus admitting to the priestly duties that complement our role as political arbitrators. In the power-key of B flat major the basses enunciate a rising scale in crotchets, while the upper parts scurry in canonic demisemiquaver scales. Bit by bit the imperious crotchets pervade all the parts, ending with the sopranos who, over a pedal point, rejoice in their high B flats. Our reward is that God, still at our right hand, is eager to 'shatter' inimical kings on his Day of Wrath; and the succeeding, very brilliant, movement is sung mainly by the soloists since exceptional talents – such as Handel as 'composing mortal' and these cantillating virtuosi – are called for at the day of reckoning. The movement opens as a trio sonata for two violins and continuo in D minor, a dangerous key apt for human pilgrimage. Beginning with flickering quavers in scales and arpeggios, the two violins also exploit the trio-sonata technique of chains of suspensions, dissonant but controlled. When the sopranos take over from the violins, animation is enhanced, leading to a dominant modulation to A minor and to wide-flung arabesques and immense leaps from the solo bass. A climax of considerable nervous intensity occurs when the five-part chorus joins the soloists canonically, with the theme tightened by the intrusion of a diminished fourth. Although the shattering of our enemies is enacted in short silences and broken beats, the moto perpetuo of quavers continues ruthlessly. This virtuosic movement, the high point of the score, has more to do with the power of man's will and his inventive ingenuity than with the promptings of a holy spirit.

Unabashed, the next chorus concerns the inevitability of God's law, proclaiming the Old Testament God's power to 'judge among the heathen and fill the places with dead bodies' (!). Unsurprisingly, this is a rigorous five-voiced fugue on a theme incorporating a rising major triad of earthy F major; the plurality of the nations unleashes ascending scales in quavers, which the orchestra diminishes to glittering semiquavers. The 'shattering' ('implebit ruinas') coruscates in whirling scales and clattering arpeggios, climaxing in a shift from duple to triple time, setting the word 'conquasabit' to a thumping beat. Finally, and devastatingly, the word is splintered. But when the psalm's next verse tells us, in the beautiful version of the Book of

Common Prayer, that 'he shall drink of the brook in the way; and therefore shall lift up his head', human, even Christian, compassion is for the first time evident. The strings' level procession of quaver chords is slow (*adagio*) and sometimes acutely dissonant in minor seconds and major sevenths as well as in predictably horrendous diminished sevenths. The tonality droops down the cycle of fifths from the work's initial G minor to C minor and to 'lugubrious' F minor: though the soloists' freely canonic entries 'exult' in rising sixths and reiterated crotchets. Public values are in part redeemed by private feeling in what may be construed as an incipiently democratic process.

This momentary awareness of the private as distinct from the public life is, however, only a means of gathering impetus to approach the dazzling finale, which sets the doxology, paying homage to God the Father, Son, and Holy Ghost, here identified with Church and State. Significantly, Handel returns to his original key of G minor and produces music that, if superabundant in energy, is far from being blandly blessed. We marvel, admittedly, at its technical dexterity, recognizing that the trumpeting repeated notes, sizzling scales, and bounding arpeggios exhibit man's justified pride in his skills – such as negotiating long passages of coloratura and piercing processions of high B flats, while at the same time disciplining such wanton showing-off with a contrapuntal *cantus firmus* on the words 'sicut erat in principio'. God's law is as it always was and ever will be: so the work may end with a grand fugue in *stretto* on a theme that begins with repeated notes quickening from minims, to crotchets, to quavers, these literally superb reiterations appearing throughout the five-voiced texture, trumpet-like in majesty. No less typical are motives for both voices and strings that frisk through octaves, in emulation of trio-sonata violins. These convolutions are, however, ironed out as the original fugal theme reasserts itself, clarion-like. However worldly this music's effect, there is something super-natural about such red-hot genius at the age of twenty-two.

Not long after writing this resplendent apprentice-piece Handel embarked on the career that established his international reputation as a maker of Italianate heroic operas dealing, in highly stylized conventions, with heroic men and women who, pursuing power in this world, elevated themselves to superhuman stature as gods or monsters. At the height of his celebrity he moved to England where, always a canny businessman, he hoped to sell *opera seria* to Britain's rapidly rising middle class, who could well afford it. It seemed as though the venture would succeed, with the help of the box-office appeal of imported Italian singers who had the charisma and notoriety of modern pop-stars. But the glamour proved short-lived; and clever Handel, having misjudged his audience, decided to abandon *opera seria* in favour of English oratorio, which he more or less invented. In fact, English oratorio used exactly the same conventions – of recitative, arioso, aria, and ceremonial chorus, dance, and march – as did *opera seria*: the only musical difference being that Handel gave an important role to the chorus, representing us the people, alongside the soloists who played the people's often tyrannical leaders or oppressors. A further difference was that Handel now found his stories not in classical mythology nor in political history, but in the biblical Old Testament: the one book the British middle class knew like the back of its hand. The Old Testament tales dealt in humankind's contradictorily ambitious will and the fight between it and the inevitably mysterious Will of god. These stories contained political themes and counterthemes apposite to a society bent on imperialistic adventures; on the basis of them Handel created the most powerful, and for that matter the most heroic, examples of Heroic Opera ever made. Although they were not fully staged, Handel's oratorios were almost always performed in theatres rather than in churches.

All Handel's Old Testament oratorios turn on the fatal paradox of Man's attempting to play God. In *Saul*, arguably the greatest of these works, Saul is at once hero and villain; and the oratorio asks what happens when the Leader, who is not God – however god-like his powers – is subject to human infirmities. Jealousy may overthrow reason; madness may bring ruin not only to himself but also to the state for which he is responsible. This is why the chorus – in the oratorios but not in the operas – becomes a (perhaps *the*) central protagonist. Handel's humanity is nowhere more evident than in his incipiently democratic realization that public destiny inevitably embraces the destinies of private people.

Despite its biblical precedents *Saul* is not a religious work but a human tragedy cast in the form of an *opera seria* without (or, possibly, on occasion with) stage action: in which there are two related themes, one personal, one epic. After an expansively public overture we enter the fray with an Epinicion or Song of Triumph. What is being celebrated, with trumpets, drums, and martial rhythms, is the defeat of the baddies (Goliaths and Philistines) by the goodies (Israelites), in a resonantly public C major; current political parallels to these historical events are encouraged. Everybody, especially the adolescent girls, praises David the pop-star hero who in slaying the foul fiend has released us from bondage. Only Saul, the King and Wise Man who framed the laws, has doubts, though he offers his elder daughter Merab to David as a bride and maybe bribe. The compliment is double-edged, for Merab is a prissy prop of the Establishment whose *da capo* aria displays more patrician pride than human heart.

But if Merab is the moribund side of Saul – the letter of the law – his other children illuminate what he once was. The younger sister Michal is all sweetness and light and loves David with virginal passion; her brother Jonathan also loves David with a love that 'passes the love of woman'. The central characters have now been introduced, and a lapse of time is indicated by a bucolic welcome-song, scored for carillon. The song's innocence is barbed because, like the tinkling carillon, it is inane; and when the carolling girls rashly claim that David has slain ten thousand of the enemy to Saul's one thousand the flame of jealousy, already smouldering in Saul, flares into fire. In dark arioso – the realities of experience intensified – Saul tries to murder David by hurling a javelin at him; and his aria of frustrated rage sunders convention by stopping in midstream, without the reassurance of a *da capo*. Impotent himself, he commissions his own son, Jonathan, to slay David; in response Jonathan sings a superb arioso and aria debating the battle between personal feeling (friendship) and filial duty (respect for the law). He decides – at this date we cannot readily appreciate how brave this is – in favour of common humanity.

The second act opens with a chorus enacting the chaos that human fallibility lets loose in the world. In chromatics and enharmonic modulations opposed to tonal relationships socially accredited and intellectually understood, virtue 'sickens in blackest night'. Jonathan appeals to his father to relent; and Saul pretends to acquiesce, offering Michal, to her delight, to David as a bonus since Merab will have no truck with him because he's a commoner. But Saul reveals his dark heart in arioso which reflects ironically on the dreamy wedding-music; the ultimate climax occurs when Saul accuses his son of disloyalty and attempts to murder *him*, as well as David. The Leader, who should be the Law, is anti-law; chaos is come again. From this point Saul–Othello turns into Saul–Macbeth: 'from crime to crime he blindly' (and chromatically) 'goes; no end but with his own destruction knows'. In Act III Saul recognizes, in his famous 'lost' aria, that he is the author of his own ruin. Since Heaven has deserted him – he is unable to pray – he appeals to Hell, seeking the Witch of Endor, of course in F minor, the traditionally infernal key which Purcell had also employed in his spine-chilling *scena* on the story. The Witch offers scant consolation. Saul has 'had it': though the reason she gives is not the moral one that through rage, envy, and malice leading to madness he has denied his humanity, but the to us trivial one that he disobeyed God's decree in failing to slaughter the 'accursed Amalekite'. The irony is enhanced when David, the new Hero, *doesn't* spare the Amalekite but acts too late since the heathen have already finished off the wounded Saul and Jonathan, fighting at bay. The ethics are confused. We may hope that the irony suggests that Handel found them as monstrous as we do.

That such may be the case is suggested as the oratorio attains an Orphic consummation in an Elegy that, centred on C major to balance the initiatory Epicinion, proves to be a victory for compassion. The Dead March reasserts Saul's one-time grandeur; and in this case the simple, triadic C major sounds more solemnly funereal than the most doleful minor key since it reminds us of hopes unfulfilled. David's aria reviews the positive aspects of Saul's and Jonathan's lives and deaths – a third higher than the Elegy's C major, in E major which Handel (and most classical baroque composers) usually reserved for celestial moments. The repeated crotchets of the theme are at once a caress and an affirmation, and the musical images for 'sweetest harmony' and 'bravely died' are as poignant as they are simple. When the chorus joins the *da capo* in universal consolation, the orchestra appends, on cellos and basses, a regeneratively rising scale.

Meanwhile David (another soprano emulating a semi-divine castrato) interjects reminiscences, in the tonic *minor*, of his personal love and loss. This is one of the supreme moments in Handel, and is the end of the personal tragedy of youth versus age and of the public epic of a threatened civilization. A coda is added, however, returning us to Augustan England and the advance of imperialist expansion. We have to learn again and again that military might cannot be independent of personal qualities of love, justice, and reason. In some form the story will happen again – perhaps even, as has been hinted at in the incident of the Amalekite, to David. So the threnody in *Saul* is no longer a puff to our pride but a stirring of the bowels of compassion; and the distance Handel has travelled between the brave but blunt confrontation between power and pathos in *Dixit Dominus* and the profound comprehension of conflicting human purpose and error in *Saul* is evidence of Handel's humane democratization of ethical morality, if not of religious belief.

A third, consummatory, stage in this process occurs in the only Handel oratorio that takes its texts not only from the versions of the Psalms that featured in the Book of Common Prayer and from the Books of the Old Testament (in this case Isaiah), but also from the New Testament Gospels of Luke, Matthew, and John, and from St Paul's Epistles to the Romans and the Corinthians. *The Messiah* is the most popular of Handel's oratorios because it is a repository of common sentiment – the values on which not only Augustan civilization but also succeeding, more democratic societies at least hoped to be founded. Although in *The Messiah* common man's lot is viewed in the light of the story of Christ, it is about Man before it is about God. The 'vision' that Handel claimed to have seen may have been 'spiritual' but its significance lay in its relation to a moral code: he hoped and believed that his music would make people *behave* in a more Christian spirit. So the French overture now celebrates *our* potential heroism, rather than that of a God–King. The double dots and dissonances convey a toughly human fortitude which the animation of the fugue converts into action. The texture is sinewy, the tonality a purgatorial E minor; but the bounding leaps of the lines, the thrust of the rhythms, and the rising chromatic bass generate an élan the more powerful because it does not deny the pain in the introduction. The vigorous unity of fugue can thus, overriding contrarieties, lead to *comfort*, and even to *exultation*. So for the tenor arioso 'Every valley' the key changes to seraphic E major; the pulsing rhythm, regular as a heartbeat, the sustained vocal notes, and the symmetrical sequences all promote the comfort of assured belonging. Although the music is not spritual in Bach's sense, it affirms faith in human postulates, as arioso burgeons into aria in which 'every valley may be exalted'. The aria adds to regular rhythm and symmetrical sequences a measure of operatic display: a virtuosic expression of pride that is also an assertion of common humanity. We are asked to look, listen, and feel how in this melodic line we have made 'the crooked straight and the rough places plain':

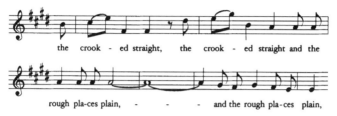

There it is, made straight instead of curly; and that we hear birds chirruping in the orchestra affirms our place in ubiquitous Nature rather than in court or market-place.

Against this exultation consider the opening of Part II: which faces the irremediable facts of evil and of death. 'Behold the Lamb of God that taketh away the sins of the world' is set to music in no way transcendental nor even lamb-like. In dour, potentially tragic G minor – like the opening and closing choruses of *Dixit Dominus* – it is concerned more with our sinfulness than with divine revelation. Once more, the piece is about fortitude: ours, though the hammered repeated notes in dotted rhythms, sounding fierce rather than heroic, threaten us like the Wrath of God, while being at the same time a Rock we might try to cling to. If they are a rock, it's because we have made them so by way of our courage; and that turns our minds to Christ's sublimely greater courage as he is presented, in 'He was despised' as a scapegoat for you and me. An outcast, he is also a man who brings balm in the key of E flat major, flat submediant to G minor, a tonal relationship that in Baroque and Classical music usually promotes relaxation. The vocal line of this aria has the immediacy of arioso: as is manifest in the screwed-up diminished fourths, the fragmented rhythms, the expectant silences, the gut-disturbing tensions of the Neapolitan progressions. Yet although this arioso-like line bears us through the guilt and pain that human beings may suffer within the mind, anguish is 'contained' within the formality of a *da capo* aria that embraces, in its middle section, a shift from metaphysical to physical agony as man's inhumanity to man becomes incarnate in a ferocious 'smiting' motif. This aria is the essence of tragedy; and it is typical of Handel's humanity that the middle section's physical body-rhythm takes over, engulfing the succeeding chorus which, in the 'evil' key of F minor, equates Christ's suffering with ours. 'Surely he hath borne our griefs'; and he does, in the fast fugal chorus 'And with his stripes', with its diminished-seventh-punctuated theme and its remorseless duple rhythm. Corporeal suffering wilfully makes whole that which was broken, just as the paradisal 'Happy valley' aria had made the crooked straight.

The full psychological depth of this is revealed only in the transition from this fugue to the mainly homophonic chorus 'All we like sheep', with its fatuous F major tune garlanded with idiotic semiquaver scurryings as the sheep wander blithely 'astray'. Their gambols are as inane as the repeated notes in which we humans insist on following Each/His/Own/Way. That the effect is farcical is evidence of the adult sense of humour that is part of the mature Handel's democratic stance; and it's significant that Handel's farcical irony coexists with his tragic sense: as is revealed in the *adagio* postlude to the chorus, in a chromaticized F minor no longer evil, but purgatorial, as the Lord lays on Christ 'the iniquity of *our* sins'. Only from Handel's genius could we accept such devastating honesty about our fallen selves. So after all, evil and death prove to be *not* irremediable.

This is why the rebirth celebrated in the exquisite Nativity music – in which Handel seems to have preferred a natural boy treble to an unnatural male castrato or an operatic female soprano – can prelude the faculty to rejoice, even in a fallen world. The most famous example of such jubilation is, of course, the Hallelujah chorus, in which Handel's heavenly vision is identified with soon-to-be-industrialized Augustan England, newly redeemed and technologically fulfilled. The Kingdom of this world has indeed become, as the text tells us, the Kingdom of the Lord; so the glory of British Baroque resonates on D major trumpets and military drums, and is marshalled sequences and homophonic antiphony, always thrusting sharpwards *up* the cycle of fifths. No wonder George II rose to his feet in awed response to our pride in being human, paying homage to Handel as composing mortal, to himself as monarch, and only vicariously to God as creator of both King and composer. In reference to an Empire-building potentate it cannot of course be literally true that 'he shall reign *for ever and ever*'. None the less it was in some such wishful thinking that a convention was established that at this point we the audience should also rise to our feet; and Handel could persuade us to do so because – as 'He was despised' and the still more heart-rending arioso 'Thy rebuke hath broken his heart' abundantly prove – he knew most that was knowable about human suffering, as well as pride. Alone among Handel's oratorios *The Messiah* is not an opera because it is centred on the chorus of us the people, its soloists are not 'characters', and it tells no story, though that of Christ is enclosed within it. Yet in a sense it is the greatest of all heroic operas since it envisages the ultimate apotheosis of the theme: its Hero and Heroine are you and I. The New Testament elements in *The Messiah* differentiate it from the Old Testament sung dramas; it may not evoke the numinous or summon the Holy Ghost but it does tell us that humankind may democratically attain its own divinity without presumptively elevating itself to Godhead. In saying 'so be it' to that, Handel concludes with a chorus on the word Amen that in contrapuntal scope, sonorous splendour, and harmonic density may challenge Bach himself. In *The Messiah* it is difficult to perceive any distinction between Glory to Man, and Glory to God, in the Highest: which is fair enough, since man invented God, who created us.

Part III:
From Enlightenment to Doubt

13

Light in the Church's Darkness

From Haydn's early Roman Masses to
The Creation (1798)

In his youth Haydn (born in 1732) composed a fair amount of church music
to commission, in the accepted rococo styles. To object to the frivolity of
these styles is irrelevant, for frivolity was appropriate to the garishly
decorated churches and to the spirit of the people who worshipped in
them, with the merry music's help. In the sixteenth century, church
polyphony and the court or domestic madrigal were basically in the same
idiom, though the liturgical manner dominated the secular. In Haydn's day
it was the other way round: the opera house effaced the church to such an
extent that ecclesiastical buildings began to look like opera houses, though
proffering a different kind of illusion. Haydn felt no qualms about the jollity
of the masses he composed in the 1750s, remarking that 'since God has given
me a cheerful heart, He will forgive me for serving Him cheerfully'.
Although he regarded himself as a fervent Roman Catholic, he had little
interest in the mysticism of Catholic dogma. When in his mature years he
discovered the nature of his own faith it was conditioned not so much by
churchy traditions as by the spirit of rational enlightenment: which he, more
than anyone, had made musically 'incarnate' in perfecting the forms of the
classical symphony and string quartet – the latter likened by Goethe to 'four
sensible people conversing in a drawing room', the adjective 'sensible'
meaning both commonsensical (in English) and *sensible* (in French).

When Haydn claimed that in his opus 33 string quartets he had explored
'a new way of composing' he meant that he had discovered an approach to
form whereby one thing evolves embryonically into another, reconciling
contradictions and thereby helping life to function more efficiently because
more humanely. From the 1770s onwards Haydn's music celebrates the
Discovery of Man through the 'becoming' which is sonata. For his efforts he

was revered by fairly common people everywhere: for they recognized, more readily than the declining aristocrats, that Haydn's musical adventurousness helped them to discover themselves. His commercial success, which enabled him to become a freelance musician no longer dependent on aristocratic or ecclesiastical patronage, is thus inseparable from the spiritual victory manifest in the Apollonian classicism of his mature years.

It follows that when Haydn, towards the end of his long life, composed his great, not merely jolly, masses, their structure depended on their fusing the grandeur of the Handelian High Baroque with the drama of the new sonata principle: which meant that these masses were not concerned with unblinking faith but with faith remoulded in the spirit of ethical enlightenment. Such faith entails a voyage of exploration not dissimilar from that which Haydn embarked on in his 'London' symphonies. In particular the big choral and orchestral works of his old age – conceived after he'd become familiar with Handel's 'English' works – generated an on the whole ebullient optimism – as is still evident in the very last of Haydn's Roman masses, composed just into the nineteenth century in 1802. This work was called the *Harmoniemesse* (though not by Haydn) because of the domination of its scoring by wind instruments, especially clarinets, flutes, oboes, and bassoons. These blown, rather than bowed, instruments, being woodwind rather than festive brass, produce a 'harmonie' not that of nations as potentates, but of Goethe's 'sensible people' who are seeking to fashion, in sobriety and enthusiasm alike, a new society.

Like all his late liturgical works, Haydn's *Harmoniemesse* is open, 'natural' and, if grand, never pompous and circumstantial. It is music for newly democratic man who rejoices in the High Baroque power-key of B flat major, knowing that the future will be his. The initial Kyrie has, like a sonata first movement, a dualistic structure since it celebrates God the Father, the source of life, and Christ the Son who, having a mother, was half human. Neatly enough, Haydn equates the Father and Son with the first and second subjects of his quasi-sonata form; and opens the second subject in G minor, the relative of B flat major, in a more closely wrought, near-homophonic style apt to the person of Christ in being more human and humane. The recapitulation is orthodox although, in sonata style, what had happened in the development affects the way we re-hear the material that is not only repeated, but also re-created. In particular the soloists' arabesques, in parallel thirds, sixths, and tenths, are more extended, lyrical, and even spiritually ecstatic in effect; although no other movement is as close to sonata style. The Gloria and Credo – which follow eighteenth-century precedent in dividing the text into an alternation of choruses with arias and ensemble numbers for solo voices – contain dramatic startlements such as we are familiar with from the London Symphonies. Especially in the big Amen choruses New Democracy holds its own with classical autocracy; indeed, Haydn's Amen choruses seem, in their excitation at discovering new potential, to be worthy successors to Handel's Hallelujah Chorus; like that famous piece, they hint that Glory to Man in the Highest and Glory to God in the Highest need not, even should not, be differentiated.

But for the quintessential church music of his last years Haydn abandoned the Roman Mass in favour of forms derived from English oratorio as practised by Handel. The key-work is *The Creation*, composed in 1798, a decade away from the French Revolution and on the verge of a new century. In it, Haydn transmutes Handel's heroic recitative, arioso, aria, and chorus into more intimate terms, while sometimes transforming Gluck's choral homophony into ethical prayer comparable with Haydn's own noble hymn for the Emperor. To translate heroism into domesticity is not to deprive it of drama, or even of grandeur. On the contrary, drama may be intensified by the recognition that conflict is no longer merely a matter of class distinctions and divided loyalties, but is also a search for unity within the mind. In a democratic society each person, like each member of the classical orchestra that Haydn brought to fruition, had to be responsible both for his own destiny and for the public weal. Whirlwinds will ravish the sensibility, as they will violate Nature, but although one cannot control their incidence, one may steer their course in humanity's interest – helpfully, if not as surely as day succeeds night and calm follows storm.

The text of *The Creation* was put together by Haydn's illustrious friend, the Masonic Baron von Swieten, who offered a German translation of a rhymed rehash by Thomas Linley of bits of Milton's *Paradise Lost*, with addenda from the Old Testament in the form of connecting links sung in recitative or arioso by three angels purloined from Milton under the names of Raphael, Gabriel, and Uriel, two of whom also impersonate Adam and Eve. The verse is utterly un-Miltonic since it divests God of spirituality and man of the sense of sin. 'An Object must be found', announced the Baron, 'for music which, by its fervour, its universal sufficiency and perspicuity, may take the place of the Pious Emotions of former days'; God turned into a working mechanic and the story of the Creation into a Masonic parable. Light triumphs through Reason; but what makes the victory significant is the fervour and perspicuity of *mankind*. In this context Haydn 'stood for' us, and his audience responded to his evocation of Light in awed amazement, as though he were Orpheus reborn.

The first part of the work describes the birth of Order from Chaos; the second deals with the evolution of Created Nature; the third with human love, as manifest in the story of Adam and Eve. The 'argument' of *The Creation* thus makes explicit what is implicit in all Haydn's mature sonatas, symphonies, and string quartets. The creation of Order from Chaos is the impulse behind the marvellous Prologue, wherein the lucidity of 'white' C major is painfully *established* through chains of dissonant suspensions and tonality-veiling diminished sevenths – the rootless Chord of Horror consisting of two devilish tritones interlocked. Although the symbols of disorder are themselves elegantly stylized, the interweaving strings and wind instruments create sonorities prophetic of romanticism, not excluding Wagnerian sequential chromatics:

Only because Haydn's renewal of convention was thus radical could the famous blaze of C major of the words 'Let there be Light' have had so cataclysmic an effect on contemporary audiences. The juxtaposition of minor and major triads was not in itself revolutionary; here, however, on the relatively large band of the recently 'perfected' classical orchestra, the C major triad sounds not merely complementary to C minor, but also like Enlightenment Itself – a force that had, to some measure, refashioned the world. The tenor aria that succeeds Light's apocalypse enacts the process whereby 'the gloomy Shades of Night / Vanish before Thy Holy Beams'. From youthfully buoyant A major Hell's spirits slink in panic into the 'Deep Abyss' of a remotely turbulent C minor, riddled with serpentine chromatics: until the chorus, in formal fugato with urgent *stretti*, sweep us back to an A major that is also a 'new created world' of a homophonic simplicity and symmetry that accords with men and women who, proud to be common, 'spring up' in jauntily leaping sixths.

The remainder of Part I offers more august instances of God's refashioning of the firmament, each introduced by one of the angelic soloists in heroic Handelian recitative. Nature's 'furious tempests', aggressively Vivaldian in imagery, are briskly subdued, their tonal instability conquered by a C major aria for soprano, with choric commentary, praising the 'Marv'llous Work'. After the soprano angel has whizzed up to a high C the number ends in dotted-rhythmed fanfares. A bass aria, with chorus, then disposes of recalcitrant floods, the main key being 'obscure' D minor, with whirling arpeggios and shooting scales. Nature's destructive forces are given a good innings, only to be routed by man's beneficent ingenuity and ushered into 'glorious' D major.

A famous soprano aria, 'With verdure clad', is in pastoral B flat and 'Arcadian' siciliano rhythm, with operatic ornament sweetly domesticated. If this represents personal fulfilment, public rejoicing follows in a fugal chorus in, of course, D major, with a sturdy theme based on a rising triad and upward-leaping sixths. In it God 'clothes' both heaven and earth as if they were eighteenth-century gentlemen adjusting their perukes. The number ends with an Amen cliché that habituates us to routine followed, however, by an anthropomorphic arioso describing the splendours of the 'azure sky' wherein the Sun and Moon let off fireworks for our delectation. Although this reminds us that the transformations taking place in the universe are far from commonplace, Part I concludes with a symphonically constructed chorus in common time as well as rational C major, presenting Man as God the master-mechanic, in music resolutely homophonic and regularly metrical. Yet there is a moment of aberration when the three quasi-angelic soloists claim that God's purpose is by us 'never unperceiv-ed, *ever* understood'. Singing these words, they're left frailly on their own, with no support from orchestra or chorus as the accredited voices of Society, and wander into 'errant' D minor, being humans of exceptional talents who threaten to grow too big for their boots:

The hitch is not, however, serious: their momentary Fall into wish-fulfilment, or even doubt, is soon banished by the chorus's tight fugato in what amounts to a widely modulating sonata development section: leading into a coda wherein, with dominant-tonic cadences approached by fulminating 'German sixths', the wonders of the firmament are displayed for our approval and (possibly) benefit.

Part II of the work is at first less symphonically organized and more episodic since it mostly exhibits the prodigality of Nature, beginning with a soprano aria paying tribute to the birds in pastoral F major, but with modulatory adventures that differentiate between predatory eagles, cooing doves, and merry larks. The birds provide opportunities for vocal virtuosity while being anthropomorphically domesticated and aesthetically formalized. They're succeeded by the 'great Whales', who alarmingly multiply as they swim through the 'finny deep', inevitably in 'errant' D minor. We find this hilarious, but shouldn't assume that Haydn expected us to take his leviathans portentously; a lively sense of humour – and a 'recognition of other modes of experience that may be possible' – was an aspect of demotic democracy that, already latent in Handel, in Haydn directly threatens the Heroic ideal. The next movement, embracing the gentler aspects of Nature's fecundity, demonstrates this in being 'serious' enough, but also domestic, with purling parallel thirds. True, that 'immense Leviathan' unexpectedly pops up again on burbling bassoon; but if he makes us laugh out loud, that puts us in the mood for a canonic trio from the three angel-soloists, expressing admiration, in both senses, for the multiplicity and to-us-inconceivable variety of God's inventiveness. That Haydn can chuckle at it slightly elevates man at God's expense:

th'im - mense Le - vi - a - than

Here the almost-divine soloists are humans so enlightened that they can execute a three-part ensemble that explodes in coloratura before climaxing – now bolstered by the chorus – in symphonic drama fuelled by a rising chromatic bass.

Even so, given the demotic bias of his late, semi-Anglicized works, Haydn follows urgent energy with descriptive arioso portraying, in irresistibly risible aural imagery, the 'chearful, roaring, tawny Lion', the 'flexible Tiger', the 'nimble Stag with flying Mane and fiery Look', alongside placidly lowing cattle and 'fleecy' sheep, the 'unnumbered Hosts' of the insects and, climacterically and chromatically, the 'Worm who in long Dimension / Creeps with sinuous Trace'. I'm sure Haydn meant us to reward with a belly-laugh this creature literally of the underworld: whose grotesquely scored music introduces a seriously grand D major aria for the bass, saluting the Wonders of the World while pointing out that the ultimate crown to God's creation was still missing: namely, US. This makes sense if God created us in his own image, as he claimed to have done, though when the tenor-angel sings an aria about 'our native Worth and Honour' it is not in glorious D major but in rational C major, albeit illuminated, after trumpery trumpetings, by 'visionary' modulations wherein God is miraculously mirrored in (not very) humble us. At the end, however, we 'find our place' in folksy simplicity, with cadential trills permissible but discreetly marked *pp*.

The tenor aria, though the apex to Part II, is not its end, for it is capped by a big Handelian chorus in the power-key of B flat major: which encloses within itself a 'middle section' in the form of an aria for the three angel-soloists, representing us a bit larger than life, in the Masonic key of E flat major, appropriate to the newly restored world. Significantly, this trio embraces both our potential (E flat major) nobility and our mortal terror (in dark E flat minor): but ends by modulating from E flat to its dominant B flat for a *da capo* of the power-chorus. This may tell us that man needs his fellow-creatures as well as God, for the public chorus is extended into a dynamic fusion of the monism of fugue with the dualism that Beethoven will eventually develop to unsuspected heights and depths. In the Haydn example, the two forms, or rather techniques, may be associated with God and Man respectively; in any case, it's significant that by the end of Part II the progressive, 'symphonic' aspects of Haydn's music are reinstated and lead bravely into Part III, wherein we learn that the angel (agent) of social regeneration is *human* love, as potentially manifest in the loves of all us descendants of Adam and Eve. Haydn and the Enlightenment inherited the Christian doctrine of redemption while believing that the catalyst was Man become God, not God become Man. The humanism of the classical baroque was physical, sensual and emotional; Haydn's humanism, if less physical and sensual than Handel's, was no less emotional, while being also ethical, moralistic, and intellectual. The alternation of Darkness and Light is perpetual and, for better and for worse, we are committed to it and are also, as Fallen creatures, in part responsible for it.

Pointedly, Part III opens with a Prologue summoning a New Dawn in traditionally celestial E major – that sharpest, highest major key in common use. The succeeding arioso recreates the 'morning, young and fair', with avian flutes: music that might be called Sublime in the specialized eighteenth-century sense, since it sounds grand but pristine, like Thoreau's 'New Hampshire everlasting and unfallen, with dew on the grass'. Here Haydn's scoring is genuinely expressive if not of 'reality', at least of a vision of Eden reclaimed. But when Adam and Eve carol their duet about *their* heavenly bliss it is not in otherworldly E major but in rationally humane C major, with a wistful oboe obbligato and a rocking triplet accompaniment that recalls the temporary sojourn of Gluck's Orpheus in the Elysian Fields. The chorus, as we the people, supports our Mother and Father in triadic harmony, leading into a second duet in Arcadian F major, with choric commentary wherein everyone thanks God for our salvation and pays homage to the animate creatures with whom or which we hope, in an Eden renewed, to live in peace. This long rondo returns obsessively, from widely modulating episodes, to its dreamily hopeful tune. The dream-imagery is rudimentary, making a disproportionately thrilling effect with a slow-rising chromatic scale as all created nature, including ourselves, pays homage to the Lord's almightiness. Adam and Eve, their 'duty performed', venture to praise *one another* as 'Grateful Consorts', again in the Masonic key of E flat major, childishly envisaging a new world in which there is no sin, no temptation, and therefore no guilt and – it may seem to us – no point. This, though typical of the era, sounds piffling compared with Bach or Beethoven, or indeed the Handel to whom Haydn, in this piece, owed so much. Still, the tenor Angel warns the 'wedded lovers' against 'false conceit', and the work is rounded off by a wedding chorus again in the power-key of B flat major, *almost* worthy of Handel, and strong enough to carry Haydn into the as-it-were new millennium. Despite his youthful cheerfulness,

Haydn knew that enlightened optimism was a tricky commitment through which fingers needed to be kept resolutely crossed. Late in life he confessed that the most he hoped for was to be a 'spring from which the careworn may draw a few moments' rest and refreshment': a modest ambition in which he found 'a powerful motive for pressing onwards'. Nowadays, it doesn't seem so modest an ambition; it could keep us going, even whilst belief in life, and in humankind's potential, is subject to much discouragement.

14

From Enlightenment to Vision

Mozart as ecclesiastical successor to Haydn and as
precursor to Beethoven:
his *Litaniae de venerabili altaris sacramento*
(*c.*1772) and his *Requiem Mass* (1791)

Late eighteenth-century Vienna, the melting-pot of Europe, had a polyglot
culture within which a new musical world was nurtured. As we've noted, the
new music, known as sonata, was brought to fruition, though not conceived,
in the city. Being a discovery of unity within diversity, it reflects the Hegelian
dialectic of what is now called democracy, as do the media of the string
quartet and of the classical symphony favoured by Haydn – media wherein
each individual player can find self-fulfilment only by democratically
showing respect for his neighbours. Given the primacy of the 'democratic'
sonata and symphony, it's understandable that church music, in the
traditional sense of worship dedicated to a deity outside the self, was
relatively insignificant during the Viennese classical era. Even Haydn,
though a man of faith, found the heart of his experience in the string quartet
and the symphony and, in his old age, composed his greatest masses in a
baroque idiom modified by the interior drama of sonata. His mature faith
was discovered rather than revealed.

Mozart, second in the Viennese succession, is unique in being equally
distinguished as a composer of instrumental sonatas and of operas. In his
tragic–comic operas he reinterpreted Baroque opera's public 'imitation of
human action' in the light of the private drama of sonata, thereby animating
theatrical myths that not only mirrored the psychological story of his time
but also foreshadowed the shape of things to come. Not surprisingly, opera
was a medium more congenial to him than church music, which was obliged
to show deference to authority. Nonetheless Mozart came of a family of

professional church musicians and, during his early years in Salzburg, fulfilled ecclesiastical obligations as a fairly easy way of making money. That he did so in an idiom indistinguishable from that of his early theatre music is only to be expected. Not much more than a child, he was hardly likely to betray a lofty sense of the numinous or a profound sense of sin; in any case a mystical approach to religious music would have been inappropriate to a man of the Enlightenment who, believing in the Perfectability of Man, reckoned that anything God could do, man ought to try to do better. This is more a matter of wish-fulfilment than of conviction: which is why rococo church music, when it convinces *us*, does so through the dramatic urgency of sonata – which implies an element of doubt as complement to hope. We can see this even in a childhood work like the *De Profundis* (K93), in which the 'universal' validity of the words creates a nervous frisson within social conformity. As an instance of rococo adolescence in Mozart's church music we may cite *Litaniae de venerabili altaris sacramento*, written when Mozart was sixteen, momently visiting Paris, before shedding the dust of provincial Salzburg for bad and all.

Ever since the fourth century the chanting of litanies figured in the public life of the church, especially during Lent. Pope and people processed to a different church for Mass, these processions being called *litaniae* after the Greek word (*lite*) for a prayer. They became immensely popular over the seventeenth century; in the eighteenth century the texts were restricted to hymns in honour of the Blessed Sacrament, usually of an intimately devotional character. The intimacy no doubt appealed to the young Mozart: though this work (K243) is fairly ambitious in displaying the composer's budding talents, being scored for four soloists, chorus, strings, two each of flutes, oboes, bassoons, and horns, with three trombones and organ continuo. The trombones earn their place for their sacral associations, since this is a Eucharistic litany. That this does not necessitate solemnity is, however, immediately evident in the Kyrie, a lyrically arching melody for soloists and chorus in E flat major – a key already associated by Haydn with friendship, benevolence, and humane institutions. The sonority, over a cantabile bass line, is warmly enveloping, though there's a hint of drama in the Christe's shift to E flat's relative, C minor, indeed the Christe motif serves some of the functions of a sonata second subject. The repetitions of the words 'miserere nobis' concentrate more on God's potential pity than on our misery, and the second section ('Panis vivus') gives a further twist in being a sonata-style aria for solo tenor, brightly in the dominant. Extravagantly virtuosic roulades on the word 'miserere' belie the word's surface meaning, as though young Mozart were trying to buffet God into offering us succour. Could he resist so brave a display of youthful pride and presumption?

The succeeding 'Verbo carum facto' tells us that he could and does, for it deflates the tenor's almost ludicrous perkiness by shifting chorically to

Handelian fugato in G minor, with a dotted-rhythmed theme incorporating a diminished fourth. The sacral trombones here assume their role as guardians of ecclesiastical law, while the (human?) violins cavort in wide-flung arpeggios. And although the 'Hostias sacra' is in C major and again lyrically flowing, its grace is compromised by abrupt explosions in the minor, by sequential chromatics, and by cross accents. The cries of 'miserere' grow distraught: as well they might, since the 'Tremendum' directly confronts the Wrath of God, as the chorus declaims the dread words, supported by trombones, while the violins stutter in nervous repeated notes, and tonality wavers between C, G, and F minors.

Yet this imposing movement suggests not so much awareness of the numinous as doubt about human perfectability: which may be why its tremor of anxiety is followed by the soprano solo 'Dulcissimum convivum', wherein angels float in triplets, with chromatic passing notes, in the pastoral key of F major. After the tremendous 'Tremendum', this aria sounds like a celestial dream; but we're swept back if not to truth, at least to the Church's inexorable Law, for the 'Viaticum' is a severe cantus-firmus-style number in which the quasi-liturgical theme, sung in minims by the trebles, is punctuated by grave trombones and pizzicato strings, riddled with 'horrendous' diminished sevenths. This serves as prelude to the 'Pignus', a double fugue back in E flat major, with the trombones busy both in duplication of and antiphony with the voices. This too sounds like regression to the old Baroque unity-through-power, though jazzy syncopations render the theme precarious. Moving into the consummatory Agnus Dei, Mozart abandons any pretence of providing a mystical resolution to human anxiety, for this Agnus is another sweetly-smiling dream-song in B flat major leading, lamb-like indeed, into a recapitulation of the original E flat major Kyrie, which reasserts comfortably social – and perhaps incipiently Masonic – virtues. So the work amounts to an affirmation of *human* love anticipatory of Mozart's mature operas; music so radiant may suggest that in being fully human we're on the way to being divine.

It is significant that Mozart more or less abandoned church music as soon as his official duties no longer called for it. The only exceptions to this are the Mass in C (K337) and the Kyrie (K341), written while he was working on *Idomeneo*, his first indubitably great opera. The two church works reconcile the ceremonial majesty of the baroque with the long-range symphonic drama of the opera – a development more spaciously manifest in the big Mass in C minor (K427), and in the *Requiem* (K626) of his final year, both of which he left unfinished. Although incomplete, these two works are the climax to Mozart's ventures into ecclesiastical music, and each was written for personal rather than dogmatic reasons. The big Mass was composed at the time of his marriage as an avowal of praise and gratitude. Its models are the great baroque masters, Handel, Caldara, Alessandro Scarlatti, and above all Bach, in whose polyphony Mozart had recently discovered much to fascinate him. As Haydn had done, Mozart interprets his baroque models symphonically and dramatically, relating Italian vocal style to his own kind of operatic lyricism. The 'Qui tollis' is especially Bachian, the 'Incarnatus' especially operatic; but there is no longer any confusion of genres.

We don't know why Mozart left the C minor Mass unfinished. Perhaps the reality of his marriage proved less inspiring than his ideal conception of it; or maybe, more mundanely, he had to put the Mass aside in order to meet commitments that brought in more immediate financial return. In any case this was not the kind of music in which he was most interested. The *Requiem* is a different matter. The Mass, written for Constance, is still ostensibly Catholic in spirit; the *Requiem* he wrote for himself, possibly in the awareness that his current ill-health might prove terminal; its spirit is personal, and Masonic rather than Catholic. The anticipatorily romantic story of the Dark Stranger who came to commission it is well known and in a sense discountable. There was a rational explanation of the stranger's presence, since he was the emissary of a Count who wished to pass off the work as his own composition. To Mozart's fevered imagination he seemed an emissary from another world. He wrote the *Requiem* rapidly as well as feverishly, perhaps conscious that death was overtaking him.

Although we don't know why Mozart didn't complete the C minor Mass, the unfinished state of the *Requiem* was occasioned, *tout court*, by his own early death. Whether or not Mozart thought of it as a requiem for himself, it is certainly by far his most 'personal' ecclesiastical work, reflecting the blend of ethical humanism and mysticism that was typical of Freemasonry, especially as viewed by Mozart's vivid imagination. Its structure is that of the normal requiem service, beginning with an Introitus setting the words 'Requiem aeternam', followed by the fugal Kyrie. The sequence of shorter movements that make up the Dies Irae, climaxing in the 'Lacrimosa', leads into the Eucharistic Offering, comprising the Domine Jesu and the Hostia. A Sanctus, Benedictus and Agnus Dei then follow the normal sequence of the Ordinary of the Mass, capped by the consummatory Lux Aeterna. Only the Introitus was completed and fully scored by Mozart, who left sketches and partial scorings of all the movements up to and including the Offertorium. Most of the material was revised and emended by Süssmayr, who was Mozart's assistant, then helping with the recitatives of the new opera *La Clemenza di Tito*. Other friends, colleagues, and pupils also lent helping hands, and current opinion inclines to the view that the contributions of Eybler were more musical, and Mozartian, than those of Süssmayr. I shall comment only on the sections that are indisputably Mozart, though the much-performed work has by now acquired an almost vicarious existence in its hybrid form.

The Introitus is, as entrances to mysteries are prone to be, solemn and also awed, and slightly agitated because one cannot know precisely what the mystery portends. This equivocation is enhanced by the dark orchestration, which lends to the slow procession of chords and the syncopated rhythm a holy aura that for Mozart spelt Freemasonry, both as a 'quest' (in symphonic style) and as an illumination. In particular, pairs of clarinets, basset horns and bassoons lend plagency to the orchestral introduction with its chromatic passing notes, occasional augmented triads, and piercingly dissonant suspensions (of minor second and minor ninth); enhanced energy eventually achieves a modulation to the dominant. Both the gravity and the intensity are augmented when the voices enter in canon at the godly fifth, the theme moving mainly by steps both diatonic and chromatic, the pulse of the bass line being nobly funereal. At the words 'lux perpetua', however, the music modulates homophonically to the relative major F, and then to its subdominant, B flat. Figuration in 'weeping' semiquavers, mingled with 'broken' arpeggio patterns, indicates that 'Deus in Sion' may answer our prayers, but the harmonic, rhythmic, and figurative potency generated also suggests that Masonic rites admit that our suffering alone releases God's pity. The arpeggiated phrase, repeated, is now ornamented with flowing semiquavers in coloratura style, as the music modulates restlessly through D minor, A minor, and G minor. The hope, or even promise, of this 'perpetual light' animates all the parts in a manner that preserves an awe-ful solemnity throughout textures that are operatic both in their coloratura and in their dialogue of short, broken phrases in speech-rhythm. The movement closes back in D minor over a declining chromatic bass; we recall that during his mature operatic years in the 1780s, Mozart was peculiarly partial to D minor, a key traditionally associated with the 'obscurity' of our earthly destiny. The D minor string quartet (K421) and the D minor piano concerto (K466) are merely the most celebrated of these D minor masterpieces.

The Introitus leads into the first section from the Ordinary of the Mass, the Kyrie, which is a fugue on a double subject. The initial motif, presented by the basses, coalesces a D minor triad with a falling diminished seventh: a dramatic cliché of classical baroque music which is answered by the altos in a motif of vigorous repeated notes that flower into coloratura. The first motif would seem to indicate the urgency of our distress, while the answering motif hopefully anticipates the 'unending' plenitude of God's grace:

This collusion of contradictions offers an interpenetration of the human and the potentially divine and – developed in firmly moulded counterpoint through continuous modulations over a wide expanse – carries us irresistibly along with it. Both the agony and the courage of the 'man' theme shine through in sundry permutations; and God's glory grandly wins through in the final perorations: or it seems to, though the final cadence, after the sopranos rise up to high As that momently may imply A major itself, is savagely frustrated, breaking off on an exceptionally 'horrendous' diminished seventh, before returning to D minor at the adagio tempo of the Introitus. Human courage, and resilience, must precede God's grace, if ever that lights on us.

This ends the portion of the *Requiem* that was fully composed, scored, and revised by Mozart; though he left substantial sketches for the sequence of movements that make up the Dies Irae, along with advice, communicated to Süssmayr, about his concept of the entire work. Interestingly enough, it is in the confrontation of the dreadful Dies Irae that we may detect the most crucial relationships between the *Requiem* and Mozart's final opera, written over the same year. Although we think of the *Requiem* as a piece at least seeking peace, and of *Die Zauberflöte* as a magically fanciful *singspiel*, both works are remarkable for the strength with which they confront the perils, confusions, and alarms that beset us on our pilgrimage through our lives. The Banquet scene in *Don Giovanni* presents D minor anxieties anticipatory of those in *Die Zauberflöte* and in the *Requiem*; and Georg Knepler, in his brilliant book on Mozart, has written persuasively of the Pamina–Tamino love-story in the *Magic Flute* as a parable of human redemption having analogies with the Christian Eucharist – even though, or perhaps because, Knepler, as a committed Marxist, also stresses the social–political strands in the allegory. The 'trials' that Masonic initiates had to submit to enabled Mozart, according to Knepler, to 'maintain a stance of critical detachment toward the church without sacrificing his faith'.* In the *Requiem* the dichotomy between 'tragic' D minor and 'powerful' B flat major reflects on, or mutates, the dichotomies of *Don Giovanni*: perhaps most startlingly in the 'Rex tremendae majestatis' which, in G minor (D minor's subdominant and B flat major's relative), equates, in its heroic double-dotted rhythms in unisons, octaves, or parallel thirds, 'almighty' God with a hopefully Benevolent Despot – such as the monarch Titus, whom Mozart was currently celebrating in opera.

But the most profoundly late Mozartian – and Masonic – music in the *Requiem* is that which is furthest from classical baroque traditions and closest to the mainly homophonic, hymnic manner of Gluck. Significantly, the full flowering of this idiom appears at the Eucharistic offertorium itself, in the melody of the 'Hostias', harmonized with the utmost simplicity in the Masonic key of E flat major. The religious undertone that Mozart's Free-masonry introduced into E flat major, which was already a key associated

* Georg Knepler, *Wolfgang Amadé Mozart: Annäherungen.* Berlin: Henschel Verlag, 1991: 196, 204; trans. J. Bradford Robinson, *Wolfgang Amadé Mozart.* Cambridge: Cambridge University Press, 1994: 140, 147.

with the humane compassion of the Enlightenment, made for a kind of melody that only a composer of Mozartian genius could bring off – alike in the sublime simplicity of the original tune:

Off'-ring of pray'r and of praise we bring to thee, God of Is - ra- el, Fa-ther most mar- ci - ful;

and in the harmonic startlements, prophetic of a new kind of life, which it may generate.

Melodies and progressions such as these occur throughout Mozart's last works – not only in *Die Zauberflöte*, but also in the slow movement of the clarinet concerto, and in the short but pregnant Masonic motet significantly setting the *Ave verum corpus*. Although such pieces are associated with the triumph of Light, they are quite different in effect from the grander melodies of Handel and Gluck that were their proto-type. We may, however, consider these themes alongside the hymnic themes of Haydn's last years, and regard them as anticipatory of a type of tune evolved by Beethoven (in, say, the slow movement of the opus 96 sonata for violin and piano).

In any case, the significance of these melodies in relation to Mozart's religion is unmistakable. He associated them with the triumph of Light: but only in the negative sense that their consolatory gravity robs death of its power. This is why Mozart's Masonic music is so different from Haydn's. Haydn celebrates life; in the orthodox religion he had been reared on death was accounted for, and it is unlikely that he often thought about it. Mozart lived so intensely that consciousness of death can never have been far off; increasingly he saw death not as a mystical release from the sufferings of his and our life, but simply (and profoundly) as the context in which we exist. On this theme he wrote a most remarkable letter to his father:

> I need not tell you with what anxiety I await better news from yourself. I count upon that with certainty, though I am wont in all things to anticipate the worst. Since death (take my words literally) is the true goal of our lives, I have made myself so well acquainted during the last two years with this true and best friend of mankind that the idea of it no longer has any terrors for me, but rather much that is tranquil and comforting. And I thank God that he has granted me the good fortune to obtain the opportunity of regarding death as the key to our true happiness. I never lie down in bed without considering that, young as I am, perhaps I may on the morrow be no more. Yet not one of those who know me could say that I am morose or melancholy, and for this I thank my Creator daily and wish heartily that the same happiness may be given to my fellow man.*

---

* Letter dated 'Vienna, 4 April 1787'. In *The Letters of Mozart and His Fmaily*, ed. Emily Anderson, London, 1938; rev. 2nd edn by A.H. King and M. Carolan, London, 1966; rev. 3rd edn by S. Sadie and F. Smart, London, 1985.

Although Mozart never lost his belief in the potentialities of the human heart, he came to accept man's natural limitations.

Can we see something of this acceptance of life and death as complementary even in the smallest works of Mozart's last years? Although his life was so short, the completeness and perfection of his music leave nothing to be said. Had he lived longer, he would presumably have added something to a musical experience that seems already all-inclusive, though it is impossible to imagine what. Even Mozart's slightest works appear, in his last years, to be independent of time or place. Even the little works for glass harmonica are poles apart from the serenades and cassations of his youth. They diverted Mozart himself, no doubt, and they would divert a company of angels; but they are no longer music to eat or chatter to. It almost seems as though Mozart had given up the attempt to make music for a society in which he only half believed. He now writes in a celestial drawing-room, where the only audience is himself and silence (as he has no need to listen): just as Bach in his last years, composing *The Art of Fugue* in an outmoded fashion, played to himself in an empty church. Mozart's discovery of the 'spirit' within us, independent of accredited gods and creeds, was a necessary step towards Beethoven who, from within the Self, would attempt to invent God anew.

15

'God's Kingdom is in Ourselves'

The High Baroque and the Sonata Principle in Beethoven's *Missa Solemnis* (1819–22)

Every lock has its key which fits into it and opens it. But there are strong thieves who know how to open locks without keys. They break the lock. God loves the thief who breaks the lock open: I mean, the man who breaks his heart for God.

The Ten Rungs of Hasidic Lore: trans. Martin Buber

I have no friends, I must live alone. But well I know that God is nearer to me than to other artists. I associate with him without fear. I have always recognized and understood him and have no fear for my music. Those who truly understand it must be freed by it from all the miseries of the world.

Beethoven: Letter to Count Ignaz von Gleichenstein, 1807–8

When in the last years of his brief life Mozart created, in *Die Zauberflöte* and the *Requiem*, music animated by the numinous it was, we noted, in a spirit conspicuously distinct from that of the orthodox Roman Church. In 1791 modern, fashionable Freemasonry was a creed based, in some ways in covert opposition to the Church, on an ethical humanism that found place for mystical illumination. Technically, this involved a radical re-creation of Bachian counterpoint and of Mozartian operatic arioso. Now Beethoven's triumph was coincident with that of democracy, wherein man painfully asserted belief in *himself* rather than in a law imposed from above, whether by Church or State. For if everyone is equal in his or her sight and right, art's first task must be to define identity: which was the prime meaning of the sonata principle. Haydn, a country man reared as a Roman Catholic, composed throughout his long life church music refashioned in the light of the sonata principle, which he did more than anyone to establish. A mature Haydn mass is simultaneously a hymn of praise and a dramatic

113

conflict usually triumphantly resolved; while the work in which Haydn's church music culminated is, as we discovered in Chapter 13, not a Catholic mass at all but a post-Handelian oratorio spelling out patently what is latent in the opening of the B flat major string quartet from opus 76, the 'sunrise' it celebrates being here in this world, just over that hill, yet also within the minds of those creating a new society.

The inwardness of Mozart's awareness of 'spirit' was perhaps more potent than his well-developed social conscience, and that conditioned the fact that he was a necessary precursor to Beethoven. This wasn't immediately obvious, since in his early days Beethoven devoted little attention to religious music, being mainly concerned with the forging of an instrumental idiom in a sonata style apposite to his concerns, which were at once private and public. When, at the height of his 'middle period', he composed in 1807 a full-scale Mass for soli, chorus, and orchestra, it is in essence socially humane, an act of worship Rousseauistically simple as well as Masonically enlightened, inhabiting the world of the Pastoral Symphony, and conceived in the same year.

The dotted rhythm with which the Kyrie opens is probably a Masonic 'knocking at the door' and there is certainly Masonic symbolism in the parallel thirds for woodwind which fraternally interlace the C major lyricism of the voices. Although recurrent modulations to the mediant suggest, through the false relations they provoke, a glimpse over the horizon, climax occurs in chains of suspensions in traditional *a cappella* style, affirming the Church's social solidarity. Archaic modal relationships, hinting at mysteries and mysticism, are not, however, totally expunged; and the Gratias is gracious in a suave A flat major, countered in the next section with pantingly syncopated 'misereres', is in F minor, A flat major's relative and traditionally the key of 'chants lugubres'. There's an approach to operatic rhetoric in the soloists' dialogue with the chorus's misereres, though God's Law asserts itself in rigorous A major fugato, the Amens being quietly euphoric in sequential modulations.

The Credo is even more humanistically weighted, being at once symphonic and operatic in enacting the Passion story. God puts on harmonic flesh in the tonic minor 'Et incarnatus', garnering acute diminished fourths and tritones; Pilate imposes judgment in a nagging dotted rhythm; Christ suffers in languishing sixths and undulating chromatics. The physicality of the Crucifixion is appropriately excruciating but, after a climax of 'horrendous' diminished sevenths, Christ is calmly buried in humanely Masonic E flat major, only to be resurrected with another mediant modulation. Returned to the white key of Enlightenment, he dances again in lucent C major. Beethoven rattles through the bits of the creed that don't deeply involve him, and brushes aside the unanswered questions of the 'Et expecto' with an orthodox, rowdily jubilant fugue for 'Et in vitam venturi'.

The Sanctus's triple cry of holiness momentarily hints at transcendence, oscillating between a hymnically scored A major and its flat supertonic, and thereby mating youthful innocence with experience springing directly *ex periculo* – from or out of peril. Another mediant transition carries us to D major, the Baroque key of pomp and circumstance, as is appropriate to the 'Pleni'; and with a further lift to the mediant we reach F major and the heart of the work. In this Benedictus the chorus comment on the soloists' lyrical flights, while the orchestra 'weaves the garlands of repose' in decorated arpeggios. This blessedness, in the traditional pastoral key of the Pastoral Symphony, is that of Masonic Gluck's Elysian Fields, wherein the Common Man is reborn through the simplicity of his heart and the singleness of his mind. This may be why Beethoven's Agnus Dei is not, like that of the adolescent Mozart in his Litaniae, a dream of paradise but a lament for suffering mankind, personalized in weeping appoggiaturas, separated by silences. Though the word 'miserere' provokes reminiscent murmurs in frightened repeated notes, these soon disperse for the Mass to end as a Masonically social rather Catholically religious testament, with a literal restatement of the opening Kyrie. This now sounds, as it wings serenely up the scale of C major, consummated. Mozart's early Litany was still for privileged people, on whom we are permitted to eavesdrop; Beethoven's C major Mass is a humanist ritual directed towards all common men, but composed by a most uncommon one.

Although Beethoven's C major Mass is a social rather than a religious testament, it serves as prelude to the *Missa Solemnis* of 1822, which he believed to be his greatest work. While working on this Mass, Beethoven also composed his last three piano sonatas in which – after having in his middle years embraced the savagest dualities in 'civilized' music – he found serenity within the Promethean Fire itself. In the final piano sonata, opus 111, 'shipwrack' (in Gerard Manley Hopkins's words) becomes 'a harvest' and 'tempest carries the grain'. The beatitude the C major Arietta wins through to, after a C minor first movement fusing the contradictory principles of dualistic sonata and monistic fugue, reconciles Blake's Tyger with his Lamb: an interiorized reconciliation that also, in my view, makes the *Missa Solemnis* the most profound religious testament, at once holy and hazardous, in European music.

The instigation of the Mass was not in a formal commission but in an act of friendship. Beethoven himself decided that he would compose a Mass to celebrate Archduke Rudolf's enthronement as Archbishop of Olmütz: that Beethoven dedicated not only his *Missa Solemnis*, but also the *Archduke* Trio in B flat and the *Hammerklavier* Sonata to him suggests that Rudolf must have been a very remarkable young man. Moreover, Beethoven took his self-imposed task of mass-creation extremely seriously, restudying, as preparation, Latin declamation, the German text, and earlier ecclesiastical polyphony, especially plainchant and Palestrinian counterpoint. Given Beethoven's daimonic nature, the piece became a personal testament then deemed beyond the reach of even the most accomplished professional musicians, and it is still probably the most challenging choral work in the repertory. In a sense, contemporary opinion was right, for the unperformable nature of the Mass, as of the contemporary *Hammerklavier* Sonata, is what the music is 'about'. Beethoven paid tribute to his friend in assuming that he, the dedicatee, would understand, whereas Tom, Dick, and Harry, or Jane, Joan, and Judith, would not. Vicariously, he also paid tribute to us his successors, for at the head of his autograph score he added words indicating that the music, having come from the heart, should find its way to our hearts: 'Von Herzen – möge es wieder – Zu Herzen gehet.'

Although Beethoven uses the liturgical text, he makes symphonic drama in accord with the sonata principle. The first Kyrie is socially ceremonial music, centred in the then-modern world and rife with Masonic symbolism. Dominated by the human cry of falling minor third, in the dotted rhythm of fortitude, the textures embrace both homogeneous polyphony and antiphony between the soloists (representing individual consciousness) and the chorus (representing the Church and People). The Christe – Christ being a *man* through whom God 'saves' us – speeds up the tempo from duple to triple, shifting the key from resonant D major to 'suffering' B minor. As the initially falling thirds are absorbed into a fugue launched by rising fourths and in flowing scales, the souls of individual men and women are liberated from the Church, Masonic or orthodox, and the second Kyrie ensues as a developing (Christ-inspired) recapitulation of the first. The quasi-miraculous transition back to D major and the first Kyrie theme occurs by way of a 'transcendental' modulation into F sharp minor. The Gloria is an encapsulated choral symphony in four movements. The first has for quasi-first subject a furiously upsurging D major scale, though the descending interval of a minor third is still pervasive. This is the Life-and-Death force that used to be known as the Wrath of God; compared with this alarming upsurgence the quasi-second subject – a Masonic waltz-hymn in the lower mediant, man's B flat major – sounds graceful in more than one sense, yet also puny. Even so, the operatically harmonic polyphony is potent enough to suggest Kant's Invisible Church wherein, here on earth, 'God's Kingdom is in ourselves'; and to generate conflict that leads not to recapitulation, but to a slow movement, larghetto in $\frac{2}{4}$, in a key ambivalent between earthily pastoral F major and the D minor that Mozart thought of as daemonic and therefore apposite to uncertain human pilgrimage. The music vacillates between the soloists' quasi-operatic dialogue and the public polyphony of the chorus, the words 'Qui tollis peccata mundi' being personalized in dealing with 'our' sinfulness, while the 'miserere nobis' is anguished in dissonant suspensions and appoggiaturas.

There is a fascinating parallel between Beethoven's 'Qui tollis' and

Pamina's short but shattering G minor aria, 'Ach, ich fühl's', in Mozart's Masonic *Magic Flute*. Both themes fall through a fifth, embracing the third; Mozart rises to the sixth, then falls to the sharp seventh, while Beethoven also expansively leaps but drops to a leading note that inflicts pain. Pamina weeps because she thinks she is unloved by Tamino who, faithful to his Masonic vow of silence, refuses to speak to her. After singing her aria Pamina contemplates suicide, echoing Christ's words ('My God, why has thou forsaken me?'); but she is saved by three magic Beings who are servants of *both* the 'black' Queen of Night and of the 'white' priest Sarastro. In both the Christian myth and in the collateral story of Orpheus and Eurydice there is a sojourn in the Underworld, where the hero dies with the year, his desolation being also that of Pamina. For both, the only answer to unrequited love and apparent betrayal is death.

At the turn of the scherzo anguish is not annealed but brusquely effaced by the wrathful God's solitude ('Quoniam tu solus'), musically manifest in tonally and metrically disrupted, plunging arpeggios in double-dotted rhythm – a corporeal enactment of the Fall of God relatable to the famous-infamous opening of the Ninth Symphony. Whereas the Gloria had opened with a whirlwind ascent, this movement begins with a fall, contrarious in rhythm and dislocated in tonality, crashing down from D to G to C. The lunges of the bass line are cataclysmic; and although the tonality swings back to D major, the screeching high As are more desperate than victorious. The effect is similar to that of the transitional passage that approaches the Hymn to Joy in the finale of the Ninth Symphony; the sudden diminuendo on the word Amen chills the nerves like a douche of cold water, as do the subsequent false related triads of C and A major. The fantastic fugue that forms this symphonic Gloria finale hardly puts the fallen God / Humpty-Dumpty together again, though it certainly exhibits – like the fugal episodes in the opus 101 and 106 piano sonatas – all the power that kings, men, and horses could ever hope to muster. It is worth noting that Hegel had announced the Death of God many years before Nietzsche.

The first four entries of the theme remain strict, asserting human volition in a manner Handelian rather than Bachian. Yet there is also, in so fanatical an assertion of Law, a desperation that Bach had no need of, and by the time we reach the drunken Amens the music has become as Beethovenian as it is non-Handelian. It's as though Man, rigorously declaiming what he imagines might be God's law, is attempting to *curb* God's wrath: the Amens are frenzied rather than joyous, while the muttered As on the words 'cum sancto spiritu' are minatory as well as forceful. Such attempted dominance by merely human will can only prove inadequate. Three attempts at contrapuntal unity are frustrated, leading to two desperately faster, increasingly splenetic, codas, yelling Amens to a frantic permutation of the Wrath of God's upsweeping scale. This leaves us almost breathless (dead!), whether we be the tormented singers assaying the remorseless sequences of high notes or merely awed, possibly terrified, participators in the rite. This astonishing music – 'modern' for all time, as Stravinsky said – is countered by a Credo that offers a statement of Belief, albeit again paradoxically cast in the form of a four-movement symphonic conflict. The 'first movement', in common time and in man's B flat major, opens as fugato on a *cantus firmus*-style theme generated from the familiar falling third and rising fourth; (courageous man rises higher than he falls!). And this human assertiveness nurses the ultimate mystery of Incarnation, suggesting that for Beethoven Man made God in his own image rather than the other way round; or, as Blake (Beethoven's exact contemporary) put it, 'Jesus Christ IS the Human Imagination.' The Incarnatus is a hymn-aria-fugue in the dorian mode, garlanded with celestial trills: though the miraculous moment wherein 'Homo factus est' – based directly on the 'crying' minor thirds – shifts from the dorian mode to D major, and from adagio $\frac{4}{4}$ to andante $\frac{3}{4}$:

In the ensuing Crucifixus Christ the Dying God seems to be identified with suffering Beethoven, for the music is humanly physical rather than divinely metaphysical – tonally contorted, harmonically dissonant and rhythmically corporeal, with double-dotted notes syncopated across the bar-lines, creating an effect of tortured dislocation:

The passage is a startling instance of how high genius may reanimate apparent cliché – in this case the 'horrendous' chord of the diminished seventh, as the quasi-operatic soloists and the homogeneous public chorus savagely interlock. Beethoven-Christ expires on a 'lugubrious' F minor triad as plagal approach to a dominant C.

His Resurrection in the scherzo is anti-climactic, if not bathetic, for the friskily upsurging scales dance as though *incredulous* – even in a *Credo* – of this magical metamorphosis. Yet they counterpoise the Gloria's Fall of God and steer the finale ('Et vitam venturi') back to man's B flat major, broadcasting the tempo to $\frac{3}{2}$ for a cumulative series of fugues, all thematically related to the first, humanly Masonic, Kyrie. Historical continuity, over centuries, is thus affirmed, and instils confidence enough to return to the Credo theme in sturdy recapitulation – though (as in the C major Mass) one part, usually a deglamorized tenor, gabbles through the doctrinal bits of the creed in which Beethoven had little interest. The recapitulation does, however, eventually become a reaffirmation which is also growth, for the last of the fugues, based on repeated notes and falling minor thirds, leads into a coda marked *Grave*. The tumult subsides, and the credo closes in rising scales that gently mutate the Wrath of God into human prayer, ascending from Kant's Invisible Church that is 'within ourselves'.

With the Sanctus we enter the mystical heart of the Eucharist: a hymn-aria-fugue in the lydian mode on B, oscillating to D major; sacral trombones support the individualized voices, in which the falling thirds expand, in steady rhythm, to a godly fifth. But the 'Pleni sunt coeli' (allegro pesante in $\frac{4}{4}$) and the Hosanna (presto in $\frac{3}{4}$) abruptly switch to (mundanely) baroque power and glory in D major, manifesting, perhaps, the human 'benefits' that may accrue from the Eucharist. This latent pragmatism may be the reason why the Pleni and the Hosanna have, at least since the Renaissance, tended to be relatively worldly sections of the Eucharist, though that Beethoven still scores his Pleni and Hosanna for *solo* voices reminds us that he never underestimated human potential. It used to be considered a 'miscalculation' that Beethoven entrusted these rampageous passages to his soloists, pitted against full orchestra; and Beethoven was excused because he was deaf! Yet surely this must be his way of saying that such triumphs as we may achieve are attributable to God-in-US; and it would seem that he knew what he was doing since his solo voices, in defiance of the orchestral tutti, now sound superbly. Moreover, the Osanna precipitates the ultimate sacred moment of the Praeludium to the Benedictus – surely the most profound allegory of introversion in all music – and leads to consequent transcendence. Thematically derived from both the 'human cry' of the first Kyrie and the (divine) Sanctus, this *profanely sacred* music undulates in extreme chromaticism, prophetic of Wagner's *Parsifal* which is also profanely, if more ostentatiously, sacred. Mysteriously *veiled* in scoring, Beethoven's Praeludium annihilates time, descending – by way of rising fourths in caressing appoggiaturas and in sequences of chromatic ninth and eleventh chords – into the dark labyrinth of the Eleusian Mysteries:

The descent into the earth is also a descent 'below' consciousness, from which new life may spring. Taken over by Christianity, labyrinths were designed to decorate the floors of churches, where they symbolize both the delusions of time and space and the redemptive power of grace. It was common throughout the Middle Ages, at the New Year and the Feast of the Holy Innocents, for bishops, clergy, and choirboys ceremonially to dance through the convolutions of the labyrinth on the church floor, playing with a golden ball that was an image of Christ the Sun. While it is improbable that Beethoven knew of this practice, it is indubitable that the effect of the transition from the Praeludium's labyrinthine darkness into the Benedictus is like a shaft of *sunlight*, which dust motes may darken. The literal meaning of the word Praeludium is 'before play'; from the murky delusions of the maze floats the dancing play of angels.

The Benedictus itself is a vast aria-concerto-fugue, radiant in benedictory G major, in a spacious $\frac{12}{8}$. The movement's threefold identity as a supernal aria for solo violin; as a socially contracted concerto of themes, harmonies, and tonalities 'architecturally' disposed and embracing elements of sonata-conflict; and as the quasi-mathematical many-in-oneness of a fugue; makes it a sublime reconciliation of opposites. Authentic motives from plainchant float in interwoven canons as the solo violin, a Winged Messenger or Holy Ghost, descends from the heights:

The close of a movement whose length is indeed 'heavenly' inverts the close of the Credo: for whereas that movement had ended with 'our' prayers wafting to lofty subdominant triads on dulcet flutes and violins, in the Benedictus the structure is mirror-like – A B C D E B C D A – and non-sectional, flowing in an unbroken stream of melody, the Hidden Song revealed. This is why Beethoven embraces the Osanna *within* the Benedictus, as a canonic coda, the theme being a simple rising fourth that then declines down the scale in the lilting $\frac{12}{8}$ rhythm. During the final twelve bars the solo violin resumes its soaring song, the voices their plainchant intonation, which now, however, *rises* by a minor third from B to D, and presses up through the leading note to the tonic. The motive is an inversion of the original cry (at the beginning of the Kyrie) of falling minor third, now resolved harmonically as well as melodically. It is sung four times in canon, no longer at the fourth or fifth but in ultimate unison or octaves. This is the Mass's *consummatum est*, reminding us that the word sacrifice itself means a making holy.

Yet although Beethoven has experienced Paradise Regained and the Benedictus's final cadence is another plagal Amen through which the solo violin wings in a subdominant arpeggio over almost motionless concords, this is a moment of illumination. Grace may descend as ecstasy ascends, and time may seem to be effaced; even so, the last movement must bring us back to the earth where, in the Agnus Dei, we once more exhort the Lamb of God to purge our sins. Having been where we have been, knowing what we know, our cry is more fraught with pity and terror than it was when we uttered those declining thirds in the first Kyrie. This does not mean that Beethoven's 'misery of the world' no longer exists: as he makes manifest by beginning the Agnus as an aria for *bass* voice and, moreover, in B minor, which Beethoven himself had called 'a dark key'. The modality of the Sanctus is abandoned in favour of a sonorously scored, humanly passionate diatonicism while, complementarily, the fluid rhythm of the Benedictus gives way to a time-dominated pulse, like a slowly thudding heart. The melody is impelled by the simplest possible cry of the motivic thirds, though appoggiaturas and chromatic embellishments render them operatic, the more so when the male voices of the chorus respond to the soloist's ululations. Quasi-operatic lament resolves, however, in D major, leading into the 'Dona nobis pacem', which Beethoven calls a 'prayer for inner and outer peace'. It is at first sung by the soloists to a theme fusing a falling arpeggio with the lilting rhythm of the Benedictus. This is not, however, in the Benedictus's winging $\frac{12}{8}$ but in a more earthily dancing $\frac{6}{8}$: which suggests that the Dona nobis is concerned with the effect of our incursions into the numinous on our life in the 'real' world. When the chorus enter, their floating melodies are freely canonic, the strings' semiquavers a liberated delight. The consumatory phrase is un-accompanied.

None the less, although Beethoven has, in St Paul's words, been 'changed, in a moment, in the twinkling of an eye', and God's grace has through Beethoven's art spilt on to the world, the world *as such* remains irremediable. The section ends with the chorus repeating the word 'pacem' in paradoxically pugnacious sforzandi. If man is hectoring God, he pays the price of his presumption, for a sudden modulation into man's key of B flat major ends in belligerence all too predictably human, as timpani and distant trumpets evoke a martial music alternating open fifths (which ought to be godly) with the humanly clenched fist of a dominant ninth. We should remember that war and rumours of war were a reality in contemporary Vienna and that Beethoven – like us in the Second World War – spent some time cowering in cellars, evading bombardment. So despite that heart-rending Song of Peace, there can be no finality. Indeed, the scarily martial music recurs intermittently, and spectrally, through the final affirmations of peace on earth, including one long, purely orchestral interlude which, though beginning presto in D major, modulates through G major, C major, and C minor, and crazily dissipates through rapid sequences around 'mundanely' orientated B flat. Piercingly scored, the scatty hubbub anticipates Mahler's symphonic evocations of the world's tawdry turmoil. Although the parallel thirds and sixths in contrary motion, as the music reaches such remote regions as A flat and D flat, are crazy rather than frightful, the energy would seem to be inane and perhaps blasphemous, since its basic motives spring from the Benedictus. In a finally fierce recurrence of the minatory military march in B flat major, with dreadful drums and terrible trumpets, Beethoven lights on a profound psychological insight into the relationship between inanity and evil.

So the Gloria and Credo are choral symphonies related to one another thematically and structurally: as one would expect, since the words of the Gloria prefigure those of the Credo. These 'progressive' sections lead into the sacred heart of the Sanctus and Benedictus, their relationships being mirrored in the key-scheme, founded not so much on the baroque hierarchy of fifths as on mediants and the false relations they entail. The tonal goal of the Mass proves to be G major, lower mediant to B flat and flat submediant to B minor, for Beethoven as for Bach a 'dark' key of suffering that they may lead, 'for the *time being*', to a G major haven of blessedness. Yet Beethoven's Solemn Mass does not end by 'attaining' this goal. The end, though it is in D major which can be a 'glorious' key, simply admits that human experience is cyclical and circular. Recurrently, we descendants of Adam must stretch out our hands to pluck the fruits of the Tree of Life that flourished in pre-lapsarian Eden and that Beethoven, in his Benedictus, equates with the creative force within Nature herself. 'Nature', of course, includes Beethoven's own nature, as well as the natural world in which he exists. When Beethoven says 'It is as though every tree in the countryside said Holy, Holy, Holy! Ecstasy is in the Woods', he is close to what Blake meant in saying 'Everything that lives is holy.' In this sense the final pages of the *Missa Solemnis* affirm life, though they are not consummatory. Indeed, throughout the final coda the scoring is oddly insubstantial, divided between strings and woodwind, with staccato articulation, so that bassoons, usually solemn in this Mass, become clownishly skittish. The contrast between such delicate 'foolishness' and the melodic radiance and harmonic euphony of the hymn-like tune is a distillation of the *conjunction oppositorum* inherent in the whole Mass and, indeed, in life itself. This is why, in the sprightly figurations of the Mass's final pages, there is still a rustle of sprites and minor demons, if not of the daemonic fiends that Beethoven had confronted during the Mass's presentation of Christ's Passion and death.

So 'concludes' is too strong a word to use of the end of the *Missa Solemnis*. The Sanctus and Benedictus offer, if ever any music did, moments of transcendance, and the final version of the hymnic song give us a hint of what life within the Invisible Church might be like. But its serenity remains ideal rather than real; and the Agnus Dei demonstrates that it cannot be impervious to the frenzies of the world, whose trumpery trumpetings and feckless follies will recur, since 'God's Kingdom is not of this world.' It is evident from a letter that Beethoven wrote to the Archduke Rudolf in 1823, when labour on his Mass was behind him, that he believed that he, in his moments of *raptus*, was able, unlike the generality of humankind, to enter into God's Kingdom, disseminating Henry Vaughan's 'Bright shootes of Everlastingness'. He was an instrument through whom divine rays might light on us. Although the Blake-like 'terrifying honesty' that is the heart of his art sometimes makes us quake, it is precisely this superhuman courage that persuades us to recognize in his music the supreme achievement of modern man.

Looking back, the complex structure of the *Missa Solemnis* argues for a compositional process beyond rational comprehension. Einstein, a scientist as great in his field as was Beethoven in music, maintained that the mystical was the heart of all true science as well as art. This meant that both art and science were spiritually centred; and only on some such premise can one appreciate Beethoven's intricate interrelationships of theme, motive, rhythm, and harmony as well as key: whereby he even finds a place, in the Gloria, for 'the foolishness of God' and, in the Agnus Dei, for man's vainglory, idiot fribble, and feckless folly. The only valid comparison is with Shakespeare's *King Lear* whose tragedy encompasses, along with pity and terror, pathos that is near to bathos (Lear's recalcitrant button and his quintuple 'nevers'), and grotesque farce (Gloucester's self-precipitation over the non-existent cliff) containing a horror that, except for Shakespeare, would be unspeakable (Gloucester's blinding). No work of Beethoven so fully justifies the startling statement that, if we can respond truly to his music, we will be freed from all the miseries of the world. The wonder is – though the rub lies in that little adverb 'truly' – that works of art like Shakespeare's *King Lear* and Beethoven's *Missa Solemnis* momently convince us that Beethoven's words are not only memorable, but true.

16

Nostalgia and the Dream of God

Liturgy and Romanticism in Schubert's Mass in A flat major (1822)

Haydn, Mozart, and Beethoven were all revolutionary composers in that they reacted against elements in the society they lived in. Mozart's reaction was more 'conscious' than Haydn's, and Beethoven's was more conscious than Mozart's. Yet Beethoven no less than his predecessors still believed in civilization; at least he thought that, although change was necessary, it was feasible, and the future – to a considerable degree moulded by himself – was worth living for. Not all his calculated will to be misunderstood can alter the fact that he achieved as great a material success as any composer has a right to expect, while at the same time he was able proudly to follow through his destiny.

With Schubert one approaches the typically romantic view of the world. When he was born, in 1797, Mozart had been dead for six years and Beethoven was approaching the first crisis of his career. By Schubert's time the corruption within Viennese society could be disguised neither by the tawdry frivolity of a degenerating ruling class nor by the industry, piety, and cosy sentimentality of the middle class, to which Schubert's parents belonged. Both aristocratic triviality and the bourgeois mentality represented by the newspaper cartoon Biedermeyer – an anticipatory 'little man in the street' – were an escape from fear. Schubert had no use for either, except in so far as he absorbed Italian opera from the one and urban pop music from the other. He rather sought salvation in a communion of kindred spirits. The members of the 'Schubertiad' were university men – poets, dramatists, painters, some brilliant, most cultivated, all worldly-wise. Schubert could not have been their crony had he been the unthinking song-bird of popular myth. Far from being irresponsible, Schubert and his friends were acutely aware of political oppression in Austria, even to the

124

point of revolutionary fervour. Even Schubert himself spent a short time in gaol, hardly for subversive activities, but for being found with the wrong people at the wrong time and place. Yet at the same time the young men of the Schubertiad felt powerless to change their own or their country's destiny. All they could hope for was to find in friendship a community that, being based not on autocratic power but on fellow feeling, kept alive, rather than stifling, the human spirit. They were an intellectual minority awaiting their doom fairly quietly, but with their eyes and ears wide open.

One might almost say that Schubert was a composer of Friendship as Bach was a composer of the Church and Handel a composer of the State. And although Schubert, from adolescence, composed prolifically in all the musical conventions favoured by the Viennese classics – especially by Beethoven whom he revered only just this side of idolatry – it is not fortuitous that we think of him first as a composer of *lieder*: the new, intimate form of art-song that was linked both to Austrian folk song and to the work of the young lyric poets currently proliferating. Some of Schubert's friends were numbered among them, most notably Mayerhofer, a poet of romantic melancholy who may claim a modest distinction in his own right. The collection of folk verse published under the title of *Des Knaben Wunderhorn* also made a deep appeal to romantic sensibility, as an escape from narcissistic self-contemplation; though most of the new lyric poets were romantically subjective, Novalis dealing with frustrated love, consumption, and heavenly aspirations, Rückert, Hellstab and Heine with the ego in torment.

In an astonishingly brief time Schubert developed the primitively strophic lied into a vehicle of profound psychological subtlety. One of the most famous of his songs, *Die Junge Nonne* (written between 1823 and 1825), sets verses by Jacob Nicolaus Craigher in a manner simultaneously lyrical and dramatic, since it tells a tale and paints a scene by way of a self-contained melody economical in its arpeggiated contours, bolstered by stormy piano figuration provoked by the poem. The girl who is singing has retired to a convent as a consequence, it would seem, not of a vocation, but of frustrated love. Outside, the storm rages. She welcomes her heavenly bridegroom instead of her earthly lover; and her rapt state, abetted by the convent's tolling bell, transforms the storm's fury into ecstasy. The openly arpeggiated, hauntingly reiterated melody enshrines the young woman's innocence, while the storm figuration of the piano part – of course in F minor, the lowest, flattest minor key in common use, traditionally associated with tempest, turbulence, and terror – conveys the agitation of her heart. The keyboard's enharmonic vacillations between tonic minor and the flat supertonic offer a violent approach to a familiar tonal relationship given a highly personal significance throughout Schubert's music: for the unexpected modulation from minor to major suggests, in context, that the minor triad is 'reality', the major triad dream. The psychological subtlety of the song lies in the fact that we cannot be sure whether the girl is divinely illuminated or humanly self-deceived; nor indeed whether self-deception may not amount, in some circumstances, to a kind of truth.

In any case the song, though dreamily lyrical, embraces a passionately realistic drama that turns on faith without being strictly speaking religious. Like Schubert, the young nun is voluntarily separated from a pain-inflicting world. Having lost her earthly lover, she idealizes, and perhaps idolizes, him into a dream-lover free of the imperfections of mortality. She seeks a new Eden, as did Schubert throughout his brief life: so the young nun is a mask, as are the people in the two song cycles Schubert wrote in the last years of his life (which are arguably the greatest art-songs ever written). *Die Junge Nonne*, if not quite in the *Winterreise* class, displays a comparable fusion of very stark reality with dream; and it would seem that for Schubert religion, far from being 'binding' as the word's etymology suggests, rather implied an escape into dream that seemed truer than truth. In 1825 (probably the year in which *Die Junge Nonne* was first performed) Schubert wrote a letter to his father in which, speaking of a mutual acquaintance, he complained that

> he probably still keeps crawling to the Cross, and he will certainly have imagined himself ill another 77 times and to have been on the point of death 9 times, as if death were the worst thing that could happen to us mortals. If he could only take a look at these divine lakes and mountains, *whose aspect threatens to stifle and devour us*, [my italics] he would not be so attached to this petty existence as not to think it a piece of great good fortune to be confined once more to the incomprehensible power of the earth to make new life.

Haydn had regarded man and nature as partners in a humanitarian scheme; Mozart considered nature to be insignificant in comparison with people; Beethoven used nature as a means towards his own – and perhaps even humankind's – salvation. But Schubert, having no humanitarian morality and seeking no mystical salvation, made do with his exquisitely tuned senses, which are pitifully subject to time. If not scared of death, he is in awe of lakes and mountains because they are impervious to human feelings. He can but conquer his fear in a pan-theistic (pagan rather than Christian) acceptance of his pettiness.

The letter quoted above is an extraordinary document to come from an ostensible Roman Catholic. It seems probable that Schubert paid little more than lip-service to his church. He wrote Masses in his adolescence because they were a legitimate source of income; but he often cut out the words 'I believe in one Catholic and Apostolic Church', and his was never a religious nature either in an orthodox doctrinal or in a Beethovenian sense. His early Masses sound like the operas of Pergolesi or occasionally those of juvenile Mozart; they often have *buffo* finales. This is the theatrically Austrian aspect of Schubert's Catholicism; the other side is fervent, ecstatic, Marianic, with nothing to do with liturgical practice. It becomes personal, sensuous experience, and finds its heartfelt expression in songs like *Die Junge Nonne*, the famous *Ave Maria*, the inspired setting of Psalm 23 for women's voices, and especially in *Lazarus*, an oratorio about a non-miraculous human resurrection from what was expected to be a fatal sickness. Alfred Einstein maintained that it contains music more dramatically powerful and spiritually exalted than anything in Schubert's operas, and claimed that in creative power it far exceeded Weber's *Euryanthe* and Wagner's *Lohengrin*, which it predates. The oratorio was composed in 1825, the probable year of the launching of *Die Junge Nonne* and certainly the year in which Schubert penned that remarkable letter to his father.

Also in tune with that letter is a Mass in the unusual key of A flat major: for which Schubert made sketches as early as 1819 when he was a mere twenty-two, though it was mostly composed in 1822, and substantially revised later. Schubert regarded this Mass as his finest large-scale piece to date, and worked hard at first to perfect it, and then to promote it. His efforts proved abortive, probably because the work pays little deference to either ecclesiastical or courtly conventions, and comes out as a choral and orchestral symphonic poem of subjectively romantic character; indeed, as a Mass it might be called pan-theistic, if not quite pagan. Incorporating some of Schubert's boldest harmonic and modulatory flights, the piece is, even today, not easy to perform, and must have daunted even Schubert's most adventurous friends among performing musicians. The Mass's basic key of A flat major had been little used by Haydn or Mozart in large-scale works, and was by Beethoven reserved for moments of exceptional sensuous benignity (such as the slow movement of the *Pathétique Sonata*) or of sublime transcendence (such as the adagio of the opus 127 string quartet); the late A flat major piano sonata opus 110 embraces both the sensual and the spiritual dimensions. Similarly, Schubert's A flat major Mass is physically emotive yet aspires to transcendence. In fact, the A flat major key signature for the first Kyrie, though it hints at tonal adventurousness, doesn't recur until the Benedictus. Still, it prepares us for the Mass's dramatically long-ranging tonal architecture and for its unconventional approach to liturgical expectations. It's worth recalling that this A flat major Mass was composed over the same span of years as was Beethoven's tremendous *Missa Solemnis*. The young composer made no attempt to emulate the Master's mind-boggling means of 'making it new'; but he was brave enough to follow his own nature in being a mystic of the senses, especially in harmony and tonality.

His originality is also evident in his scoring, which uses choirs of woodwind, brass, and strings that merge into one another. This we may observe in the opening of the Kyrie, as clarinets and bassoons are answered by strings, and they by the choric voices. The clarinets' diatonic concords are 'humanized' by the bassoons' diminished fifths, against which the chorus's lucent thirds gracefully resonate. The movement as a whole is sweetly sensuous, with no overtones of incense or ritualistic pretension. When the four (SATB) soloists take over for the Christe, their lyrically expansive line (beginning in E flat the major dominant) seems to suggest Man-elevated-to-Godhead rather than God-become-Man; and with the *da capo* of the Kyrie rendered discreetly chromatic, we are aware that, for a being of Schubert's romantic sensibility, Word and Flesh are barely separable. The final *eleison* on a rocking A flat major triad is bliss at once physical and metaphysical.

It's swept away by the entry of the Gloria, in the improbable, loftily heavenly key of E major: though grammatically this is F flat major, the flat submediant to the initial A flat major – the partiality for mediants relationships being one of Schubert's many legacies from the Beethoven he so deeply revered. The music – marked Allegro and *both* vivace and maestoso – surprises us not only because the key is unexpected, but also in its triple-pulsed lilt, its seething semiquavers on strings, and its wide-prancing bass, through which the chorus declaims Gloria in Excelsis in boldly triadic figures thrusting sharpwards. After a brief return to search for the words 'Et in terra pax hominibus', the music returns even more exuberantly to the original figurations, exploiting, at 'Laudamus te', sidesteps to the lower mediant and the tonic minor. The 'Adoramus te' is more seductively chanted by the soloists on a phrase opening on falling fifths and sixths, the tempestuous whirl of string semiquavers now silenced. The first (E major) section ends by modulating to the subdominant A major; in which vernal key we offer thanks to God ('Gratias agimus tibi'), at first radiantly sung by the soloists. But when the words apostrophize God Himself up there in his heaven, 'charming' A major is replaced by dour A minor – a key that Schubert, in *his* dourer moments, was partial to; and as the chorus declaims the words metrically, strings caper upwards in *goat-like* arpeggios:

God's caprine untameableness is manifest too in the volatile tonal side-steppings the arpeggios embrace: until, with the words 'miserere nobis', awareness of the gulf between God's almightiness and us dissolves into chromatics, supported by spectrally pianissimo trombones. Such romantic fear-and-trembling calls for stern treatment, and receives it with a return to jubilant E major for the doxological 'Cum sancto spiritu', set as a Grand Fugue launched by sturdy repeated notes turning into tramping scales. The Amens are protracted, in counterpoint of considerable ingenuity, often chromaticized. But the implacable 'on-goingness' and vast length of this fugue become fearsome rather than triumphant, as though God's 'alti-tudinousness' must always be beyond our scope. Possibly Schubert decided the struggle wasn't worth this effort, for the finally final Amens sound, after so much imaginative enterprise and canonic contrivance, oddly perfunctory.

The Credo – also marked allegro and both maestoso and vivace, as though the composer were undecided whether to take it seriously or not – begins in C major, in hopeful rationality, though the hushed, low-pitched chords for brass and woodwind and then for the chorus soon modulate from C major to 'errant' D minor, and then, a step up the cycle of fifths, from G major to A minor. The effect is of awed affirmation of a faith we can barely credit, the scoring being richly mysterious. Christ's descent 'de coelis' revitalizes the eighteenth-century cliché of the diminished seventh; and the moment of Incarnation is a miracle, in limbo between A flat major, F minor, and C flat major (!) but leading, through fiercely dissonant suspensions, into a daemonic D minor. D minor, however, seeks a haven in pastoral F major, on the words 'ex Maria virgine', and shifts back to A flat major as Homo factus est. The Crucifixus is in deathly A flat *minor* over a stalking arpeggiated bass. But that God is 'sepultus' back in A flat *major* makes a psychological, and possibly theological, as well as musical point.

The resurrection on the Third Day returns to the Gloria's original C major, as though hopeful that, after the previous weird and wild music, rationality might be restored. Cheerfulness does break in, though it is hardly rational, since for Schubert the Resurrection was wish-fulfilment. His account of God's Day of Judgment comes out as almost perky, since it's beyond human comprehension: though his vision of the 'mortuous' is chromatically and enharmonically awe-ful, since death cannot be gainsaid:

This means that the doxological rejoicings are distinctly jittery, though the Confiteor finds a marvellous aural image for heart-felt and simple-minded faith by way of a bass line in marching crotchets, supporting choral harmonies that reinstate the Credo's original progression from C major to D minor to G major and back to C. The violins in the Amens flicker in quavers, somewhat tipsily, though they garner confidence by the end.

Whereas Beethoven's Sanctus, in his *Missa Solemnis*, evokes the ultimate holiness, Schubert's Sanctus is his score's most outlandish, most extravagantly romantic, moment, and possibly this extravagance was, in Schubertian context, more or less equivalent to holiness. It opens in pastoral F major and in a swaying $\frac{12}{8}$ pulse, as though we're about to enter into Gluck's Elysian Fields – a rationalist's Heaven. But the chorus's first cry of 'Sanctus' is on a fortissimo F *sharp* minor chord, after which the orchestra strays through D major, B flat major-minor, B major-minor, before wandering back through C minor to pastoral F major, now garlanded with semiquaver roulades on violins. This is no stroll through Eden's garden, though when the chorus links the Sanctus to the Pleni sunt coeli and the Osanna they convert the apocalyptic elements of the Sanctus into naturalistically conceived rural music with fanfares on (hunting) horns and strings. As had become conventional (except of course in Beethoven), these sections are brief and somewhat mundane, as though they're the best we can do in the way of jubilation. The Osanna ends abruptly, unambiguously in F major.

But the Benedictus at last restores A flat major which is supposed to be the Mass's main key, and presents the words sung by a trinity of vocal soloists (soprano, alto, and tenor), in dialogue with a trinity of woodwinds (flute, oboe, and bassoon), over an ostinato of quavers on pizzicato cello. The music is transparently homophonic, returning to and perhaps purifying the intimacy of the Kyrie. Although the music gathers ardency when the chorus join in duologue with the soloists, the music never relinquishes its smiling grace, which is a re-vision of Schubert's Paradise Lost.

The last movement, the Agnus Dei, however, is unsure whether Eden can be recaptured: as is hinted in the curiously ambiguous tonality in which it opens. The key signature is still one of four flats, though the tonality is neither A flat major nor even quite F minor since there are no cadential E naturals. The strings are echoed by the solo voices in a heart-easing phrase that droops through a fifth but then, on the words 'peccata mundi', unexpectedly twists to celestial E major, as though to compensate for the introduction's lack of sharp sevenths. Perhaps this suggests that the breath of life (God?) cometh where it listeth; and Schubert underlines dubiety by chromatic oscillations on the word 'miserere'. A dominant cadence is approached by way of a German sixth, leading into an allegretto 'dona nobis pacem' in which three soloists (SAT), soon joined by the four-part chorus, sing in A flat major in the intimately sensuous style of the opening chorus. The music attains climax on high A flats, but fades out over a tonic pedal. This is an inconsequential way to end a work so lavish and in several ways so audacious, but the inconsequentiality reflects Schubert's lack of religious certitudes. One might expect that its very dubiety would make it peculiarly appealing to us today, but although it is performed fairly regularly, one couldn't change that regularly to frequently. People want religious music that reflects their beliefs, however uncertain, but it would seem that, since religion is meant to realign (bind) us, one shouldn't stray too far from accredited doctrine. People are uneasy with Schubert in church, whereas they can 'take' Bruckner because he was by profession an organist and choirmaster.

Yet Schubert's A flat major Mass seems to me in its very oddities a transcendent masterpiece, and one can't help wondering what would have

130

happened to him, as a church composer, had he not died at the age of thirty-one – four years younger than Mozart. He is closer to Mozart than to any other composer, but the lyrical and dramatic founts of his art are more widely separated; from the struggle to reconcile them came the mingling of passion and nostalgia that is his music. Mozart is apparently impersonal in his perfection: the dancing interplay of parts seems the essence of mutability itself, whereas Schubert's singing melodies and harmonic wonderments are his own consciousness of mutability, romantic in spirit. This is why, despite his respect for the past, Schubert's music is inexhaustibly prophetic, especially of the sensuous individualism of Wagner; with him we therefore feel, as with Mozart we do not, a tragic sense of potentialities unfulfilled.

Even so, the anticipations of romanticism in all his music – perhaps most of all in this transitional Mass in A flat – are inseparable from the sense of doom that hung over Schubert and his world. He composed much superficially merry music; yet from the moment he attained personal identity the merriment is chilled by melancholy, and the spine-chilling loveliness of his late works – supremely of the C major String Quintet – is inseparable from their consciousness of death's unconsciousness. Again, the Schubertian experience is sensuous. We feel this beauty with our physical awareness of melody and harmony, and in knowing from the music (not from the books we have read) that Schubert himself had so little time in which to relish it, we become aware that for us too beauty is as transient as a dream. The music is still almost before we have heard it; the dream is past that was more real than the waking life.

17

Faith and Doubt in Mass, Symphony, and Symphonic Mass

Bruckner's Mass in E minor (1866) and Mass in F minor (1867)

The music of the Viennese Classics was balanced between tradition and revolution, between an Age of Faith and an Age of Anxiety. Haydn was born into a Roman Catholic faith against which he did not rebel, though he unwittingly transformed it from mystical dogma into ethical humanism. Mozart reinterpreted faith in personally emotional terms, so that it was no longer a faith that the Church could easily digest. Beethoven rejected the past but created new faith out of conflict. Schubert too rejected Catholic orthodoxy, with nothing to replace it but his Nature-affiliated pantheism. Beethoven said that he could have 'no friends'; Schubert used friendship, along with his music, as a bulwark against a hostile world. Yet Beethoven discovered something like belief *through* his music, whereas Schubert had to be content with fleetingly magical moments of illumination.

The changes in attitudes to belief between Haydn and Schubert parallel the slow deterioration of Austrian Catholicism. Schubert's dismissal of the Church was echoed by many of his successors as it grew increasingly remote from the realities of the nineteenth century. By the time of Francis I the identification of the Church with oppression was undeniable, and the Jesuitical spirit pervaded every aspect of life. The revolutionary stirrings of 1848 were brutally suppressed; conditions returned to an even more reactionary conservatism. The Concordat of 1855 handed over the entire educational system to the Church.

Yet that Austria preserved through the nineteenth century a fossilized feudalism alone made possible the strange phenomenon of Anton Bruckner. In him one finds again the innocence that the self-conscious mind of

Schubert had yearned for; whereas Bruckner was apparently a medieval survival in a country cut off from the evolution of Europe. He believed in his Church as unequivocally as a medieval peasant; the evils consequent on it in nineteenth-century Austria he either failed to notice, or considered to be an entirely secular matter. Anecdotes about Bruckner's naïvety are innumerable; counting stars is a fixation that has a touching, cosmically if comically medieval flavour; while his grave acceptance of a wag's intelligence that he was to be elected Emperor of Austria is as much beautiful as ludicrous. He knew that he had the heart of the matter in him: he was kingly and saintly by nature – which was more than could be said of those officially in power.

Born in 1824, the son of a schoolmaster, Bruckner spent his boyhood in the remote country where village life hadn't substantially changed for hundreds of years. When Bruckner was thirteen his father died and the family moved to Ebelsberg near Linz. Having early exhibited musical talents, be became a pupil and chorister at the neighbouring monastery of St Florian, thereby attaining his first taste of Catholic dominance and an introduction to the musical riches of Europe, both of which he accepted with enthusiasm. Grown to manhood, he became a servant of his church, working as an ecclesiastical musician at first at St Florian, later in Linz. Only after more than twenty years did he move to Vienna, as a mature composer with several large-scale works to his credit. He had to wait another twenty years for recognition, for the cultural backwater of Vienna had no more use for him than it had for Schubert. He felt no bitterness at this lack of recognition. One of the reasons why he moved to Vienna was to learn, from more able teachers than were provincially available, to compose better, since he wrote music in praise of God, for whom only the best would suffice. If he was no more aware of the fire that burned within his spirit than he was aware of the revolutionary stirrings latent in his most talented predecessors, he was, in matters that deeply concerned him, not in the least naïve, having an intuitive insight that amounted to clairvoyance.

At St Florian's he had acquired a firm basis in traditional harmony and counterpoint, though his acquaintance with the European classics was probably not wide and possibly not deep. Yet in Vienna he found, in Simon Sechter, a truly great teacher – a musician from whom Schubert, in his last years, had hoped to take counterpoint lessons. From the strangely sensuous Bachian texture of Schubert's C sharp minor *Moment Musical* we may vaguely hazard what profound technical and spiritual changes might have occurred in Schubert's music, had he lived to put this scheme into effect. In Bruckner's case the meeting with Sechter in 1855 was the most decisive event in his career: for he gained from Sechter profound knowledge of the work of Bach and of the late music of Beethoven. Whether Bruckner divined that Sechter would give him what he needed, or Sechter had the insight to see what he wanted, is immaterial. Bach was a religious composer whose techniques were based on the unities of counterpoint; Beethoven was a *modern* religious composer who in his last works fused the monism of 'old' fugue with the dualism of 'new' sonata. Bruckner was a man of faith as was Bach, yet he lived in a world that, since Beethoven had re-created it, would never be the same. To find Bach and (late) Beethoven, and to re-cognize their contradictions as complementary, was to find himself. This bears on the question asked but left unanswered in the previous chapter: had Schubert lived and undertaken his counterpoint course with Sechter he would probably have composed ecclesiastical music to a degree moulded by Bach and late Beethoven: a development that would, of course, have influenced his instrumental music also.

With Haydn, Mozart, Beethoven, and Schubert church music was an appendix to their instrumental work; they remake liturgical techniques in the light of their experience of sonata and symphony. For Bruckner the opposite happens; he starts from the liturgy of his Church, and transforms the symphony into a confession of faith. That confession cannot have been easy; the liturgical certitudes of the Church cannot, for him, have been unequivocal, since he was primarily a symphonist, and symphony is of its nature concerned with conflict. Of course Bruckner, as a 'natural' conservative trained in a monastery, had been happy to accept the liturgical styles handed down by his predecessors; yet his most direct models were Haydn, a composer of Enlightenment, of whose Nelson Mass he possessed a score; and Schubert, from whom he derived the roots of his lyricism and his harmonic sensuality. It never occurred to him, any more than it had occurred to his masters, to wonder whether his ecclesiastical styles were too theatrical. Yet the spirit of his church music, given his later date, is neither very Haydnesque nor very close to Schubert, whose church music yearned for the same lost innocence that informed his instrumental work. Bruckner had never lost his innocence, and so could transform rococo theatricality into a paean of praise, absorbing it once more into the baroque. Bruckner still possessed an instinctive sense of Glory, which most of his contemporaries lacked. Baroque grandeur involves baroque counterpoint of the type that was handed down from the seventeenth-century masters to Fux, and from Fux to Sechter. In principle Bruckner had discovered Bach before Sechter initiated him into the range and depth of Bach's contrapuntal art.

The mature E minor Mass of 1866 (substantially revised between 1869 and 1882) returns, beyond Bach, to the principles of Palestrinian counterpoint and even revives a traditional baroque scoring for double chorus, brass, and woodwind. This may have been partly because Bruckner hadn't at the time access to a symphony orchestra, and because the piece was initially performed in the open air. Even so, these fortuitous circumstances bolstered Bruckner's instincts: which were reactionary in that his melodic lines were frequently tinged, despite the Schubertian sensuality of the harmony, with the Gregorian modality on which he had been nurtured at St Florian's. As a grown man he was associated with the Cecilian movement, the aim of which was to restore the traditional plainchant intonations. Despite this deliberate archaism, it is interesting that among sixteenth-century polyphonists Bruckner was especially partial to Jacobus Gallus: whose music is often enigmatic, chromatically instable, and even secretly revolutionary in its use of ciphers inimical to religious and political orthodoxy. Did Bruckner's 'subconscious' mind reveal more of his true self than his 'conscious' one?

That Bruckner's consciousness was complex, notwithstanding his naïvety, is evident, mostly in elements in his music that derived neither from Renaissance polyphony nor from Baroque monumentality, nor even from Haydn's symphonic style, but rather from music that was immediately contemporary, and even prophetic of the future. Two supreme works exerted on Bruckner an influence that one has to call obsessive. One was Beethoven's Ninth Symphony (composed shortly before Bruckner was born), which made its tremendous impact because it is a large-scale evolutionary piece concerned with the experience of 'Becoming', while being at the same time a monumental choral and orchestral work related to the High Baroque. The slow movement has the serenity of a belief *attained* such as is typical of the adagios of Beethoven's late string quartets. The sublime A flat major adagio from opus 127 seems peculiarly prophetic of Bruckner.

The other key-work is Wagner's *Tristan und Isolde*, which Bruckner first heard in Munich in 1865, the year before he wrote the E minor Mass. Superficially, it is more difficult to understand Bruckner's obsession with *Tristan* than it is to appreciate his obsession with the Ninth Symphony: though it becomes less difficult if one thinks of *Tristan* as complementary to the sensuous abnegation of *Parsifal*. For Bruckner, Wagnerian orchestral harmony was simply the most beautiful – indeed 'ravishing' – sound he had ever heard; to have refused to use it in the praise of God would have been a blasphemy. We are told that Bruckner used to sit through Wagner's operas with his eyes tight shut. To the end of his days he had little notion of what all the palaver was about. Had he known, he might have been surprised, though we cannot assume that he would have been revolted. Perhaps the most remarkable evidence of the original force of Bruckner's genius lies in the fact that he transforms Wagnerian harmony and orchestration into a radiant spirituality that is at once liturgical and baroque, devotional and operatic.

Yet these subterranean hints of the Ninth Symphony's cosmic strife and of Wagner's cosmic egomania must surely imply some oddity in Bruckner's religious experience. Do they hint at a pre-conscious uncertainty – an intuitive awareness that after all the world was no longer medieval? Bruckner's innocent fixations were at times not far from pathological neurosis. His faith saved him from the dementia that destroyed Hugo Wolf; but faith had to win strange victories over subconscious terrors, and victory is not won without a fight. In Schubert's mature work the Beethovenian features and the anticipations of Wagner testify to a split in sensibility of which he was probably aware emotionally and possibly, to a degree, intellectually. Bruckner, Schubert's successor, was not thus aware. He achieved sublimity; but moves us so much because we know, as he knew in his heart of hearts, that his sublimity soared over an abyss.

Given its Gregorian and Cecilian proclivities, the E minor Mass may be, among the composer's major works, the least threatened by that abyss. Archaisms are evident in the opening clauses scored for trebles and altos in four parts: for the lines are notated in old-fashioned *alla breve* style, and the parts respect stepwise movement and the godly intervals of fifth and fourth. At first the second alto serves as a tonic pedal, and the second bass has the same function after tenors and basses have entered antiphonally, declaiming the Kyrie Eleison. On the other hand, more stressfully leaping intervals are sometimes permitted (the falling seventh and rising tritone in the trebles in bar 10, the tritone in the second altos in bar 14, the diminished fourth uttered by basses seven bars after their entry); while the counterpoint embraces real modulations to the dominant B minor and its relative D major, thereby to a degree counteracting modality. Support by brass and woodwind is discreet yet potent in effect. All these features are latent in the first music for tenors and basses:

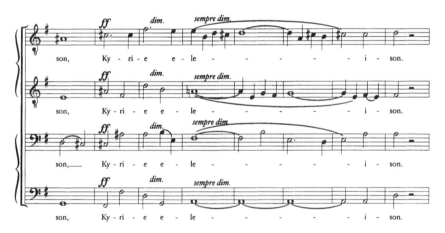

The Christe – just emerging in the alto part at the end of the quotation – is set to a more expansive, *rising* phrase which, in inversion, is diminished to crotchets. In a thrilling cadence tenors reach up to high B; which earns a fraught silence before SATB, all divided à 2, repeat the Kyrie in modified form, finally resolving by way of a 'pathetic' chord of the ninth. In a beautiful Renaissance cliché the parts sink to rest on a blissful tierce de Picardie, the second basses reverberating on their low E. This coda creates a holy hush, possibly because it evokes the *wonder* Bruckner feels at the miracle of faith.

The Gloria, having been introduced by the traditional plainsong intonation, abandons modalized E minor for diatonic C major. Tempo is allegro, with horns sustaining cantus firmus-like semibreves through each $\frac{4}{4}$ bar, haloed by crotchet arpeggios on two bassoons. The chorus appeals for peace on earth, at least for men of good will: though the procession of triads in mediant relationships hints that human existence cannot simply efface turbulence and incertitude. The wind instruments are kept busy, compared with their ritualistically supportive role in the Kyrie; but when the words switch from us 'homines' to 'Domine Deus coelestis' the regular metrics become syncopated and dislocated in a (possibly other-worldly) modulation to the flat submediant, D flat major, soon shifting to B flat and then D minor/major. The setting of the 'Qui tollis' moves, slightly more slowly, through chromatics into remote modulations to A flat major and F minor, revealing the pathos of unknowing but merges into a *da capo* of the original tune in a cross between C major and A minor. In some ways the 'Et in terra pax' and the 'Qui tollis' sections behave like first and second subjects in a sonata movement, though their keys are not clearly defined. The volatile modulations through the 'Cum sancto spiritu' give, by way of chromatic alterations and German sixths, a slightly feverish flush to the music's Glory; while the Amens, syncopated in declining tritones, don't achieve stability until a protracted plagal cadence makes a real modulation to the subdominant.

The Credo is also based on, without being in, C major, opening allegro in triple time, in textures that veer between octave unisons and block harmony. Again, there is something a shade frantic about the affirmations, accruing from the way the original motif circles around itself, getting stuck in a groove just before the descent of God 'de coelis':

The Et Incarnatus – not a separate movement but a section of the Credo – is in F major, for eight-part antiphonal choir. The Crucifixus shifts from benignly pastoral F major to 'lugubrious' F minor, with the wind band in somewhat agitated syncopations against the slow $\frac{4}{4}$ pulse. But the music narrowly evades descent to deathly A flat minor so that God may be quietly 'sepultus', back in F *major*, ready to resurrect himself in triads divided between trebles and altos, tenors and basses, encouraged by throbbing quaver chords:

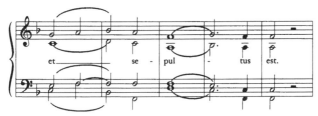

The original figuration of arpeggiated crotchets returns at the Day of Judgment, moving from turbulent C minor to orderly C, and even heroic E flat major; and back to C major for *da capo* of the Gloria melody asserting belief in Holy Spirit, Holy Church, and – in pianissimo dissonant suspensions – in the resurrection of the dead. The final Amen is a conventional dominant-tonic cadence, albeit approached by a subdominant minor chord followed by a German sixth on A flat, with the instruments jubilantly hammering quaver triplets, getting faster. This is a very economical Credo in which the eventful drama is fitted tersely into its liturgical context. The contrast between this practicability and Schubert's romantic–nostalgic Credo in his A flat Mass is trenchant.

The Sanctus is in G major, traditionally a key of blessedness. Given the modal flavour of its free-rhythmed phrases it doesn't, however, sound like straight diatonic G major; each melodic line is serene, with pentatonic minor thirds and soft-flowing scales, and although the polyphony involves imitative 'points' there is little strict canon. Perhaps freedom is the essence of Bruckner's blessedness; if you sing each line separately to yourself, you'll understand how much this music owes to sixteenth-century tradition but also how the past is newly illuminated. The climax, built on the threefold cries of 'Sanctus' on high Gs and As, is awesome, with dominant sevenths in G major sounding triumphantly *disembodied*, rather than cadential.

The Hosanna's return through remote E flat major to tonic G major mates awe with ecstasy, and is more 'spiritualized' than Hosannas commonly are.

On the whole Bruckner's Wagnerian obsession is not strongly evident in this music, perhaps because of the work's deliberate archaism. There is, however, more than a hint of Wagner in the tritonal chords and rising sequences that open the Benedictus. Bruckner's excitement at 'coming in the name of the Lord' is not the same as Tristan's anticipation of his Beloved's arrival over the 'empty' sea, but its psychological, and perhaps even physiological, effects may be similar: especially when, climactically, chromaticized C major–A minor erupts radiantly into A flat major garlanded with woodwind arpeggios. The final Benedictus 'in the name of the Lord' leads without pause into the second Hosanna, which more conventionally tames exultation into C major vivacity, albeit with chromatic sidesteps.

The concluding Agnes Dei at last restores the original quasi-modal E minor, the chorus beginning with declamatory repeated notes modulating to the dominant and aspiring to a high G. The 'miserere' prompts the woodwind to a faintly Tristaneque undulation:

It may be significant that recollection of our sins makes for a fortissimo climax on high B flats, leading into a modulation into benign A flat major soon enharmonically mutated into C flat, 'standing for' B major. The 'Dona nobis pacem' oscillates by mediants between E minor-major and C sharp minor-major before expiring through an 'excruciating' minor ninth into a plagal cadence, with the second basses moored on low E, fading *a niente.*

The spiritual quality of this E minor Mass springs from its nervous equilibrium between several pasts of liturgical music and the then present. Yet it's possible that Bruckner attained his highest point in church music when he accepted, without 'Cecilian' pretension, the style he had evolved from the models of his immediate predecessors. However this may be, the Mass he wrote in the year after the E minor is his biggest and probably greatest mass, scored in the then accepted convention for SATB solists, chorus, and symphony orchestra. Its key is F minor, traditional key of *chants lugubres* and *chants funèbres*, which seems an odd key to praise God in. It's unlikely that Bruckner consciously reflected on the implications of F minor; but it's possible that, wanting to compose a high and serious mass, he lighted on the key most aware of human trials and tribulations. Moreover, having been used for the opening Kyrie, the key does not reappear, with notated key signature, until the final Agnus Dei; even then it is abandoned in favour of F major for the 'Dona nobis pacem'.

The opening of the Mass is entrusted to the ripely Wagnerian orchestra, the theme being a drooping scale entering in canon at the fourth or fifth, until it attains a climax on a 'Neapolitan' G flat major chord. When the voices enter they chant the same lamenting phrase, while the woodwind of the orchestra diminish their twining figuration to semiquavers as the music modulates, through the dominant, to the relative. In this key, for the Christe section, the soloists take over, as is appropriate for the presentation not merely of God become Man, but a particular, identifiable man. The soloists invoke Christ in noble falling octaves, and perhaps also in the volatility of chromatic and enharmonic modulations that end up having traversed from 'flat' F minor to 'sharp' (high and heavenly) E major: from which remote point the scale motif, now both descending and ascending, returns enharmonically to B flat minor and the original declining scale:

The Gloria centres, as often in Bruckner, on 'white' C major, possibly with a hint of Enlightened rationality to temper an access of Glory. Prefaced by the plainchant intonation, it opens in brisk $\frac{2}{2}$ time, with surging scales in the orchestra and antiphony between the choric sopranos and altos, and tenors and basses. Through the 'gratias agimus' modulation is characteristically free, enhancing rather than threatening the sense of glory. Excited orchestral trills over fierce scales in quavers are Beethovenian, in the vein of the epic Ninth. The 'Qui tollis' is a separate section, if not movement, basically adagio in D minor. The chorus entries are now canonic, the theme opening with a falling fifth; the sins of the world make the tonality sink abysmally to G flat, only to recover, at the prospect of sitting at God's right hand, in a blaze of E – grammatically F flat – major. The concluding misereres are declaimed on awe-struck repeated notes, back in D minor but with Neapolitan overtones of E flat major.

The Quoniam returns to C major at allegro tempo, the vocal parts divided between soloists and chorus, the orchestra rippling in contrary motion scales. The citation of Christ's name – as usual in Bruckner – is hushed, for God's manifestation as a man is the ultimate miracle: against which the Amens, though beginning in C major with leaping octave, are instable in tonality and complex, within the regularly driving beat. The final affirmation is jubilant in this uneasy context, though it's hardly comparable with Beethoven's terrifying Wrath of God at the D major beginning of the Gloria in his *Missa Solemnis*. One might say that the drama in Bruckner's Gloria is in Beethoven's sense symphonic; and the same is even more true of the Credo, again rooted in C major at $\frac{2}{2}$ allegro tempo. A 'revolving cam' tries to stabilize the bass; but the vision of 'lumen de lumine' bewilderingly rocks between mediants, and is 'incarnated' in a tenor aria marked both 'moderato' and 'mysterioso', of course in heavenly E major, derived grammatically as F flat major in the mediant cycle. When the tenor soloist is joined by the chorus ('de Spiritu Sancto') enharmonic transitions further enfeeble the pull of the earth, as a solo violin subsides in syncopations over the strings' and woodwinds' pulsating quavers. The effect is a long way 'after' that of the solo violin in the 'Benedictus' of Beethoven's *Missa Solemnis* but the allusion, if remote, is potent. 'Homo factus est' is set to an undulating, as though introverted, motif, leading without break into the

Crucifixus: beginning a tone lower, but in E flat *major*, not minor. The thudding quaver chords and the syncopated scales on the orchestra do not abate, sliding through oblique modulations until God is 'sepultus' in a chromaticized permutation of the Kyrie's original declining scale:

His Resurrection is simple and, in its simplicity, both superb and sublime. After the E flat major burial – possibly Bruckner is making a point in burying God in the key currently associated with human heroism – the music inches up a semitone to bare fourths and fifths in military rhythm, but very softly. The neutral fourths and fifths alchemize into a blaze of E major as the music ascends into Heaven and Christ sits at God's right hand. The ultimate blaze of Glory is on a triad of D flat major – 'really' C sharp major as lower mediant to E major. The Day of Judgment proves, however, to be as metrically severe as it is in the E minor Mass, at least until it contemplates not the 'quick', but the 'dead'. God's invulnerability returns to C major with a driving (Beethovenian) dotted rhythm in the orchestra. Consciousness of death's *un*consciousness periodically induces near-breath*less* hushes, though the doxology reminds us that everything must unfold as was promised 'per prophetas'. Yet although the textures are unifyingly 'in fugato', the lines are often chromatized and sometimes almost febrile. Even though the final Amens exult in an unambiguously tonic C major, Bruckner's CREDO has been hard fought for – if not as hard as Beethoven's!

The Holy of Holies of the Sanctus, after that battling Credo, opens in pastoral F major, *sub*dominant to C and on sensuous strings that momently recall Schubert and Wagner. The vocal themes involve godly rising fourths and falling octaves, divided antiphonally between upper and lower voices. The 'Pleni sunt coeli' and the Hosanna are brief, skipping like lambs on the mountains, eschewing grandeur. Bruckner is following convention in treating these sections as relatively mundane if not trivial: thereby preparing the way for the Benedictus: which restores the four-flat key-signature – meaning not F minor, but A flat major. This, though not comparable with Beethoven's ultimately transcendent 'Benedictus' in his *Missa Solemnis*, is spaciously lyrical, and romantically emotive enough to be prophetic, in its dropping appoggiaturas, of Mahler. The solo voices at first sing the heart-easing tune in close canon in an A flat major almost unsullied. The soprano, on the word 'benedictus', is seraphically echoed by a flute; but although the polyphony flows flatwards through a 'middle' section, the canonic *da capo* is also developmental: leading through a chain of mediant modulations into the repeated Hosanna. The peremptory conclusion again oscillates between D major and F major.

At last, for the Agnus Dei, the tonality of F minor is reinstated. The opening orchestral theme fuses the falling scale of the Kyrie with drooping fourth, fifth, and tritone, thereby allying God with the Devil, his complementary opposite. The vocal theme presents the scale rising as well as falling, and the first clause modulates to the subdominant, B flat minor, as the soloists wail 'misereres' to a weeping semitone, and the syncopated orchestral rhythm recalls the moment in the Credo at which 'Homo factus est.' The choral polyphony modulates to G minor-major and then, exultantly, to A flat and F majors. Remembrance of 'peccata mundi' brings back the darkness of F minor with semiquaver orchestral undulations: until darkness is banished for the 'dona nobis pacem', lyrically in F major with the declining scale marked 'ruhig'. The ghost of Beethoven hints at distantly military drums, reminding us that this peace has been attained through strife; the transformation of the theme in the last section, with perfect fifth of C minor, followed by a plunging diminished seventh and a trilled cadence into C major, re-enacts the symphonic conflict in microcos. Finally, the original Kyrie theme droops down the scale in F major, then curls up through a godly fourth. In the orchestral coda F major triads shine seraphically, the more so because the descending scale momently clashes semitonically with the choral euphony.

Bruckner's sopranos and altos were of course boys when his liturgical music was performed in churches, though we are now habituated to female sopranos and altos when works like the F minor Mass are sung as concert pieces. Both boys and women are 'right', given that the F minor Mass is, as a confession of faith, at once traditionally 'religious' yet also profoundly 'modern', in a way that honourably succeeds, though it can hardly compete with, Beethoven's *Missa Solemnis*. This becomes even clearer in the symphonies that are the crown to Bruckner's achievement, though they have no explicit liturgical dimension. Even if one never comes to recognize and accept the logic of Bruckner's vast symphonic structures, there are still moments when, listening to the adagios of his last three symphonies, we wonder whether, since the late works of Beethoven, European music has reached this point again. The climax to the adagio of Bruckner's Seventh Symphony – and therefore to the whole work – is a conflictless paean of bells on a C major triad, which evolves out of slowly upsurging scales on violins. It is naïve, if you like; yet it also renders Glory *incarnate*, and only a man who had seen and heard this glory could have composed the threnody (in heavenly E major) with which the adagio concludes: funereal music, inspired by the death of Wagner – for Bruckner a human being of godly stature – in which there is regret, but no shadow of fear. In such moments Bruckner seems, in his very innocence, to belong to a race nobler than our own. It is a sober statement of fact that we will not look upon his like again.

18

God and Classicism, Agnosticism and Romanticism

Berlioz's *Grande Messe des Morts* (1837) and Fauré's *Requiem* (1887)

Although an heir to Haydn, Mozart, and Beethoven as a Viennese classicist, Schubert was also a harbinger of romanticism who created, in his Mass in A flat major, perhaps the earliest High Romantic Mass. Berlioz, in some ways the High Romantic composer *par excellence*, was overtly an agnostic who, in making music peripheral to ecclesiastical tradition, did so in the spirit of his formidable originality, which was even more conspicuous than Schubert's. His initial work of genius, the *Symphonie Fantastique*, 'came to me' (as he put it in 1830) 'in my manhood, a voice out of the burning bush': proffered by Shakespeare in the guise of Harriet Smithson in the guise of Ophelia, the personal being inseparable from the literary revelation. Although the *Symphonie Fantastique* was autobiographical, its romantic musical techniques were orientated with classical precision; complementarily, Berlioz's supreme public, as distinct from private, work – the *Grande Messe des Morts* – was prompted by specific historical circumstances, though its public dimensions serve as a frame for inward psychological verities. Both the private and the public work tore Berlioz to tatters; frequently he threatened to faint over the kettledrums, and was thrilled by the visceral effects – 'a *reasonable* degree of weeping and trembling' – his music aroused in other people. So an artist's musical autobiography became, in ancestrally Roman Catholic but nationally self-conscious France, a generalized myth, allied to the contemporary cult of the Colossal – which was itself a product of the age's expanding science and technology. Material 'progress' was inseparable from the evolution of the human spirit.

Whereas Schubert was a great but intimate composer who, as a person, was far removed from Beethovenian aggression, Berlioz – who revered Beethoven no less than did Schubert – was Beethovenian in dynamism. He bitterly contested the machinations of enemies who were scared of his 'Babylonian' images of Glory; and triumphed when, in his *Grande Messe des Morts*, these images were fully 'realized' and were later capped, in his mammoth Virgilian opera *Les Troyens*, with a vision of a Good Life unrealizable in fact, yet in a sense more real than reality. Today, Berlioz's Virgilian opera, which he never heard in its entirety, stands as a work so rich in invention, so electrically charged in rhythms, so rapid (especially by nineteenth-century standards) in harmonic pacing, and so acutely heard in sonority, that it justifies its composer's belief that it co-exists not merely with Gluck, its closest historical analogue, but also with Virgil, Shakespeare, and Beethoven: in which sense art would seem to have superseded religion.

For this reason, too, Berlioz's *Grande Messe des Morts* occupies a crucial place among Europe's choral masterpieces. The particular public event that triggered the work was a commission for a large-scale memorial piece for those who had died in the 1830 July Revolution. In typically Berliozian paradox the work was thus at once revolutionary and establishmentarian; and, as was frequently the case with Berlioz's dealings with establishments, it was exceptionally accident-prone. Cantankerously competitive administrators did their best to wreck the project, and only the adventitious death of a colonial General fighting in Algeria enabled Berlioz's work to be diverted to an alternative subject for public lament. When the Mass, completed in 1837, was eventually performed in 1840, its galvanically unconventional energy could not be gainsaid. An immediate success, it has remained one of Berlioz's supreme achievements; indeed, quite late in life he remarked that if he were threatened with the destruction of all his works save one, he would 'claim exemption for the *Grande Messe des Morts*'.

Like all major composers (with the exception of Bruckner) who came to fruition in the mid-nineteenth century, Berlioz was not a man of faith but a confessed agnostic who, by definition, did not *know*. Vividly endowed with a sense of the numinous, he celebrated the *un*known and unknowable: so that his requiem for the dead is an awe-ful but not strictly speaking religious creation. He scored it for gargantuan forces that were unlikely to be assembled in the course of diurnal acts of worship, acceding to the cult of the Colossal endemic to the Revolutionary era, when proud man recognized that he had something to prove. Several 'sublime' gestures in revolutionary French music of the nineteenth century have gone with the wind, while Berlioz's sublime gesture remains today as alarming as it was when first penned, since its 'Babylonian' and 'Ninevehan' splendours are uniquely authentic and authentically unique. Moreover, Berlioz's colossalism is tempered by restraint; much of the Requiem's most disturbing, as well as beautiful, music is diaphanously scored.

This public Requiem has roots in the traditional liturgy, beginning with a Kyrie and climaxing in a Sanctus and Agnus Dei. The main body of the

144

work is, however, a setting of Thomas of Celano's thirteenth-century Latin poem on the *Dies Irae*, which Berlioz divides into five sections wherein all the 'colossal' episodes occur. Even in these, the operatically and classically trained Berlioz obeys his own precept to 'do coolly the things that are most fiery'; and the form of the whole work is conceived not only with objectifyingly theatrical panache, but also with architecturally crafted gravity. In the preludial Requiem-Kyrie the theatrically expressive accents and corporeal gestures never threaten ceremonial grandeur. The opening theme – in G minor with chromatic side-steps – starts simply as a rising scale. The theme seems in equilibrium between the inevitable declension of death and the prospect of a *world* redeemed; static and progressive elements are mated in the technique itself, since the movement is structured as an operative set-piece in which the instrumental figurations grow gradually more animated, while it is an embryonic sonata-form with a second subject (for the 'Te decet hymnus') in the relative major. Feverish tremolandi make for a briefly intense development section with a thrilling climax, for the word 'luceat', on a D major triad. The drooping chromatic scale, reinforced with sobbing appoggiaturas, fades over funereal drum-beats in false related triads of G minor and major.

The first section of the Dies Irae, the 'Tuba mirum', does not immediately contradict the quasi-liturgical Kyrie since it begins in a devotional aeolian A minor, as though recounting an old tale, 'as David and the Sybill prophesied'. Plangent chromatics and more tremolandi soon discount sobriety, however, leading to the first of the notorious outbursts on four strategically placed brass bands, blared in heroic E flat major, at the furthest possible pole from modal A minor. The tussle between apocalyptic forces and terrified human beings is furious, though the section ends terror-numbed ('Mors stupebit et natura') in a quiet, if hardly tranquil, E flat major. Berlioz borrowed these brass fanfares from a *Messe Solemnelle* he had composed a dozen years previously, in 1825 – a work that has quite recently been restored to the repertory. In their new setting in the *Grande Messe*, however, they have a savage venom that makes the contrast with the next section, 'Quid sum miser', the more astonishing. As the words switch from cosmic cataclysm to 'my' plight, the thinly scored music in a modal G sharp minor with chromatic vagaries is at once piteous and pitiful; still proud in its 'coolness', it fades into a weirdly elliptical Neapolitan cadence:

Immediately plumbing down a third to E major, the fanfares return even more exuberantly and a semitone higher than on their first appearance. If this makes them more assertive, their E major status hints at celestial matters only in the sense that the Last Day Judge seem impervious to human concerns: a disparity underlined in the next section, 'Quaerens me', which appeals to the crucified Son to help us since God the Father won't. This music, sung by chorus unaccompanied, has a tender radiance almost reminiscent of sixteenth- or even fifteenth-century polyphony, and is in the traditionally youthful key of A major, E's subdominant. A few dissonant suspensions and a faintly minatory incantation on repeated notes occur when the text evokes Mary Magdalene and the Penitent Thief: for Berlioz, being humanly sinful may be a gateway to grace. The peculiarly Berliozan flavour of the passage lies in the way in which human compassion functions by way of a cool, chaste, quasi-divine (?) impersonality.

Yet again private compassion is engulfed in public lament, for in the 'Lacrymosa' we the people, arraigned before the Last Judge, weep for our fallibilities rather than our guilt – to which brave Berlioz, like braver Beethoven, was reluctant to admit. This movement, the longest in the work, is also the most fiercely physical, in an acrid A minor with upshooting scales and arpeggios dislocated by syncopations. In every bar both choral singers and instrumentalists *enact* weeping and wailing:

Although relief is offered in a quasi-second subject, in the relative major, the lurching $\frac{9}{8}$ declamation remains both virile and aggressive, hanging on, like early Verdi, for grim life, however harsh life's horror and frigid death's fright. The *da capo* of the original A minor motif sounds even more volcanically eruptive, and though it is assuaged by a return of the quasi-second subject, this too is progressive action since the return happens not in the relative but, sonata-wise, in tonic A major. The coda is also in the tonic major but is, if triumphant, more beastly wild than human.

The Offertorium, again using Christ as intermediary, shifts from the apocalyptic to the intimately human. Schumann thought this movement the crown of the work, and it is certainly the point at which human redemption occurs, whatever function in it God has or has not. Lucently scored in the dorian mode with chromatic alterations, the invocation to 'Domine Jesu Christe' oscillates semitonically between A and B flat, instrumentally accompanied by figurations that, while remaining gentle, grow rhythmically more complex as we gird ourselves to confront 'hell and the deep pit'. Again, Berlioz's religious sense seems to consist mostly in admiration (in both senses) of human courage: the reward for which seems to be something we can only call transcendence, when the reference to 'holy light' provokes a mutation of the chromatic oscillation into D major, with diatonic triads luminously juxtaposed in sixteenth-century style.

The setting of the Dies Irae concludes with the 'Hostias', our offering of sacrifice and prayer on behalf of the battle-slain. This notorious passage – perhaps the most extraordinary in Berlioz, which is saying a lot – auralizes the vast gulf between us as miserable offenders and the imperturbability of God. Declamatory passages for male voices in grammatically unrelated triads are pierced by minor triads scored for piercingly high flutes and sepulchral trombones, swelling from *pp* to *sfz*, then fading *a niente*. The sound stabs us in the solar plexus, leaving us tottering over that abyss: from which, in the nick of time, we are rescued by the return to traditional liturgy in the Sanctus. Yet characteristically, Berlioz makes a non-doctrinal point in scoring this for a solo voice, stressing that redemption, should it occur, could be only a personal matter. Unsurprisingly, the soloist is a Heroic French Tenor who makes magic when, like Christ incarnate, he transforms a radiant D flat major melody, by a single enharmonic alteration, into the remoteness of D major: after which the music winds and wins its way home through a tremolando diminished seventh. Here D flat major 'stands for' C sharp major, the most 'upward' key in tonal music – in analogy with Janáček who, habitually using D flat major as his love-key, thereby evaded C sharp major's plethora of double sharps.

The Sanctus is capped by a relatively orthodox, and brief, fugue for the 'Hosanna in excelsis' which here, as normally, concerns the manifestly mundane benefits of the Eucharistic act. This reinstatement of the public world can only momentarily override the terror of mortality and of the super- (or sub-) human, if not our awe of the unknowably divine. The final movement – the Agnus Dei – proves to be profoundly consummatory in Berlioz's and in man's terms, if not in God's. It opens with hushed, unrelated concords in 'archaic' style, and reincorporates the Hostias's stratospheric flutes and cavernous trombones, which again threaten to open the ground beneath our feet, hurling us to hell: though it is typical of Berlioz, as we saw it to be of Lear-like Beethoven in his *Missa Solemnis*, that knowledge of the depths is a necessary prelude to even a nodding acquaintance with the heights, Beethoven bluntly remarked that if his demons left him, so would his angels, with one accord. However this may be, after startling enharmonic shifts, music from the original Kyrie returns, transmuted. The rising crotchet scale, the drooping chromatics, and the quasi-second subject in the relative major, with its weirdly gyrating accompaniment, all recur; but this time the initial G minor scale winds its wandering way to G *major*, traditionally a key of blessedness; and the final bars, threatened by funereal drum-taps but bathed in celestially arpeggiating harps, enact the peace that passes understanding, though it indubitably, if mysteriously, exists. The 'Neapolitan' A flat major triad in the approach to the final cadence sends a chill down the spine that itself validates the ultimate quietude which is death.

Berlioz's *Grande Messe des Mortes* is a crucial work in that in it even modern non-believers may recognize that there are 'more things in heaven and earth than are dreamt of in your philosophy'. Berlioz was indeed a Hamlet-like figure, combining manic extroversion with depressive introversion; and by now we know that not even many massive books – including David Cairn's recent, magnificent two-volume biography – let alone the Player's tootling recorder in *Hamlet* – can hope to expound his 'mystery'. Berlioz, like Hamlet, is an agelessly modern type, inexhaustibly fascinating to, if never comprehensively understandable by, us who are his heirs. Ironically enough, that makes him a bit like the God he so deeply mistrusted.

Although Berlioz was in several obvious ways a revolutionary he was also a maker and guardian of civilized values who aided, rather than threatened, the cultural traditions that France revered. Indeed, that France became in the second half of the eighteenth century a melting-pot in which were generated Europe's political revolutions, was not unconnected with the fact that French aristocracy and autocracy had been so deeply entrenched. Certainly, Gabriel Fauré's conservative discretion, which looks like an opposite pole to Berlioz's iconoclasm, was really, if opposite, also complementary. In this respect Fauré's Requiem may be revealingly considered alongside the earlier composer's grander and greater Requiem. Fauré, after all, had a composing span of over sixty years, stretching from the mid-nineteenth century to the first two decades of the twentieth. He lived through political and cultural turmoil, including the musical revolutions associated with Wagner, Debussy, Stravinsky, and Schoenberg; and while it would be excessive to say that they left no mark on him, one could validly claim that he continued to follow his own path – that of conservatory rather than of revolutionary France.

Whereas Berlioz, although profoundly French, was a conspicuous loner, Fauré was in several ways a representative Frenchman. His family was of durable stock that might even be called ancestral; and his family history followed the opening up of French society that occurred after 1789 through the rise of the bourgeoisie and the encroachment of industrialism on a largely agrarian economy. His immediate forebears were higher civil servants, and had links with the Church. Fauré himself was sent to the recently founded Niedermeyer school of religious music in 1854, at the tender age of nine. Since the school had been founded expressly to counteract the bland secularity of contemporary French church music with a return to the modal traditions of plainchant and of French liturgical music of the Renaissance, and was also grounded in the study of Bach, Mozart, and Beethoven, this was musically advantageous. Its influence is evident in the earliest distinctively personal music Fauré was to create, such as the affecting, punningly titled lydian-mode setting of Leconte de Lisle's 'Lydia'. That Gabriel was sent by his parents to the Niedermeyer school may mean that they envisaged his future as that of a church musician – as a professional occupation, if not as a destiny. In any case Gabriel was not a rebellious, any more than a revolutionary, type; did well at the School; and embarked on a number of minor church appointments before becoming, through the good offices of his teacher Saint-Saëns, organist and choirmaster at St Sulpice's in Paris. In 1877 he moved to the Madeleine, where Saint-Saëns had himself presided, staying there until 1895.

Yet Fauré was not temperamentally a churchman, but was representatively French in being an *homme moyen sensuel*, indolent, charming, civilized, irresistible to women; he was described by Renaldo Hahn, that ornament of the salons, as a 'gregorianizing voluptuary'. Though he married, somewhat late, and produced children, he continued to live a life that Debussy, himself a voluptuary, considered to be mindless socializing. He was sobered, however, by his dedicated work as head of the Paris Conservatoire, and by his devotion to the craft of composition, working mostly in small forms such as the *mélodie*, and in sequences of piano pieces in the categories that Chopin called preludes, nocturnes, barcarolles, and impromptus. His first great success was with a violin and piano sonata in A major, his opus 13. Subsequently he favoured chamber music, especially that mating strings with piano; but he wrote little orchestral music and (in his indolence?) usually handed over the scoring to his pupils.

The originality of Fauré's apparently conservative art is first revealed in his songs: as is evident in the already-mentioned 'Lydia', in the simple but appropriately mysterious 'Le Secret', the radiant 'Nell' whose unforgettable tune soars over a singing bass and tremulously broken chords on piano, and the proudly arching hit-tune of 'Après un rêve'. The climax to Fauré's song writing occurs in the Verlaine cycle called 'La Bonne Chanson' which, triggered off by his passion for Emma Bardac (later Debussy's second wife), is distinguished by a lyrical afflatus outrageously unbuttoned for Fauré, yet qualified by an austere modality, and by what one might call harmonic evanescence. Indeed on the evidence of these songs one might say that the *strength* of Fauré's art lies in its Bach-like characteristics; his long, serene melodies and basses, his unfailing, unbroken rhythms, his as though pre-ordained command of canon and counterpoint – these being elements that one might expect to be faith-inspired, though Fauré was no believer in Christianity, nor in any established creed. What he did believe in was an ideal rather than immediately real civilization, distilled from the continuity of the present with the past: in which respect, however improbably, he resembles Berlioz. Complementarily, the *charm* of Fauré's art is synonymous with 'le parfum impérissable', to cite the title of a magical song of 1897: a European, Mediterranean grace manifest in the delicacy of his elliptical transitions, recalling the modal polyphony of seventeenth-century French composers as they gravitated towards the metrical, harmonic, and tonal certitudes of the High Baroque. Fauré was a between-worlds composer apposite to the transitional civilization he lived in: melodies and basses tend to stability, while harmonies and textures are in flux; what makes this contradiction possible is the regularity of the pulse, as powerful as the turning earth. While this is evident in the songs, it is still more patent and potent in the chamber music of Fauré's middle years, especially in the Second Piano Quartet in G minor, written in 1887. Fauré said that the first movement's fierce opening theme sprang from recollections of an iron-works in Montgauzay – a formidable industrial aural-image that had haunted his childhood: whereas benign and rural childhood images surface in the adagio's tolling bells, which Fauré associated with nature's overtone series and with 'a yearning for things that perhaps do not exist', though they give aural substance to our dreams. A fusion of Berlioz's apocalyptic fire with Schubert's domestic fancies may, in this masterly Quartet, have encouraged Fauré to spread his wings. Certainly, in the same year of 1887 he conceived the Requiem that has become his most frequently performed, and best loved, work. It would be another three years before the work assumed definitive form; and Fauré disavowed the rumour that it was intended as a personal tribute to his father, who died in 1885. According to the composer, the work was a product of his normal ecclesiastical duties, originally designed for modest forces consisting of soprano and baritone soloists and mixed chorus, with a small band of divided violas, cellos, and basses, harp, timpani, and organ, plus a solo violin in the last movement: these being resources that could be assembled in parish churches throughout the land. Later Fauré made, or caused to be made, a version with normal symphony orchestra, since from its first performance the Requiem achieved a public success that the composer hadn't bargained for and wasn't accustomed to. Though it was meant to be performed liturgically, it soon established itself in the concert hall, and is still the most frequently performed of Fauré's larger works. Nowadays, we usually hear it in the full orchestral form, and cannot be certain how much of the scoring is Fauré's. Still, he kept a wary eye on his helpmates, and seems to have been pleased with the scoring we commonly hear, however much or little he was responsible for it.

Although the idiom that Fauré adopts is the conservative one of Gounod or Saint-Saëns in their ecclesiastical guises, he transmutes this idiom into a language of Bachian nobility, if of slighter range: as is immediately evident in the opening bars of the Introit and Kyrie which, in their reticent sobriety, seem light years away from Berlioz's grandeurs – until we remember that the most piteously poignant moments of Berlioz's *Grande Messe* are even more lucently economical than is Fauré. Although the opening words simply ask God to give us peace, gently declaiming them on a tonic chord until the intonation rises through a pentatonic minor third, it is significant that the basic key is D minor, which already had a long history (through Haydn, Mozart, Beethoven, and Schubert) as a tonality or modality associated with peril and pilgrimage. The 'answer' to the uplifting third of the first clause invokes 'lux perpetua' by starting on the minor third above the tonic D; then wavers between D, E flat, and C on the words 'luceat eis'; but returns to a dominant of D minor by way of a $^6_4$ triad of F major. Despite subservience to the sacred text, the level rhythm and upward-expanding thirds create a luminosity that serves as 'introit' to the main theme – which tells us that Fauré's strength lies in the memorability of his melodies, which are not demoted by being called 'tunes'. This was why the work attained, to the composer's surprise, so great a popularity. In the opening of the 'dolce espressivo' main theme we may note how its memorability depends on its firm basis in the pentatonic falling fourth and rising minor third. A still, almost motionless phrase balanced by an arpeggiated rise through an octave, gives both nobility and ardour to our appeal to God; while the string choir, flowing with rather than accompanying the voices, traces variations on the rising arpeggio over a singing bass.

The balancing phrase ('Te decet hymnus') modulates to B flat major and G minor without disturbing the lines' equable flow, though a climax occurs when, in the relative major, Fauré somewhat brusquely demands that God should harken to our prayer. A point is made when the F major triad slightly shifts to form an augmented fifth; lifts its drooping arpeggio a semitone from F to F sharp; and cadences back to D minor by way of an augmented fifth on F. The *da capo* of the main tune is intensified by chromatic passing notes as well as augmented fifths, but the movement ends calmly, with the words 'Kyrie eleison' subsiding on tonic Ds.

The Offertorium is distinguished by the harmonic and textural 'charm' that complements Fauré's melodic 'strength'. Tonality is elusive, for although the strings open in dotted-rhythmed canon in D minor, with chromatic passing notes, and the choric altos and tenors also enter 'dolcissimo' in canon at the fifth, the ambiguous key ultimately proves to be B minor – a key, as we've often noted, with a tragic heritage. The close-textured vocal lines retain a modal flavour, as of liturgical declamation, and don't aspire to drama even when their entries rise sequentially in pitch, until B minor is definitively established. The strings support the voices in fluttering minor thirds in semiquavers; but fade, through a modulation to F sharp minor, not back to B minor but into a cadence into its relative, D major. At this point the baritone solo sings the 'Hostias et preces' mostly to declaimed repeated notes doubled by violas, while the other parts bear the melodic burden in their patterns of floating quavers. The undulating textures of the strings are a magical instance of Fauré's 'évanescence' – a dreamy sensuousness through which the lines preserve melodic identity:

The *da capo* of the opening of the movement is in four-part canon. As coda, the strings double the voices in radiant B major with its five-sharped key-signature, effacing the earlier modal ambiguities on the ritualistic AMEN.

The Introit and Kyrie of Fauré's apparently gentle Requiem were basically in 'errant' D minor; the Offertorium is in a modalized B minor, with intimations of its relative D major. The Sanctus, surprisingly, is in the remote key of E flat major – a Neapolitan relationship to D minor, with something of the disturbing effect the E flat major chord has as preface to a dominant-tonic cadence in D minor. That we are on the threshold of an 'other' world is suggested too by the scoring which, until the final bars, is restricted to strings and harp, the latter making its first appearance. The opening, in a moderate $\frac{3}{4}$ crotchet pulse, presents divided violas playing spread arpeggios in contrary motion, con sordino; the harp murmurs the same triad. Sopranos, followed by tenors and basses in unison, chant the holy word in undulating seconds around the fifth, with an obbligato for solo violin woven within and around the voices, hinting at celestial matters. Sliding from E flat to D major, the solo violin 'speaks' more expressively, though only momentarily, since the chorus, back in E flat, still 'sempre dolcissimo', pays tribute to God's glory, with the solo violin now doubled in octaves, rotating on its godly perfect fourths. After a *da capo* of the main tune the obbligato violin fades seraphically into trills. Instead of the traditional Benedictus, Fauré introduces the Pie Jesu as a solo number, written for a female soprano, but often sung by a boy treble. The intimacy of the movement, at first accompanied by organ only, hints that one fairly innocent person is praying to Jesus in a slow, simple tune freely derived from the fourths and the stepwise movement of the previous Sanctus. The first phrase begins with a rising fourth, immediately expanded to a fifth; pentatonic ritornelli separate the two clauses. This initial phrase modulates sharpwards from B flat to F major and then, after three interludial bars, returns to tonic B flat major. Adding the word 'sempiternam' to 'requiem', the tranquil tune slightly warms up in chromatic passing notes, modulating to D minor as a way back to B flat. The *da capo* is strict and in the final bars a solo viola succours the child-like voice. The harp's pentatonic figuration adds plangency to the final bar.

The Agnus Dei is usually the peak point of a Mass setting, as it is of the Eucharistic ritual. *This* Agnus is the peak of Fauré's Requiem too: though not for the usual reason but rather because it is the movement in which most happens. We have often pointed out that D minor, the basic key of the work, was considered 'obscure' and therefore apposite to our human pilgrimage. This piece, being a Requiem, has inevitably been preoccupied with death, but its Agnus reaffirms *human* life – in a way that bears on Fauré's agnosticism, despite the calm piety most of the work distils. The key of this Agnus is F major – D minor's relative; and the six-bar introduction for strings is lyrical in melody, impulsive in rhythm, rich in sonority. The melodies sweep in generous curves, mingling arpeggios with stepwise movement, the vocal tune being at first chanted by all the tenors, once more 'dolce espressivo'. When the words link the Lamb of God to 'peccata mundi' the music, now sung by full choir, modulates vigorously between G minor, E minor, and A minor, rising and falling in arches, with the harmony enriched by horns and bassoons. This passionate 'middle section', prompted by human sinfulness, is not long sustained and when the F major tune returns, again sung by all the tenors, the cello and bass line is songfully sustained. The final section approaches the visionary, for the words 'sempiternam requiem' release an 'out of this world' sequence of modulations by mediants, gradually building to a climax as we meet with, or perhaps ourselves become, the 'saints in glory'. Through the 'visionary' passage the chorus chants homophonically, each part having a noble line to sing; violins and violas weave their patterned arpeggios. The saintly visitation culminates in a modest forte, and resolves back to D minor, in which key the quietly declamatory opening to the whole work is repeated, 'as it was in the beginning'. This time, however, the declamation flows into a coda in which the lyrical opening theme of the Agnus is sung by the strings not in F major, but in a D major fulfilled and fulfilling. Cello and bass lines, both arco and pizzicato, grandly support the arches of the grand tune.

So the Agnus Dei has become, for agnostic Fauré, not the still heart of the Christian mystery but a resurgence of human life: which is why the movement is developmental, both within itself and in the context of the whole work. Yet although or because it's a *growing*, it cannot be The End; and the Requiem service plays into Fauré's hands in that, unlike the Ordinary of the Mass, it does not conclude with the Agnus Dei but appends two more movements. The first, 'Libera me', offers us a chance to make a more desperate appeal that God should 'liberate' us from the horror of death; and characteristically Fauré sets the words with strong dignity, for baritone solo accompanied by strings and organ in a syncopated, almost panting rhythm that lends nervosity to the noble tune:

This melody, with its godly rising fifth, almost seems strong enough to free us from hell's eternal fire: which the chorus invokes in telling us that the Day of Judgment will bring all flesh to desolation. Hammered repeated notes on brass and marcato scales on strings thrust upwards in triple pulse, fast and almost furious, while the choral parts progressively, or perhaps regressively, decline both in pitch and in tonality.

Fauré's fit of the horrors is, however, brief and classically disciplined. At the verbal reference to 'eternal light' tonality sharpens and the rhythm shifts from the Dies Irae's $\frac{6}{4}$ back to the syncopated $\frac{2}{2}$ pulse. Again in D minor, the baritone soloist's haunting tune is now chanted in octave unisons by the choir, boosted by double-stopped strings that reinforce the ardent if slightly frantic beat. At the end the baritone solo takes up his tune again, perhaps to emphasize that salvation is a private matter, while the chorus whisper the words 'libera me' on unison Ds, finally resolving, by way of a dissonant seventh chord, on to a long sustained but implacably *minor* triad of D.

When this 'real' end to our human pilgrimage is followed by the coda of an 'In Paradisum' in almost-unsullied D major the effect is of palpable wish-fulfilment, albeit a wish-fulfilment we have deserved because the Agnus has shown that we still believe in life, if not in life-after-death. The tune is levelly in triple time, built on a rising D major arpeggio sung by sopranos only. The accompaniment is for strings with obbligato organ that utters dulcet arpeggios, like angelic pipers. As the tune soars it discreetly modulates, but soon returns to D major since heaven, even in dream, is atemporal. Modulation perhaps provides evidence that life and movement may continue to exist even as we die; but after plashing harp has joined the tinkling organ the fleeting shifts between tonic D major and seventh chords on the dominant of F sharp minor don't amount to authentic modulations, while the bass line is innocently pentatonic. When the words refer to the apparent resurrection of the real man Lazarus from deathly coma there is a momentary, but real, modulation to F major, key of the crucially humane Agnus Dei. The final bars, almost unmoving in harmony and unruffled in figuration, evoke eternity with a conviction that, for an agnostic, is mysterious though not incredible.

Nadia Boulanger, a fervent admirer of Fauré's Requiem, as conductor as well as teacher, maintained that 'No disquiet or agitation disturbs its profound meditation, no doubt tarnishes its unassailable faith.' That cannot be true, for Fauré himself claimed no more than that the work conveyed what he felt about death which, after life's fretful fever, would at least and at last bring peace. Many years later, not long before his own death, Fauré wrote to his wife that 'the best that man can be offered is oblivion, the Hindu Nirvana, the Roman Catholic Requiem aeternam'. It would seem that Fauré was a 'Christian agnostic' like Vaughan Williams, and possibly like Elgar, his almost exact contemporary, whose art also sprang from tension between spiritual aspiration and a materialistic, mercantile Empire. This may be why Fauré's Requiem has exerted so wide as well as so deep a spell. The music's quiet courage sheds balm even on those who, like Fauré, do not claim to know. No less than Berlioz's bold bravado, Fauré's quietude elevates the spirit as we recognize that the achievement of a harmonious equilibrium between mind and senses may be itself a kind of paradise: which, though it cannot outlast us, may make us feel *momently immortal*. As Fauré beautifully said: 'L'artiste doit aimer la vie et nous montrer qu'elle est belle. Sans lui, nous en douterions.' (The artist should love life and show us that it is beautiful. Without him, we should be in doubt.) Though modestly put, that is, on reflection, a noble claim, to which Fauré proved equal.

19

Two more Agnostic Requiems

Verdi's quasi-Roman Requiem of Life (1874) and Brahms's quasi-Lutheran Requiem of Death (1857–68)

A case might be made that Verdi was the first great musical democrat whose music dramas, created over a long life, were initially concerned with political issues. Born in 1813, he had the emotional and spiritual toughness to weather the cultural turbulence of Italy during the early nineteenth century; coming of peasant stock, he spoke soberly when, late in life, he said 'My life was hard.' While Verdi was growing to manhood, political affairs could hardly have been more exacerbated, while the musical outlook, with Rossini in early and indolent retirement, Donizetti in the madhouse, and Bellini prematurely dead of consumption, was no less distraught. As a boy, Verdi exhibited some precocity and much pertinacity in acquiring a musical education in the face of odds; when he took up a professional career, it was without extravagant ambition. He wanted to compose music for the town band and to produce operas, a people's medium, on the conventional, and therefore saleable, models. Like any craftsman, he expected to learn his trade the hard way, partly by study, more by practical experience. The familiar operatic clichés – such as those horror-struck diminished sevenths in tremolando – were survivals from eighteenth-century conventions which the nineteenth century had demeaned to their lowest common denominator. Verdi accepted them without a glimmer of shame; no more than Bellini or Donizetti did he seem to be aware that an Austrian instrumental tradition had recently come to fruition, changing the course of musical history.

Yet the provinciality of the tradition in which he worked had compensations. If he was not tempted to experiment, neither was he lured from his course by distractions that might prove extraneous. Even the incompetence of the opera-house orchestras meant that in restricting the orchestra to a few provenly effective gestures he could concentrate – as had Bellini and Donizetti – on what most interested him. And he had one quality that Bellini and Donizetti lacked: an ardent sense of a more than personal destiny. Buffo frivolity was not for him, nor was the luxury of personal lament. His opera was to be as serious as he could make it: only its seriousness was part of its popular appeal. Directly or indirectly, he made a People's Music that expressed the passion for freedom that was to unite Italy under Cavour. He chose social–political themes not, with Meyerbeer, to encourage daydreams of grandiosity, but to stimulate real people, many of them 'peasants' like himself. He probably hoped that stimulation would provoke political action; grandeur his early operas hardly aimed at, but energy and power they achieved since their primitive techniques were servants of a passionate integrity.

Nabucco made Verdi famous overnight partly because it had a political theme to which, in 1842, the audience saw a contemporary parallel, identifying themselves with the enslaved Jews labouring under oppression. Yet its success could not have been so overwhelming but for the raw force of Verdi's music – especially the choral music, that of *hoi polloi*. As he matured, Verdi, a born opera composer, relived his understanding of historical–political themes through his understanding of specific human creatures: a development that coincided with the growth of his passion for Shakespeare, and of the appearance within his operatic style of musical–dramatic techniques suggested by Beethoven. Two operas in particular mark this transitional phase: his version of Shakespeare's *Macbeth*, which plumbed psychological depths uncharted in the conventional Italianate libretto; and *Luisa Miller*, in which Verdi's political awareness and his interest in the human psyche meet in the destiny of an 'ordinary' middle-class girl sacrificed to bourgeois convention. Her story is gloomy indeed but never – like that of bourgeois opera – sentimental. Verdi's passion is not here heroic, like that of Berlioz; but it is no less powerful for being intimate, in unequivocally tragic terms as compared with the simultaneously tragi-comic realms Mozart had explored.

In his 'late' period Verdi was to fuse his early historical–political preoccupations with his intensifying awareness that social issues germinate from individual passions – as is manifest in *Simon Boccanegra*, *Un Ballo in Maschera*, and *Don Carlos*. The only dimension missing from these powerfully complex human panoramas is a sense of the numinous – of the spiritual values that lie behind organized, or merely incipient, religions. Significantly enough, at the turn between the big 'transitional' operas mentioned above and the two final Shakespearean masterpieces, *Otello* and *Falstaff* (one tragic, the other – for Verdi – uniquely comic), Verdi unwontedly turned his attention to church music, since in 1874 a grand Requiem was commissioned from him, in memory of Alessandro Manzoni, with whose social and political causes Verdi in part identified.

Although Verdi's Requiem can hardly be said to be preoccupied with the numinous, it is about death as the cessation of life, the vicissitudes of which Verdi had explored through the long cycle of his operas. As one might expect, he concentrates on his text's most overtly, even crudely, dramatic aspects, as manifest in Thomas of Celano's medieval Latin poem of the Dies Irae. This offers a theatrically dramatic survey of the terrors of mortality – as we noted in reference to the Requiems of Berlioz and Fauré – and lends itself readily to division into sections: 'numbers' in the form of arias and ensembles with or without chorus. Verdi can thus unabashedly create operatic scenes displaying his habitual immediacy; and only after this large-scale span of theatrical music does he admit, in the Offertory, Sanctus, and Agnus Dei, the spiritual dimensions of the Eucharist. Even then, the traditional disposition of the Requiem service appends an additional section (the 'Libera me'), which allows him to end with a modest victory for human courage, rather than in metaphysical grace.

The introductory Requiem and Kyrie establish a mood and hint at a theme: for it is a dualistic structure alternating between dour A minor and radiant A major. The theme introduced by the orchestral basses consists of a falling minor triad followed by a declension down the scale. The chorus sing-speak the words *sotto voce*, first on a bare fifth A to E, then on a dominant triad in four parts. The hushed urgency of the appeal for peace is contained in sighing, syncopated descents by four sopranos only: until at the words 'et lux perpetua' the key shifts to 'youthful' A major as the orchestra sings a lyrical pentatonic phrase 'dolcissimo', while the choir transforms its declamation into song.

The 'Te decet hymnus' shifts the tonality to the lower flat mediant F major – a relationship to which, we've noted, both Beethoven and Bruckner were partial. It also speeds up the tempo, the melodies being in canon at the fourth or fifth. The rising scales stretch out longer, like pleading arms, as our appeals grow more urgent; and the pattern of minor–major duality is repeated. The Kyrie that traditionally rounds off the Introit is entrusted to the soloists, who enter sequentially in A major, as though in an operatic aria. The soprano mounts to a high B; the orchestra diminishes its quavers to semiquavers; and as the music soars to the upper mediant C sharp major, the chorus joins with the soloists in rhetorically leaping sixths and octaves. When Christ is petitioned in the words 'Christe eleison' the key changes back to A minor and the movement closes in an extended Neapolitan cadence through triads of F major and E flat major to the dominant and tonic of A. This Introit is recognizable as liturgical ritual while being also a dramatic event.

It prepares the way for the overtly operatic Dies Irae, which opens with no holds barred, in 'tragic' G minor, with thumping orchestral chords and screaming ascending and descending scales representing the yells of the damned, meaning us:

The chorus, entering fortissimo on high G, wail in descending chromatics against a sustained tonic. This savage devastation prompts a motif rather than a tune, rotating chromatically between A flat and F; gradually, the lines subside in nervy tremolandi, the solo voices declaiming in terror-struck repeated notes. The chorus, returning, literally stutter – breath stifled by rests – through the words 'Quantus tremor est futurus', until a blazon of brass announces the 'Tuba mirum'. This is music-theatre exceeded in potency only by Berlioz's 'Tuba mirum' in his *Grande Messe des Morts*. The choric voices bellow on single notes or rock on triadic fanfares, while the orchestra's brassy paeans splinter into chromatically whirling scales. The Judge inspires Dread, rather than offering absolution; 'everyone' (including us) is swept into panic such as may overwhelm Verdi's operatic characters in dire extremity. Verdi presents this DIES IRAE as our inescapable human lot, writ very large; and the direst of dire moments occurs in the 'Liber scriptus', when the mezzo soloist defines, in repeated As and Es, God's irremediable Law, while the orchestra trembles in chromaticized triplets. The section is rounded off with a *da capo* of the undulating choral motif, gradually drooping on to a dominant seventh of G minor.

But the next section, 'Quid sum miser', for soprano, mezzo, and tenor soloists, offers palliative release from terror in compassion, as the three human beings together ask who might help them. The interweaving of the solo voices in a slow-swaying $\frac{6}{8}$ pulse is physically agonized in a manner familiar from Verdi's operatic ensembles; but the Rex Tremendae himself, invoked in an indeed tremendous phrase sung by choral basses in unison, seems oblivious to our appeals, complacently 'heroic' in his double-dotted metres. The cry of 'salve me' is banded between the soloists, with choric comments, covering the whole 'gamut' of Verdian emotion from awe to desperation, with aggressively leaping sixths and volatile modulations, now violent, now dulcet. After the soprano soloist has climbed to a lacerating high C the rising-sixth-pervaded tune finds resolution in white C major, soloists and chorus interlacing in eight canonic parts. Eventually, however, reiterated Cs prove to be dominants of F major: in which pastoral key the soprano and mezzo soloists remember, in the 'Recordare', that Jesus Christ – a *man*, as distinct from that Rex Tremendae – may hopefully succour us. The tune sways between tonic and major third over an orchestral ostinato of rising fifths whilst high up, on woodwind, the Rex Tremendae reminds us that the Judge misses nothing, having open ears. The music grows more animated and chromaticized before admitting that the Father and the Son are one, as the two solo voices chime in thirds and sixths.

An aria for tenor solo, a tone lower in E flat major, seeks the intermediacy of the Virgin Mother in a swinging pop-style tune, 'dolce con calma' in a marching pulse decorated with triplets. The tenor soloist appeals – as might you or I or anyone – that *he* should be saved from the universal conflagration, becoming vainglorious in his desperate asseveration. The bass's much longer aria, a semitone higher in E major, tends even more crudely to vainglory, only because he has a bigger voice with which to insist on his claims for exemption from the fire; he even mentions his palpable superiority to the 'cursed rabble'. Still, he humbles himself sufficiently to *pray* for salvation; though God isn't deceived, or at least doesn't weaken. For he gruffly dismisses the bass's plea for 'comfort' at the last hour by returning to the full fury of His Day of Wrath! The original G minor Dies Irae music sounds, in context, even more ferocious; but the tears of the Lacrymosa – which will contribute something to Britten's comparable movement in his *War Requiem* – has a grandeur that keeps us afloat and aloft. The tune, sung by the mezzo, is symmetrical in a funeral march beat, enclosed within a rising and falling fourth. When she is joined by the other soloists she soars to the heights, echoed still higher by the soprano who sighs in syncopated, *upward*-thrusting appoggiaturas, doubled by violins. The luxuriance of the polyphony makes the quietude that the interlacing melodies win through to seem miraculous. The telescoped triads of B flat major and G major effect a new mutation of a device common in sixteenth-century modal polyphony; the breathless hush reminds us how Verdi has, throughout this movement, learned much from Beethoven's masterly use of silence.

The Dies Irae has been a self-contained sequence of numbers that *enact* human life and death in the raw. It speaks, sings, and yells in the voice of us the People, all variously alive yet all commonly aware of the fact of death. The rude, crude, irresistible tunes – consider that swinging 'Lacrymosa' – have the flamboyance of middle-period Verdi, and their tub-thumping eloquence asserts human resilience and the will to endure. When the Requiem service returns from this overt theatre to dramatized ritual, as happens in the Offertory, the rhetoric is scarcely abated, though the 'Domine Jesu' is scored for the four soloists rather than for the chorus as *hoi polloi*. The key is initially A flat major, and the memorable tune, rotating in stepwise movement around a fifth, sticks in the mind no less limpet-like than one of Verdi's operatic 'hits'. He relishes its catchiness by eschewing modulation for some time; mezzo, tenor, and bass twine around one another in the hope of Christ's, if not of God the Father's, help until – now with a startling modulation to A major and thence to remote G flat – the soprano solo enters with a long-sustained E natural, over which soars a solo violin. With the other soloists' help she steers the music back to A flat major, and thence into choral fugato in a fast duple beat and in strict canon, to demonstrate the irrefutability of Abraham's Old Testament Law. Despite the metrical rigidity, the lines turn chromatic, revealing Verdi's – rather than the People's – horror of the Law's moribundity: which can be healed only by a resurgence of the private passions of particular human creatures. Tenor solo transforms the 'Hostias et preces' into a lyrical aria of praise, with commentary from the other soloists, so that an aria becomes a quartet: leading into a *da capo* of the stretto chorus about Abraham's Law, with the chromatics now disturbing the harmony as well as the tune. Back in A flat major, the original 'hit-tune' returns, sung by all the soloists firmly, but softly and sweetly, fading through string tremolandi.

The Sanctus in masses usually celebrates the Holiest of Holies. Verdi scores his grandly for double chorus, but as ceremonial public music hymning mundane rather than celestial glory. The key is pastoral F major, the pulse an unremitting $\frac{2}{2}$, the texture that of a double fugue with the first subject built on a rising arpeggio and the second theme combining a rising scale with a falling tritone. The rhythmic drive is formidable, the contrapuntal skill impressive, the energy of the rhythms almost Handelian; modulations are boldly self-assured though they culminate in fearful B flat minor. Unexpectedly, the 'Pleni' and the 'Hosanna' begin dolcissimo, back in F major and in conventionally 'ecclesiastical' minims, though the moto perpetuo of dancing quavers never lets up. Finally, both choruses merge in massive homophony in 'white' minims, while the orchestra splinters into chromatics, with trombones jubilant, though in no way celestial.

The Agnus Dei offers a kind of peace, but no holy illumination. It consists simply of a tune repeated six times, first sung unharmonized by soprano and mezzo soli, then by the chorus in octave unisons; the effect depends on the plainness of the unaccompanied tune; after all Verdi's histrionics and his contrapuntal ingenuity, the voice of the Lamb of God proves to be a diatonic tune in C major, moving by step until the falling fifth at the first clause's end. The second half of the tune answers the first half with six instead of seven bars; the chorus repeat the whole tune still in octave unisons, unharmonized. Although the stepwise melody does not remind us of holy plainchant, it is indubitably plain, like a pop rather than a folk song, and is in tone more urban than agrarian. Perhaps this is the best Plain People can do, and Verdi is honouring their plainness; but with the third repeat, again scored for soprano and mezzo soloists, the key changes to a more charged C minor, and the orchestra softly doubles the tune in thirds and sixths, with an obbligato of repeated notes on woodwind. There is still no hint of evolution, let alone development, and dynamics remain dolcissimo. The fourth repeat, back in C major but now with orchestral doublings, is again melodically unchanged, but leads into a fifth repeat in which the tune wears a halo of flowing quavers on woodwind. The sixth and final repeat is scored for the soloists with the four-part chorus, bolstered by strings. In a brief coda the basses fall through a C major arpeggio to land on A flat – possibly a recollection of the opening of the Offertory. The orchestra counters the basses' declension with upward-floating C major arpeggios on strings and angelic flutes; but these angels are the plain hearts of plain folk, not celestial visitants.

Although this Agnus Dei is the most touching admission of Verdi's agnosticism in the Requiem, it's followed by a 'lux eterna' for solo mezzo, tenor, and bass that is the closest the work gets to the metaphysical. Even so, the key is 'earthy' B flat major, with hushed string tremolandi through which the mezzo declaims the holy words, floating through enharmonic modulations:

When the bass solo takes over, the key is dark B flat minor and the rhythm is in the dotted pulse of a funeral march, though Light shines when the three soloists chromatically wind back to B flat major. The orchestra finally dissolves in floating arpeggios, 'dolcissimo con calma'.

If this trio hints at beatitude, it is in no beatific state that the work ends. For (as already noted) the Requiem service adds an extra movement to the Ordinary of the Mass: the 'Libera me', which offers us trembling mortals another (last?) chance to appeal for a grudging God's mercy. The chorus begins by muttering the words to an heroically human E flat major triad – which is perhaps a phrygian flat second to D minor. At 'tremens factus' the soloists take up the prayer, mingling repeated notes with piteously wailing chromatics. But after paradoxically – or might it be hopefully? – modulating to C major on the word 'timeo', there's a *lunga pausa*: out of which thunders a literal repeat of the chromaticized G minor opening to the Dies Irae itself. This further Dusty Answer from the Almighty stimulates the chorus, as Us the People, to action, in lines mingling chromatic deliquescence with sturdy repeated notes that hang on, as it were for grim life. Gradually, the murmured words 'Dies irae' fade in chromatic undulations between triads of G flat and F major; the succeeding homophonic chorus in B flat minor heart-easingly recalls the crucial 'Lacrymosa', before ending with its drooping triad inverted into a rising perfect fifth, and then into an upward leaping octave to a high B flat for the soprano soloist – optimistically marked *ppp*!

A Verdi Requiem cannot, however, conclude with so palpable a wish-fulfilment; and the last substantial movement in the work reminds us of Verdi's confession that 'My life was hard.' To counterpoise the grand

Handelian fugue in the Sanctus, Verdi offers us a massive fugue in $\frac{2}{2}$ time, with a comparably dotted rhythm and grandiloquently arpeggiated subject. Beginning in C minor, the music modulates widely and wildly, with a telling excursion into infernal F minor, followed by outlandish enharmonic transitions that threaten to open the ground beneath our feet, ending in remote B major. This reignites the fires of hell, though the high soprano, aloft, steers us through the hazardous enharmonies, and eventually persuades the fires to simmer down, thereby to some extent (we hope) damping the efficacy of divine judgment. With a shift into massive homophony in C minor veering to F minor, the chorus tries to chivvy God into liberating us miserable offenders, while the soprano solo climbs to a piercing, but also thrilling, high C. Even so, that climax knocks the stuffing out of us, as the texture thins through truncated inversions of the thematic rising arpeggio; orchestral entries in canon also dissipate, while the chorus whispers the words 'libera me' on low Cs. True, we are offered the palliative of a C major tierce de Picardie, on which the music dissipates over remotely funereal drums. This 'resolution', if that's what it is, can only be the indubitable peace of oblivion; and in this the virile and sometimes virulent Verdi is one with the sensuously civilized Fauré.

Verdi's Requiem deals with living and dying with the same immediacy and splendour as does *Aida*. The passion of its soaring tunes, of its violent harmonies and tonalities, and of its glowing, sometimes garish, orchestration is so extravagant as to seem sublime, though the music has none of the visionary singularity of Berlioz's Requiem, which Verdi knew and admired. The sobs of Verdi's Lacrymosa are grander, but identical in technique and spirit, with those of Violetta in *Traviata*, for this requiem is of the earth, earthy. Perhaps it is also of the sun, sunny, for the fury of its Dies Irae terrifies us because it tells us that, when the grave shuts out the sun, we become Shakespeare's 'kneaded clod'. This stark opposition between being alive and being dead is the heart of Verdi's Requiem, as it is of his Shakespearean opera *Otello*, which, a dozen years later, proved to be Verdi's ultimate masterpiece, on the ultimately tragic theme of proud Man, whose destiny is to destroy what he most loves. In face of that tragedy, there may be nothing we can hope for except the neutrality of oblivion. So Verdi is a composer greatly human and humane, though not 'religious', though he lived in, and served, a Roman Catholic community.

Verdi was an Italian maker of operas; Brahms was a German maker of songs, piano music, chamber music, and symphonies in German–Austrian tradition, based on reverence for his predecessors, especially Beethoven. Yet although we tend to think of Brahms as a bearded sobersides, he was in youth wedded to romanticism, an avant-garde movement. Schumann, whose disciple Brahms was proud to be, called Brahms the Young Eagle, and it was hardly surprising that Clara Schumann fell, albeit discreetly, for the eagle's exceptional physical beauty and probably loved him for years, while his (unmarried) charm was gradually sullied by self-assertive grumpiness.

Musically, Brahms's adolescent enthusiasm for the presumed spontaneity of folk song and gypsy music didn't desert him. Never mind that, according to the ethnic purism of a Kodály or a Bartók, Brahms couldn't recognize a folk song when he heard it. The spirit mattered more than the letter, as it had done when Ossian's forgeries swept Europe, carrying the distracted Brahms with them. Brahms's trigger to creation was a duality between such romantic spontaneity and a rage for order. In this he was a more self-conscious successor to his god Beethoven, who came near to breakdown round the time of the Moonlight Sonata and devoted the rest of his life to reconstruction. Beethoven's pilgrimage was an ultimately triumphant search for a faith, or a substitute for it. Brahms made do without a faith; if this makes him a lesser figure than Beethoven, it also explains his popularity throughout the late nineteenth century and his durability today. In an age of unfaith, he spoke for mankind's fortitude, often enlightened by sensibility and joy. His greatest work is probably his fourth and last symphony: a post-Beethovenian symphony brave enough to admit that for modern man no transcendental resolution was possible. For the last movement he calls on the old-fashioned baroque form of passacaglia, which in its heyday imposed the unity of unalterable law (the repeated ground bass) on transience and change. Yet not only does Brahms's Fourth Symphony embrace his most austere use of an inherited classical form, it is also the most modern, because the most deeply 'motivic', of his large-scale works. Indeed, the contrapuntal intricacy of its textures effects a bridge between traditional symphonic thinking and the inner necessities of thematic serialism, whether it be chromatic or not. This is why Schoenberg, in a remarkable essay, hailed 'Brahms the Progressive'.

Despite his agnosticism, Brahms was reared in and respected Lutheran traditions; which entailed reverence for the German master J.S. Bach, whose classical baroque techniques proffered not only a craft but also a haven in a sea of chaos. This became evident quite early in his career when, in 1866, at the age of thirty-three, he composed his German Requiem, which immediately made him a celebrity in his native land, and before long throughout Europe. The work is not a liturgical requiem but a choral and orchestral work suitable for performance in concert halls, if perhaps happier in churches; its biblical text was sensitively assembled by Brahms, mostly from Ecclesiastes and the Psalms. The words proffer comfort to the bereaved rather than metaphysical sanction for the dead; but although the work is not Christian in its theology, its message may be Christian in implication since the key-words of 'comfort' and 'patience' preserve spiritual values through, and even because of, the work's unflinching confrontation of death. Indeed, composing the piece may have been Brahms's way of bolstering himself against the lunacy and subsequent death of his friend Schumann and the death of his beloved mother. This personal intimacy no doubt encouraged him to use the vernacular German, rather than Latin, text, and to score the work in rigorous polyphony and stable homophony for mixed chorus and orchestra, paying tribute to Lutheran Bach and his predecessor Heinrich Schütz (who had set the German 'Selig sind die Toten' in his *Musicalische Exequien* of 1636). At the same time, in using a soprano and baritone soloist in an idiom not remote from the personalized style of Brahms's lieder, the work abandons Lutheran public tradition to become part of Brahms's personal life, paying reverence more to his mother and his grievously distressed friend than to an abstract, or even to a personally romanticized, God. It was probably this fusion of an inherited creed with private sorrows that led to the work's remarkable success with a middle-class German public. Brahms told his friend Siegfried Ochs that the whole piece was fired by the chorale 'Wer nur den lieben Gott lässt walten'; and the German public enjoyed this sense of 'belonging' as they detected, in the opening theme and in the second movement's triple-rhythmed funeral march, a rising and falling curve similar to that of the hymn. An arch-shape conditions the whole work, while the careful ordering of key sequences offers musical support to the notions of 'comfort' and 'patience' as a refuge from pessimism. Although Brahms was temperamentally remote from Frederick Delius, both men's requiems hymn what Delius called 'human courage and self-reliance' – which may, *in extremis*, amount to spiritual values.

The basic key of the work is F major – traditionally the pastoral key, and therefore earth-rooted. The first chorus has words from Beatitudes ('Blessed are they that mourn'); and the bright violins, along with clarinets and trumpets, are here silent. The pervasive sonority – mourning, though not mournful – is of violas, while the level pulse of moderate-paced crotchets over low pedal notes on F provide the frame in which the stepwise rise and fall of the chorale-derived tune enters in canon at the fourth or fifth. A chromatic inner voice on cellos reminds us of mortality just before the chorus sings, in plain diatonic concords, the words 'Blest are they', at first unaccompanied, reminding us that the courage that makes for salvation is *our* responsibility. The words 'who goeth forth in weeping' are set to the chorale-related first theme, with the weeping stressed in a diminished fourth. What follows hints at a sonata development but in fact returns to the original theme and the bass pedal notes, at first in D flat major, then shifting to F major for the spiritual source of 'comfort'. Two arpeggiated harps look prophetically towards the comfort in which the whole work will end.

By the close of this first movement we recognize that, whereas Verdi's agnostic requiem is as vividly theatrical as are his operatic imitations of human action, Brahms's agnostic requiem remains soberly within Lutheran tradition. The disparity is confirmed in the second movement, which is a triple-rhythmed funeral march in the minor of the subdominant, B flat. Just as the first movement pivots on the relationship between F major and D flat

165

major, so the funeral march veers between B flat minor and *its* lower mediant, G flat major. The full orchestra is now involved, though the elegiac violas still 'lead' in that the theme is entrusted to them, doubled by muted violins. The bass line, rocking between fourths and fifths, has the 'feel' of a passacaglia, though the ground bass is not here a strict ostinato. The words, reminding us that 'all flesh is as grass' are chanted by the lower voices in octave unisons, the theme undulating up and down the scale, with the second degree sharp in the ascent, flat in the descent. The vocal theme is incantatory, while the orchestra pleads in rising arpeggios. The clause ends in the dominant but shifts to the subdominant, E flat major: until a faster middle section, in the euphonious upper mediant G flat major, introduces the theme of Patience, awaiting the advent of Christ returned. The theme is at first homophonically harmonized but, with the falling third stretched to a fourth, grows contrapuntal at the reference to the waiting husbandman, with canons between sopranos and basses and between altos and tenors, flowering in enharmonic modulations for the ripening of the earth's 'precious fruit'.

Several times the triple-lilting funeral march returns in rondo style, getting gradually louder and more inexorable, since the withering of the grass and of the flesh cannot be gainsaid. The reiterations, though formidable, are not scary since they are testimony to human courage, the more so because they are in octave unisons, never in block harmony. Brahms's scoring, featuring plangent violas with a pallid piccolo that has lost all trace of pristine perkiness, underlines the elegiac mood.

With the prophecy that 'the ransomed of the Lord shall return', B flat major is re-established and rhythms become sturdily metrical, though orchestral syncopations and enharmonic modulations respectively promote the 'gladness' and 'wonder' associated with Christ's coming. The final section is a vigorous fugue on an arpeggiated theme in dotted rhythm; contrapuntal complexities simmer down over tonic-dominant pedal-notes until only fragments of the fugal theme flicker among rising and falling scales of B flat major, recalling, albeit faintly, those at the end of the Credo of Beethoven's *Missa Solemnis*.

The third movement, back in F major, introduces the baritone soloist who declaims in noble phrases, asking God what the measure of his days may be. But the distance between man and God is suggested through enharmonic modulations, and the basic key shifts from F major to relative D minor which, as already noted, had become associated with the obscurity of our earthly pilgrimage. The theme surges in tempestuous waves on the orchestra, accompanying first the soloist, then the chorus. Turbulence finds a haven when the words admit that 'my hope is in Thee' – in D *major*, in a series of stretti soaring up in triplets to a high A, and merging into a fugue in $\frac{4}{2}$ on a sweeping theme over an unbroken tonic pedal. The unremitting pedal is a Rock from which we may hopefully levitate, while the basses hammer out their presumptive conviction that redeemed souls are in God's hands. This section is potently Brahmsian, for the whirling of the melodic lines in wide-stretched arpeggios testifies to the turbulence of his gipsyish youth, while the unbroken pedal notes grittily, and a shade desperately, affirm his 'rage for order'. The tense balance between linear freedom and harmonic density intoxicates, as sopranos and tenors whirl in ornate melismata that threaten, but cannot destroy, the pedal note.

The next movement (from Psalm 84, 'How lovely are Thy dwellings') is in E flat major – in dramatically Neapolitan relationship to the D minor of the previous chorus. The orchestral prelude begins with a falling arpeggio which, inverted, becomes the main vocal theme, unambiguously diatonic after the chromatics of the previous fugue. After its initial paragraph, the movement vacillates in tonality, as though the loveliness of the heavenly dwellings were something that humankind might *dream up*, if of good heart – the dreaminess being manifest in the volatile modulations, usually flatwards. The vocal textures are now in fugato; stretto entries carry the sopranos to a high A, with breathless syncopations; and so to a *da capo* of the E flat major melody. The concluding song of praise is less wavery in tonality and is freely canonic. Although the sequences yearn for the 'loveliness' of heaven, the human security of E flat major is affirmed.

Benediction is attained in the beautiful soprano solo in G major, traditionally a key of blessing, and again in (upwards) mediant relationship to the previous movement's E flat. Gentle quavers on strings float over a stepwise moving bass in crotchets in $\frac{4}{4}$; above, the soprano solo floats with a lyricism that seems validated by the occasionally bitter-sweet chromatics. The chorus softly succour the soloist who, in a middle section, drifts through many keys, as far as remote B major, before rediscovering G major (this time the *lower* mediant). Passing references to E flat major recall the previous movement, but the final resolution is a plagal Amen in G major. Sorrow and comfort have become one.

The dream-like quality, and perhaps therefore the irreality, of this moment is affirmed in the next chorus that hints (in words from Hebrews 13) that in this world we have no abiding home. The pulse is still in common time, but at a moderate rather than slow tempo. Pizzicato strings trudge in crotchets, initially in C minor, but gloomily drooping to very dark F minor as we seek a home that might be eternal. Confusion is worse confounded when the baritone solo lures us into F sharp minor – with a Neapolitan progression to suggest how all will be 'changed' at the Last Trump. But the Day of Wrath is not theatrically expatiated on, as it is by Verdi, though it *is* dramatic; and finds itself in the previous movement's heroic E flat major when the baritone solo asks Death what has happened to his victory. The chorus supports the soloist, abetted by a 'revolving cam' and syncopated cross-rhythms in the orchestra, hoping and perhaps believing that the human will is unconquerable. Metaphysics don't come into this exuberance, which turns into a sturdy four-part fugue in C major, ballasted by an orchestral ostinato of thrusting crotchets. The complexity of the counter-point, riddled with augmentations, diminutions, inversions, and stretti, somewhat desperately hopes that man might be a match for the Almighty: as perhaps he is in that Brahms's courage doesn't falter through the restless modulations, or even through the lulling orchestral figure that seems momently to hint at a divine amnesia! If God takes an occasional nap, man, in the shape of Brahms, doesn't: for the movement climaxes and ends in a breath-taking fugal stretto, so triumphantly jubilant that we may be tempted to call it godly, if indubitably man-made. In this sense it may be valid to say that an agnostic composer can create religious music.

If this seems too much to be credited the epilogic chorus is a more validly modest apotheosis, with words from Revelation ('Blessed are the dead'). Brahms returns to the key, F major, and to some of the thematic substance, of the opening movement. Orchestral quavers slide in pairs across the beat, while sopranos launch the spacious theme. The 'spirit', credibly promising us rest from pain and labour, encourages the chorus to wing through melodies in youthfully renewing A major, and to aspire to celestial E major, with Brahms as agent and angel, and then to B major a further step up the cycle of fifths, albeit partnered by its relative, G sharp minor, as a dark shadow. But the chorus wind back to A major by way of a brief *unaccompanied* passage (as though testing the truth of the dream?): whence they droop once more to the lower flat submediant – which of course is the initially pastoral F major. In this key the orchestra's procession of sighing quavers recalls, a tone lower, the soprano's magical aria of benediction; and the Requiem ends with quotations from the first movement's 'Selig sind', with harps that shed on weary souls a bliss that is a haven, if not a heaven, that Brahms's courage has created. Brahms's requiescat, though it is only a cessation, may count as a bliss well earned, as is the oblivion at the close of the Requiems of Berlioz and of Fauré. There is also a precedent for a later, more uncompromisingly agnostic requiem, that of Delius: though Brahms, from the fortress of Lutheran tradition, displays regret over, rather than pride in, his lack of faith.

In this country Brahms's Requiem is often sung in the English of the Authorized Version: which I have used in the musical quotations since the words matter as a devotional act, however much or little doctrinal belief they entail. Even so, the German vernacular of the Lutheran Bible accords better with Brahms's sinuous or sinewy melodic lines, and so better reveals the composer's equilibrium between the public and the private dimensions of his art. This may explain why Brahms's Requiem preserves a numinous aura that Verdi's Requiem lacks; and in this context it is pertinent to add a note on one of Brahms's last works, the *Four Serious Songs* written in 1896, thirty years after the Requiem, to words from Ecclesiastes that reflect the essence of his death-sense. The style is a compromise between that of a Bach cantata and of the Brahmsian lied; and the third song is a closely wrought structure based on the same descending third motif that pervades the passacaglia of the Fourth Symphony, in the same key of E minor – incidentally Bach's Crucifixion key.

Brahms's obsession with falling thirds, especially in his late work, is unmistakably associated with his potent but never febrile awareness of death: from which point of view we may contrast him with Bruckner. For Bruckner, death is a liberation that generates long soaring melodies with intermittently ecstatic leaps. For Brahms, the falling thirds root the music harmonically to the earth, as dust returns to dust. In the magical *Intermezzo* in B minor, from the opus 119 set of piano pieces, drooping thirds interlace in suspended triads, creating an illusion of polytonality; if in the E minor symphony's passacaglia and in the third of the *Four Serious Songs* the drooping thirds return the body to the earth, in the *Intermezzo* it is as though human dust were dissolving into air, and sun, and rain.

But in the fourth and last member of the song cycle the text refers to the 'faith, hope, and love' which are what remains when Death has done his worst. These were precisely the values that Brahms celebrated in his Requiem, thirty years earlier. In the late song the baritone line swells in this stupendous phrase:

It's as though human love has itself become winged and angelic; and so although Brahms never learned to transcend death, as did Beethoven; or to accept it, as did Mozart and perhaps Schubert; or not to brood over it, as did Haydn; we may say that he arrived at a point not so far distant from Haydn, but with this difference: for Haydn, human love might regenerate an Enlightened but Fallen world; for Brahms, it was a dying man's solace for the follies of the past.

Yet this is not quite all. If we look again at that winged and angelic phrase we may note that its huge leaps suggest the bitter-sweet anguish of Mahler and early Schoenberg, as does the main theme of Bruckner's Ninth. So, after all, Brahms comes to terms with Bruckner, often considered his rival and polar opposite. It would seem that, if love is the seed of creation, it doesn't greatly matter whether we think of it as human or as divine.

Part IV:
From the 'Death of God' to
the 'Unanswered Question'

20

The Victorian Crisis of Faith

The Roman Church, Science, Cardinal Newman, and Elgar's *Dream of Gerontius* (1900): Delius's pagan *Mass of Life* (1904–5) and his pagan *Requiem* (1914–16)

When Handel, early in the eighteenth century, settled in Britain in an attempt to sell Italianate *opera seria* to the mercantile British, he was a composer of operatically dramatic conflict who remained unrivalled except by Mozart, being superb in pride but always humane and never complacent. The sturdy British were tickled by his star singers for a while, but didn't remain faithful to the 'exotick and irrational' entertainment of opera, though they responded enthusiastically to Handel's invention of English oratorio, which was in effect *opera seria* on Old Testament subjects. Even so, over the years Handelian oratorio was deprived of its dramatic intimacy as the pieces were performed with giganticized forces, in theatres and in public assembly rooms: for as the Victorian age unfolded, Handel's oratorios were increasingly construed as hymns to Industry and Empire. High Victorian composers themselves – still under the influence of foreigners, such as the adolescently brilliant Mendelssohn, and Spohr who lacked Handel's energy and humanity – tended to be hollow at the core. Only the oratorios of Sir Hubert Parry – an Etonian English Gentleman of considerable cultivation and an agnostic with Christian aspirations anticipatory of Vaughan Williams – hinted that music might restore spiritual values to a fallen world. It is, however, significant that Parry's last major work, composed during the War-to-end-all-wars, was entitled *Songs of Farewell* and is, though indubitably choral, English and noble, explicitly valedictory.

A good if by no means goody-goody Victorian, Parry lacked what

T.S. Eliot called Blake's 'terrifying honesty': as is patent in his setting of lines from Blake's *Jerusalem* which, in defiance of the poet's intentions, he turned into a patriotic hymn rather than a summons to spiritual renewal. Keeping a stiff upper lip, Parry nurtured the Imperial Dream, making music collateral with Arne's 'Rule Britannia'; only whereas Arne's perky tune had in 1740 asserted the mindless optimism of the Common Man in his martially and materially prosperous nation, optimism had, by Parry's time, turned sour. Parry was a composer of genuine talent; but to make energy spiritually re-creative, genius, rather than talent, was called for. Such genius appeared, after our long musical desuetude, in the work of Sir Edward Elgar, to whom we instinctively accord the accolade of his title, as we do to Parry. For Elgar accepted, indeed revelled in, the Pomp and Circumstance of the world celebrated in his marches, one of which, with Benson's words attached, became as 'Land of Hope and Glory' a national institution no less potent than 'Rule Britannia' or 'Jerusalem' – with still greater justification, since it is a magnificent, ripely harmonized tune that can still send shivers down reluctant and even resentful spines. In this jingoistic vein Elgar had a literary peer in the young Kipling; and the electrical energy of both author and composer is disturbing enough to indicate that their face-value wasn't the whole truth about them. It is not fortuitous that Kipling's supreme achievement, *Kim*, written at the beginning of the new century in 1901, should be simultaneously about the Imperial Dream and the adolescent innocence necessary to sustain it, nor that Kipling's late tales should be deeply perturbed and perturbing, at times even morbidly sado-masochistic. *Kim* would have been inconceivable after the 1919 Amritsar Massacre.

The parallel with Elgar is exact, down to the brilliant technical expertise the composer attained by hard experience, in provincial Worcestershire, with little formal training. Profoundly English though he was, Elgar's technique was basically German, as was that of all British composers of his day – a fact not without socio-political implications. By means of it Elgar was able, in an England whose musical traditions were moribund, to rival the composer–industrialist Richard Strauss in virtuosity, and to assume the existence of a symphonic tradition that in Britain had never happened. Even so, Elgar's virtuosity is not what makes him a great composer, for his mature work turns out to be a *threnody* on Edwardian opulence and material might. The top-hatted, morning-coated Sir Edward, chatting and 'sharing a joke with' the rich and titled at the races, is a mask for the man of deep spiritual intuition who conceived his sweeping themes while striding over the Malvern Hills, often embracing within his Teutonic idiom the inflections of English folk song – explicitly in his *Introduction and Allegro* for strings, implicitly in many of his most characteristic themes. This is evident in his first fully representative work, the *Enigma Variations*, written in the last year of the nineteenth century when he, understandably a slow starter, had already turned forty. Significantly, the *Enigma Variations*, although a large-scale orchestral piece ending in a blaze of public rhetoric, is at heart local and intimate, since it celebrates neither Church nor State but his dearly loved friends, enigmatically personified in the sequence of variations; for good measure he includes, among those dearest friends, a portrait of himself.

Immediately after the *Enigma Variations* Elgar produced, in the first year of the twentieth century, the first religious work of his maturity, *The Dream of Gerontius*. Sir Adrian Boult, who knew more about Elgar than most people, having conducted his major works, maintained that the high point of his religious music was the oratorio *The Kingdom*. But this piece never caught the public imagination, probably because it did not centre on a suffering seeker after faith. In this respect Cardinal Newman's poem offered Elgar what he needed, since it was not a rehash of biblical precedents but the personal testament of a man in some ways similar to Elgar, but differing in that Newman was a trained theologian who, as poet, was a non-starter. He could therefore provide the theological substructure that Elgar needed but was indifferent to, while leaving the imaginative flesh and blood to the music. This Elgar provided, for his Gerontius, albeit old as his name implies, is no spiritual aesthete but, in Elgar's words, 'a man like us, not a priest or a saint, but a sinner . . . no end of a worldly man in his life, but now brought to book. Therefore I've not filled his part with church tunes and rubbish but a good, healthy, full-blooded, romantic remembered worldliness.' Elgar liked the part to be sung by a 'big' Italianate tenor and justifiably hazarded that Verdi himself wouldn't have been ashamed of Gerontius's 'Sanctus fortis' aria.

At the end of the score Elgar transcribed some words from Ruskin: 'This is the best of me: for the rest, I ate and drank and slept, like any other; my life was as the vapour, and is not. But this I saw and knew; this, if anything of mine, is worth your memory.' If we think of *The Dream* in the sequence of Elgar's religious pieces it is indeed defined by its personal intensity. This is why its debt to English oratorio from heroic Handel to aspirational Parry could be modified by its debt to late Wagner. *Tristan* and *Parsifal* were the apex to Europe's deification of will and ego. The elemental realities of sex and death, love and war, here attained so orgiastic a climax that the surge of harmonic passion and the luxuriance of orchestral sonority – itself a product of nineteenth-century industrial technology – must needs be released into extreme chromaticism, enharmony, polymodality, and even atonality. Elgar, having absorbed late Wagner, could supersede Parry's diatonicism in lines no less majestic yet in perpetual volatility, modulating in sequential paragraphs that outstrip Parry in exultation.

Accepting *The Dream* as a successor to *Tristan* and *Parsifal*, we may ask how far Elgar 'believed' in Newman's theology, which had more backing from a religious tradition than had Wagner's emotive metaphysics. We cannot doubt the sincerity of Elgar's Catholicism; but neither can we ignore the conflict and doubt inherent in his music's chromaticism and enharmony, and even in its structural complexities. In this respect we may contrast Elgar with Bruckner, the only great nineteenth-century composer to be inspired by a traditionally Roman Catholic faith: yet also a composer who embodied this faith in symphonies employing sonata forms that are by nature concerned with conflict and contradiction; even his vocal liturgical music allows for chromatic and enharmonic insecurities that, in subverting traditional modality and tonality, undermine faith's certitudes. Only they seem not to do so; though he was far from being a medieval peasant, Bruckner's music attains a simple sublimity that has excusably if misleadingly been related to some such person.

Not remotely could such a collocation be entertained in reference to Elgar, a complex, sophisticated Edwardian responsive to the religious, scientific, and political cross-currents of his age. Yet Elgar, whatever his doubts, had *no* doubt that *Gerontius* was a religious experience. Newman's poem boldly if foolhardily confronted whatever may be 'beyond' our diurnal activities: for Part I presents the Old Man on his death-bed, in failing communication with his earthly friends; while Part II describes his passage 'through the veil' momentarily to glimpse his God, enthroned in judgment. The self-lacerating torments he suffers in this rite of passage seem to some of us poetically extravagant, grotesque, even repulsive. The mystically reverential Bach, the heroically human Handel, the subjectively re-born Beethoven, even the sensuously seismographic Mozart and Schubert, suffered no such traumas in embracing the inevitable fact of death. Only after Nietzsche's proclamation of the Death of God and Wagner's deification of the human ego did the mere certainty of our mortality seem, no less than Yeats's 'the fury and the mire of human veins', too much to be borne. Yet if Newman threatens hysteria and doesn't count as a poet, Elgar profited from the fact that music cannot, of its nature, be theologically explicit but can *reveal* what Newman's verse prosily talks *about*. Occasionally, listening to Elgar's *Dream*, we may mistrust so much palaver about the mere act of dying and may thank God (or whomever) for a Janáček – Elgar's exact contemporary who, living in an agrarian rather than industrial community, could accept man and nature as interdependent, and life and death as perpetually self-renewing.

Even so, Elgar wins us over because we recognize that his re-birth, like the supreme instances in Shakespeare and Beethoven, takes place within his psyche. Newman must have believed in his allegory more literally than Elgar, or you or I, needed to. Elgar's Dream may be 'only' a dream, and he always referred to it as 'the Dream', never as an oratorio; yet what matters is the Dream's inner truth, prophetically adumbrated in the orchestral Prelude which previews both the musical themes and the dramatic motives in both the psychological and the Wagnerian senses.

The basic tonality is D minor, a key associated, as already noted, with strife and doubt by the Viennese classics and traditionally, way back to its origins in the dorian mode, considered 'obscure' and therefore appropriate to our uncertain earthly pilgrimage. The theme is first presented as monodic incantation, chromatically undulating but merging into a godly rising fifth, expanded into an aspirational sixth. If the monody suggests a *cantus firmus*, its tonality is far from firm, and its slow unfolding (marked 'mistico') leads into chromatic sequences wavering in dotted rhythm:

Apprehension becomes agitated aspiration that ends in a stepwise motif of Prayer; though this in turn flows into dotted-rhythmed chromatic undulations – sound-images for the dreams and nightmares in a sick man's slumber. Slowly and tentatively a noble, forward-thrusting march evolves, later to be associated with the soul's 'going forth'. Chromatic passing notes and dissonant appoggiaturas intensify rather than enfeeble the exultation, which none the less relapses into the Dream motif. Gerontius initiates the psychological 'action'; in arioso wavering between B flat major and G minor; and this arioso is closer to Verdi than to Wagner, reminding us that Elgar favoured an Italianate tenor for the role. Even so, the line is beautifully 'framed' to the life of the English words: as is further evident when a chorus of commiserating friends enters in fugato, offering to succour Gerontius on his journey. Their 'everyday' music is plain diatonic or incipiently modal and, even when chromaticized, never surrenders its direct lyricism.

Lyricism climaxes in the work's first aria, the tremendous 'Sanctis fortis': the dying man's appeal, in a traditional *miserere*, to God. The solo line teeters between the major and minor triad of B flat, in a swaying triple pulse. Neither the false relations nor the declining chromatics, with the dotted-rhythmed 'Dream' motif undulating beneath, undermine the Verdian fervour, to words offering an anglicized version of the Creed. This desperate if still wavering attestation of belief ends in a region in more than one sense unearthly: for the final appeal to the 'Judex meus' is engulfed in serpentine chromatics anticipatory of the demons Gerontius will encounter when his soul has 'passed over'. 'For the time being', however, a Priest, Parsifal-like in solemnity, calls on Gerontius to 'go forth in the name of the Lord'. The chorus – his human friends, boosted by sundry 'Angelicals' – solicit Mary to succour him in fugato havering between life-affirming E flat major and deathly A flat minor: evolving into a grandly fugal peroration burgeoning from the 'Go fourth' theme of the Prelude. Ultimately, a wide-spaced Elgarian melody in D major heals the Prelude's D minor, its spaciously arching Parry-like mobility now ecstatic.

In Part II Gerontius's soul is released from his body in what may be the simplest, and possibly the most beautiful, music Elgar ever wrote. Floating from god-like fifths and fourths it is at first not only diatonic but modal – initially mixolydian on F. Limpidly scored, the music alchemizes materiality into spirit and materializes spirit, since Gerontius's soul, in limbo, converses with an Angel whose music is poised between Gerontius's dreamy enharmony and modally pure alleluyas:

This is the first, and possibly the only direct, intimation of Vaughan Williams's music in Elgar; as Vaughan Williams was himself to do later, it equates the vision of Albion with a New Jerusalem attainable within the mind, if not outside it. For the moment Edwardian Sir Edward becomes a Blakean Bard, 'calling among the ancient trees'. Elgar didn't tell us whether the bard calls in vain because he didn't know, apparently accepting Newman's limbo-theology that had left Gerontius, after so much anguish, still awaiting God's chancy verdict. In the light or dark of this Elgar's angelic music passes understanding almost (though not quite) as much as does the Agnus Dei of Bach's B minor Mass, the Benedictus of Beethoven's Missa Solemnis, or the entry of Shakespeare's King Lear with Cordelia, dead, in his arms. In all these, tears 'burst smilingly', and the individual tragedies of heroes become acts of transcendence outstripping their puny selves. Similarly, if less sublimely, Gerontius's personal *angst* envisages a new world embryonic within his society's rampant industrialism and imperialism.

Nor does it finally matter that Elgar lived to recognize that his vision had been betrayed by the enormity of the First World War and the lunatic criminalities of the human race, in which we must include ourselves who did not, in the biblical sense, 'prevent' the politicians, industrialists, and imperialists whom Elgar's gibbering demons represent. The common objection that they don't sound supernatural is precisely the point: they are all too distressingly *mundane*. That Elgar's Land of Hope and Glory never had existed or could exist 'on land or sea' would seem to be admitted in the valedictory works of Elgar's later years. The magnificent Second Symphony, in humanly heroic E flat major, opens with sweepingly grandiloquent paragraphs while admitting that Shelley's Spirit of Delight 'cometh but rarely': for the sonata allegro is followed by a funeral march both private (for a dead friend) and public (for the recently deceased Edward VII); and these solemn exequies lead to a scherzo as neurasthenically nightmarish as Mahler, and thence to a 'Malvern Hills' finale that is none the less in dualistic sonata form, and ends with a dying fall.

Similarly, Elgar's last two major orchestral works turn into elegies. *Falstaff* is a dazzling symphonic poem describing the life and death of Shakespeare's ambivalent hero, presenting him, warts and all, as the archetypal Englishman that Elgar would have liked to be, and perhaps was. Finally, the Cello Concerto opens with the most spacious of Elgar's 'Malvern Hills' tunes, makes only fleeting, slightly macabre reference to Pomp and Circumstance, and ends in introverted appoggiatura-laden self-communion – capped only by a brief, almost perfunctory, gesture of renewed energy. Elgar wrote no major work after 1918 though he lived until 1934, occasionally grousing that 'they no longer want my kind of thing'. In a crude sense he was right; but in a deeper sense he was wrong, for his Land of Hope and Glory did exist *in his music*, and does so still, when that music is heard. In the two symphonies, and perhaps in the concertos for violin and for cello and in *Falstaff*, Elgar created music greater than *The Dream of Gerontius* which, back in 1900, he had said was most worthy of our memory. Even so, the choral work does occupy an in more than one sense sacred place in the Elgar canon: for the D major beatitude he wins through to in the final chorus offers a truly blissful consummation of the work's hazardous D minor pilgrimage, so that in silent awe we may – whether or not we call ourselves Christians – join in those lucent Amens.

Elgar, though the greatest, was not the only composer of genius (as distinct from talent) to reanimate our music at the turn of the twentieth century. He had a complement, and also a polar opposite, in Delius, who was born in 1862, five years later than Elgar, and died in the same year as he, 1934. Whereas Elgar ostensibly relished the Edwardian, materialistic world he celebrated whilst being at heart a spiritual seeker assailed by doubts, Delius reacted violently against his heritage, abominating alike industrial Bradford where he was born, and all churches, which he believed to be shibboleths born of man's shaming frailty. In his poem 'Ego Dominus Tuus', published in 1919, the year after Elgar virtually relinquished composition, W.B. Yeats remarked that

> The rhetorician would deceive his neighbours,
> The sentimentalist himself; while art
> Is but a vision of reality.
> What portion in the world can the artist have
> Who has awakened from the common dream
> But dissipation and despair?

We might say that Elgar, in his pompous and circumstantial response to Edwardian society, ran the risk of being, in the sense defined by Yeats, a 'rhetorician'; whereas Delius, in deliberately depriving his music of social and religious context, courted the possibility of being a 'sentimentalist'. Both men, however, evaded such a fate by virtue of an emotional, and perhaps spiritual, toughness; if Elgar's attitude to the world he lived in was, at the end, tinged with despair, he was never dissipated; if the hedonistic Delius had his moments of dissipation, he exhibited a high courage that amounted to a kind of triumphalism.

The experience that fired Delius's imagination was narrow but intense; it was also the heart of his Englishness, despite his in part Teutonic descent, his Scandinavian affiliations, and his Wagnerian approach to his art. Thanks to the grudging generosity of his businessman father, he had the wherewithal to leave Bradford and seek havens in the Bohemian life of Montmartre, the solitudinous mountains of Norway, and the orange and grapefruit farms of Florida – in which his father somewhat wanly hoped he might find a 'career'. As composer, Delius carried the Wagnerian deification of the self a stage further in that in his most typical music there is *no* human population, only himself and solitude. So the essence of Delius's music is the flow of sensation – to him 'the only thing that matters'. Even in an abstractly musical work like the Violin Concerto the initial Wagnerian appoggiaturas – sighs of the overburdened heart – generate a fluctuating woof of chromatic harmonies, while the lines that comprise these harmonies are, individually considered, vocal, modal, often pentatonic in contour, as though each singing melody were seeking, beyond the temporal flux, a oneness incarnate in the violinist's soaring song. Delius's music, like Richard Jefferies's prose, is 'the Story of my Heart' or, like Whitman's 'free' verse, is 'a Song of Myself'; yet this story and song can find consummation only in surrender to the impersonal forces of wind, sky, and sea. This violin concerto, discovering an equipoise between the Innocence of pentatonic melody and the Experience of 'advanced' chromatic harmony, defines the basic Delian theme of the self alone in the populous world; it is one of his most beautiful and fully 'realized' compositions.

Even so, Delius's *most* consummately realized work has as soloist a *human voice*, with full chorus and symphony orchestra. This is *Sea Drift*, written in 1904, significantly a setting of part of a poem by the aboriginally American Walt Whitman. The experience with which it is concerned could hardly be more elemental, since it deals in the life and death of two animate creatures, one avian, the other human, against the eternity of the all-encompassing sea from which emerges, and into which dissolves, the self. Whitman symbolizes the self as a sea-bird who sings of his separation from his (probably slain) mate. The solo baritone, who enunciates Whitman's free-flowing words, is Delius himself, who alchemizes words into music, and is also you and I, 'insensible of mortality' yet, like everyone else, 'desperately mortal'. But the soloist is also Delius as the small boy of the poem, or any small boy at the moment when he first apprehends the immutability of death: 'my mate no more, no more, with me; we two together *no more*'. Borne on the natural rhythm of the words, the vocal line recurrently flows into the pentatonic formulae that are most natural to the human voice; whilst the orchestra, with uncanny immediacy, dissolves their rudimentary humanity into the surge and sizzle of the sea. In acknowledging the fact of death the boy loses innocence, while the sea remains eternally unconscious. The loss of love – the sea-bird's dead beloved – and the boy's loss of innocence are interdependent: which is why Delius's final recognition of lost happiness ('O past, O happy life, O songs of love'), in a traditionally Edenic E major, is even more heart-rending than the immediate cognition of death. The music's dissolution into sighing appoggiaturas on the chorally reiterated 'No mores' sounds at once like the eternally breaking waves and the wail of a new-born babe. Paradoxically, the symphony orchestra was a triumph of nineteenth-century technology; yet at the end of this work the sighing orchestral appoggiaturas seem to *be* forces out there in the natural world: breaking waves that are also our breaking hearts at the dawn of consciousness – specifically consciousness of the *un*consciousness of death.

This is a – perhaps *the* – essential religious experience: despite the fact that Delius did not believe in God and was contemptuous of people who affected to embrace any creed invented in his, her, or its name. Unsurprisingly, Delius abominated English oratorio, deprecating the time Elgar wasted on it, though he offered a crumb of comfort in admitting that Elgar wasn't as desperate a case as Parry, who would have set the whole Bible to music had he lived long enough. Yet even so, Delius composed two works that couldn't have existed but for the tradition of English oratorio. The earlier of them, *A Mass of Life*, was begun at the turn of the century and finished in 1904, the year of *Sea Drift*. It is his biggest work, and possibly his greatest, though it is not as completely fulfilled as *Sea Drift* and his later choral and orchestral masterpiece, significantly titled *A Song of the High Hills*. Certainly, the Mass is Delius's most comprehensive testament wherein he identifies himself with his hero Nietzsche, celebrating man's 'high courage and self-reliance' in the face of his own irremediable death, and of Nietzsche's 'Death of God'. For man to be totally self-responsible is an ultimate exultation, and an ultimate terror. Delius carried fanatical belief in the self to a point at which he could tolerate no music but his own – except possibly that of late Wagner to which he owed so much, and that of a few younger composers who had dedicated works to him. This, if magnificent, is also foolhardy; to carry it off an artist needs to be consistently inspired: which, over the not-far-off-two-hour duration of *A Mass of Life* is asking a lot. But although Delius is not quite equal to the challenge, he produces enough inspired music to win the day. Despite the post-Wagnerian idiom, the evocations of the stillness of summer noon and of midnight are as original as they are heart-rending;

while the opening and closing choruses remind us, in surging impetuosity and in control of the vast paragraph, of the young Delius's superabundant energy, which so potently animated his nostalgia. Both the life-celebrating virility and life-transcending nature-worship are musical equivalents of Nietzsche's *Also sprach Zarathustra* which furnished Delius with his text, set in German. Since the magic of such music may be explained only as an act of *faith*, it is not surprising that there should be a parallel between the monumental choruses of State-supporting but God-aspiring Elgar in his *Gerontius*, and these monumental choruses of a composer who professed to believe neither in God nor State, but only in himself.

The opening chorus of *A Mass of Life* is in several senses breath-taking. The immense sweep of the paragraphs; the wide range of the vocal parts; the freedom of their chromaticism which remains vocally grateful because 'spontaneous' pentatonic formulae recurrently inform the tonal exuberance, the complementing of the vocal parts by orchestral lines that are, despite their chromatics, vocal in contour; and the sheer luxuriance of the orchestration: all these make for a dizzying affirmation of Life which needs quoting in full score if it is to be adequately meaningful. Nothing could be more remote from the image of Delius – old, frail, blind, paralysed in his wheelchair – that has become part of the popular imagination. Delius was around forty when he composed this music, which is a sublimation of his handsome Byronic youth, with heart pounding, pulse beating, blood seething. One might even say that this chorus is Delius's quintessence, the prime source of the virility from which his life and art sprang. Yet since he was on his own admission a 'pagan', fulfilment of the senses and of corporeal desire implied too a recognition that 'fulfilment' involves an acceptance of our ephemerality and of the inevitable *loss* of the beloved such as is the heart of *Sea Drift*. Perhaps a notion of the paradoxical religious atheism of Delius can be best revealed by way of commentary on the final movement of Part I of the work, and on the early sections of the Second Part.

The opening chorus, notwithstanding its apparently unconstrained chromaticism, is centred on pastoral F major, and the final chorus of Part I also begins in F, over low tonic pedal notes on string basses. The soft sonorities of woodwind and horns stir almost imperceptibly, in slow-swaying $\frac{6}{4}$, as the baritone solo invokes the 'fountain of human love' as the source of renewal. The slow expansion of the baritone line, with reiterations of the leaping sixth, that interval of aspiration, enacts the flowering of love in what both Nietzsche and Whitman call the Soul, reinforced by strings in flowing parts, bathed in liquid harp arpeggios. The chorus nourish both the sentiments of the words and the ripeness of the orchestral textures. sometimes adding wordless ah-ahing and la-laing to the orchestral instrumentation. The end of the song is magical, with the soloist aspiring to what are (for a baritone) lofty heights, but dreamily drooping into quietude for a final resolution in B flat major, a fifth lower than the original F. Although the tonality wanders as freely as it does in the surging opening paragraph of the first movement of the piece, the meandering is never aimless. The tonal destiny of that hushed B flat major seems inevitable: though how far Delius consciously knew what he was doing is tricky to estimate and is hardly the point, since the 'technique' – a word that Delius mistrusted – *is*, if it works, the enacting of the 'experience'. Here, it *creates* the bloom of love in the heart or 'soul'.

The ultimate revelation follows at the opening of Part II: which opens with distant horn-calls on the mountainous heights, murmuring pentatonic figurations, echoing through divided strings con sordino, over cavernous pedal notes on C, shifting to F. The horns, calling through rising fourths and fifths and falling thirds, are pristine, magically effacing any modern concert-hall or even any church, should the pagan piece be granted entry. The strings, anchored to their deep pedal notes while bearing the chromatic burden of our weary hearts, offer perhaps the sublimest instance of the Delian equilibrium between pentatonicism and chromaticism; the music finally fades on a triad of 'innocent' A major marked *pppp*: A major being the upper mediant to the original F.

That A major triad serves to introduce the first movement proper of Part II: an invitation to 'arise' into life reborn, scored for double chorus, full orchestra, and the four soloists. Initially, the key is still spring-empowered A major, and the eight choral voices all launch themselves through literally rising intervals, dominated by the familiar leaping major sixths. The strings also surge upwards in rising arpeggios in tremolando; although vocal tessitura is dizzily high, the writing is grateful enough to sweep the chorus along 'con elevazione e vigore'. Climacterically, the sopranos leap through an octave to a high C: indicating how man may be 'neighbour to the sun' and sweeping the tonality from the chorus's basic F major back up to A, again with the rising sixths, resplendently reinforced by trombones. Here the corybantic ecstasy that characterized the opening of the work attains to an ultimate exultation; and although the free tonality and the opulence of the orchestral sonority owe much to late Wagner, Delius's pagan pantheism remains unique, perhaps because no other music so totally liberates human passions – especially sexual passion – in the elemental context of Nature. Yet characteristically Delius's euphoria doesn't surrender awareness of the reality that humanity, according to him, will do 'anything to escape'. The climacteric movement, mostly for the solo voices, invokes midnight as symbol for the hopefully gentle closing of our lives, making for a quietude that balances that of the penultimate movement to Part I. The final double chorus triumphs *through* the acceptance of death in the context of life seasonally, and on those terms eternally, renewed. The music, dominated by leaping octaves as 'fulfilled' permutations of the familiar leaping sixths, and frequently surging in Delius's favoured $^6_4$ lilt, wings through many keys before coming to rest in a coda (largo, con solennità) with a key-signature of B major – a key which, being a step further up the cycle of fifths from

traditionally celestial E major, acquired for Delius transcendental implications (it is the key of the fine, early violin and piano sonata without opus
number, recently restored to the repertory by the performances of Tasmin
Little). Certainly the end of *A Mass of Life* effects an apotheosis of B major
as both soloists and chorus soar pentatonically around high Bs before
'dying' on a B major triad with added sixth, leaving a pure major triad on
strings, horns, and woodwind that in turn evanesces into nirvana. We
remember that B major is the key in which Wagner's Tristan lingeringly
expires; and Delius can sustain the comparison.

Although it has no connection with the Eucharist, Delius's *A Mass of Life*
is aptly titled. His later Requiem, written during the First World War, is a
Mass of Death; and the two works prove indistinguishable in intention, since
for the Delian humanist life and death are interdependent. Though less
massive than the Mass, the Requiem is scored for comparable forces and its
text, cobbled together by Heinrich Simon with Delius's promptings, is
mostly adapted from Nietzsche and from Ecclesiastes, a biblical source
remote from Christian mysticism. The composer was careful to point out
that his Requiem was 'not a religious work . . . The proud spirit casts off the
yoke of superstition, for it knows that death puts an end to all life and
therefore fulfilment can be found only in life itself.' This was not what the
British oratorio public expected from a memorial tribute to young men
martyred in the War, and in 1916 moral disapproval of the text – especially
of the second movement's Hymn to Free Love – spilt over into dismissal of
the music. What used to be liabilities now count as assets; and although the
big choruses of the Requiem cannot rival those of *A Mass of Life* in
exhilaration, there are 'progressive' moments in the piece that suggest how
Delius's music might have evolved, but for the syphilitic paralysis that slowly
destroyed him.

These numinous moments occur mostly in the final movement. The
soprano solo tells us that we should 'honour the man who can love life,
and yet without base fear can die'. Thus we may win 'the crown of life', these
words being exultantly echoed by the chorus. The soloist sings of a brave
man's ascent to the mountain top, whence he may fearlessly watch the sun
decline as evening spreads its hands in blessing, lulling us to 'long and
dreamless sleep'. The soprano soloist is joined by a baritone to form a
regenerative pair of lovers who twine in pantheistic homage to nature's
eternal renewal in the spring of the year. The section wherein the soprano
honours the 'brave man' is so free in tonality as to be almost a-tonal;
although marked 'slow and solemn', Delius encourages us to perform it
'with energy'. When 'the star of life' sinks into the darkness whence it had
risen, the soprano solo declines flatwards into silence: whence emerges the
'visionary' final section that wavers pentatonically between celestial E, B,
and F sharp majors, with pentatonic clusters on celesta and harp. Lydian G
sharps in what becomes basically D major lend tingle and tang to the

sonority, creating a scrunchy sound, as of sap rising. We've noted how, throughout Delius's music, pentatonic innocence seems to be the goal of chromatic experience; here, at last, pentatonicism takes over unsullied, except for those 'healing' lydian fourths. Blithe birds and babbling brooks twitter and tinkle through drones on a pentatonic paradise of harp, celesta, and glockenspiel. While the common view of Delius as a psychologically regressive composer can never be adequate since his evocations of the life-force attain such glory, this epilogue is unique in his music: a prelude to life's seasonal renewal wherein non-Western, quasi-Balinese sonorities are harbingers of what's to come – including the 'oriental' elements in Holst's *Hymn of Jesus* and in the 'magic musics' of Vaughan Williams's final phase. The difference between this new Delian *ex-stasis* and his earlier exultations (such as the opening of the *Mass of Life*) is that the new music has relinquished the earlier music's will-fulness.

Yet although the myth of the blind and paralysed Delius, recollecting in tranquillity in his garden at Grez, discounts the Byronic magnetism of his youth, there is nonetheless allegorical import in that Delius, crippled, became a spectator of his own imaginative life. His nostalgia, and its complementary nature-mysticism, if 'limited', are also perennial and universal experiences: which is why, though his weaker works have faded, those in which inspiration flowered remain impervious to fashion. We may admit that the experience by which he was obsessed is unlikely, in our technology-dominated societies, ever again to seem as significant as it did during the first two decades of the twentieth century, when Delius was most vigorously creative. On the other hand, it is also unlikely, in any foreseeable future, to be meaning*less*. No welfare state, nor even the Kingdom of Heaven, can appease the unsatisfied cravings of man. Although Delius would have expunged the 'wretched', he wouldn't have apologized for the pride, and his 'message', albeit from a confessedly irreligious man, was in the deepest sense spiritual, and also religious, though it totally denied the bondage etymologically inherent in the word.

21

Cosmic, Social, and Personal Mysticism and Apocalypse

Holst's *Hymn of Jesus* (1917),
Vaughan Williams's *Sancta Civitas* (1925), and
Howells's *Hymnus Paradisi* (1938)

Our discussion of the Crisis of Faith in Victorian and Edwardian England covered music of those polar opposites, Edward Elgar and Frederick Delius, finding in Elgar's *Dream of Gerontius* an experience of the numinous latent in the anti-poetry of Cardinal Newman's confessional verse and, in Delius's *Mass of Life* and *Requiem*, a comparable transcendence in the ecstasy of Nietzschean 'high courage and self-reliance'. But what were the choices open to British composers of the next generation, who couldn't passively imitate Elgar whose social values no longer seemed tenable, and who would find it increasingly tricky to withdraw, with Delius, into a nostalgia that could be validated only by pristinely inspired genius? At this date we can see that, in the early years of the twentieth century, there were two composers who had the honesty and integrity to know what had to be done: Holst and Vaughan Williams. In the case of Elgar, genius triumphed in spite of adversity in the shape of a basically materialistic society; in the case of Delius, genius triumphed *because* of adversity, since his alienation released his creativity; but Holst and Vaughan Williams triumphed *over* adversity: which is why they are not composers of greater talent, but figures of such crucial importance in our musical history.

Holst was naturally alienated by his Danish ancestry and Teutonic affiliations; he dropped the 'von' from his name of Gustav von Holst during the years of the First World War. Living and working in indus-trialized London, he began by composing in Teutonicized conventions he later referred to as 'good old Wagnerian bawling'. Traces of this may still be detected in his music which he and we came to accept – notably in the orchestral suite *The Planets*, which is his biggest and most frequently performed work. But despite the nineteenth-century legacy of an immense symphony orchestra used with Wagnerian opulence, the music of *The Planets* is also at least superficially responsive to the neo-primitivism of early Stravinsky; and its finest moments delineate the authentic Holstian universe, within the aegis of the astronomical and astrological themes latent in the work's planetary subject. This Holstian world is a brew of violence, perhaps related to advanced industrialization, and of alienation, favouring notions of human destiny remote from our 'Western' world. This must be why Holst, an Outsider, veered towards oriental (especially Indian) philosophy and music, and especially towards quasi-oriental theosophical notions that had crept into Christian Gnosticism.

But as an Englishman by adoption, Holst could find himself only by rediscovering the basic nature of English musical tradition, before its Teutonic hybridization. This he did in a series of small but telling works: such as the *Four Songs* for voice and violin of 1916, which set medieval texts in rhythms as non-metrical and freely word-related as are folk song and plainchant. The vocal line of Holst's setting of the lovely medieval carol 'I sing of a maiden that is makeless' is at first purely aeolian, and such bar-lines as it has are without accentual significance, since there is no 'beat'. What makes the slight song 'modern' music is the tonal precariousness whereby, at the approach to his mother's 'bower', a single chromatic alteration deflects the melody into an 'other' world, distanced from medieval peasant or cleric. The change of vista, if only momentary, is startling; and when the melody rediscovers its aeolian roots we hear it with new ears.

Such music penetrates to the heart of the matter, being at once ancient and pristine; and it is not surprising that in a work like *Sāvitri* (written in 1908 when Holst was embarking on his Indian Rig Veda series), he should have used free-rhythmed declamation in a modality that fused oriental with early Christian elements. The piece, though not strictly an opera, is a mystery-play in music that may, of its nature, go on longer than a lyric carol. The snag lay in the fact that such modal monody didn't lend itself readily to theatrical works calling for dramatic development: as becomes palpable in the later stretches of *Sāvitri* when Pucciniesque passion, intruding into the love music, fails to establish a convincing relationship with the modal declamation. This dichotomy remained a problem throughout Holst's creative life, especially in purely instrumental music. He came closest to solving it in the choral and orchestral *The Hymn of Jesus*, written to a Christian Gnostic text in 1917, the year after the triumphant *Planets*. Next to that work, *The Hymn of Jesus* is probably Holst's most frequently performed piece.

For many years Gnostic texts were classed among the New Testament apocrypha, their authenticity as Christian documents being dubious. Fairly recent research has revealed that Holst became acquainted with this and other Gnostic texts by way of his theosophist friend G.R.S. Head, who had published an edition of a post-resurrectional gospel in 1896. Its appeal to Holst was immediate and understandable, since it mated Christianity with the Vedaic preoccupations of his Indian phase. He opens the work literally with monody: a single line not 'based on' but directly quoting the plainchant 'Pange Lingua', played by a tenor trombone impersonating an 'abstract' metaphysical priest. The 'Prelude' to the work derives direct from this antique monody; and another chant, 'Vexilla regis', is introduced on sundry solo instruments against a backcloth of sustained strings loosely tethered to G minor. This second chant was probably written by Bishop Fortunatus in the year 569 and was later used as a marching hymn by Crusaders; later still it was appropriated by several art composers from Gounod to Holst to Jonathan Harvey.

In this introduction monody is reinforced by other techniques that tend to deny temporal progression: for instance, a reiterated broken triad of G major played on three flutes in slow, level quavers, painfully pierced by an appoggiatura on F sharp drooping to E sharp, played on plangently unisonal oboe, cor anglais, clarinet, and viola. This 'piercing' appoggiatura is probably a legacy from Amfortas's 'wound' music in *Parsifal*, wherein Wagner himself revealed Buddhistic proclivities. More overtly medieval is Holst's use of organum – the multiplication of a single line by the addition of fourths and fifths, the 'absolute' consonances with so little harmonic implication that they almost count as unisons. Holst's organum is here played on divided strings and woodwind, doubled by piano and intermittently by organ garlanded with celesta. The return of the original 'Pange Lingua' tune, 'freely' chanted by 'a few tenors and baritones', prepares us for the Hymn that succeeds the Prelude, setting the Gnostic words in Holst's own translation.

Immediately, the Hymn reveals that, while most European music since the Renaissance has been based on harmony as alternating degrees of tension and relaxation existing in time, Holst does his best to evade this concept. Despite his admiration for (especially English) sixteenth-century composers, there is in his own music little genuinely harmonic polyphony of the kind that depends on tension between 'horizontal' line and 'vertical' harmony. Holst's partiality for bitonal effects (as referred to above), springs positively from his austerely linear approach and negatively from the almost pathological horror of luscious seventh and ninth chords which he nurtured in reaction against Wagner. Unexpected linear relationships between diatonic concords condition his harmony in a manner comparable to Debussy's, especially in organum-derived pieces such as *La Cathédrale Engloutie*.

The self-contained nature of Holst's modal melodies and the lack of progression in his harmony together mean that he had to rely on rhythm, or rather on metre, to keep the music going over a relatively long span. The most primitive method of achieving continuity – of 'going on' at all – is the ostinato: as is demonstrated at the Hymn's outset, when cello and basses, boosted by bassoons and piano, reiterate descents down the scale from C to E, with the precise disposition of the scale shifting slightly to accord with the choric harmonies. The chorus is 'double', allowing for two groups to be used antiphonally; and to be echoed by a third, 'distant' semi-chorus. At first the two choruses are together on unison Cs, fanning into an E major triad in second inversion:

The 'out of this world' effect depends on the massive oneness of the two choruses before they become divisive; on the 'distant' dimension of the semichorus; and on the obstinacy of the ostinato, which simultaneously measures time and obliterates it since an ostinato, always returning to the same point, never 'gets anywhere'. Eventually, the ostinato settles into the aeolian mode on soft strings and piano while the hushed chorus *speak* the act of glorification, which the upper strings adorn with pentatonic triplets. As the music swells in dynamics, the bitonal shifts between triads of C major and E major recur, and the choruses sing the Amen antiphonally, boosted by a triple forte C major triad on organ.

Up to this point the music has been communal and celebratory. In the next section, however, the two choruses, antiphonally divided, explore the heart of Gnostic paradox by uttering pleas that are distinct and per-sonalized, one pleading to *be* saved, the other *offering* salvation: while the distant semi-chorus, now in parallel minor instead of major triads, inter-polates Amens apparently confirmatory of two totally contradictory atti-tudes. Unsurprisingly, tonality becomes vague, often enharmonic, and the textures grow sparer, even gaunt, as in the 'piercing' that is indeed a FALSE relation. It is remarkable that Holst, in 1917, should have made choral and orchestral music so remote from the opulence of Edwardian oratorio; perhaps the desperate climax to the First World War helped rather than hindered Holst's exploration of alternative vistas. In any case this episode of 'lost' tonal bearings and textural divisiveness closes in a pentatonically celestial E major: and moves into another ostinato pattern, now in a lopsided $\frac{5}{4}$ falling from B to E in the bass, with fully scored E major triads in a dynamic ostinato metre similar to that which Holst had deemed appropriate to war-celebrating Mars, fiercest of the planets.

The words of this section – bandied between the antiphonal choirs and bolstered by Amens on $\frac{6}{3}$ chords from the semichorus – indicate that a holy but orgiastic dance is being enacted. Early Stravinsky is distantly evoked, though the unstable mediant transitions and oscillating false relations also have precedents in English Renaissance music. The words ('The Heavenly Spheres make music for us, the Holy Twelve dance with us') prompt music almost tipsily corybantic, with sizzling scales on strings, blares from brass, and screeches from woodwind, strident piccolo aloft. Occasional bitonal blasts on organ delineate stages in the terpsichorean revels as Holst achieves an impressive broadening by the simplest of means – an interjection, within the $\frac{5}{4}$ pulse, of augmentations into $\frac{5}{2}$. The ultimate climax of this Gnostic work hymns divisiveness, not unity: for while the second chorus tells us that 'I have no resting place, I have no temple' the first chorus affirms that 'I have the earth, and I have Heaven.' For the climacteric words of the poem – 'to you who gave, a Lamp am I' – the two choruses, moving in $\frac{6}{3}$ chords organum-style, create acute passing dissonances of F sharp major against F major before shining, lamp-like, in the resonance of D major:

The semichorus still append their rotating Amens in parallel triads in false relation; the fierce passing dissonance is repeated in a telescoping of triads of B flat and A majors; and subsides flatwards into the 'Pange Lingua' intonation, ending the $\frac{5}{4}$ ostinato-dance. A 'religious' work based on the ultimate contradictions of Gnosticism seems apposite to the apparent disintegration of 'Western' civilization in a War that did nothing to 'end war'; but so fundamental a contradiction has nothing to do with the 'binding' that is implicit in religion.

The final section of the work, however, seems to seek an atemporal reconciliation of opposites in going back to the beginning. The orchestral ostinato now undulates in level crotchets on whole tones and major thirds, while the women of the choruses chant the 'Vexilla regis' hymn in the aeolian mode on B. This holy song is, however, again disrupted by the preludial ostinato on a rocking triad, pierced by the *Parsifal*-like chromatic appoggiatura; and leading into a coda admitting that, but for the magical intervention of the Word, we could have knowledge of nothing at all. Though it begins with a rising, innocently pentatonic scale, this is the only passage in the piece that faintly recalls the 'good old Wagnerian bawling' that Holst justifiably claimed to have expunged from his music. Perhaps he momently felt that Gnostic paradox was a bit too much to swallow; if so, we must applaud the efficacy with which the famous and infamous 'passing dissonance' returns on the words 'Behold in me a couch', finding a release that seems sheer magic on a first inversion E flat major triad. The original ostinato bass to the Hymn, in something between C major and the aeolian mode, takes over in interweaving pentatonic canon, with the semichorus's Amens still in minor triads undulating between A and C. The augmentation of the pulse to minims in $\frac{5}{2}$, stressing the mystical vision of the 'holy souls', is heard in the last, and most awe-ful, of the passing dissonances which, since it resolves on a whole-tone ambiguity, doesn't really resolve at all. The final paragraph repeats the music of the opening of the Hymn ('In my end is my beginning'), with the last Amens rising through a minor third canonically, and the semi-chorus, at half speed, rising from an A minor triad, through B flat major, to C major. From the final pianissimo chord all trace of bitonality has evaporated, though the burden of the poem, and of Holst's music, has been the interdependence of duality and unity.

The lucent C major in which *The Hymn of Jesus* ends is perhaps a wish-fulfilment that may be called 'mystical', if anything may; and a comparison with the tone-poem *Egdon Heath*, which some consider to be Holst's 'quintessential' work, suggests that the basic Holstian experience, far from binding people together as religion is supposed to, is in essence solitary. Holst is alone on the bare heath, as Delius is alone in the high hills; and his *Hymn of Jesus*, however 'mystical', seems to be without social context and therefore without the consolation of an accredited faith. There is a sense in which Holst was a necessary and significant, but also a negative composer whose place in our music is fully intelligible only in relation to his friend and colleague, Ralph Vaughan Williams. *He* was in no sense an outsider, but British enough to become, over the years of a long life, a figure of the type now often called iconic.

Vaughan Williams's British legacy embraced the landed gentry, the Army, the Church, and the lost agrarian England. He owed a general debt to people such as Spenser, Shakespeare, Milton, Herbert, Crashaw, Vaughan, and Traherne, whose poetry and prose he set to empathetic music; while he owed a more specific and life-long debt to another figure who strode our turbulent seventeenth century and may still claim to be part of popular consciousness. John Bunyan reinterpreted Coverdale's Bible in the light and dark of the religious turmoil thrown up by the Civil War. He was a common man, by trade a tinker; and tinkers were outcasts from civilized society, sometimes genetically, and usually temperamentally, gypsies. Bunyan's most famous book, *The Pilgrim's Progress*, exerted an obsessive hold over many social levels of people throughout more than three centuries. The gentry could not ignore it, if only because they were afraid; in middle- and working-class homes it became, during the eighteenth and nineteenth centuries, the most revered book after the Bible. As a personal testament about the salvation of Tom, Dick, and Harry, and even of Jane, June, and Joan, and as a vision of a redeemable Promised Land, it struck to the hearts of common men and women – and of some uncommon ones, including Vaughan Williams who approached it as a traditionalist who loved fairy-tales. His first major work, *A Sea Symphony* (1903–9), was about a pilgrimage; the journey of Bunyan's progressive pilgrim is more specifically tied to English tradition, though it is no less elemental in range. Significantly, despite the Christian eschatology of the book, Vaughan Williams did not call his hero Christian, as did Bunyan, but simply the, or a, Pilgrim.

For Vaughan Williams his opera on *The Pilgrim's Progress* was literally the labour of a lifetime. Its inception dates back to 1906, or even to 1904 in that in that year he composed, or 'dished up' from a folk tune, his sturdy setting of Bunyan's hymn 'He who would valiant be', included in his *English Hymnal*. The opera's initiation is thus contemporary with Vaughan William's earliest published works. Much later, in 1922, the cantata *The Shepherd of the Delectable Mountains*, with text concocted from Bunyan's book, was published and performed, and was followed by other fragments of Pilgrim work-in-progress over the years, including a substantial score of incidental music for a BBC dramatization of the book. It was many years before Vaughan Williams completed the 'operatic morality' as it now stands; but much Pilgrim-music found its way into non-theatrical music of his vintage years, notably the Fifth Symphony, begun in 1938, on the threshold of another war, and completed at the war's peak in 1943. Vaughan William's thirty-year-long obsession with the book suggests that his relationship to our religious, social, and political traditions was direct, as that of Holst, an outsider, could not have hoped to be. The monody of folk song was a part of this tradition, but was only one aspect of the unfolding pattern of British music from the Tudor polyphonists to Purcell, to Elgar and Delius. Whereas Holst found inspiration mainly in medieval and early Renaissance models, Vaughan Williams responded directly to Elizabethan and Jacobean vocal polyphony wherein the interrelation of independent melodic lines generated harmonic substance, and therefore the possibility of evolution and even of development. This may be why Vaughan Williams left his operatic morality on Bunyan's book for long unfinished and, even when completed, open to several different interpretations. Fundamentally, it describes a spiritual or – as we would be likely to say – a psychological pilgrimage such as we all may, and perhaps must, embark on. We may also take it, if so inclined, as a Christian journey to an after-life. Either way, it is also a parable about the making of a New Jerusalem born of the rebirths of individual men and women. Its religious, social, and political implications colour most of the works of Vaughan Williams's later maturity, whether they carry a literary text or function by way of symphonic argument. A key-work is the oratorio *Sancta Civitas*, composed between 1923 and 1925, just after the cantata *The Shepherd of the Delectable Mountains*.

The relation between *Sancta Civitas* and Vaughan Williams's Bunyan-inspired works is intimate though its text is drawn not from Bunyan himself but from one of his prime sources, the Authorized Version of The Revelation of St John. In Greek this is the 'Apocalypse', composed or compiled around AD 96 by St John of Patmos, a man distinct from the author of the Johannine Gospel. No book of the Bible has exerted a deeper hold over the human imagination, for Revelation brought apocalypse into the centre of Christian eschatology. Its images are archetypal: pagan myths of sun and moon-worship; fertility cults; the zodiacal signs and the prognostications of astrology; the magic of numbers centred around 3 (divine perfection), 4 (creation), and their magical addition 7 and their multiple 12: the old symbols of the man on a white horse, and the death-dealing but life-creating dragon – all these and more offsprings of the collective unconscious lurk in this revelatory book. They speak to us over hundreds of years, even though the original text was rewritten, perhaps many times, by Hebraic prophets who bent it to their own purposes, and was refashioned yet again by Gentile Christian apologists whose message was different from, and often opposed to, the pagan world-view.

The apocalyptic theme flowered under Jewry, though apocalypses can be dated back as far as the Chaldeans and Egyptians. The Judaic prophecies of Enoch, Daniel, and Esdras all start from a recognition of crisis within the world; pronounce judgment on sinning people presumed to have precipitated that crisis; and enunciate a stage wherein, the elect having been vindicated, society may be reborn. The difference between apocalyptic and pagan prototypes lies in the application of an ethical yardstick whereby degrees of sinfulness and severity of punishment may be adjudicated. Political overtones are almost always involved in this, since the Lord's People are oppressed by pagan aliens through whose influence the elect may be themselves corrupted. Although there was a factual basis for this oppression, Babylon – the original persecutor of Israel – became a symbol for any top-dog, whether of race or class, who seemed to be having a jollier time than one did oneself. Patriarchs wept as they waited for a deliverer and a Day of Judgment – a notion taken over by Gentile Christianity when, in Europe's Middle Ages, ecclesiastical exegetists combed the Old and New Testaments for numerical and astrological evidence of the precise date of a Second Coming. *Dies illa* must be *dies irae*, for although the doctrine of the Fall implied redemption, blind terror was stronger than hope.

Over three centuries, whilst the modern world was in labour, millennial prophecies increased in extravagance; men of Milton's generation, obsessed with the traumatic year 1666 (the number of Apocalyptic Beast preceded by 1 to indicate its imminence), looked for a millennium soon realizable in both spiritual and material (political) terms. Cromwell was regarded as a middle-class millennial Messiah and Bunyan, a member of the labouring class, considered his visions to be a passport to pragmatic fulfilment. In the mid-seventeenth century the young Dryden, in his *Annus mirabilis: the Year of Wonders 1666*, had given a down-to-earth account of the New London, post-plague, post-fire, as a 'Citty of more precious Mold, Rich as the gold which gives the Indies name, with Silver pav'd and all Divine with Gold'. Gold and silver may have symbolic divinity but are also base metal – hard cash. The New Jerusalem *is* this prosperous modern, mercantile community. But for Shakespeare certainly, and probably for Milton, the 'new heaven and earth' spoken of in Revelation is not a *thing* proffered to erring but redeemable mortals but is rather man's potential to create, from the maelstrom of error, a new self. In this context Shakespeare's successor is Blake, who spoke as a self-styled prophet in biblical tradition, or as a Bard who 'Present, Past, and Future sees' (*Songs of Experience*), hymning the cycles of history at the onslaught of the Industrial Revolution. When, in *Jerusalem*, he said that all he knew was in the Bible he added that he understood the Book 'knowing of no other Christianity and no other Gospel than the liberty both of Body and Mind to exercise the Divine Arts of Imagination . . . To labour in knowledge is to build up Jerusalem.' It was in this Blakean spirit that Vaughan Williams viewed the apocalyptic theme, though he was not averse to the cruder amelioration of a William Morris.

It may have been the latter strain that prompted him to call *Sancta Civitas* an oratorio, though it has little in common with the Victorian prototype. Ethical and political implications are manifest in the City's disaffection; wars, rumours of war, and apocalyptic disasters were rife in the world at large; and if Holst's *Hymn of Jesus* had proffered a *vision* of apocalypse, Vaughan Williams's *Sancta Civitas* gave apocalypse immediate reality – even to the extent of achieving its first performance on the Day of Judgment of the General Strike! Even so, these social and political dimensions were merely a physical backcloth to a work that is at heart metaphysical, demonstrating how, in Vaughan Williams's words, 'the object of all art is to obtain a partial revelation of what is beyond human sense and human faculties'. He prefaced his score with a quotation (in Greek) from Plato's

Phaedo, admitting that 'a man of sense will not insist that things are exactly as I have described them, but I think he will believe something of the kind . . . and he must *charm his doubts with spells like these*' (my italics).

The opening of the oratorio is so metaphysically mysterious as to be, like faith, elusive. The large orchestra is hushed in a quietude ambiguous rather than serene, and although the score has a key signature of one sharp, the music is far from the beatitude of G major. Nor is the tonality E minor, Bach's key of Crucifixion, for the cavernous bass starts on, and recurrently returns to, a low C which rises slowly up the scale to F *natural*. An ostinato chord on three flutes hovers pentatonically between E, A, B and D, E, A; the implicit but never defined modality may be phrygian on E:

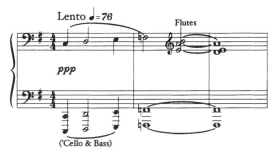

The rising scale then *starts* from F natural, aspiring to B flat and supporting a piercing motif on solo oboe – a rising fourth from A to D, drooping through C sharp and B natural. Tonality becomes even more obscure when the baritone soloist begins to declaim the Revelatory words, taking up the oboe phrase in speech rhythm. The baritone is Blake's Prophet, as the flutes' pentatonic chord vacillates on strings, while the main chorus sing distant alleluyas derived from it, at first chordally, then 'horizontally', in canon. Perhaps on the precedent of Holst's *Hymn of Jesus*, there are three choruses: a full chorus, a semi-chorus, and a Distant Chorus. The composer directs that this third chorus should be literally distant and if possible invisible. It should consist of boys' voices, and is not only a third choir but also a Third Dimension, over the horizon. Being supernatural, the voices are changeless, sufficient unto themselves; their key is always A flat major, perhaps in indeterminate whole-tone relation with E and C (the A flat standing enharmonically G sharp).

These equivocal mysteries are almost spelt out when the boys' chant, opening with the rising fifth A flat to E flat, is heard over a pedal bass, which is not A flat but the C the work had crepuscularly emerged from. The voices are homophonically triadic, in swaying triple rhythm, though chromatic alteration, producing a whole-tone augmented fifth, disturbs the euphony:

The effect is 'planetary', like the semi-chorus in Holst's *Hymn of Jesus*, and the modality remains indeterminate between C, A flat, and E natural – tones that together form a rootless whole-tone augmented fifth, on which the section climaxes. The pedal bass rises, however, from C to E and a song of praise ensues, flowering from Vaughan Williams's familiar upward-flowing pentatonics. The full chorus's alleluyas in $^6_3$ chords are close to the Amens in Holst's *Hymn of Jesus*, though Vaughan Williams is more disturbing in tonal ambiguity; if paradise is in the offing, it is still remote. Meanwhile the baritone solo calls on God omnipotent, shifting between aeolian and lydian E. The three choruses meet for the ultimate invocation, swaying between parallel triads of E, G, and F sharp, and proceeding to C sharp, which changes enharmonically to D flat:

In this key (really C sharp major as lower mediant to E) choirs and orchestra bound in pentatonic fanfares in triple-rhythmed fugato. The invitation to 'gladness' is sustained only briefly, for the marriage of the Lamb to his Church is a chancy prospect, if only because the Spirit is presumptively eternal whilst the Church is an institution man-made. As the notation changes back from flats to sharps the key-signature is that of heavenly E major though the bass is still rooted on C natural. When the first section – it might almost count as a 'movement' – simmers down in retrospective references, the ambiguous C-founded bass wriggles in (devilishly?) serpentine triplets tied across the beats. The baritone's solo hyming of marriage is in pentatonic E, which is also compromised by devilishly tritonal lydian overtones. The Distant Choir and their annunciatory trumpet are still in A flat, their false-related triads perturbingly extended.

The first part of this apocalyptic vision has thus invoked God Omnipotent in his Glory, but in its bi- and tri-tonality and its interior divisiveness has also revealed – as did Holst's *Hymn of Jesus* – that God, being self-contradictory, may have feet of clay. Division becomes the essence of the next movement, which starts with St John's vision of the White Horse and Horseman, making another abrupt shift to a mediant that might be mixolydian G though it is undermined by triads in false relation – especially on B flat minor, a devilish tritone away from the tonic E. The tumultuous false relations in the bit about the Horseman's two-edged sword are particularly Holstian. The Rider, named Faithfull and True, is clearly related by Vaughan Williams to Bunyan's Pilgrim: his triple-rhythmed march, like Bunyan's hymn, 'He who would valiant be', is energetically corporeal and harshly scored, with jazzy cross-accents suggestive of the post-war 1920s, though there is nothing topical and local about the Vision of the Angel, yelled by full chorus in homophonic major triads in the dorian mode on a very sharp B major. Bitonality is technically a doubleness which in this central section is of the essence since it depicts the War between Heaven and Earth, the issue of which is the obliteration of Babylon, the Sinful City.

An introductory fugato in a Holstian quintuple metre may be in the phrygian mode on A, the flat seconds pressing hard on the tonic. The war-music is an astonishing inspiration, more tri- than bi-tonal and spiked with chromatically altered intervals, especially devilish tritones. When the orchestra lurches into wailing triads, starting from G minor, the bass alternates between A flat and E flat in a 'fallen' version of the distant trumpet. The words 'Babylon the great is fallen' are set to a weird howl, dropping through unrelated triads:

This becomes a refrain that recurs, always on the semi-chorus; here it evolves in grave fugato on a theme basically pentatonic on G, though the orchestral bass still teeters between the opening notes of the magic trumpet-call, A flat and E flat. The repetitions of the refrain are never altered, for the wild despair seems to be no less 'eternal' than the supernatural music of the Distant Choir. When the Distant Choir congratulates 'Heaven' on its vengeance over sinful mankind, the sweet serenity of sonority and rhythm sound, in context, spine-chilling. Once again God's 'mysterious way' baffles mere mortals, including Vaughan Williams.

The Angel's hurling of the avenging millstone is recounted in the baritone's narration, in a dorian B minor. The orchestra's wailing chromatic triads recapitulate the undulations around G, still over the bass's A flat – E flat ostinato. The Voices of the Bridegroom and his Bride (God and his Church) peter out in fragmented pentatonics, with echoes of the semichorus's tritonal refrain on 'Babylon is fallen.' What happens then is one of the most magical moments in Vaughan Williams's music. The bass A flat punningly changes to G sharp: which serves as a first inversion bass to a solo violin that almost imperceptibly emerges from the orchestral depths to float pentatonically into paradisal E major:

This is the 'New Heaven and Earth' of St John's vision, and not even *The Lark Ascending* or Elihu's 'Dance of Youth and Beauty' in *Job* is a more marvellous image of innocence reborn. Only the bass pedal's being in first inversion rather than in root position imparts to the slow ascent a hint of vulnerability: which echoes that of the Distant Choir's alleluyas, to which the pedal is always in first inversion. It is fascinating to note that this juxtaposition of the G minor Fall with the E major Paradise recapitulates by inversion the famous 'Fall' motif of the serpent-nipped Eurydice in the arioso of the Messenger in Monteverdi's 1607 *L'Orfeo*, at precisely the same pitches.

According to Michael Kennedy, this E major passage was adapted from an early unpublished Whitman setting; so it is New World music not only in the mystical sense of the Book of Revelation but also in the psychologically topical and local sense. Whitman's free verse borrowed some of its cadences from the apocalyptic books of the Old Testament, thereby making a link between New World (American) Whitman and Old World (English) Blake For the specific vision of the Holy City the key signature is that of luminous E major though the sevenths are often flattened and the (lydian) fourths sharpened. Imperceptibly the pedal bass flowers into a pentatonic melody echoing the solo violin, which now mutates into that ascending lark. The lydian fourths gently propel the music towards G sharp minor, the arabesques being picked up not by solo violin, but by a more plangent oboe. The bitonal texture here resembles the sensuous exoticism of *Flos Campi*, composed in the same year. So it would seem that the vision of a New Heaven and Earth is a *consequence* of division, as was hinted at in Holst's *Hymn of Jesus*. Later, the philosophical and theological burden of Vaughan Williams's *Job* and of the fifth and sixth symphonies will make the same point.

In the final section 'Glory and Honour' flow in impulsive cross-rhythms and hunger is banished in parallel triads in lydian A major. The contemporary backcloth of the General Strike underlines Vaughan Williams's identification of spiritual with (politically) material themes, but the primacy of the spiritual is indubitable when the pentatonic incantation on solo violin returns as the people of the New City 'see God': who is presumably not new, except that in being reborn he needs us no less than we need him: a Blakean theme shortly to be explored in *Job*. Eventually the Lark descends from the heights, borne on alternations of a second inversion E major triad with an augmented fifth on D. From thence the bass falls to the work's initial C: above which the Distant Choir and Distant Trumpet again chant their false-related triads undulating around A flat, unchanged because God is changeless.

In the doxology the three choirs sing antiphonally, offering thanks to God for having (we hope) restored us. All the choirs sway in false-related triads veering between mediants (E, C, and A flat). The key of the unwavering angelic trumpet, A flat major, dominates but the music, for brass in organum-like triads, shifts enharmonically back to C, with C natural still the pedal bass. Very softly, the opening of the oratorio is repeated 'as it was in the beginning' and a high tenor (not baritone) solo declaims, on E, the words 'Behold I come quickly, I am the bright and the morning star.' This is possibly the most marvellous moment in a piece full of marvels. The tenor's elevation to high A, followed by G sharp and E, may owe its poignancy to its reminiscence of the semi-chorus's 'Babylon is fallen' refrain, during the War in Heaven. The Morning Star promises light to the City, though not yet: for the full orchestra's whispered Amens fade into the original embryonic bass creeping up from C natural to F, supporting the pentatonic ostinato-chord, D, E, A. We the people are left waiting as, deep in the bass, the 'off-key' phrygian F hums to silence.

Sancta Civitas was Vaughan Williams's favourite among his choral works, probably because it confronts head-on the issues of private and public responsibility in the then-modern world, and no less in ours. Although it offers no answers and ends on a question mark it tempers hope with strength; and in so doing has much in common with Blake's approach to religious and social experience. Blake, a visual artist as well as a poet, lived at the onset of the Industrial Revolution, as did Samuel Palmer, the visionary painter who was profoundly influenced by him. Vaughan Williams – an admirer of and successor to Blake and Palmer – lived at a time when the dire as well as the beneficent effects of industrialization, foreseen by Blake as bard and prophet, seemed inescapable. Vaughan Williams did not advocate escape; he rather showed how, in a world changing with bewildering rapidity, hope may reanimate tradition, while tradition succours hope.

In the *Hymn of Jesus* of Holst the outsider speaks in Gnostic and somewhat cosmological terms; Vaughan Williams's *Sancta Civitas* is rooted in the revolutionary book of Revelation, in the transitional England of John Bunyan the visionary tinker, and in the modern industrialized world, with all its social and political overtones. But apocalyptic disasters may also be private; and another English composer, twenty years younger than Vaughan Williams, made a large-scale choral and orchestral piece that discovered an apocalyptic vision within a private grief. He is Herbert Howells, whose *Hymnus Paradisi* cannot be denied a place among the major achievements of English choralism.

Howells, like Vaughan Williams, had a rural background, having been born in Gloucestershire; and although he was not actively involved in the rediscovery of English folk song, it coloured his imagination, enabling him to resist the Brahmsian Teutonicism favoured by Stanford, his – and, it sometimes seems, everyone's – teacher at the Royal College. Credit must go to Stanford, who was not notably encouraging to young composers, for recognizing the talent displayed in the chamber music written by Howells as a student. The Phantasy Quartet and the Piano Quartet, composed during the First World War in 1917 and 1918, are works of true nobility and individuality; and it is worth noting that the latter was dedicated to Ivor Gurney, the English poet and composer who, although not killed in the war, suffered a nervous breakdown during its aftermath. Nor was the dedication merely an act of friendship, for Howells included, alongside Gurney's name, the *places* (Choden and Churchdown Hill) which were the haunts of Gurney's and of Howells's youth, being spiritually lands of lost content obliterated by the ravages of war. Musically, these two works owe more to Vaughan Williams than to Stanford, effecting a compromise between sonata form and modal polyphony.

Professionally, Howells started as a cathedral organist at Salisbury. This appointment was curtailed by ill-health, so that Howells spent much of his working life as a visiting professor at the Royal College of Music and at London University. His creative affiliation remained, however, with the Anglican Church, for the liturgy of which he composed more prolifically than any of his contemporaries. His decision to become a composer who was more than a servant of the Anglican Church was prompted when, in 1910, he heard the first performance of Vaughan Williams's *Fantasia on a Theme of Tallis* at the Three Choirs Festival in his beloved Gloucester Cathedral. Howells was not, like the elder composer, a 'double man' in the sense that made the *Tallis Fantasia* not only a rediscovery of England's past but also an expression of a contemporary dichotomy, based on 'English' false relation, that had roots in the fifteenth and sixteenth centuries while being relevant to the then-present. Howells didn't follow Vaughan Williams in being a trail-blazer; he hardly could have done, while producing so much music for the Established Church in a conservative idiom based on Merbecke's anglicization of plainchant and on the unbroken tradition of Anglican services and verse anthems stretching from Tallis to Stanford. In his Service for St Paul's and his *Collegium Regale* for King's College, Cambridge both the stepwise movement of the modal lines and the syllabic declamation are shaped by the majestic prose of the English Prayer Book: so that Howells does consistently what Vaughan Williams did intermittently on his occasional forays into liturgy. But for Vaughan Williams's example, however, it is doubtful if Howells could have effected so moving a metamorphosis of churchy liturgy into terms pertinent to us without being exactly 'modern music'.

Whereas Holst embraced Gnostic mysteries in part because he was an outsider, and Vaughan Williams because his mind and senses were so sensitively aware of the physical and metaphysical potential of contemporary life, Howells needed a personal calamity to release awareness of heaven-and-hell. This occurred when, in 1936, Howells's beloved nine-year-old son unexpectedly died. The shattered musician composed in his memory a Requiem for unaccompanied voices in an idiom that refines the techniques of his everyday liturgical music to a purged austerity that is deeply affecting, and worthy of the texts that Howells assembled from the Latin Vulgate versions of the Psalms and of the Missa pro Defunctis, and in English from the 1662 Book of Common Prayer and the Salisbury plainchant diurnal, the latter perhaps in tribute to the cathedral wherein Howells had first officiated. Although Howells realized that in this requiem he had made music at a level of intensity higher than his wont, he made no attempt to promote or publish it, though he continued assiduously to revise and expand it over more than a dozen years. Although the newly expanded work was shaped by 1938, it wasn't offered to the public until 1950, when it was performed at the Three Choirs Festival as a large-scale work for soloists, double chorus, and full symphony orchestra, under the title of *Hymnus Paradisi*. In some ways the non-liturgical version of the requiem dilutes, in enlarging, the potency of the original version, since one listens to *Hymnus Paradisi* as a concert work, rather than participating in a rite. Even so, the grandeur of the large-scale choral and orchestral piece, when performed in a large building, preferably a church, is appropriate to our now largely secular society; and Howells was justified in maintaining that, although the requiem had been inspired by personal loss, the new version legitimately dealt with the 'transient griefs and indestructible hopes of mankind'. We cannot deny that the expanded version fulfils the genius of a composer always quietly distinguished, but seldom thus emotionally charged and intellectually animated.

The six-movement form borrows only the 'Requiem aeternam' and the Sanctus from the traditional requiem service, and precedes the former with an orchestral prelude that, in its chromatic introversion, leaves us in no doubt that this music, though ritualistic, is also deeply personal. For the prelude and the 'Requiem aeternam' the music equivocates between faith and doubt, joy and sorrow, as does Elgar's *Dream of Gerontius*, though Howells is more austere, less operatically emotive. The basic mode is dorian on E but the tonal meanderings are free, in intricate polyphony for double chorus and independent solo voices; and the more complex the textures, the more Howell's idiom acquires its own identity: which involves an amalgam of his three greatest immediate predecessors, Elgar, Delius, and Vaughan Williams. The repeat of the 'Reqiuem aeternam' text in a, for Howells, harshly harmonic–polyphonic explosion in effect releases us into the more personal and domestic setting of the Twenty-Third Psalm.

This opens as a soprano solo directly evoking Vaughan Williams's 'English Eden' – indeed the psalmist's descent into the valley of the shadow of death provokes music closely aligned to that made by Vaughan Williams for his death-defying Pilgrim, with enharmonics that flirt with, without precisely being in, bitonality. The simplicity of this setting, after so much polyphonic intricacy, creates an appropriate aura of idealized domesticity for this well-known text, without sacrificing the music's nobility. The tenor's final cadence, claiming that he 'lacks nothing', lands us unexpectedly in verdantly pastoral F major.

The apex to *Hymnus Paradisi* occurs in the following dual movement, fusing the traditional Sanctus with the setting of Psalm 121 in which the poet hopefully lifts his eyes to the hills. This stimulates a corybantic climax to Howells's personal apocalypse, in a radiantly six-sharped F sharp major, albeit often with mixolydian flat sevenths. The choric jubilations mell with brass fanfares while the solo entries shift the mode to dorian on F sharp, the solo voices floating up canonically while the chorus carol ever more ecstatic cries of Sanctus, culminating in a startling modulation to lydian C major, announcing the appearance of the Lord. Ultimate transcendence occurs as the Sanctus leads into the 'Pleni sunt coeli', marked 'deliberato ma elato'. It may be significant that this section, usually treated as a declension from the afflatus of the Sanctus, is here the peak of Howells's euphoria, attaining a dionysiac abandon challenging even that of Delius's *Mass of Life*. Perhaps the personal, even autobiographical, source of Howell's jubilation validates the identification of private ecstasy with holiness: a point reinforced at the close of the movement when, in a pentatonic-flavoured F sharp major, the music simmers *up* rather than down, ending – on the words 'for evermore' – oscillating between earthily pastoral F major and potentially celestial F sharp major.

Equivocation remains in the magical opening for tenor solo of the Voice from Heaven, whose chromatic alteration strangely disturbs. But chorus and semi-chorus finally offer rest to the dead, if not the living, in glowing D major, with resounding low Ds from the second basses. The last section begins with soft trumpet fanfares over a pedal note long sustained on B flat. Pentatonic polyphonies curl over the unchanging bass, gradually illuminating even death with the Holy Light of the Salisbury Diurnal. Christian sublimation, moral dubiety, and Nietzschean inebriation meet in Howells's final marriage with his three great predecessors (Elgar, Delius, and Vaughan Williams) who had refired our music at the turn into the twentieth century.

Howells was not himself, as they were, a regenerative flame; but he is here inspired to an incandescence that, in healing personal grief, leaves him free of his sources. The quiet close is in E flat major, plainly diatonic, a semitone lower than the dorian E minor the work had opened in, but a semitone higher than the sublime D major of the 'Voice from Heaven'. We may recall that, at least from the eighteenth century onwards, E flat major has been associated with human heroism and perhaps with ethical morality. Howells's small son, in this context, sounds dead, yet also blessed: which was probably the most the composer thought he could hope for. 'Religious' music needs no further justification if it makes it possible for us to survive.

22

Twilight of the Gods

Life, War, and Death in Western Civilization and in Britten's *War Requiem* (1961–2)

The work that first testified to Britten's genius, when he was still in his teens, was appropriately called *A Boy was Born*, the boy in question being Jesus Christ. The work that made Britten internationally famous, a few years later, was the *Variations on a theme of Frank Bridge* for strings: a work that, harking back to the Edwardian heyday of his teacher Frank Bridge, created a sequence of variations on Bridge's theme that placed the then-present in the context not merely of Britten's and Britain's past but also in that of Europe's past, in that the variations turn into pastiches or even parodies of European models that, over the young composer's lifetime, helped to make him what he was. The Variations were thus at once a (Mahlerian) funeral oration for the Death of Europe and a (Brittenesque) harbinger of spring's renewal. *The Winter's Tale*, Shakespeare's late, great romance of death and birth, is so called because the child Mamillius, son of a mentally sick king, remarks that 'a sad tale's best for winter; I have one of sprites and goblins': to which the comment of an Old Shepherd, later in the play, might almost be seen as a retort: 'Thou met'st with things dying, I with things new-born.' Benjamin Britten did not live, like Shakespeare's Old Shepherd, in an agrarian community but in an industrial society that had been twice racked by war; even so, 'things dying' and 'things new-born' are the prime motivation of the *War Requiem* he was commissioned to compose for the regeneration of Coventry Cathedral, destroyed in a savagely wanton air-raid. The reconsecration service took place in May 1962. I was present, and have no hesitation in saying that the occasion is among the most moving memories of my long life.

Like most artists, Britten was a man of religious sensibility though he was not formally a member of the Church of England nor even, strictly speaking, a man of faith. This makes him representative of the majority of people in our community; and since the piece was meant to be a public testament, he decided to use the still universal Roman rite of the Missa de Profundis (in Latin), set for large chorus and vocal soloists with symphony orchestra, in the manner adopted by most eighteenth- and nineteenth-century composers of large-scale works for festive occasions. But Britten's *War Requiem* could not be merely ceremonial; the appalling scale of the calamity – which in conjunction with the not distant First World War seemed to spell for many people an end to Western civilization – meant that this requiem had both a public and a private dimension. The world needed to mourn; but Britten and the individual mourners, including you and me, had to act and suffer – a dualism that Britten tackled with typical ingenuity (a word related to genius). He set the Latin text, with the weight of tradition behind it, for large chorus and large orchestra: but interspersed within this text settings of poems by Wilfred Owen, scored for soloists and a chamber orchestra such as he had employed in his chamber operas and 'church parables', conceived in intimate terms for his English Opera Group. Owen was the finest poet to have experienced and died in the First World War; his poems are obsessed not only with its horror but also with its futility, it is to the point that a mid-twentieth-century requiem should have dual dimensions, public and private, for duality is the essence of 'modern' democracy.

Britten opens with a processional Introit (which is not part of the Ordinary of the Mass), to which the celebrants enter whilst the mixed chorus, sitting, declaims in speech rhythms (rather than sings) over the orchestra's deep dominant pedal on A. For the tonality is a chromaticized D minor which, as previously noted, was traditionally an 'obscure' key deemed appropriate to life's uncertain pilgrimage. Uncertainty is also implicit in the many tritones – augmented fourths or diminished fifths – that pervade both the choral and orchestral textures: this interval being (as also previously noted) associated with the Devil since it undermines tonal coherence ('Si contra fa Diabolus est', as the medieval tag put it). Here, D minor has a long-range significance in that the ultimate consummation of the work – the duet in the battlefield's limbo between the young but dead English and German soldiers – ends in D major with lydian sharp fourths: while the very last Amen unexpectedly resolves on a triad of F major, D minor's 'relative'. At the outset, however, obscure D minor is obscurely defined, for above the orchestra's deep pedal notes the orchestra sways slowly in irregular quintuplets, the point of which will be commented on later. The section closes with the choir chanting tritones on F sharp and C natural, reinforced by tolling bells:

Softly, almost imperceptibly, the processional music is invaded by a 'distant' chorus of boys who impersonate angels, intoning the 'Te decet hymnus' in what would be modal innocence were not the mainly stepwise movement undermined by whole-tone ambiguities in enharmonic notation – an ambivalence such as we've previously noted in Herbert Howell's 'private' requiem for his nine-year-old son. 'Heaven' would seem to be Wallace Stevens's 'fictive music'; and celestial matters are rudely interrupted by the first of the solo songs with chamber orchestra, a setting of Wilfred Owen's 'Anthem for Doomed Youth', gravitating around the 'dark' key of B minor. The smaller, more soloistically conceived forces mean that the music can generate denser and tenser textures, giving vividly immediate expression to what the Holy Boys had told us about human impermanence. Owen's poem is in sonnet form, for long a medium for introspection: and the music's electrical energy makes the young men's eyes 'shine the holy glimmers of goodbyes' and transmutes the girls' 'pallor' into their 'pall'.

The postludial 'Kyrie eleison' is sung by the full chorus unaccompanied in six-part chords oscillating around the original tritone F sharp to C natural, but surprisingly subsiding onto an F major triad marked *pppp*. The extraordinary effect of this cadence fuses Britten's instinct as an operatic composer with an awareness of liturgical function. The miracle is effected by way of the neutrality of the tritone, which is perhaps the Devil's way of contributing to the divine plan. That the human and pastoral key of F major has, after all those sharpwards undulations, the last word may be Britten's way of handing the palm to us fallen human creatures:

Certainly, if the Poetry is, as Owen said, 'in the Pity', the pity is in the music, which was indubitably created by a human being, Benjamin Britten.

The visionary moment of this Kyrie is, however, brusquely displaced by the Dies Irae, the late medieval Latin poem by Thomas of Celano on which we've commented in reference to the requiems of Berlioz and Verdi. It tugs us earthwards, partly in displaying God's Wrath at us miserable offenders, partly because its portrayal of the Day of Judgment is as obstreperously physical as the Resurrection paintings of Stanley Spencer. As had become customary, Britten divides the Latin text into sections allotted to soloists and choir, and further intersperses these sections with numbers from the Wilfred Owen song-cycle with chamber orchestra. The movement opens with military fanfares an arpeggiated triads in bitonal relationships. Though the key-signature is that of earthy B flat major, the tonality is volatile, as the vocal parts stutter in staccato crotchets separated by rests, at first hushed in stupefaction, in an irregular $\frac{7}{4}$ pulse possibly recalling Holst's partiality for such lop-sided metres. With the 'Tuba mirum' tonality grows ferocious, only to be stifled by awe at the appearance of the Judge, when the vocal lines, again in $\frac{7}{4}$, parade up and down in school-masterly crotchets. The section ends in terror on telescoped triads of B flat major and G major in false relation, ushering in the second song of the Wilfred Owen cycle, prompted by the 'Tuba mirum' since the words evoke bugle-calls. Their effect is ambiguous since, although they are heroically fanfare-like, they also sound provincially domestic, like the bands the boys might have played in at school. Both the bugle-calls themselves and the chamber orchestra's triplet arpeggios (derived from the Day of Judgment music) now sound remote, even wistful, as they 'sadden the evening air' while the young men sleep by the river-side, dreaming of what's to come. The song shivers, or almost bathetically tinkles, out on the tremulous triplets, though the triad finally sustained is that of 'youthful' A major. The disparity between vernal A major and the pervasive chromaticism and enharmony attains a violent climax when the 'Liber scriptus' sets the Written Book of the Law against our hoped-for liberation from the eternal fire. The Verdian vehemence of this music reminds us that Britten's protagonists – himself, Wilfred Owen, the people in Owen's poems, and you and I – are common humanity, retrospectively including those medieval peasants who really did quake and quail at the prospect of Judgment Day. The ancient terrors are unlikely to be totally eradicated: as Britten stresses in the solo song about the great, grim gun, 'towering' to heaven and yet about to 'curse'. The public and the private realms gradually overlap until the Owen poem ('Move him into the sun') is interlaced into the choral lament, which is itself evolved from the solo song. This is a further indication of how public War has become democratically identified with private experience; and may also be why Britten's highly 'physical' Lacrimosa owes much (on Britten's admission) to the even more directly corporeal Lacrimosa in the Requiem of Verdi – a confessed agnostic. In human terms, we might think of this absorption of public into private experience as a process of *growing up*; the grandly arching vocal line is at once aspirational and fragmented:

That another, decisive, stage has been reached in the Eucharistic pilgrimage is suggested when the Dies Irae ends with a literal repeat of the six-voiced Kyrie that had closed the Introit, now on the word AMEN, again disturbingly resolving, from its hyper-sharpness, onto the humane radiance of an F major triad. The effect is even more magical than it was the first time since it emerges from the Liber Scriptus's Day of Wrath itself; and leads into another crucial shift of perspective since in the Offertorium we ask the Archangel Michael to lead us into the Holy Light as, in Judaic destiny, God had 'promised to Abraham and his seed for ever'. This is the point at which the Old Testament prophecy is supposed to be fulfilled in the New, though Britten makes it the nadir of his Requiem, following Owen in suspecting that the promise has been *betrayed*. The boy angels, sounding even more distant, intone the words in (genuine) plainchant over a chord, sustained on chamber organ, that telescopes an imperfectly devilish diminished fifth with a holy (and wholly) perfect fifth, over a C sharp pedal note that we may think of as the original C natural of the tritone C natural to F sharp 'corrected', rather than 'altered'. The sound of the drone-chord on the chamber organ weirdly suggests another dimension – poised between life and death, Old Testament and New; and it is indeed a crucial moment when, in the succeeding duet, the Old and New story of Abraham and Isaac is 'acted out'.

In the duet the baritone Father represents the Old Testament and the tenor Son the New. Here Britten adapts the music from the wonderful setting of the biblical story that he had recently made as his *Second Canticle*; and since Owen's poem on the theme, set for soloists and chamber orchestra, is incorporated into the music for big choir and orchestra, the Owen poem and the Biblical story contradict one another. Owen equates Abraham's sacrifice of his son with the war-lords' betrayal of everyone's sons; Britten musically refers back to the 'Anthem for Doomed Youth'. When the boy angels (still distantly) chant the liturgical 'Hostias et preces' there is *no* fusion of body and spirit and no metrical synchronicity between the angelic chant and the jaunty duet between baritone and tenor, which ironically jitters around the heavenly key of E major! The duet ends, however, in E minor (Bach's Crucifixion key) in sundry manifestations, including the purgatorial phrygian mode. The music vanishes in a sulphurous puff of smoke.

We've noted how, throughout the Dies Irae, the incidence of 'present moment' solo songs grew progressively more frequent in relation to the atemporal liturgy until, in the Lacrimosa, the two dimensions became one. For Britten, coincidence between private reality and public ceremony is what makes the Eucharistic offering meaningful: which is why, at the close of the terrible tale of Abraham and Isaac, an *acclamation* of holiness occurs in the threefold Sanctus. It may be significant that the acclamation is made by a woman – the soprano soloist – who declaims boldly the first and second Sanctus on F sharps in octaves, prefaced by the flat seventh below, with tolling bells on F sharp (without the tritonal C natural), haloed by tremolandos on piano and percussion. The key signature is that of B major, one step up the cycle of fifths from heavenly E, although the third cry of Sanctus, marked 'brilliant', sounds like skipping children in a round-game, bringing in Britten's habitual Eden-theme in so far as the children are pretending to be Seraphim. That bright B major triad collapses through arpeggiated triads of G and F major while the bells continue with their F sharp major clatter that reminds us that the Fall was a *felix* culpa. Holiness depends on innocence even though innocence of its nature cannot evade a Fall, since from Heaven there is nowhere to go except *down*! It's difficult to think of another composer (except Beethoven, and possibly Haydn) who so serenely evokes divine playfulness or what was sometimes called, by medieval folk, the Foolishness of God. This is an awesome moment which deters the chorus from competing with the angelic voices since the 'Pleni sunt coeli', usually set rumbustuously as man's celebration of Nature's fecundity, is here not sung at all but spoken, albeit on more or less pitched tones. In any case the graceful humility of the Pleni and the Benedictus leans towards D major, the Requiem's ultimate goal. But this is prophecy, not present reality, and the work descends to its nadir when, after the jubilation of the D major Hosanna, the next Owen poem links modern war's mechanization to the death of the spirit, musically imaged in rigorous canons *rectus et inversus*. The music rumbles out on declining tritones on double basses, from C natural to F sharp.

The Agnus Dei, always the pivot of the Eucharist, initiates potential rebirth, after the 'nadir'. Significantly, the personal Owen poem now *precedes*, and is then accompanied by, the chorus's intoning of the Latin liturgical text. The tempo is vastly slow (semiquaver = 80!) and the key-signature is that of B minor, by Beethoven called 'black', and favoured by Bach in connection with suffering and holiness. The chamber orchestra's strings remotely hum an ostinato in $\frac{5}{16}$, the bass falling in B minor from F sharp to B, then rounding back to C *natural* to climb up to G in 'white' notes, like the serpent of eternity swallowing its own tail. The ground bass thus rotates on the work's fundamental tritones of F sharp to C natural; and it remains constant while the tenor solo, moving by step like the string bass, sings the opening of Owen's poem, 'One ever hangs where shelled roads part.' Since this brief twelve-lined poem in three octosyllabic stanzas equates Christ with the slain Unknown Soldier, the personal and the universal themes are identified. When the chorus enters with the liturgical text, *ppp*, they duplicate the ground bass exactly, so there is no differentiation between the myth of the Unknown Soldier and that of Christ. In seventeenth-century music ground basses were often associated with God because they *go on* atemporally. Numerology lends further authority to holiness since the chorus chants the words 'Agnus Dei qui tollis peccata mundi' *five* times, always in $\frac{5}{16}$, and rounds off the upwards and downwards scales with godly perfect fifths. Only in the final stanza about the difference between the State's Law and that of God does the soloist respond to the human burden of the words, for now the previously hushed vocal line is marked both 'forte' and 'animated', though there is no hastening of the basic pulse and no ruffling of the stepwise movement. The chorus's ultimate clause, adding the word 'sempiternam' to 'requiem', puns on the identity between B sharp and C natural to resolve on a four-part F sharp major triad, over which the chorus at last abandons Owen's poem and commits itself to the Latin liturgy while making a small but significant change in its musical setting. For the vocal line now rises from F sharp up the scale of B minor, only to curl back from C sharp to C natural, and thence to float up the scale not of C major, but of C *minor*. We probably hear the E flats here as D sharps so that the passage becomes – like the coda to the Introit – another miracle wherein 'suffering' B minor and 'celestial' B major are mysteriously identical. The tenor's high G then sinks back to F sharp, fading *a niente*.

Britten's numerology may have conscious parallels with Bach's: for his *War Requiem* starts from those limping quintuplets in the processional Introit, and quintuplets recur throughout the work until its consummation, the Agnus Dei, is *in* $\frac{5}{16}$ time, hieratically slow yet unwavering, being the 'Mind of God' brooding 'over the waters', and bringing that which sub-sists in matter into ex-istence outside matter. This process is enacted in the tenor's final ascent that annihilates the distinction between B minor and B major. But the Requiem service, unlike the Ordinary of the Mass, does not end with the Agnus; it appends another section, the 'Libera me', which allows us to make another appeal for liberation from sin, hell, and damnation. Returning from the mystery (miracle) of the Agnus, Britten's 'Libera me' opens with a rigid march, rustling on percussion with neither melodic nor tonal identity and with little metrical definition. This vagueness suggests the spiritual no-man's land we find ourselves in, in the aftermath of war; and when the lamenting chorus creeps in snake-like, their theme undulates chromatically around itself, becoming a permutation of the serpentine Agnus Dei theme itself. And at this point the limping quintuplets, first heard in the Introit, recur to hint, in their suppressed energy, at a sundering of shackles:

Throughout a long crescendo the music is simultaneously a yell of despair at the prospect of hell-fire and also an appeal for, even a shot at, liberation. But the comfort of the resurrection seems dubiously available, as references back to the 'Liber scriptus', the tablets of the Law, are identified with multi-tudinous evils, including the mass-murders of the Wars. Yet even so, since the Fall's *culpa* turns out to be *felix*, the *liber* may hopefully be alchemized into *liber*-ation! Of course, Britten didn't believe this literally, any more than he believed in hell-fire and damnation: though he knew that modern life had equivalents for these states and recognized the psychological links between law and liberty. Britten's supreme skill here lies in his maintaining a momentum that is simultaneously negative (the orchestral march is riddled with aggressive dotted rhythms and raucous dissonances) and also positive (the introverted snake-theme unwinds into sturdier rhythms and diatonic fugato). At the words 'tremens factus' tempo accelerates as the soprano solo ascends to a high C, no holds barred. The threat of redemptionless death climaxes in 'horrendous' diminished sevenths themselves *redeemed* from cliché, while the chorus precipitately cascades in a flurry of canonic scales.

At this point, with words recapitulating the cry of 'Libera me', the music returns to thematic rotation around high G, G sharp, A flat, F sharp, and G: reminding us that throughout the work Britten's sense of human drama and divine mystery has centred on puns between the diminished third and the major second. In equal temperament the two intervals are of course identical, whereas in just intonation and in some mean-tone tunings the diminished third is slightly the larger interval. Through much of his music, and consistently in the *War Requiem*, Britten equates this technical pun with his humane equivocation between tonally compromising man and justly intoned God. The chorus joins the soprano solo in these dubieties, while the orchestra sustains an ostinato triad of G minor through which the bass line etches the quintuplet-rhythmed, sixth-and-seventh-prancing melody of the 'Anthem for Doomed Youth'. Gradually, the choral textures splinter in snatches of the undulating snake theme that derives both from the Dies Irae's chaos motif *and* from the purgatorial Agnus Dei theme, making a point at once musical, psychological, and theological. The rest of the work is devoted to the process whereby the 'tense' interval of a diminished third is translated into an 'open' major second: an aural phenomenon that, in context, creates the peace that passes understanding. This technical and spiritual consummation occurs in the last of the Wilfred Owen settings, which is the Requiem's ultimate climax.

'Strange meeting' is not only the greatest of Wilfred Owen's poems, it is also, in making 'present' the confrontation between the two young but dead soldiers, one British, the other German, by far the most dramatic, even operatic, of his verses. It may even be possible that Britten's desire and need to set this poem was the trigger that released the *War Requiem*, the greatest of Britten's non-operatic works. Given the crucial significance of this text, it must be quoted complete (here, in Britten's slightly adapted version):

TENOR SOLO

It seemed that out of battle I escaped
Down some profound dull tunnel, long since scooped
Through granites which titanic wars had groined.
Yet also there encumbered sleepers groaned,
Too fast in thought or death to be bestirred.
Then, as I probed them, one sprang up, and stared
With piteous recognition in fixed eyes,
Lifting distressful hands as if to bless.
And no guns thumped, or down the flues made moan.
'Strange friend,' I said, 'here is no cause to mourn.'

BARITONE SOLO

'None,' said the other, 'save the undone years,
The hopelessness. Whatever hope is yours,
Was my life also; I went hunting wild
After the wildest beauty in the world.

For by my glee might many men have laughed,
And of my weeping something had been left,
Which must die now. I mean the truth untold,
The pity of war, the pity war distilled.

Now men will go content with what we spoiled.
Or, discontent, boil bloody, and be spilled.
They will be swift with swiftnes of the tigress,
None will break ranks, though nations trek from progress.
Miss we the march of this retreating world
Into vain citadels that are not walled.
Then, when much blood has clogged their chariot-wheels
I would go up and wash them from sweet wells,
Even from wells we sunk too deep for war,
Even the sweetest wells that ever were.

I am the enemy you killed, my friend.
I knew you in this dark; for so you frowned
Yesterday through me as you jabbed and killed.
I parried; but my hands were loath and cold.'

TENOR AND BARITONE SOLOS
'Let us sleep now . . .'

The verse is in deccasyllabic couplets all of which are in half-rhyme. Owen was a master of this technique, here, perhaps, using it to suggest the limbo in which the protagonists meet (in lines which Britten omitted from his setting the meeting-place is called hell, but limbo is more accurate since none of Owen's poems passes judgment on the multitudinous victims of war).

Britten's musicking of the poem is, as it ought to be, the high point of his score. It's wonderfully appropriate that a triple piano chord of G minor in first inversion (not, in this limbo, in root position) should be sustained on the chamber organ, outside time in human terms, as had been the Agnus Dei's serpentine ground bass musically, philosophically, and theologically. G minor was Mozart's 'tragic' key, in which he composed some of his most profound music – the G minor string quintet and the G minor symphony, and Pamina's brief aria of redemption in *The Magic Flute*. It's even possible that Britten had Mozart consciously in mind in calling on G minor in this context – especially in relation to what is to be the work's ultimate consummation in D major. In any case the tenor solo, personifying the British soldier, begins 'slow and quiet' in speech-rhythms mostly unbarred, his theme being meditatively 'speechified' from the introverted theme of the 'libera me' and the snakey undulations of Agnus Dei's ground bass. Stepwise movement, wavering chromatically and enharmonically, is countered by 'open' perfect fifths and 'closed' diminished thirds to make incarnate the two soldiers in that 'profound dull tunnel', the reverberations of which are simulated by the verse's congested u-sounds and assonances, and by the music's quasi-echoes:

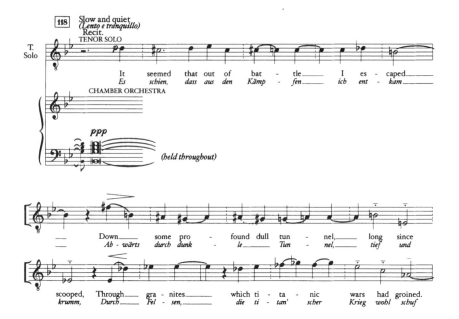

The first clause ends on C sharp, a tritone away from tonic G, recalling the opening of the Offertorium, to which universal testament the personalized Strange Meeting offers a particularized complement. But when those 'distressful hands' offer blessing, the G minor chord remains unaffected, though the strings inject fragmented dominant seventh chords on top, while orchestral basses reinsert the quintuplets leaping through sixths, hinting at new life – perhaps even physically grasping after it, without quite catching it.

Why are these disembodied dominant seventh chords, played on strings with swelling portamenti, so emotively potent? I suspect it may be because, throughout European music of the eighteenth and nineteenth centuries, the chord of the dominant seventh was intrinsic to cadences and especially to modulation, and therefore to *going on.* Here, in the limbo of the battlefield, the humanly expressive strings suggest the possibility of continuance which may also be hope – especially in contrast with the pallidly neutral tone-colour of the chamber organ that sustains the ostinato chords. Even though the dominant sevenths soon expire, they reverberate through that profound dull tunnel, hinting that it may also be the womb from which might emerge those 'things new-born'. When the dead English boy addresses the dead German he does so on the work's basic tritone of F sharp to C natural; only when the German youth answers does the ostinato organ chord shift from G minor in first inversion to a telescoping of an E flat major triad with is dominant: which irons out into a pentatonically neutral chord of D F G D, so that the distant touch of E flat major's tonal activity dissolves in limbo (I am not claiming that Britten 'thought out' these quasi-symbolic codes of

214

tonal behaviour though, given his 'cleverness', it is possible that he did; in any case, his genius lies in their happening).

Solo oboe and bassoon entwine in ghostly dialogue with the voice, recalling the serpentine undulations of the 'Libera me' and of the Agnus Dei. But when the German youth recalls the childhood in which he went 'hunting after the wildest beauty in the world', fragmented retrospects of military fanfares on wind instruments sound both heroically relevant to the Chase and martially wanton in destructiveness, possibly admitting that man is generically a hunter and that 'wild beauty' might possibly accrue from his predatoriness. That the organ's ostinato chord is very slowly mutated into 'tragic' B minor for the verse's reference to 'the pity of war' intimates that God's will involves a synthesis of positive and negative forces; and something like human passion, as well as divine mystery, flows from the vocal and orchestral enharmonies. At the reference to 'the swiftness of the tigress' (again it may not be fortuitous that the big cat is female), the ostinato chord becomes sharply dissonant while a distant military drum pounds in a dotted rhythm 'with no connection with the main tempo'. The ironic climax on the word 'progress' reintroduces metrical patterns mechanistically similar to those that followed the Hosanna, now played not on brass, but on harp and soft drum.

At the poem's reference to 'baptismal wells' Britten reminds us of the (failed) baptismal redemption in the 'mechanistic' arioso, 'After the blast of lightning'; and the baritone solo takes up the undulating ambiguities of the Agnus theme, again with the paradoxical diminished third which both is, and is not, a major second. The intrusions of obbligato instruments grow benign on harp and in violin and viola harmonics, and then in tremolandi muted for the 'wells sunk too deep for war'. The ostinato chord on organ finally returns to G minor, still in first inversion, with intermittent interjections on strings of those fragmented diminished seventh chords, *falling* through mediants from G to E to C minors, and ending in an A minor that turns out to be major – or perhaps a dominant of D major in the lydian mode. The two boy-men of different and inimical races sing the words 'Let us sleep now' in duet, the German now preceding the Englishman:

At first they sing not in plain diatonic A major but in a pre-diatonic, almost pentatonic, A rounded off by an explicit modulation to what seems to be that pristine key. It's as though they are indeed children 'new born' – a point reinforced by the entry of the chorus of angel-boys to chant the plainsong In Paradisum, moving by step in an ionian A major unsullied. Only it turns out not to be A major after all, for the chamber orchestra twines into the counterpoint, now with pedal point on a *pppp* D, making the basic tonality lydian D major, with sharp fourth. That the lydian mode was traditionally associated with healing was certainly known to Britten and he may, like Blake, have suspected that the lydian mode's therapeutic properties had something to do with its embracing the Devil's tritone within it!

There is no further modulation until the epilogic blessing and Amen, since Paradise has no before or after. This is a state to be seen only in visionary glimpses: such as Britten has as the tenor and baritone soloists lull one another into (dreamless?) pentatonic slumber, while the full chorus (with full orchestra merging into the chamber band) intone the plainchant In Paradisum in canon *rectus et inversus*, seraphically echoed by the soprano soloist, now perhaps equated with the Great Mother who is the source of creation. Joined by the boy-angels, she stresses the high E as though the major second, D to E, might be identified with paradise itself: as it momently may be, in distinction from the diminished third that has epitomized so much of the personal anguish of these two young soldiers, who momently discover peace in and out of war.

Penultimately, the caressing polyphony rests on the tritone F sharp to C natural, sustained on the chamber organ whilst the 'still distant' boy angels repeat the tritone to the words 'Requiem aeternam dona eis', as though accepting the tritonal devil as a necessary condition of sanctity. Ultimately, the full choir intones the plainchant In Paradisum in eight-part canon *rectus et inversus* (as well as *dexter et sinistra*) while the two soldier-soloists cease, without resolving, their drowsy pentatonics on D and E. We may note that this cessation, rather than ending, exactly repeats, at the same pitch, the closing bars of the adolescent Britten's first two masterpieces, the choral *A Boy was Born* and the string orchestral *Variations on a theme of Frank Bridge*. Moreover, the soprano solo, marked *mf* alone among the multiple pianissimos, declaims the invocation of the Chorus Angelorum on repeated Es. Although E major was traditionally the celestial key, here the repeated Es are part of a dominant chord of D major and at the same time a major second to the D major tonic, now literally reinforced by the angelic boys. The English tenor and German baritone also cease, but do not conclude, on an open second D to E, which can no longer be confused with a diminished third. High aloft, the soprano solo soars in an undulation that recalls her once brilliant and blissful cry of SANCTUS.

Although the two soldiers' lullaby brings them rest on their open second that could no longer be mistaken for a diminished third, there is no intimation of an 'after-life'. The stilling of enmity in human peacefulness must be its own reward; and that there can be no final answer to first and last things is confirmed when the work returns, for its close which is no conclusion, to the six-voiced unaccompanied homophony of the epilogic coda-Kyrie to the Introit. Again, the tritone is notated as B sharp to F sharp, leading, by way of its alternative punning notation as C to G flat, to the 'strange meeting' of a resolution into F major. The ultimate evidence of Britten's genius as distinct from his talent is that this third statement of a tonal miracle tells us that on the third day the human spirit, which may *be* God, 'rose again', and that this third resurrection is as startling, yet assuaging, as it was the first time at the end of the Introit, or on the second occasion at the expiration of the nightmare of the Dies Irae. Perhaps, indeed, it is *more* startling yet assuaging, given all that has happened on Britten's Eucharistic pilgrimage from the original procession into the cathedral: a *process* which may stand as an orthodox Christian testament for those who can take it on those terms but which, for those (now the majority) who cannot, may still purvey abiding truths about the human heart, mind, and spirit – or what used to be called the 'soul'. I can think of no work that more profoundly re-creates Old Testaments in New forms, thereby becoming a phoenix risen from its ashes – Coventry Cathedral being, of course, not merely a hallowed but demolished building, but also a symbol of human endurance and survival against the odds, as well as of the unknown and probably unknowable mystery called God.

Significantly, the last sounds we hear are neither a triad of 'healing' lydian D major nor the neutral tritone of C natural to F sharp from which the entire requiem seems to have emerged, but rather a triad, sustained as though 'for ever and ever', of humanely and earthily pastoral F major: a key collateral with *The Winter's Tale*'s Old Shepherd who countered the child Mamillius's 'things dying' with 'things new born'. No wonder Britten's third repeat of that magical cadence leaves us breathless. Those 'things' were Lambs – who 'taketh away the sins of the world'. And Britten's magic cadence almost persuades us that they could – while leaving us not in heavenly E major, nor even in humanly victorious D major, but in pastoral F major, on the still-nurturing earth.

217

Part V:
The Ancient Law and the
Modern Mind

23

Earth Transcendent

Fertility rites and Christian liturgy in Janáček's *Glagolitic Mass* (1926)

Part IV of this book was occupied with British traditions in religious music from the crisis of faith and doubt rooted in the Victorian age to the Second World War – specifically from Elgar's *Dream of Gerontius* of 1900 to Britten's *War Requiem* of 1962. For the book's fifth part we return to the motivations of belief that link Christian faith with pre-Christian earth-worship, first in Janáček's awesome *Glagolitic Mass*, then in Messiaen's fusion of Roman Catholic mysticism with ethnic elements from oriental cultures and from Latin America; while the last three chapters of Part V will deal with more ancient roots of Christian orthodoxy, Greek, Russian, and Byzantine: as manifest in Rachmaninov's *Vespers*, in Stravinsky's *Oedipus Rex* and *Symphony of Psalms*, and in Arvo Pärt's *Passio Domini nostri Jesu Christi secundum Joannem*.

Janáček is a good place to start from since, as one of the great originals, he is oblivious of time and place. One wouldn't expect him to be, since his work sprang from a specific locality and agrarian tradition. Spatially, he would seem to belong to a world that has vanished; temporarily, to a moment that is present but unformed. Yet somehow – which is shorthand for the alchemy of genius – the topical and local elements in Janáček's music become universal. We find his music simply extraordinary, and at the same time extraordinarily simple. This is why it makes an impact on the sophisticated and the unsophisticated alike.

As a theatre composer Janáček preserves many of the qualities of folk ritual – as we may hear in his pulsing rhythms and hypnotic reiterations, his incessantly shifting, yet grammatically unmodulating, tonality, and his ceremonially lucent scoring. Even so, the agitated fluctuations of his solo lines and the shimmering ellipses of his harmony are musical realism, acutely sensitive to the agonies and ecstasies of the individual psyche. So Janáček both reflects and recreates – as did the great Russian novelists whom he deeply admired – an old-fashioned 'organic' community: which is paradoxically inhabited by misfits! He reminds us of what communal life once was, while being responsive to the nervous stresses that make us 'modern'. We may thus respond to his earthy vigour whilst recognizing, in the mirror of his honesty, our frailty.

Born in 1854, in Moravia, Janáček acquired a late Romantic, Teutonic technique only to discard it when his identity was revealed to him. He composed almost all his characteristic music over the last twenty years of his life, and in this music looked not to the Western European civilization that his predecessors Smetana and Dvořák had yearned for, but eastwards, exploiting those elements in Moravian folk song that rely more on additive than on divisive rhythms, and more on subtleties of melodic nuance than on extended harmonic and tonal development. He is a musical 'natural' in that each phrase is a bodily gesture, which of course carries psychological implications. Janáček's humane optimism is evident in his first masterpiece, *Jenůfa* (1894–1903), for although village folk cruelly threaten one another in this opera, there is sufficient harmony between man and nature to make for a convincing happy ending; and although the later *Katya Kabanova* (1921) has a tragic denouement because small-town small-mindedness destroys reciprocity between humankind and the instinctual springs of life, the heroine's death is a casualty that doesn't carry the community with it. A 'real' folk artist doesn't expatiate on the seasonal processes of the year as a vindication of his humanity; he accepts the world he lives in because it never occurs to him that he has a choice. But Janáček, in *The Cunning Little Vixen* (1924), deliberately gives Nature priority over man, admitting that we must in part surrender 'consciousness' if we are to learn to live with it or in despite of it. In his next opera, *The Makropoulos Case* (1926), Janáček deals with the same theme from the human angle; based on a play of Karel Čapek, the story is set at the turn of the century, in a decaying provincial community. Against a backcloth of century-old litigation, we learn that human passions necessitate a finite context; if one lived for ever – or merely, like this heroine, for 300 years – all experience must seem equally illusory. The heroine's great monologue in the last act is a death-wish that is also an affirmation of human life; and one can say as much of the confessional utterances of the prisoners in Janáček final opera, based on Dostoevsky's *From The House of the Dead* (1928), since they too, singing of defeat and death, paradoxically reassert human resilience.

Although Janáček's approach to his art was – even when he composed string quartets – humanistic and therefore dramatic and potentially operatic, and although he adhered to no religious creed, he was reared in the countryside near Brno, singing not only folk songs on the village green, but also liturgical music in the village church. Moreover, he was educated in a monastery school wherein his musical precocity involved him in the performance, and to a degree in the creation, of music for worship. Between the ages of seventeen and twenty-one he composed short introits and motets in a style encouraged by the Cecilian Reform musician, Josef Forster, the aim of the Cecilians being to re-establish a liturgical tradition rooted in the golden years of the Renaissance. Palestrina, Lassus, and Victoria were revered models; and although Janáček didn't find either the monastery or its music particularly congenial, Forster's desire to 'purify the dialect of the tribe' offered a launching-pad pertinent to Janáček's first creative stirrings. In being brief, plain diatonic, and in the tradition of plainchant (albeit mainly homophonic or in primitive canon), these pieces instil in us a sense of open-eared wonder, with dew on the grass: in which sense they are prophetic of grown-up Janáček.

There is not, however, much connection between these juvenile efforts and the *Glagolitic Mass* which, written in 1926, two years before the composer's death, was the apex to Janáček's work in the non-operatic field. Unlike the operas, it is not specifically concerned with sin, guilt, and conscience and is non-mystical, possibly even non-Christian, albeit written in an ancient Czech language to a text that echoes the Ordinary of the Roman Mass. The work opens with a purely instrumental introduction that suggests performance in the open air. Timpani roll and brass blare primitively pentatonic fanfares based on fifth, fourth, and pentatonic minor third, in celebration of the majesty of God – though the key is E flat major, associated over the last two to three hundred years with the heroism of *man*. Although the modality doesn't 'modulate' in grammatical progression, it shifts between mediants and between keys centred a tone apart. Phrases – more accurately described as 'gestures', such as might be used by characters in a drama – sometimes introduce massively scored but grammatically unrelated concords as support for the reiterated pentatonics:

and although there is no harmonic progression in the 'academic' sense the shifting modal centres elevate the tonality by a semitone to 'heavenly' E major, just at the time when the procession enters the church.

The first section of the Mass, the Kyrie, borrows thematic material from the Introduction; presumably the fanfaring brass instruments, having processed with the timpani into church to join the rest of the orchestra, now fulfil normal orchestral roles, though their phrases continue to resemble corporeal gestures. A 'speaking' motif, first heard on cellos through sustained trombone chords, makes bodily actions almost vocally communicative, here in deathly A flat minor – though there is no darkly seven-flatted key-signature since Janáček doesn't use them, presumably because his tonal shiftings, rather than formal modulations, are so volatile. The sustained chords, and the trills with which they are garlanded, suggest the eternity of Nature within which we human creatures struggle to speak. Our first appeal to God, asking for his 'mercy', is uttered softly over an A major triad in first inversion, but immediately slithers to A flat. Although the persistent pentatonics sound pristine, the fluid enharmony of the modality undermines assurance. When the soprano solo takes over she too veers between E major and A flat major, giving vigourous identity to our appeal while the orchestra, also enharmonically notated, doubles the vocal line and appends a 'spread' rising arpeggio that looks in score, and maybe sounds to our ears, like hands raised in prayer. The chorus supports her with rootless whole-tone chords, yelled minatorily as though (like Verdi, only with more direct belligerency) we are trying to bully God into assent. The section is at once highly theatrical (operatic) and at the same time ritualistic, because the chorus is a 'crowd' taking action, hoping to affect events. The chorus chant their cry in what might be pentatonic E major; the orchestra passionately reiterates the spread arpeggio through sustained trombones; and the Kyrie ends with the initial cello 'speaking gesture' now a semitone lower but sliding back to E major with sharp 'lydian' fourths. The lydian mode, especially in peasant communities, often had associations with healing, which may bear on the 'message' the chorus has been trying to communicate. The sharp fourths are sustained in the E major chord, left to fade *a niente*.

Against this tragic–pathetic fade-out the Gloria ('Slava' in the ancient Czech language) is a pantheistic shout of joy in a surging $\frac{9}{4}$. Initially, the unambiguous pentatonic tune is sung by soprano solo, offering glory to God and to men of good will. The key begins as heroic E flat major, the tune being introduced and supported by bell-like tollings of E flats alternating with fifths of D flat and A flat. The soprano tune is doubled by clarinet which also introduces cross-rhythms (4 in the time of 3), such as seem to be endemic to the Moravian language. Mediant transitions from E flat to G flat, and then from F sharp ('standing for' G flat) to D natural, complicate the textures and transform the blithe rising fourths into slightly more urgent sixths and *diminished* fourths. The exuberance in which the movement had opened is further exacerbated by dizzy triplets and even stained by chromatics; enharmony grows freer and the orchestrally reiterated quavers surrender their synchronicity. Momently, the chorus is silenced and the orchestral quavers chase one another in two-part canon. Their helter-skelter turns, however, into homophonic affirmations of praise and blessing, somewhere between 'heroic' E flat major and 'deathly' A flat minor.

In Janáček's works praise and blessing generate something like frenzy, as well as jubilation: the cross-rhythms of fours against threes, the chromatic intrusions within pentatonics, and the rapid teeterings between tonal centres are all prompted by the text's reference to the 'sins of the world' which *we* are responsible for, and which cannot be effaced by Nature's mindless trilling. Pleading for mercy, the chorus becomes a dichotomous community aiming at 'togetherness', yelling their declining cries in parallel thirds in canon, doubled by orchestral voices yet countered by the fours against the triple pulse. The soloists, high in register, add a new edge to the babble, and although the music finds its way home to E flat major over a tonic pedal, that key is no abiding sanctuary. The Amens, beginning in a chromatically oscillating allegro in $\frac{6}{4}$, quickens to presto in $\frac{4}{4}$ before unexpectedly shifting to savagely barked chords of celestial (!) E major over clumping fourths on timpani. Whether this is a victory for man or for God or a bemusement for both is unclear, though we have no doubt about Janáček's perpetual renewed and renewing energy. This Gloria pays homage to Almighty God simply in asserting the life-force.

The Credo offers, as one might expect, the most overtly operatic music, since the words are a tremulously hopeful confession of, or yearning for, belief. The first sounds are the trills of Nature's going-on-ness – on D flat, which is Janáček's key of love! Through the trills, cellos and clarinets 'speak' little phrases that are, of course, wordless. Enharmonically notated, they are at first pervaded by whole-tones, though when the pedal note inches up from D flat to E flat the music trembles on the verge of knowledge, hopefully professing belief (CREDO) on a chord of the thirteenth:

The chorus 'lists' the objects of their belief, reinforced by Amens from the soloists, while intermittently the yearning, rather than affirmatory, chord of the thirteenth recurs, growing louder and more animated. The words tell us how the Holy Spirit 'came down' from heaven in the human form of Christ, the tenor solo declaiming through whole-tone or diminished-third trills that provide a context of 'Nature'. Gradually, however, the Credos on the chord of the thirteenth decrease in energy, finally fading from *p* to *ppp*, as credence falters.

The next section, dispensing with words, tells the gospel story in orchestral music that, being self-subsistent, becomes itself theatre. The opening depicts – through rising fourth to fifth and tritonal spread chords – Christ in the Garden, his destiny being *obscurely evident* (a telling contradiction) in the enharmony. Obscurity momentarily clarifies when processional music swaying in $^6_4$ portrays Christ carrying his Cross, the key being a lucid C major and the bass in an unflagging ostinato rhythm. Gradually, however, the obsessive syncopated figure (crotchet, dotted crotchet, quaver) grows unstable while whole-tone trills induce panic rather than awareness of Nature's munificence. Christ is crucified to extraordinary, fragmentarily chromatic music on harsh-registered organ, speeding from a furious allegro to a ferocious presto. At the scary climax the chorus return to shout in four homophonic parts and in deathly A flat minor while the orchestra, in a weird passage over A flat minor timpani, teeters between triads of (hellish?) A flat minor and (heavenly?) E major. The section – almost a movement – that follows enacts the resurrection on the third day, not by way of any levitating angels but by alchemizing infernal A flat minor into celestial E major. Yet, at the precise moment when a dominant seventh of E major is about to resolve on to its tonic, the bass changes enharmonically from B natural to C flat, leading into a return of the almost-forgotten chord of the thirteenth as heard at the Credo's opening. The chorus's citation of what they (hope to) believe in, in the original fragmented phrases, is still affiliated to A flat minor though the orchestra loudly subsides therefrom to a dominant of C, followed by an empty – yet fraught – bar of $^2_4$ marked with a G.P.

This silence launches the final section of the Credo which, for the first time, flows in long-fast-surging paragraphs, with rising C major arpeggios with added sharp fourths, boosting the choir's now grand affirmation by way of a German sixth within C major:

With the rising arpeggios moving between A, G, and D flat, the tenor solo, high in register, even proclaims belief in the Catholic and Apostolic Church: though there's a degree of desperation in the music's undermining of tonal security. Looking for the resurrection of the dead, the chorus reinstate *human* E flat major, hinting at the triple-rhythmed sway of the Gloria. The 'life of the world to come' enters in C major with German sixth, flowing through F sharp major and E major, to lead into Amens on an E flat major motif very close to the Gloria; and although the last pages shilly-shally

between 'human' E flat and 'heavenly' E major, it's the humanly lower key
that wins through. The final swinging motif is thrillingly reinforced by
organ, breaking off abruptly and echoing into silence in a way that recalls
Bruckner: who also told our redemptive story in the context of an eternal
silence.

The Sanctus, evoking the Holiest of Holies, opens gently in E major, in
a moderate $\frac{2}{4}$ pulse, with melodic violins, harp and celesta over pedal Bs on
cellos and basses. Heaven, however, proves elusive, for the keys and pedal
notes are repeatedly in flux, especially after the soloists have entered on
cries of 'Sanctus', falling through sixths or sevenths, usually from a lofty
note. When the bass solo enters, the pedal note is inverted to high B flats
on flutes; and an inverted pedal on piccolo even shapes a full E major
triad above rocking quavers during the 'Pleni sunt coeli', though tonality
vacillates in less than total assurance. The Hosanna enhances jubilation
with a medley of straight crotchets and quavers with triplets of both, as
the soloists recapitulate their praises from high notes, glinting and glowing
in E major, but stopping in mid-stream in F major – undeniably a tone
higher than E flat major and a semitone higher than E major, the keys
that have dominated, earthily or celestially, the previous movements.
Janáček, a man of the earth, doesn't feel the slight mistrust of the 'worldly'
Pleni and Hosanna that most nineteenth-century religious composers
harboured.

We've noted that the Agnus Dei is the crucial point of the Eucharistic
rite. It is the apex of Janáček's Mass too, and it is probably not fortuitous
that its 'misereres' startlingly recall, and its orchestral postlude directly
quotes, the closing bars of Act II of *Katya Kabanova*, Janáček's most
uncompromisingly tragic, and probably greatest, opera. The Agnus opens
adagio, with muted trombones oscillating between triads of G minor and
B flat major, beneath desolate chromatic undulations on violins and flutes.
The chorus sing homophonically in $\frac{6}{4}$, vacillating between what might be
dark E flat minor and light E major. The orchestra repeats its prelude a
semitone higher, followed by the chorus's reiteration of its original phrase
now veering between E flat minor and F major. A further repetition slides
from D flat minor into an 'enhanced dominant' of E flat: in which key the
soloists personalize their pleas, now syncopated slightly off-beat. Persistent
enharmony means that there is no clearly defined tonality until the 'middle
section' returns to the original theme at the original adagio tempo; the
orchestra now oscillates between D flat minor and F flat (equals E) major.
In the orchestral postlude the weirdly scored bitonal undulations between
major and minor third convey the same longing for peace as do Katya's
heaven-aspiring flutes and violins, by precisely the same technical means,
coming to rest on a remote, infinitely tender triad of A flat *major*:

The music tells us that both Katya and we, the human race, yearn for something more than the mere cessation of pain.

Whatever it is we long for is brutally swept away by the thunderous Organ Solo, which is an even savager re-animation of the Crucifixion music (also played on organ) in the Credo. Ironically, the Organ Solo opens on the pedals in lydian *E major*, with the manuals in furious cross-rhythms with the pedals' ostinato. Gradually the ostinato is transferred to treble register in a chromaticized A flat minor, with the manuals' syncopated motif also in A flat minor: so any Dream of Heaven is ruthlessly obliterated by the stark fact of death. Moreover, tempo inexorably speeds up as texture splinters into frantic exchanges between two-part canons in quavers and massive chords in minims, frozen across the bar-lines. Contrarieties between fours and threes and enharmonic puns between A flat minor and E major sweep us alarmingly into a presto, and then a prestissimo, with the pedals bellowing the ostinato bass in deathly A flat minor, the tonic chord being oddly approached by a dominant seventh of F. The ultimate immensely loud tonic triad of A flat minor seems – especially in contrast with the A flat major triad that ends the Agnus Dei – as black as death:

The tremendous impact of Janáček's *Glagolitic Mass* springs, of course, from the fiery impetuosity of his genius: though it also owes something to his direct relationship to an agrarian community – such as Holst and Vaughan Williams, in industrialized London, could have only in imaginative retro-spect. This is spelt out at the end of Janáček's Mass in a post-ludial procession that balances the Intrada. The Agnus Dei's moment of visionary pathos had seemed to be obliterated by that terrifying Organ Solo; yet the final processional movement, as the congregation 'proceeds' out of the church, makes a virtue out of 'the fury and the mire of human veins'. For although the processional music is far from peaceful, it is positive in effect as the marching $\frac{3}{2}$ pulse drives onwards in cross-accented quavers, initially in C major over timpani on C and G. The thematic substance consists of the preludial pentatonic fanfares on brass, now sounding a tone lower, and then a tone lower again, in B flat and A flat. Cross- and counter-rhythms run riot until the final cadence, three times repeated, consists of an F flat major triad (identical with E major) in first inversion, followed by an A flat *major* triad with dissonantly semitonic appoggiatura. The silences between the triads are indeed 'pregnant'; we recall the infinitely pathetic A flat major triad after the tragic death of Katya Kabanova. In the Mass, the death commemorated is that of Christ and of all of us; and Janáček, having capped the visionary cadence with his spine-chilling Organ Solo, can likewise cap *that* with the pentatonic procession out of the church, into the sun, the rain, the wind, and the earth which is our temporal home. No composer believed more unequivocally in life, however dubious he may have been about man's morality, God's goodness, and the inequities and obliquities of fate.

24

Un saint sensuel *and 'Le Jongleur de Notre Dame'*

Messiaen's *Quatuor pour la fin du temps* (1940), *Cinq Rechants* (1948), and *Chronochromie* (1960): Poulenc's *Gloria* for soprano solo, chorus, and orchestra (1959)

It is to the point that although Messiaen was a man of the Old Faith and an heir to one of the oldest of European cultures, his religious roots stretch tentacularly beneath Christian traditions. For Christianity, in becoming the hub on which Europe revolved, also became the religion of 'Faustian' man: the pioneer–pilgrim who, as traced in previous chapters, was a Protestant who protested on behalf of individual conscience, as against the idolatry of frozen creeds. So many of the central conventions of European music (such as sonata and symphony) are aural incarnations of this Western pilgrimage – a concept that barely touched Messiaen who, rather than asserting ego and will, sought release from them at a primitively physiological, rather than theological, level. From his earliest creative days he tried to free the sensory moment from before and after, even more comprehensively than did Debussy himself. In the earliest of his works to be accepted as a masterpiece – *Le Banquet Céleste*, for organ – the movement of the chromatic chords is so slow as to seem almost stationary, while the chords themselves are so engulfed in 'added' notes as to have virtually no defined identity. Similarly, the relationships between the chords are as disturbingly without harmonic direction as are the comparable passages in the 'Rose Croix' works of Erik Satie, such as the *Messe des Pauvres* which Varèse described as being, in its lack of connections, like hell. Satie's Rose Croix pieces, written in the 1890s, are indeed 'poor man's masses' in that they offer numinous experience pre-existent to or independent of faith; and although Messiaen seems never to have lacked that faith, it was probably, in his early days, almost pre-conscious. This could even be true of a major work of his early maturity, the piano suite *Vingt Regards sur l'Enfant Jésus*, in that each 'peep' at the Holy Child is without momentum, being based on an alternation of two or three chords, an ostinato, a pedal point, or a reiterated figure. This is an expansion of the static techniques explored in tiny works of Satie and in the 'spatial' aspects of Debussy's music. Messiaen's music thus evades concepts of beginning, middle, and end, denying Europe's time-sense; we may validly describe much of Debussy's music, most of Satie's early music, and all of Messiaen's music as 'mystical' in the dictionary sense, in that it is not only 'mysterious, occult, and awe-inspiring' but also seeks 'by contemplation and self-surrender to obtain union with or absorption into the deity'.

Messiaen plumbs depths below the surface of New Testament theology, for his rampant cult of Mariolatry, like that of the medieval troubadours, views the Eternal Beloved as at once the Virgin Mary and as a pre-Christian Earth Goddess redeemed. For the heretical Gnostics Jesus was a Holy Spirit (which was female in Hebrew) who 'moved on the face of the waters', while Mary – the name of the mother in whom Christ was made flesh – means 'of the sea'. It seems that Messiaen's Virgin Mary was not far removed from Aphrodite, the 'wise one of the sea'. A return to the unconscious waters is thus latent in Messiaen's Christianity, so it's unsurprising that, in uncovering the remotely mythological roots of his religion, he should metamorphose Christian chastity into fecundity, in a riot of ornament more oriental than occidental and in a harmonic luxuriance that may attain ecstatic sensuality.

Not only does Messiaen call on Eastern melismatic decoration, he also employs Indian *rāga* and *tāla* in both pure and adapted forms. Sometimes his chord-formations are 'vertical' arrangements of a traditional or invented *rāg*; sometimes, complementarily, linear motives may be a 'horizontalized' version of a 'mystic chord' – a procedure analogous to that of Scriabin, a still more esoteric musical theosophist who, in depriving sensual harmonies of progression, aimed to effect a Mystery embracing all accredited and a few previously inarticulated creeds and dogmas. When ultimately performed in a hemispherical temple in India this Mystery was to induce in its participants a 'supreme final ecstasy', after which the plane of consciousness would dissolve away, to be succeeded by a world cataclysm and, presumably, total cessation. It is not surprising that, in the apocalyptic era we have lived through, Scriabin has again become fashionable.

Messiaen, belonging to an orthodox Roman Church however unconventionally interpreted, is not thus atomically literal. Even so, the work that sums up the first phase of his creative life was written in a prison camp in

1940, the year in which a world cataclysm was undoubtedly unleashed; and the *Quatuor pour le fin du temps* for clarinet, violin, cello, and piano – the scoring being dependent on the musicians available in the camp – directly relates Messiaen's prison experience to the Christian Apocalypse as recounted in the Revelation of St John. Seven magic movements parallel the six days of creation and the seventh day of rest, while an eighth movement wings us from time into eternity. The brief first movement, 'Liturgie de cristal', is preludial: its birds, chittering at dawn, are annunciatory, heralding the book of Revelation's 'mighty angel' with a face like the sun and a rainbow round his head. At first the Angel appears in awe-ful majesty, but sings his 'vocalise' in plainchant-like incantation divided between violin and cello, accompanied by what Messiaen calls, in accord with his hermetical sound-colour chart, 'blue orange' chords and carillons on piano, resonating atemporally:

The end of time, and of consciousness, is prophesied, though the consummation is not yet.

Prophecy does, however, release the bird of the spirit who sings alone, impersonated by solo clarinet from the 'abyss' of time itself. Monody and Spirit are here identified in bird-music that mates Messiaen's Catholicism with his Pan-theistic awareness of Nature as a non-human reality. The bird-cantillation employs not only *rāga* and *tāla* formations in 'pre-ordained' additive rhythms, but also microtonal pitches that don't occur in 'Western' contexts. All birds sing microtonally, and Messiaen's birds are at once Nature's voice and God's. The two voices are not identical though both mirror man's desire for a heaven or haven 'beyond' consciousness.

But this liberation of the voice of the bird cannot be an end for Messiaen, who had Europe's human past behind him. The next movement offers an odd, even slightly debunking, instance of this, for the brief, scherzoid piece *opposes* the bird to the abyss it had sung from, since the abyss is now manifest not in supernatural wonders but in the trivial round of our lives. The dancing music combines charm and grace with a faintly comic pathos; it sounds very French, at times almost café-orientated, with a final dominant-tonic cadence that might, in context, erroneously be taken as irony:

*) *Ce glissando prend toute la valeur des "Si" croche et noire.*

There is even a hint of Poulenc who – as we'll see – is far from being Messiaen's polar opposite. But if this represents our human frailty, it leads – perhaps logically if not commonsensically – into the Christian heart of the work: for the Word become Flesh is audible in an 'endless' cantilena, marked 'infiniment lent', for solo cello, accompanied by the piano's slowly pulsing chords in an isochronous rhythmic pattern that goes nowhere, being pre-ordained in a medieval and perhaps oriental sense. Although the chords are richly chromatic and humanely sensuous, Christ's cello melody spirals over and through them, so that through him our (harmonic) sensuality, pain, and consciousness of mortality may be (melodically) assuaged. This happens as the tones of the melody grow gradually more sustained, the pulse slower and slower.

Only after this Incarnation may the seven trumpets of the apocalypse blazon forth. They are entirely monodic since the divine voice, whether represented by bird-song or by God Himself, cannot admit the intrusion of duality, and therefore of harmony. Played by a melody instrument, usually doubled by the piano in octaves, they resound in a non-retrogradable metre, rotating in an eternal circle. When the Angel of the Apocalypse effects the destruction of Time in the seventh movement, the mating of Word and Flesh is consummated. This is a long movement – the destruction of Time takes time – wherein melismatic arabesques are absorbed into sensuous piano harmonies and jazzily corporeal rhythms. But this climacteric movement is not as long as the Epilogue after Time has been abolished: an epilogue which, indeed, ought to be end*less*. Although this is not feasible, Messiaen works a miracle in making music that, moving in time as all music must, *seems* to efface it. Scored for violin and piano in the traditionally paradisal key of E major, it has a pulse so slow as to seem immobile. The 'endless' violin melody floats higher and higher until, with quasi-oriental melismata, it fades into the stellar spaces, barely audible as well as pulseless, while the piano still *only just* pulsates, senses suspended on a chord of the added sixth:

That this Debussyan chord – which had been prophetically anticipated five to six centuries back in the work of a Renaissance composer such as Cornyshe – also became a cliché of twentieth-century cocktail-lounge jazz hints at how eroticism may, at a variety of levels, be a gateway to paradise!

Messiaen's wondrous *Quatuor* lives in equilibrium between the human and the divine, or at least the other-than-human: as does most of his later music in which organization grows less harmonically and tonally European, more dependent on magical–oriental kinds of serialism both linear and metrical. By the time of *Cinq Rechants* – another masterpiece, written in 1948 for twelve unaccompanied voices – Messiaen has created what he calls a 'chant d'amour' that is simultaneously physical (sexual) and metaphysical. It has two musical sources: the Harawi, a love-song from the pagan folk-lore of Equador and Peru; and the medieval alba or dawn song that warns lovers of the approach of day. Presumably a warning is necessary since troubadour lovers were usually illicit, though this doesn't make any difference to the visionary (and Christian?) implications of Messiaen's sexuality. The text, by Messiaen himself, is partly in surrealistic French springing from beneath those unconscious waters, and partly in an invented pseudo-Hindu language that dissolves meaning into musical sounds, often mutated into cries of insects, birds, and beasts. References to legendary but human lovers such as Tristan and Isolde, Vivian and Merlin, Orpheus and Eurydice surface alongside specifically contemporary references – for instance to the flying lovers in the paintings of Chagall. Although the movement of the note-values is usually rapid, the structures are non-evolutionary and often circular, the harmony non-progressive. In particular the tritone – that 'devil' of the Middle Ages – becomes not so much satanic as neutral in its lack of commitment; and thus at least potentially a stepping-stone *between* disparate worlds. There's an interesting parallel, in this sense, between Messiaen's tritones and those that pervade the Epilogue to the Sixth Symphony of a very different composer, the 'Christian agnostic', Ralph Vaughan Williams.

If the forms of *Cinq Rechants* have little relation to post-Renaissance tonal development, they have close affinities with medieval variation techniques and with oriental serial permutation. The title, 'Rechant', is in fact borrowed from the French *Renaissance* composer Claude le Jeune, who experimented with numerical proportions derived from verbal inflexions. In a literal sense, 'in the beginning was the Word'; and after a free monodic incantation in the invented language, the first *rechant* introduces the legendary lovers either monophonically, with wildly whirling leaps controlled by the (pre-ordained) Indian *decitala* pattern of $\frac{2+2+2+3}{16}$, alternating with $\frac{2}{8}$; or in brutal, somewhat Stravinskian homophony in which several chords are telescoped in a timeless moment.

Interspersing permutations of these brief motifs are more extended lyrical 'couplets' in two- or three-part polyphony – these being a formal device derived from late Renaissance and early baroque French music, perhaps even stretching as far forward as the rondeau 'couplets' of François Couperin. The prevalence of thirds and caressing passing-notes imbues the quasi-medieval linearity with a tender voluptuousness appropriate to the words of this section, which describe the crystal bubbles in which Hieronymus Bosch enclosed his lovers. Whereas Bosch, medievally biassed, saw the dawn of the humanly orientated Renaissance as a nightmare, Messiaen, at the twilight of the Renaissance, reverses the process, relinquishing tonal perspective analogous to the visual perspective that Bosch was at once aware and scared of. Antecedence and consequence dissolve into discontinuous time and space.

Each of the five *rechants* is structured on the same principle: an introductory invocation; the *rechant*, derived from the refrain of troubadour song and alternating with rondeau-style couplets; and a coda that returns to the invocation. Form is thus circular, so there is no climax within the individual movements, though the central (third) rechant makes an apex to the whole work. It begins not in monody, but with an undulating tritonal cantilena accompanied by wordless, sensuously static chords. From this sensuality it attains a climax of magical impersonality since the three verses are in reversible metre, augmentation being balanced by diminution of the note-durations. In the third verse the effect is, in Messiaen's words, 'intensified by a long crescendo which unfurls like a veil of sound in twelve-part canon', with each entry occurring a tone lower than the previous entry: a 'collective cry that falls back into a soft, supple, and tender coda'. This astonishing passage amounts to a vivid aural image of the act of coition and its tranquil aftermath; could it even be that the benignly saintly Messiaen was permitting himself, in his use of the technical term 'couplet', a saintly sexual innuendo? Certainly the riot of neutral, not devilish, tritones in the passage admits to a Blakean 'reconciliation of opposites'.

The basic theme of the fourth rechant *starts* from the medieval *mi contra fa* that 'stands for' the *diabolus*: and the love-ululations of the couplets are in tritonal organum! This bears on Messiaen's crucial place in the story of Europe's music. The tritones that Wagner's Tristan yearns to be released from have become, in Messiaen, a monodic positive as the Flesh becomes

Word, to complement the Word's becoming Flesh. Tristan no longer needs to die in order to metamorphose flesh into spirit. Debussy, in depriving Wagnerian harmony of even the desire for resolution, had shown the way to a musical apotheosis of the flesh; Messiaen completes the process in alchemizing harmonic tension into unaccompanied melodic line. The work ends with the tickings and clickings of animate creatures, into which the voices insinuate, *bouche fermée*, the magical vocable 'UM' from which creation emerged, here sounding on unison D flats dissolving into the neutral tritone, A flat to D natural.

It would be difficult to imagine a more complete reversal of the will-domination of post-Renaissance Europe than the *Turangalîla-Symphonie* that forms the second panel of the 'triptyque of love and death' of which *Cinq Rechants* was the first. In *Turangalîla* – still probably Messiaen's best known and most notorious piece – the fast sections are allied to the new–old primitivism of jazz in the hypnotic repetitiousness of their riffs and in the blatantly scored opulence of their harmonies. However fast, they are as time-obliterating as are the vast slow movements that evoke the sensual haven of a Garden of Love wherein the birds – represented by a gamelan of piano, vibraphone, celesta, and Ondes Martenot – ecstatically twitter, both tonally and rhythmically independent of the near-static string homophony. Such a pantheistic identification of man, God, and nature increasingly pervades Messiaen's music, beginning with *Reveil des oiseaux* which, in 1953, inaugurated a series of works based on bird-song. The writing tends, as in *Cinq Rechants*, to be monophonic or heterophonic in principle, even when the strings are divided into thirty-two parts! The fascinating sonorities are an ultimate expression of Debussy's desire to 'reproduce the mysterious accord between nature and the human imagination'. Of the sensitivity of Messiaen's imagination and of the uncanny acuteness of his ear there can be no doubt: though there are moments in the immense *Catalogue d'Oiseaux* when one wonders whether Messiaen hasn't carried 'l'atrophie du moi' a shade too far. Birds may be angel voices that have something we have lost; none the less one remains dubious about Debussy's statement that there is more to be gained by watching the sun rise than by listening to the *Pastoral Symphony*, since sunrises, like birds, have never lost something a human composer had because they never had it to lose. In fact, birds chirrup microtonally, too fast and too high to be humanly comprehensible, though nowadays they may be trapped on tape. Yet we still cannot know what they are 'saying' in their songs, and may suspect that their territorial messages are far from benign. None of this, of course, validates Messiaen's stylizations of their songs in relation to his mysticism or even, by inference, to his theology.

This becomes evident in another Messiaen masterpiece, *Chronochromie* for large orchestra, written in 1960. One of those rare pieces that make history, *Chronochromie* consummates Messiaen's retreat from humanism into magic, for its structure is based not on human awareness of progression in time, but on metrical proportions inherent in nature, at once pre-ordained and permutatory. In this Messiaen owes something to Edgard Varèse, the French disciple of Debussy who in 1916 became an American citizen and, living in New York, composed over the 1920s a series of works that rejected harmonic progression in favour of structural principles derived from nature, such as crystal and rock formation and the intricate, mysteriously unique, symmetries of snow-flakes. For Varèse, nature's law merged into the sciences of architecture and engineering, in which he had been trained: so that his monolithic music paid simultaneous tribute to the nature he youthfully loved and studied in his native France, and to the machine culture of New York where he found his second home. Messiaen was never tempted to effect this tie-up between nature and the machine – even a 'human machine', which is the term Stravinsky used to describe his music. Even so, Messiaen did see and hear nature as a cosmos overriding human subjectivity. The ego and the ticking of Time's clock were alike extraneous to this concept, and the melodic substance, derived from the stylized and categorized imitation of specific birds, has no more need of 'development' than have the blithe avians themselves. *Chronochromie*'s astonishing and, indeed, alarming dawn-chorus for a plethora of solo instruments is a climax only in its attaining a maximum of heterophonic freedom. Hermes was a winged messenger, Papageno a feathered child of Nature, and Messiaen's birds are flying angels free of humanly imposed restraints such as tonality, periodic metre, conventionalized harmonic progressions and even timbres. They are manifestations of the flux and possibly of the female principle, as are the waterfall images recurrent throughout the score.

The return to nature as an escape from human turmoil has a long history in European music, a least since the advent of romanticism. The birds in classical baroque music – especially in Couperin and Rameau – tend to be man-made artefacts, humanly contrived while reminding us of pre-human life-styles; but the bird that warbles in Wagner's *Siegfried* from the depths of the dark forest is an other, non-human presence, as are the birds and beasts in the musics of Debussy, Ravel, Delius, and Sibelius, and in the forest-musics of Janáček and Bartók, dizzy with buzzing insects, babbling birds, and barking or braying beasts. In all these nature's otherness is seen or heard as distinct from the human. The fragmented cor anglais phrase that meanders through Debussy's *Nuages* suggests man's disconsolate littleness against the vast and timeless panorama of the natural world. Apart from Varèse and Janáček, Messiaen is the first composer to reassert human validity not in juxtaposition with, or in opposition to, but as part of, the 'eternal' principles of Nature. More than any composer he exhibits man's weariness with a literate, will-dominated, patriarchal culture, and his desire to rediscover a 'matriarchy' that worships the White Goddess and the Terrible Mothers.

It is not fortuitous that Messiaen's sequence of 'anacrouse-accent-désinence', potently manifest in *Chronochromie*, parallels the lunar calendar, nor that the processes of metrical and intervallic metamorphosis that he brought to fruition in *Chronochromie* have affinities with the techniques of medieval alchemy. That alchemy has again become a respectable subject, explored in its psychological connotations by Jung, is part of our age's rediscovery of the irrational, our consciousness of the unconscious. Varèse referred to Debussy as 'a fantastic chemist', and detected alchemical analogies in the *Messe des Pauvres* of Satie, and in his own music. In the same sense Messiaen was a sound-alchemist, obsessed with the 'material' of sound itself; with the possibility of *changing* sound-matter by understanding its laws; and ultimately with the possibility of man himself being alchemically reborn. Messiaen was not embarrassed to talk in such grandly metaphysical terms, though he knew that opening oneself to chthonic forces may be perilous, since evil may be released along with, or instead of, good, as happened in Nazi Germany. But Messiaen was justified in believing that, buttressed by his faith, he was strong enough to make white magic. The strophic and anti-strophic structure of *Chronochromie* is genuinely analogous to Greek tragedy, and the work achieves a genuinely Greek catharsis wherein the wellsprings of love are renewed. Messiaen healed the breaches that Christianity had committed us to, reaffirming the validity of the sexual impulse and the identity of the creator with created nature. This is why his appeal has been widespread, even in countries that are not Christian, let alone Roman Catholic.

Messiaen wouldn't have been able to do this had not his Catholicism been a matter of spontaneous conviction. The Greek origin of the word 'theology' signifies the knowledge of God, while the word religion implies – as often remarked on – a bond adhered to. I doubt whether Messiaen admitted to a distinction between theosophy as intuition and theology as rationally argued law, for his belief is more a matter of heart than of head. The words of Robert Graves, attendant spirit of the White Goddess, are pertinent:

> Circling the Sun, at a respectful distance,
> Earth remained warmed, not roasted; but the Moon
> Circling the Earth, at a disdainful distance,
> Will drive men lunatic (should they defy her)
> With seeds of wintry love, not sown for spite.
>
> Mankind, so far, continues undecided
> On the Sun's gender – grammars disagree—
> As on the Moon's. Should Moon be god, or goddess:
> Drawing the tide, shepherding floods of stars
> That never show themselves by broad daylight.
>
> Thus curious problems of propriety
> Challenge all ardent lovers of each sex:
> Which circles which at a respectful distance
> Or which, instead, at a disdainful distance?
> And who controls the regal powers of night?

If Messiaen, unable or unwilling to answer those questions, would seem to be a theosophist rather than a theologian, he is left in the heretical position of believing that an artist is indistinguishable from God. St Thomas Aquinas had committed himself to stating that 'Unumquodque tendens in summam perfectionem, tendet in divinum similitudinem'; and in this sense – that everything that aspires towards its own perfection aspires to likeness with the divine – the sound-alchemist Messiaen, though not himself God, strove to embrace 'the divine essence which is bliss itself'. Sometimes he succeeded: most notably in the three works discussed in this chapter, the *Quatuor pour la fin du temps*, *Cinq Rechants*, and *Chronochromie*; and perhaps, more amorphously in the two immense works of his last years, his operatic parable about St Francis and the orchestral *La Transfiguration de Notre Seigneur Jésus-Christ*, the latter being the closest he came to a theological testament and an epiphany on his life's work.

As an appendix to this discussion of Messiaen, the great French composer who translated the Old Faith into the global terms of the twentieth century, we may consider a religious choral work of another Frenchman born nine years earlier in 1899 but dying prematurely, in 1963, at the age of sixty-four. We usually think of Francis Poulenc as a hedonistic composer of wittily debunking music born in the aftermath of the First World War: irrepressibly secular music conceived in the media of eupeptic or seductive piano music and songs, or in theatrical terms, especially for the dream-art of ballet. His youthful ballet *Les Biches*, which made him deservedly famous, makes an idealized re-creation of the secular paradise of Louis XIV's court, and sums up our image of Poulenc's music as a 'piece of froth' that, produced in the giddy 1920s, has proved unexpectedly durable.

Tragedy doesn't, of course, have a monopoly on durability; our fleeting follies may contain an awareness of the comic pathos of our impermanence. And in Poulenc's case there was another side to his sensibility since he was a Roman Catholic by birth and nurture who 'lapsed' during his fairly frantic youth but was, when in trouble, by no means impervious to conscience, or to God's calling. He was a homosexual with intermittent bouts of doubt about his sexual orientation; a young lover called Lucien, who liked but didn't reciprocally adore him, compounded Poulenc's guilt with mental distress, while another close friend and possible lover, the composer Pierre-Octave Ferroud, was horrendously decapitated in a car-crash. This event triggered a visit by Poulenc to the shrine of the Black Virgin of Rocamadour; and that pilgrimage led him back to the Church. For the rest of his life, 'on and off', he wrote vocal music to Christian texts, much of it for liturgical use. The *Quatre motets pour un temps de Pénitence*, written at the beginning of the Second World War, are truly penitential music at once sensuous and solemn, while a large-scale, non-liturgical choral work, *Figure Humaine*, composed during the German occupation, is a tragic masterpiece. As climax to his career as composer stands by far his longest work, the opera *Dialogues des*

Carmélites which, being about faith and betrayal, is both religious and purgatorial, painfully entwined with the saga of Lucien.

Poulenc also composed three sizeable works on religious texts for soloists, chorus, and orchestra, usually performed as concert-music but apposite to, and perhaps happier in, churches. Probably the deepest and therefore the most remarkable of these works is the *Sept Répons des Ténèbres*, written in the composer's last year; but the most popular, and most frequently performed, is the *Gloria* for soprano solo, chorus, and orchestra which, written in 1959, has deservedly become a repertory piece. Its origins were not unconnected with the belated triumph of the opera *Dialogues des Carmélites*, for that success prompted the Koussevitsky Foundation to offer Poulenc a commission for a major work in memory of the two Koussevitskys, recently deceased. After some prevarication Poulenc opted for a Gloria which could be not only a tribute to the dead, but could also pay off a debt of gratitude to God with whose help Francis had not only laid the ghost of Lucien, but had also achieved, with his opera, international renown. The occasion was thus more happy than melancholic; Poulenc composed the piece quickly yet carefully, shortly after his sixtieth birthday, three years before his own death.

'When I wrote this piece', Poulenc remarked, 'I had in mind those frescoes by Gozzoli where the angels stick out their tongues. And also some serious Benedictine monks I had once seen revelling in a game of football.' So Janus–Poulenc, self-styled 'Jongleur de Notre Dame', fused his roles as *enfant terrible*, as *dévôt*, and as *bonhomme* in a single work that is symphonic in concept and more highly organized but less self-conscious than his previous religious–choral work, the *Stabat Mater*. The piece's simultaneous frivolity and solemnity is nothing new in Poulenc's *oeuvre*, and since the work pays off a debt to God it's appropriate that it should reconcile the contrarious strands from which all his music had been woven. The symphonic introduction, dominated by brass fanfares, harks back to the youthful *Les Biches*, for its majestic gait and double-dotted rhythms recall the France of Louis XIV, for Poulenc an ideal, if unreal, civilization. That this dream-world is impermanent is patent in the closing bars of the prelude, when the brazen sonorities dissipate and tonality shifts from joyous G major to tragic G minor, the music now scored for quasi-medieval woodwind in parallel fourths and sevenths. Clouds disperse as the chorus enters, chanting Glorias in heroic double-dotted rhythms through surging parallel thirds in crotchets, over a bass pounding in minor thirds of B minor. Equivocation between merry G major and melancholic B minor pervades the entire work, on and off; and it is interesting to note that this equivocation recalls the elegantly balletic ritual of *Les Biches*. In the *Gloria* the basic ambiguity between G major and B minor is intensified as the music modulates through such keys as E flat, B flat, and F minors. At the references to men of good will (whom God may bless), declining sequences carry us back to G major, with the oscillating thirds in the bass. But the brass fanfares of the opening reappear and the movement closes in paeans of praise, with pulsing semiquavers making B minor triads over a pedal G as bass. This overt synthesis of blessed G major with suffering B minor will recur, and is a clue to the work's sublime end.

A hint of Stravinsky's neo-Russian primitivism, latent in the first movement, becomes patent in the 'Laudamus te', marked 'très vif et joyeux', and for a considerable while in 'white' C major. The music differs from Stravinsky in being 'enfantine' rather than savage in manner, with short phrases bandied between the voices often over an oompah bass. The sixty-year-old composer's glorification is as youthful as the 23-year-old's wedding music for *Les Biches*; and when modulations occur they bounce us back to C major. After an 'altered' subdominant chord and a long silence, Poulenc offers one of his glimpses 'over the rainbow': altos sing 'gratias agimus' in a mode slightly chromaticized and haloed by string harmonies. This intimation of mortality, or possibly of immortality, recalls *Les Biches*'s never-never-land: as does, more exuberantly, the resumed allegro, now in E flat major over an oompah bass. The concluding lauds, back in C major, are glitteringly scored; since tonics, dominants, and subdominants resound simultaneously, in Stravinskian neo-classical style, time is liquidated in primitive fiesta. The effect is enhanced by the perverse Latin accentuation, also probably picked up from Stravinsky's handling of Latin texts, though whereas the effect in the Russian's music is austere, in Poulenc it is naïve.

Yet Poulenc's *Gloria*, though intermittently child-like, is no reversion or retrogression. The next section, turning from us celebrating mortals to Domine Deus Himself, testifies to Poulenc not only as 'dévot' but also as grown-up. The triple tempo is 'très calme', the key 'suffering' B minor, and the words are chanted by solo soprano to a noble phrase based on a falling fifth:

In a middle section the tempo changes from $\frac{3}{4}$ to $\frac{4}{4}$; ripe modulations are resolved through a Neapolitan C major triad, serving as transition to a B major tierce de Picardie. Characteristically, the solo horn touches in a 'blue' flat seventh, suspended in time and space through the final triad.

Always mistrustful of grandiosity, Poulenc tempers this presentation of the Godhead with music that again depicts the worshippers as God's children. 'Domine fili unigenite' is back in G major and is as ludically 'vif et joyeux' as the most unbuttoned moments of *Les Biches*. The lines frolic in scales and arpeggios, plain diatonic if with sidekicks to grammatically unrelated keys; the vocal parts are often pentatonic, like childish runes. Regular recurrences of the rondo tune mean that our feet, however frisky, retain some contact with the earth; even in the final section, when modulations move flatwards, the manner is playful. Perhaps this is the bit inspired by the footballing Benedictines: in any case this fleet-footed scherzo serves as foil to the climactic movement which celebrates both Domine Deus and his human Lamb–Son.

After two introductory bars, the first in fierce false relation, the orchestra swings in a slow aria scored for woodwind, with a pendulum-like accompaniment in B flat minor. There's a high Baroque flourish in the woodwind skirls that introduce the soprano solo, whose opening phrase embraces both an augmented fourth and an augmented fifth, making for whole tones that in no way compromise the nobility:

As the soloist dialogues with the chorus, her phrase gives birth to a new theme whose stable repeated crotchets affirm certitudes in a shadowy world. Climax comes when the theme, originally in B flat minor, returns a tone lower in 'deathly' A flat minor. But the soprano solo – a Virgin and a Mother? – again proves a saviour, for her 'Qui tollis' steers us back to the wide-flung tritonal theme in B flat minor, the texture grandly divided between woodwind, strings, and horns. The movement ends with a *ppp* triad of E flat minor, a fifth lower than the initial B flat: with an effect indubitably depressive, yet also resolutory, perhaps because resolute.

From the final setting of 'Qui sedes ad dextram patris' the sacrificial Lamb is at first banished. The chorus intones the words addressed to God in his solitary omnipotence in unison, in the work's initial G major, interspersed with brazen blasts from the orchestra. Yet the heroic double-dotted figure and the simultaneous G major–B minor triads also creep back, and the main setting of 'Qui sedes' turns into a fast symphonic movement implying some 'symphonic' conflict, and its potential resolution. The tempo is a fast $\frac{4}{4}$, with a walking bass in quavers and galloping semiquavers in the inner parts. The babble of G major is often assaulted by orchestral eruptions of the double-dotted figure as the padding quavers and tripping semiquavers cavort through many keys, periodically called to order by brass fanfares that grow more urgent and more frequent, to counter the spate.

The justly famous final section recapitulates the words of the 'Qui sedes' while the orchestra, 'extraordinairement calme', weaves a texture of G major and B minor arpeggios, over a pedal G. Comparisons are often made with the end of Stravinsky's *Symphony of Psalms*, though the serene modality of the vocal lines and the radiance of the harmony are closer to Ravel, a benign attendant-presence throughout this work. But the idiom remains essentially Poulenc, and the final 'misereres' reassert the parallel sevenths and ninths of the first movement with a nobility that banishes any hint of self-pity, though Poulenc admits that the pity of God might not come amiss. The end mutates the work's contradictions into eternity, if not into finality. The chorus reaffirm the first movement's simultaneous triads of blessed G major and tragic B minor, while the orchestra blazes in double-dotted fanfares; the ultimate choral–orchestral triads of G major and B minor synchronized are capped by the solo soprano, who floats an Amen on D, aloft. So the 'lost' state of the earlier *Stabat Mater* and the purgatorial agony of *Dialogues des Carmélites* meet in a work that is hearteningly positive, but never evasive. This is why the unassuming 'petit bonhomme' Francis Poulenc deserves to be bracketed in this chapter with the saintly Messiaen. Both men were sensualists and hedonists; Messiaen made out of sensuality a 'transfigured' cosmos; Poulenc within hedonism a faith as pure as a child's. Momently, Poulenc is a *great*, if 'minor', composer.

25

The Ancient Law and the Romantic Spirit

Rachmaninov's Russian Orthodox
Vespers or All-Night Vigil (1916)

Janáček – born in an old-style agrarian community in the mid-nineteenth century yet in tune with the tensions and terrors of our modern minds – is a one-off in that we will not look upon his like again. He turned East rather than West; and had many qualities in common with Russian civilization before its Marxist Sovietization. Given the vast size of Russia and the relatively rapid industrialization of its cities, there are few Russian composers, and no major ones, who are products of a self-enclosed agrarian society such as Janáček belonged to; but we do find White Russians who, exiled from their native land by the Revolution, belonged simultaneously to the Old World they had lost and the international societies wherein they pursued their 'careers'. Two very different Russian composers, Rachmaninov and Stravinsky, who both led peripatetic lives, are in this respect oddly related. In this chapter I'll discuss Rachmaninov: followed, in the next chapter, by Stravinsky, the greater and, in the story of Europe, the more 'representative' composer, though he cannot rival Rachmaninov in popular appeal.

In White Russia Rachmaninov was of noble descent, though patrician pride didn't carry with it confidence in his own considerable musical talents, since he belonged to an aristocracy in decline and on the verge of defeat by revolutionary forces. Even so, his training under Ziloti, and at the Moscow Conservatory under Zverev, was thorough; as a performing artist he developed into one of the greatest pianists of his day, while as a composer he acquired skills, based on current German, French, and Italian traditions, that Tchaikovsky himself would have admired – and possibly did admire, since Rachmaninov was born in 1873 and Tchaikovsky lived until 1893. Rachmaninov's celebrity, at first local, then international, accrued from the fusion of his two talents: for although he composed operas, symphonies, and chamber music in a late nineteenth-century romantic idiom – including many works such as the magnificent Second Symphony that have become established in the European repertory – his name became a 'household word' by way of his piano concertos, which he initially played himself. Two at least of Rachmaninov's four piano concertos are still among the most frequently performed works in the classical–romantic canon. People relish their big tunes, opulent harmonies, stream-lined orchestration and sometimes extra-vagant emotional ardour whilst goggling, wide-eyed as well as open-eared, at the audacity of the keyboard pyrotechnics. There is piquancy in that Rachmaninov should have been Top among the Pop Classics while being himself hypersensitively White Russian in nervous instability. This suggests that we the people are prone to revere artists in whom we can admire strengths and skills that are beyond us while gratefully recognizing that they, too, share some of our weaknesses. Over the years Rachmaninov, born of an aristocratic family and embarking on a professional career in his native land, ended up as a European internationalist, travelling the world as a piano virtuoso and to a lesser degree as a conductor, with intermittent 'homes' in Russia, Scandinavia, Paris, and finally New York: whence he returned, annually for some of the summer months, to his property in 'neutral' Switzerland, on the lake of Lucerne.

Despite his international life-style, the White Russian lost world of his childhood continued to haunt Rachmaninov. Although the music he was and still is famous for is, like Tchaikovsky's, eclectic, cosmopolitan, and Russian–German–French–Italian in its sources, he remained deeply re-sponsive to the world of his childhood: which still had a surviving incarnation in the Russian Orthodox Church. In composing liturgical music for the Church Rachmaninov created some of his most distinguished work: which, since he was not a 'believer', would seem odd were it not that the Church almost literally 'enshrined' many of the values his ancestral family had lived by. The collection of fifteen anthems or part-songs usually known as the Vespers is strictly speaking a setting of what is called in Russian the 'combined prayer service' or 'all-night vigil': which includes both the Evening Service (continuing until midnight) and Matins, which welcomes the dawn of a new day. The rites consist of traditional prayers led by a priest with musical interludes by the church choir, some of them based on traditional liturgical texts and plainchant hymn, others newly invented. In 1916, on the eve of his departure for America, which became his home-from-home, Rachmaninov paid homage to his very ancient world, in an access of exultation and devotion. If he did not believe in the doctrines the Church promulgated, he revered the lost world that both the Church and he himself stemmed from. Although this work lasts around seventy minutes without the religious service it is designed to adorn and intensify, Rach-maninov composed it with fervour, completing the score in less than two months. He allowed himself a large choir divisible into seven, eight, or nine parts expertly deployed in an ecclesiastical idiom poles apart from the luxuriance of his concert music. The vocal techniques of the Vespers manage to be simultaneously opulent and austere; in them the innocent face of his childhood survived.

Certainly, although Tchaikovsky and Rimsky-Korsakov had composed music for the Russian Church earlier than Rachmaninov, neither they, nor others less famous as musicians but more orthodox as Christians, had attained the mingle of humane passion with spirituality that distinguishes Rachmaninov's work. The first number, known in English as 'O come let us worship', is an invitation to prayer introduced, after the priest's initiatory words, by two chords of C major in eight parts, two each of SATB. After that perhaps symbolically white introduction – more White Russian than whitely Enlightened – the music flows in syllabic declamation at speech-tempo, not in C major but in the aeolian mode on A, with the thirds sometimes sharpened and the seconds occasionally, especially at cadential points, flattened. There are no bar-lines since the rhythms are verbal rather than metrical, thereby indicating that the Word(s) matter more than the music; the parts move note-for-note like plainchant intonation, with virtually no polyphony, let alone counterpoint. Each melodic line, moving mostly by step, is gracefully moulded and grateful to sing, massively sonorous is the concourse of its (in this case seven) parts. The closing bars, ending in the mixolydian mode on G, will illustrate the nobility of the separate lines and the ripeness of the whole concourse, the sensuality of which is light years away from that of the composer's piano concertos. The 'form' of the anthem – and that of many though not all of the others – is conditioned by the declamation of the words, liturgically. The second number, 'Bless the Lord', takes its text from Psalm 104 and is based on an ancient Greek melody, initially sung by alto solo. The tune itself, moving stepwise at a moderate minim pulse, is in modern C major, or at least in the ionian mode on C; but the texture of the choral polyphony veers between aeolian on A and lydian on F, and is entirely 'white note' until the approach to the consummatory glorification when chromatic B flats intrude while G sharps in the tenors hint at a modulation to A minor. The end, however, blesses the Lord and us in a radiant C major unsullied, with divided basses resonating on bottom C and the E a tenth above it. The celebrated low Russian basses are obligatory in this music, for the spirituality of Russian music, as of Russian souls, seems to be rooted deep in the earth.

This movement, though liturgical in approach like the first movement, is barred in $\frac{4}{2}$, probably because the singers are divided into antiphonal groups, and barring may assist synchronicity. Organ-style drones are sustained in inner parts by way of a 'bouche fermée' technique; but the next number, 'Blessed is the man', is again unbarred, with sectional voices narrating the text in plainchant-like lines in the aeolian mode on D; in the cadences the sevenths are usually, though not always, sharpened. Each clause of the text, sung by a section of the choir, is capped by Alleluyas for full chorus, with each successive jubilation growing louder and bolder. The enhanced animation culminates in a 'real' modulation, albeit to the subdominant of aeolian D (G minor). During the doxology something approaching corporeal momentum takes over from liturgical declamation. Consummatory alleluyas reverberate over low Cs but the piece ends, as it had begun, in aeolian D, often with sharp sevenths.

The next number concerns the Supreme Light of holiness, though the Russian has been cringe-makingly translated as 'Gladsome Radiance'. The severe liturgical melody comes from Kiev; and is appropriate to physical conditions as well as to mystical metaphysics since by this time in the service twilight is deepening to night. It may be because the words concern both natural and supernatural light that this song is the most adventurous thus far both harmonically and texturally, as is evident in the shift from E flat minor to E ('really' F flat) major. Seven parts sway over basses rooted on low E flat, though at the end the music swivels back to aeolian on C, with another cavernous bottom C firmly if softly sustained.

The next two numbers have words familiar in many languages. The Nunc Dimittis again borrows a tune 'from Kiev tradition' sung by tenor solo moving by step, mostly in levelly barred $\frac{4}{4}$. The words, we recall, are those of the aged Simeon, uttered when he first sees the infant Jesus and becomes cognizant, in the encroaching dark, of his own sensibility in contrast with the new life of the holy babe. The mode is aeolian on B flat, and the soloist's chanting of the words is haloed in soft-swaying chords rocking through step or third. At the reference to the Light that may lighten the Gentiles the music flows polyphonically and even – as is rare in this communally prayerful music – into rudimentary fugato. At the end the second basses plummet to low B flat, deeper than the by now familiar low Cs, albeit *ppp*.

Companion to the Nunc dimittis celebrating the new-born Child is the Ave Maria, hymning the human mother through whom he was made flesh. Appropriately, this is the simplest song in the sequence and the only one in a straight diatonic major key (F). Perhaps it should be termed ionian on F; there is no accidental throughout the lyrical parts that pay homage to the fruit of the Virgin's womb.

The seventh movement offers Glory to God in the Highest at the (magically seventh) stage in the night-long vigil for, with midnight past, the new dawn is awaited. Musically, this number lives up to the moment's liturgical import for, beginning with a tune from 'Znamen tradition' in the aeolian mode on C, the mode frequently veers to Ionian E flat, the act of glorification being hushed in awe until it blossoms into a thrilling climax of tolling bells, with sopranos, altos and tenors all divided à 3. Bells may owe their supernal acoustic significance to their reverberating in the 'natural' overtone series that may be presumed to have *super*natural implications; the exquisite coda to these chimes is 'in' diatonic E flat major, occasionally subsiding to the subdominant A flat major, with touches of C minor. Here is the transition from bells to bliss in music which, though barred, is asymmetrical:

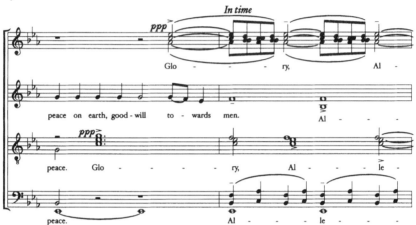

'Laud ye the Name of the Lord' is based on another Znamen chant, sung in octave unisons by bold altos and basses, adorned by sopranos and tenors singing a version of the theme in five homophonic parts. Sopranos and tenors are subservient to the cantus-firmus-like altos and basses who should, according to the composer, be equally weighted. Through several repetitions the chant grows more luxuriant in scoring in ionian A flat major with the sevenths sometimes modally flattened. More tintinnabulating bells on the word Alleluya convey gratitude to God; unsurprisingly, ecstasy and gratitude would seem to be oblivious of time for there is little movement and virtually no modulation in this chant. Nor is there much tonal activity in the next (also Znanem) chant, 'Blessed art Thou', which is not only long but also the climax to the whole sequence since it relates the emergence of dawn from darkness to the story of Christ's Resurrection. Tenors and basses start at speech rhythm in the aeolian mode on D, requesting that the Lord should teach us 'the statutes'. This he does when altos and sopranos reply in a resonant sonority at a slower, heavier, appropriately more time-measuring beat. The roles are reversed when tenors chant the Law to a cantus firmus of repeated tonic Ds: after which the original plea is reiterated, 'religiously' *bound together* by drones in closed-lips humming on a dominant and tonic of A and 'bottom' D. There is an intimation of evolution, if not development, when an angel appears to deliver to the weeping women the glad news of Christ's resurrection. The modal centre becomes aeolian on G as 'a few tenors'

tell the weepers that the time of their mourning is past. The mellifluous modality approaches E flat major, and when the women 'draw nigh' to the sepulchre there is a further access of harmonic momentum, leading to climax in a long crescendo through which we human supplicants join with the angels to honour Christ's victory over death and hell – diurnally reenacted with each oncoming dawn. Rachmaninov was proud enough of this passage to quote from it in his last major work, the *Symphonic Dances* for orchestra. The doxology and final alleluyas return to the speech-rhythms of the opening, the textures enriched by internal pedal notes; but the hymn ends in an austerely modal cadence, with no whiff of a sharpened leading note.

Rachmaninov's symphonic adaptation of part of that chant suggests that the apparently sensual world of his concert music may not be all that remote from his liturgically White Russian heart of hearts. Corroboration is offered by the opening of the next number, 'The Veneration of the Cross', which, recalling that the Resurrection was possible only by way of the agony of the Cross, opens with octave unisons on tenors and basses, chanting a theme very close to the noble, convoluting melody that launches the D minor Piano Concerto at exactly the same pitch. Rachmaninov gives no 'traditional' source for this chant, presumably because there isn't one. This may bear on the potent durability of the D minor Piano Concerto, which may coruscate in glittering piano ornamentation and seductive chromatic harmonies but which opens in these sustained motives of adoration. In the anthem, when the words speak overtly of the Resurrection, the voices move in plain diatonic concords in six-part homophony in the dorian mode on G. For the rest of the piece cantus-firmus-style plain chant and modally homophonic declamation are interchanged, often in eight parts. The victory of the Cross is momently loud, though the close is hushed in austere modality, over a basso profundo D.

In Rachmaninov's setting the words are not identified with a specific female soloist but are distributed between the voices in a masterly equilibrium between liturgical function and musical meaning. The plainchant intonation is clearly defined in aeolian G; the first altos and tenors declaim on a single D; but after the introductory clause the words are 'spoken' syllabically with no modulation until the 'magnification' at the end of the clause. This resolves melismatically in B flat major, to which the second basses belatedly offer the rock of their bottom B flat. The rest of the setting of the extensive text follows the same pattern, with sections of linear polyphony (but not counterpoint) followed by speech-rhythmed declamation. Each clause ends melismatically on a B flat major triad; but the third section moves slightly faster, introducing rudimentary counterpoint to bolster God's almighty power. The fourth statement has phrygian A flats, hinting at E flat major as well as phrygian G, but again ends melismatically on a B flat major triad. God needs more tonal movement and rhythmic energy to 'put down the mighty from their seat'; but when the higher voices return to syllabic declamation to invoke the Virgin Mother, the B flat major cadence is both more melismatically intricate and more harmonically defined. The verses about god's promise to Abraham and his seed are back in aeolian G, with level repeated crotchets; subside through $\frac{6}{3}$ chords into quietude; and are capped by the upper voices' syllabics, lightened by the sharp sixths of the dorian mode. This time the melismatic B flat major cadence shifts to the basic tonility of aeolian G minor.

The succeeding setting of the Great Doxology, with its fundament in a Znamen chant, is even longer and grander than the Magnificat. The tonality is at first ionian E flat major, with no accidental until the appearance of the human Son hints at the tonal variety of C minor. But E flat major is re-established, perhaps to indicate that 'peccata mundi' have now been absolved. The first basses, in speech rhythm, present Christ sitting at the right hand of God the Father, over the second basses' low E flat. This climaxes in another visionary moment of peeling bells. The praises 'for ever and ever' are in eight homophonic parts weighted to the bass, concluding in a grand affirmation moving from C major to E flat major to G major in glorious, if or because false, relation. False relations trigger, moreover, the succeeding stretch of the Great Doxology, in textures animated by triplets within the duple beat. But when we welcome God as a 'refuge and dwelling place' dynamics hopefully quieten and altos create a painfully expressive (rather than conventionally lachrymose) dominant ninth – a rare chord in this work, though it is common in secular Rachmaninov. The sopranos' parallel thirds gradually stimulate a homophonic texture of repeated-note chords in block harmony, seeming to enact the words 'world without end, AMEN'. After so much liturgical modality, the final cadence sounds like modern C minor, as is appropriate to a modern man composing music in celebration of a faith he can accept only in so far as it re-creates the White Russia of his lost childhood.

Musically, this might have been the End of the work; but liturgically the service called for four more short chants proleptically thanking God for the salvation he has offered, or may offer. The first, on a traditional Orthodox text and a Znamen melody, gravely welcomes salvation along with the newly dawning day, flowing in an aeolian mode in slow-paced crotchets, albeit with occasional chromatics and livelier semiquavers in recognition of God's being the Author of our Life. This piece is regularly barred in $\frac{4}{4}$; but the next, being a hymn of Resurrection, is free-rhythmed, modally equivocating between dorian and aeolian on D before cadencing on, but not in, the dominant of C. It's 'as though' we are waiting on the threshold, both of a new day and of a resurrected life; and the final number seals this in being a hymn of the Virgin Mother, beginning in white-note aeolian but modulating, almost in nineteenth-century fashion, through A minor to G major, and so to C major where, after sonorous melismata long protracted, it finally rests on a tranquil C major triad over the second basses' low Cs.

We must remember that this is not the end of a concert performance of a number of 'numbers' but of an All-Night Vigil in a Russian Orthodox Church in which the music is accessory to prayer. In this context Rachmaninov's disposition of the chants – beginning with liturgical declamation, gradually embracing degrees of expressivity from the communal to the personal, and climaxing in the liturgical grandeur of the Magnificat and the choral majesty of the Great Doxology before serenely subsiding through the four final, short movements – produces a masterpiece of religious choral music written at a time of crisis in Rachmaninov's life, as well as at a climax to the horror of the First World War. Wherever we stand in the matter of faith, we cannot doubt that Rachmaninov, by way of the Russian Orthodox Church, incarnated spiritual and psychological verities still pertinent to 'all sorts and conditions of men'. His achievement, in thus reconciling very ancient musical techniques with techniques pertinent to himself and to (some of) us, remains impressive; and will possibly prove more durable than his ubiquitous piano concertos, though there is as yet no evidence of any diminishment in the obsessive appeal of, at least, the C minor and D minor concertos.

For the most part Rachmaninov, whether in Russia or in exile, didn't bother overmuch about indigenous Russian culture but accepted, for his concert music, the European idioms that were his legacy from Tchaikovsky. Even so, the power and grandeur of his music for the Russian Orthodox Church demonstrate how deeply potent was the Old Russia in his psyche: so that there's an element of irony in that the Vespers Service remained virtually unperformed in Russia at the time when it was written in 1916. It was launched, somewhat tentatively, in the *New* World, when in April 1919 a single movement was performed, in Russian, by the Schola Cantorum, followed by another movement, sung in English by the New York Oratorio at its Spring Festival in 1920. Sporadically, a few more of the anthems were sung over the next few years, though not in the liturgical performances that should be the heart of the matter. Nowadays, however, it is recognized that these Vespers are great music that gives both universal and contemporary validification to ancient liturgy that, seemingly remote from us, proves to be pertinent to our fragmented world. The music of another White Russian, of upper class if not aristocratic lineage, discovered a *via media* between Old Russia, cosmopolitanly timeless Paris, and abrasively disruptive New York, in all of which he created music perhaps more widely and deeply representative of the twentieth century than that of any other composer. Over a long life, Igor Stravinsky moved through several distinct geographical worlds in many apparently distinct artistic directions. Although he composed a little music for the Russian Orthodox Church and later became a fervently practising Roman Catholic, Stravinsky was perhaps a clinical ritualist rather than a man of God. Even so, two of his major works – the opera–oratorio *Oedipus Rex* and the choral and orchestral *Symphony of Psalms* – are arguably the closest the twentieth century came to the creation of masterpieces of religious music that neither cheat nor resort to wish-fulfilment.

26

The Ancient Law and the Modern Mind

Stravinsky's *Oedipus Rex* (1927), *Symphony of Psalms* (1930), and *Requiem Canticles* (1965–6)

If we accept Stravinsky as the central representative of twentieth-century music, we have to admit that he is representative in a paradoxical way: for he has displayed, as composer, a deliberate denial of what we are accustomed to call 'expression', turning his back on many of the values and assumptions that have made us what we are. His representativeness is that we too are mistrustful of the beliefs on which we have been nurtured. The Stravinskian dubiety is also ours: though his art's admission of dubiety is more honest, less afraid, that most of us can hope to be.

We live at the end of a civilization that, starting with the European Renaissance, has been founded on man's belief in his ability to control his own destiny – an ability he has attained, or thinks he has attained, through reason and the power over the natural world that reason has given him. The natural world includes, of course, our own nature, especially our agile minds; the preoccupation of post-Renaissance art with expression and communication has been largely a manifestation of the belief that man, through the ordering of his passions, may influence the emotions and through them the behaviour of other people, so that an artist's personal identity is also a social force. Now Stravinsky – partly because Russia bypassed the Renaissance – never viewed music as expression-and-communication in this way. He once described his music as 'a human machine': by which he must have meant that while he, a human being, had 'invented' the music, when once it had come into existence it 'worked' on its inner mechanism, fulfilling its destiny.

In this it not only resembles a machine but also a ritual – even though, as a modern man thrice deracinated, Stravinsky lived mostly in societies that have forgotten what ritual means. In early works like *Le Sacre du*

Printemps and *Les Noces* (which dethroned both melody and harmony in the interests of 'primitive' polymetricality) he was able, as a Russian, to reinvoke the rituals of a remote past, thereby performing a negative and a positive act simultaneously: negative, because the violence of the act seemed to parallel that of our deracinated civilization currently erupting in the First World War; positive, because this barbarity reminded us of the instinctive passional life that modern man had lost. From this point of view Stravinsky had to recognize that the ritual wasn't true: which is why he objectified it in the conscious artifice of ballet – an art significantly of Russian origin that came to fruition in sophisticatedly cosmopolitan Paris. Classical (really romantic) ballet has been an artifice of dream in which the perturbations of real life were momently resolved. Stravinsky's *Les Noces* is a dream too, though the artifice it starts from is rudimentary. 'Let's pretend', it says, 'that we self-conscious beings of the twentieth century can enter into man's animal nature and can even (in the bell-tolling coda) re-experience his spontaneous yearning for the unity that is love.' But the geometric pattern-making of the music, the black-and-white abstraction of the choreography (and for that matter the black-and-white penguin-suits of the orchestra and of the affluent audience) admit that the artifice is a pretence. The game, though a game, is still beautiful, its effect cathartic.

But the burden of consciousness cannot be brushed aside merely by a revocation of the primitive springs of life; and that Stravinsky was aware of this is evident in war-time works such as *The Soldier's Tale*, wherein the theme of human guilt and responsibility queasily resurfaces in a puppet-like parody of the Faust legend. Techniques and conventions from widely separated bits of Europe's humanist past are disturbingly reintegrated, while the primitive aspects become a sophistication of elements derived from ancient Russian peasant-music – alongside twentieth-century black jazz, the music of an alien people themselves alienated and oppressed! The queasiness, even the cynicism, were serious enough in purpose and effect; and had positive direction in that they led Stravinsky to explore, in the neo-classic works of his middle years, his relationship to Europe's humanist traditions. Like his Renaissance and Baroque predecessors, he took his themes from classical antiquity rather than from Christian traditions, for at this point he was not concerned with a dichotomy between flesh and spirit. He started rather from those conventions of the Baroque world that had suggested that Man himself might be Hero, even to the point of supplanting God. In effect, however, he inverted the significance these conventions had had when they were invented, since he mutated the deification of man into a recognition of man's ephemeral insufficiency. This process began in 1926–27, in his opera–oratorio *Oedipus Rex*, a keywork in his career and the only one to make direct use of the rigid conventions of baroque opera. That he called it both an opera and an oratorio affirms his role as the Great Compromiser – a dualism on which his 'representative' significance rests.

A real heroic opera – and this, as noted, applies also to Handel's oratorios which are heroic operas on Old Testament subjects – was simultaneously a ritual of humanism (a masque or state-ceremonial) and a drama dealing with the perversity of human passions, which makes paradise-on-earth a difficult ideal. Stravinsky preserves the 'heroic' closed aria form and the atmosphere of ritual festivity; at the same time he admits that we 'belong to' this ritual hardly more than we can share in the primitive ritual of *Les Noces*; and this he symbolizes by returning to the authentically Greek stylization of the mask, and by having the opera acted and sung in a dead language (Latin), interspersed with narrations in modern French by a man wearing modern evening dress – in the original performance, Jean Cocteau, the librettist. This smart, 1920ish convention becomes, in the hands of a master at the height of his powers, unexpectedly moving. It tells us that we, like the narrator, are cut off from the fount of passion; then gradually we realize that the tragedy is ours, after all. We may not be Kings or Heroes, but we too are subject to the destiny that hounds us, and it is only our pride that prevents our seeing that that destiny is the guilt within us all. It is significant that Stravinsky chose, for this central work in his career, a myth that more buoyant humanists of the heroic age had preferred to leave alone. His Oedipus 'stands for' both the ego's pride and its insufficiency: which is why the humanist ritual in this piece is linked to the primitive ritual of earlier works but also heralds the religious rituals of the later, ostensibly Christian, pieces.

After the spoken Prologue in which Cocteau summarizes the story in (beautifully spoken) French, the chorus, masked like living statues, sing of the plague that ravages Thebes. They are the citizens of Thebes but also mankind, whose burden of suffering is a burden of guilt. The anti-expressive syllabic recitation, the ostinato patterns over chugging B flat minor triads (B flat minor being a further fifth down the cycle of fifths from hellish F minor) have affinities with Stravinsky's primitive phase, though the effect is not of orgiastic excitement. Indeed, falling minor thirds have long been a musical synonym for the domination of earth and therefore of death, and the feeling here is of claustrophobic restriction; we sense that this music is complementary both to the 'primitive' pieces and to the Christian liturgical works that Stravinsky (like Rachmaninov!) was currently composing for the Russian Orthodox Church.

In the static lamentation there is virtually no harmonic movement, though there is harmonic tension created by the telescoping of tonic, dominant, and subdominant chords. *Very slow* momentum is hinted at as the chorus calls on their King, Oedipus, to help them: until, out of the prison of the falling thirds, Oedipus, a godly high tenor, chants a prancing, dotted-rhythmed figure in ornate coloratura. 'EGO Oedipus', he pronounces; and although the coloratura suggests the sublimely silly assurance of a worldly God–King and derives from the exhibitionism of baroque opera, it also has qualities suggestive of liturgical incantation and of exotic display-music, sometimes with quasi-Asiatic effect:

Oedipus's freedom seems to be itself imprisoned, not only by the nodal oscillations around a fixed point, but also by a slowly revolving ostinato in the bass that fetters the clarinets' prancing arpeggios and reasserts the B flat minor obsession against the voice's aspiration towards traditionally rational C major. Here the fateful minor thirds insidiously persist into the *Serva* chorus wherein the men of Thebes (no women admitted) ask their Leader what may be done that they may be delivered.

Oedipus says that Creon, the Queen's brother, has just returned from consulting the oracles at Delphi. Immediately, the promise of or even the desire for spiritual sanction banishes the B flat minor obsession, replacing it not with C major but at least with sonorous G major chords, G being traditionally a key of benediction. As they become ordinary men, the chorus loses its monumental austerity, becoming primitively Moussorgskian since they, like us, are closer to peasants than to kings, Creon, as surrogate for the gods, sings a strict *da capo* aria in which there is no development since perfection is unalterable. Yet there is ambivalence in his music, as in the baroque age itself. The middle section of the aria recalls the B flat minor obsession as it refers to the old, dead King, while there is a hint of frenzy in the aria itself, even though it attains the goal of 'rational' C major. The arpeggiated tune is crude with the brass-band vigour of early Verdi rather than with the grandeur of Handel; and the ostinato on four horns (instruments that can create their 'natural' pitches) reveals terror beneath the surface. Man–god complacency wins through, however. After he has informed the People-chorus that the oracle has admitted that the murderer of King Laius is among them, Creon concludes with a tremendous C major arpeggio: APOLLO DIXIT DEUS.

Responding to the challenge, Oedipus boasts of his skill at solving riddles – which 'stands for' man's ability to control his density through reason. He promises to save his people by discovering the murderer: in an aria in E flat major, traditionally a key of humanity allied with both reason and compassion. Beginning with pridefully arpeggiated phrases emulating those of Creon, it embraces hysterically agitated sevenths, emphasizing the word 'ego' in tipsy narcissism:

Œd.   e - go, eg'   Œ - di - pus   car - men di - vi - na - bo.

Over the sustained E flat bass the voice resolves its fourth onto a major third, with an effect that is superb in the strict sense. But the chorus seems to suspect there is something phoney about it, for their reiterated 'deus dixit tibi' phrase is alchemized back into the fateful minor thirds, now screwed up a semitone to B minor. They call on Tiresias, a blind prophet who can see in the dark as ordinary folk cannot, hoping that he'll be of more assistance than any merely human leader, however mighty. In solemn repeated notes and grandiose arpeggios Tiresias proclaims that he cannot reveal the truth, though he lets slip the knowledge that the King's Murderer is a King. For the first time the tonality presages D major.

At the moment we don't realize the significance of this: for Oedipus takes over the sustained D natural, only to force it back to his man-key of E flat. Yet although Oedipus has been ruffled by his encounter with the prophet, it marks a stage in his pilgrimage, for his second E flat aria is only superficially similar to the first. Though his line is derived from the 'superb' aria, it is now chromatically fragmented as, for the first time, he reveals his weakness which is also his humanity. As he accuses both Creon and Tiresias of plotting against him, and continues to brag about his abilities as problem-solver, his melodic line begins to temper pride with pathos, and even tenderness. Significantly, he ends unaccompanied, on his own, singing the chorus's falling thirds in C minor, relative of man's E flat major and complement to C major, whether rational or godly. In seeing himself as one with the many he shifts from pride to humility, accepting fate and death in his music, if not in his words. Formally, this song is not a *da capo* aria but a rondo in which the episodes change the destiny of the theme. His absolutism disintegrates even in the process of his assertion of it: which is why the act can end with a Gloria (so titled) celebrating Jocasta's arrival in Stravinsky's white-note diatonicism, and with ceremonial music more closely related to his music for the Russian Orthodox Church, and even to his 'primitive' works, than to the ceremonial choruses of Handel. This chorus strikingly anticipates Stravinsky's *Symphony of Psalms*.

Oedipus's rondo-aria, which has more harmonic momentum than any previous music in the opera, and the ensuing Gloria, which has no harmonic movement at all, form the axis on which the work revolves. The Gloria concludes the first act, and is repeated as prelude to the second: which follows the path to self-knowledge. At first, Jocasta pours scorn on all oracles; her music has a human, almost Verdian, lyrical sweep and a harmonic momentum such as Oedipus acquired only in his rondo. The key, G minor, is *dominant* of C and *relative* of fateful B flat. Her defiance, in the F major middle section of the *da capo* form, turns into insolent ridicule.

To clattering clarinet triplets she points out how the oracles often lie, and obviously lie in this case since the Old King was killed at the cross-roads, twelve years ago. Her repeated quavers sound, however, panic-stricken, and when the *da capo* returns, its syncopations and chromatics affect us differently, seeming to drag in anguish rather than to prance in defiance. Probably at this point we realize that those original minor thirds are padding beneath the impassioned lyricism. Jocasta too struggles against destiny and if, being a woman, she is more humane than Oedipus, she is also less heroic and is not, like him, absolved.

Oedipus's assurance is finally shaken, however, by Jocasta's reference to the past, for he recalls that, twelve years ago, he killed a stranger at the cross-roads. 'Ego senem kekedi' he stammers, to a phrase that inverts the falling thirds, accompanied only by scary minor thirds on timpani:

This is the moment of self-revelation, when he recognizes that guilt is within us. At first, revelation leads to chaos, only just checked by the rigidity of the ostinato pattern. Jocasta screams that oracles *always* lie: while Oedipus in duo moans a bewildered lament confessing to his past history. So the wife–mother and the son–husband sing together in C minor, relative of the man-key E flat major and tonic minor of C major, key of a rationality that seems in this piece to be equated with the gods. The scene closes remorselessly, however, on an ostinato of fateful B flat, as Oedipus demands to see the shepherd who was the only witness of his crime.

An anonymous Messenger, as in Greek tradition an agent of destiny, enters to inform us that Jocasta's reputed father, Polybus, has died, revealing that Oedipus was an adopted son. The Messenger, ostensibly a low character, sings in peasant-like Moussorgskian incantation, oscillating around a modal point. The chorus take up the words 'falsus pater', stuttering, horror-struck; words, line, and rhythm are all broken, the harmony gelid. Momentarily, when the Messenger reports that Oedipus was found as a baby on Mt Citheron, the chorus chant in modal innocence that a miracle has occurred: Oedipus will be revealed as the child of a goddess, in a Virgin Birth. But the shepherd–witness confesses the truth, carrying the music back to fate's obsessive B flat minor, The Shepherd's aria, accompanied by two bassoons and timpani, induces a state of terror in everyone except Jocasta who, now knowing that she is the wife of her own son who was his father's murderer, rushes out.

Oedipus pretends to think that Jocasta has run off in shame at the discovery of his lowly birth; and makes a desperate return to his earlier arrogance in a scornful Italianate aria over a bouncing bass. The key, F major, is that of the insolent middle section of Jocasta's first aria, and it may be no accident that F major is the *dominant* of B flat, the key of fate. Here Oedipus's coloratura acquires a horrifying inanity, as though he is trying to cheer himself up, against all humanly reasonable odds. He climaxes in a cadenza of hysterical exultation, in descending chromatics that sweep from F major to 'obscure' D minor. At this point the thudding minor thirds return, along with the hammering *kekidi* rhythm. *This* exultation, we realize, is not entirely synthetic: Messenger, Shepherd, and Chorus declaim the truth on repeated Ds; woodwind and strings alternate the *kekidi* rhythm in false relations between D major and minor; and Oedipus chants a brief arioso that, beginning in 'suffering' B minor over pedal Ds, miraculously transforms the falling minor thirds into unsullied D major on the words LUX FACTUS EST:

Light floods the spirit as Oedipus decides to put out his eyes since, like Shakespeare's Gloucester in *King Lear*, 'I stumbled when I saw.' So Stravinsky stresses the Christian implications he has discovered in, or imparted to, the myth; while Oedipus rediscovers the Christian liturgical chant that was implicit in his first utterance, now purged of egotism and self-will.

The discovery of Light is the consummation of the tragedy, but an epilogue is needed to place the revelation in the context of our lives. So the visionary moment is followed by a trumpet fanfare in a tonally ambiguous area between B flat major and G minor. The Messenger announces that Jocasta has hanged herself and the chorus recount, in a lurching $\frac{6}{8}$ rhythm, how Oedipus blinded himself with a gold pin from her dress. The music refers back to the C minor duet of horror and bewilderment that Oedipus and Jocasta had sung at the moment of discovery.

After each phrase of the narration the trumpet fanfare returns in rondo style, giving the human tragedy an epic impartiality. On the words 'spectaculum omnium atrocissimum' the C-minor–E flat dichotomy seems to resolve itself on a solemn brass triad of D major; but this acts as a dominant of G minor, in which tragic key the upward-shooting scales of the opera's opening are reinstated. Oedipus totters in, blind, and the chorus bid him farewell – ironically, except in so far as he carries their guilt as well as his own. Gradually, thudding minor thirds of the fate motif take over, back in B flat minor, but are soon tugged down to G minor. As the minor thirds fade out on cellos, basses, and timpani, the opera tells us that although man is 'dominated' by destiny, he may improbably find redemption, for G minor, though the relative of destiny's B flat, is also a gateway to the light which is D major.

The Christian, and possibly mystical, implications of Stravinsky's Heroick opera–oratorio are fulfilled in a sequence of works that followed, most notably in the *Symphony of Psalms* which, for me, is Stravinsky's ultimate masterpiece. Written in 1930, the work was, according to Stravinsky, 'composed for the glory of God and dedicated to the Boston Symphony Orchestra'. This wry equivocation is appropriate to a work that takes as its subject the relationship between man and God. The texts are holy, from the Latin Vulgate version of the Psalms; but the resources are those of a twentieth-century concert-hall, involving chorus and symphony orchestra, though the latter is not entirely conventional since Stravinsky omits the dangerously expressive violins and features other instruments, such as a piano, that are not normally found in a classical–romantic orchestra. The piano lends itself well, especially in league with harp, to pattern-making pertinent to Stravinsky's ritualistic purposes. Formally, the work resembles a baroque concerto in three movements, toccata, double fugue, and finale; yet even in the opening bars the harmonic behaviour is remote from baroque convention. A barking E minor triad is chased by toccata figuration in semiquavers, alternating dominant sevenths of E flat and C:

After further appoggiatura-like embellishments and intrusions of rootless whole-tone progressions, these ambiguities seem to be banished by a plain phrygian E minor – but prove, instead, to be the embryo from which the entire tonal structure germinates.

As in *Oedipus Rex*, Stravinsky adheres to an 'allegorically' doctrinal tonal plan. During his middle years Stravinsky didn't abandon classical tonality, as many composers did, but rather imbued it with more rigidly defined symbolism. In the *Symphony of Psalms*, as in *Oedipus Rex*, E flat major – whose humanistic associations extend from the compassion of Bach to the

Freemasonry of Mozart, to the heroic will of Beethoven – emerges as man's key; while C – the white-note key in the major and E flat major's relative in the minor – is the key of God. Between these poles, E minor is the key of prayer and intercession. When the chorus enters, singing the Psalm text in the Latin Vulgate, they entreat God to hear our prayer as the orchestral bass returns to the alternating dominant sevenths of C and E flat. The latter are now enharmonically notated, visually and harmonically in accord with the vocal lines, though the aural effect is unchanged:

A related ostinato figure of alternating thirds appears in middle register, inducing a climax that is also a release on the words 'Give ear unto my cry', for the choral reiterations lever the alternating dominant sevenths towards C major. After a moment's pause, the prayer is answered when, over a 'timeless' chord telescoping tonic, dominant, and subdominant of C, a semiquaver motif descends in dove-like fluttering. This is a briefly revelatory interlude before a return to the prayer's phrygian E minor and the Example 8 music. The alternating thirds in middle register are now combined with their transposed and augmented reflections.

The middle section remains subject to the 'revolving cam' whereby the music is tethered to a white-note or a chromaticized version of the phrygian prayer on E. There is no real modulation until the closing bars of the third and last section, and the toccata ends triumphantly when a resonant tuba descends from prayerful E to approach a consummatory G major triad: which we hear both as relative to the E minor prayer and also as the dominant of God's C, in which sense it is at once an end and a beginning.

The meaning of the Prelude's tonal dichotomy is now apparent, for the second movement is a double fugue in which God's fugue is in C while man's fugue is in E flat. The subjects are never interchanged though they are variously interrelated. God's theme is first stated in C *minor* to which man's E flat is appositively *relative*; and although it sounds pristine, we also feel that we've heard it before:

So we have: for the theme is a linear release of the ostinato of alternating thirds which had dominated the first movement. The pain inherent in the acute leaps of major seventh and augmented fifth (caused by octave transpositions) is neutralized by the theme's static nature. It is perhaps dangerous to speculate as to whether the introduction of God's theme in C minor – the relative of man's E flat major – means that Stravinsky admitted that man had precedence in the order of events!

Since God contains all humanity but doesn't 'progress' his theme doesn't either; and although there are four fugal entries in strict classical sequence, the texture that accrues from the tortuous lines is not classical at all. The harmonic fortuity of the sound, accentuated by the woodwind scoring, is 'Gothically' late medieval – closer to Machaut than to high Baroque Handel, or even Bach. Indeed, this God-fugue is scarcely fugal in Bach's sense, since it doesn't depend on tension between linear independence and harmonic progression. Not until figure 4 is there implied modulation, when God's 'dominant' G minor hints at the minor of its relative B flat. From there, one further step down the cycle of fifths leads to man's E flat *minor*, in counterpoint still dissonantly linear, scored for flutes and piccolo. Striking, in this context, is the humane harmonic pathos that occurs in the chromatic descent before the first choral entry. In that this 'subito dolcissimo' descends from the heights of the God-fugue, it is an Annunciation of what follows when the sopranos chant the subject of the man-fugue:

As a 'human' theme, this is distinguished by the poignant chromatics on the emotive word 'expectavi' and by the rising minor sixth curling back to the fifth on the word 'Dominum', the minor sixth being a traditional sound-image of yearning. Throughout the movement the chorus is restricted to this 'human' theme, though God's fugue-subject persists in the orchestra. The 'man' theme, like God's, is presented in four orthodox entries though, unlike God's, it involves harmonic movement in time since its sense of temporality is enhanced by the post-Renaissance technique of suspension. So harmonic pathos complements linear fortitude, and for the first time Stravinsky's idiom is remotely comparable with Bach's.

At figure 9 occur transitional bars wherein the momentum of the God-fugue is increased by (as though) divinely impersonal canonic stretti. On the word 'preces' (in the fourth bar) an enharmonic pun translates the F flat of the man-fugue into E natural and an E minor triad effects a 'Neapolitan' approach to the cadence. As the orchestra ceases on the dominant of man's E flat, the voices launch into a fugal stretto on the human theme, more or less in its original form. Sopranos begin in F minor, altos follow in B flat minor, tenors in E flat minor, basses in A flat minor, the entries being in sequentially declining fifths. That the 'Lord has set my feet upon a rock' is symbolized in the chorus's singing without support from the orchestra, and also in that their telescoped keys affirm the tonal props of baroque tradition. Yet their human edifice of stretti fallibly breaks, to be replaced by an orchestral interlude that returns to 'metaphysical' canons on the God theme over a pedal B flat (dominant of E flat). As the bass descends to a pedal G – dominant of God's C – the God-theme is rhythmically transformed in the style of a Heroic French overture:

If in the Lullian overture man (Louis XIV) was playing God, here God demeans himself in man's image; and a moment later, after a bar of silent stupefaction, man responds with the New Song that God has 'put into his mouth'. In the resplendently 'Byzantine' dissonance of this climax dominants of God's C major and of man's E flat major are telescoped with 'enhanced dominants' on D and F: so this strictly musical climax totters between the human and the divine.

Towards the end of this wonder-inducing blaze the God-theme renounces its mundanely heroic dotted rhythm but slides down to man's E flat, and the chorus restates the man-theme on the words 'many shall see it, and fear'. This awe-ful fright might be called dualistic since the intervallic contraction of the original 'Dominum' figure has resulted in a starkly exposed tritone, or *diabolus in musica*. But in the movement's coda the devilish interval is exorcised and the crucial F flat is transmuted. While the chorus intones that 'many shall put their trust in the Lord' the lower strings turn the head of the God-theme into an ostinato in quavers. The fourth note of the ostinato, F flat, is now notated as E natural: which is the prayer-note of the first movement but also the major third of God's C. Through this a muted solo trumpet interjects the original version of the God-theme at half speed and at the original pitch, beginning on C. The trumpet's last two notes, C and E flat, ring through the orchestra's closing chords in which are conflated tonic, dominant, and subdominant triads of man's E flat, thereby defusing the basic means of modulatory progression in European music.

The finale begins with a triad of C minor: God's tonic minor but, with its three flats, man's *relative*. The intercessory E natural appears in the strangely scored chord that accompanies the chorus's intoning Cs on the word 'Dominum'. During the dance-song of praise that follows this praeludium, horns recall the first movement's supplicatory chant, so that our ears are attuned for the allegro's corporeal animation, combining flat-seventhed C major with the first movement's barking triads which, being C major triads in first inversion, emphasize the thirds, E to G. When this music returns at the end of the allegro it sails exultantly towards man's E flat, with horns and trumpets cavorting in almost Straussian abandon. Towards the close of the orgiastic dance some tempering of the rampage is achieved as a new harmonic vista unfolds:

The altos' lilting arpeggio in dotted rhythm reminds us of the 'heroic' motif quoted as Example 11; but the freely lyrical line is now the New Song which the fugue had promised but had failed to deliver. With the imitative entry of the basses, G major turns into G minor, thence into C minor, and finally into its relative, man's E flat major. Since the rising arpeggios are liberating, it's remarkable that the hymn that now unfolds over a ground bass of godly fourths reverts to undulations around a static point. This creates, from almost total stasis, genuinely consummatory fulfilment. First, the quadruple pattern of the ground bass contradicts the triple pulse of the melodic parts so that the unchanging pulse seems dis-embodied. In themselves, the melodic voices are nearly immobile, while creating together a sumptuous homophony. Sopranos move stepwise between E flat and C; altos alternate between A flat and B flat; tenors shift between C and its flat seventh; basses oscillate around B flat, sometimes with octave transpositions. The orchestral voices abound in parallel seconds and chromatic passing notes which enrich the sonority without disturbing the near-immobility.

After a hushed reminiscence of the preludial 'Laudate Dominum', chromatic harmonies over the ground bass create what Henry Vaughan called 'the Chime and Symphony of Nature'. The orchestral sonority suggests sap seething and bubbling as the voices exhort 'everything that hath breath' to praise the Lord. When the vocal jubilation ceases, the orchestra is left burning on a chord of the dominant eleventh whose top note is the intercessory E natural. While the ground-bass swings through the last of its six-bar rotations, the orchestral strands float upwards; it seems that we move most freely when most anchored, whether to the earth or to God's will, or to both:

The chorus ends with a retrospect of the finale's initial Alleluyas, which the orchestra caps with the same mysteriously spaced chord of C major: which is in context a revelation, sounding like nothing we've ever heard before, including chords of C major. This sublime closure is perhaps the supreme instance of Stravinsky the Great Compromiser. The tonality of the ground bass's rocking fourths is indeterminate between man's E flat and God's C minor, though man possibly has the ascendancy; the ultimate wide-spaced triad of C major is, however, unanswerable, or irremediable, according to one's point of view.

The 'universality' of the *Symphony of Psalms* springs from the interplay of its contradictory elements: the primitive depths 'below' consciousness; the humanizing concern with reason and feeling; the priestly preoccupation with musical metaphysics. These Contrarieties (in Blake's sense) prove to be inseparable: for the first movement, though it resembles a baroque *da capo* aria and toccata, behaves more like primitive ritual-music in its metrical energy, and more like liturgical intonation in its quasi-monodic lines. Yet it clearly isn't ritual dance or liturgical ceremonial, for neither its corporeality nor its spirituality is fulfilled. Similarly, the double fugue is double because it's concerned with doubleness within the psyche. The God and man themes are complementary aspects of human consciousness, for if God made man in his image, we certainly made Him in ours. That God and man have become disassociated in our modern post-Renaissance dilemma; during the double fugue the poles finally, if ambiguously, meet, through the marriage isn't easy, as the 'Byzantine' climax magnificently demonstrates. Nonetheless, marriage is consummated, so in the finale the barbaric and the civilized are fused. This is why Stravinsky, as Great Compromiser, is also the most crucial and probably the greatest composer of the twentieth century.

The third stage of Stravinsky's religious pilgrimage was already implicit in the *Symphony of Psalms*, which was in turn latent within *Oedipus Rex*. This third phase opens with works like the *Mass* and the *Cantata* (1952) which are still tonal but, starting from medieval texts, also borrow medieval musical techniques in the form of non-harmonic modal ostinati and a kind of pre-ordained serialism which is at first not totally chromatic but is in part derived from the modal serialization of the old plainchant cantus firmus. Eventually, Stravinsky embraced Webern's total chromatic serialism – though he waited for Schoenberg to die before taking so bold a step. Even then, Stravinsky did not employ serialism in a Webernesque spirit but rather in an extension of medieval serializations. Stravinsky's serial music sounds like no-one but himself; and a few of his very late serial pieces count among his most inspired utterances, for his search for serial unity was a spiritual quest before it was a technical adventure.

There hasn't been a great religious composer, at least of the stature of the diametrically opposed Bach and Beethoven, over the last two hundred years, and perhaps we can hardly expect such a composer to have arisen in the world we had made. Yet Stravinsky, the most representative composer of the twentieth century, was creative over a longer span than any other contemporary composer: in his early days he was potently inspired by primitive (Russian) notions of Godhead, while in his middle years he celebrated the humanisms of seventeenth- and eighteenth-century (European) civilizations, in the process reminding us of humanism's insufficiency and of the relevance of the Christian message of a God who *homo factus est*. Only in his last years did he make music that was theological rather than humanistic in orientation; and we have already noted, in considering the *Symphony of Psalms*, that there is deep significance in the fact that Stravinsky, our spokesman, was in some ways a composer of denial for whom the 'human machine' was not always an act of incarnation, though it was always a historical necessity. He *had* to embrace his world's fragmentation of line and disintegration of rhythm, and he knew that something similar had happened before in European history, at the time when the Middle Ages, the supreme eras of

Christian faith, expired. The linear and metrical contortions that crop up in Ars Nova music of the thirteenth and fourteenth centuries sometimes sound to us grotesque rather than life-enhancing; and they were not the creative musical heart of medieval faith, in which Gregorian chant had revealed the basic human instinct for flow and continuity, both within and outside time. Yet the dislocations of Ars Nova were themselves historical necessity that disrupted the pulse and heart-beat in favour of an imposed order that presumptively equated the Will of God with mathematics. If some such mathematical salvation was needed at the expiration of the Middle Ages, how much more desperately was it called for as the post-Renaissance cycle of Renaissance humanism drew to its close in the mid-twentieth century! When, at the very end of his long creative life, Stravinsky took over chromatic serialism, to the surprise of most and the dismay of many, it was to salvage the, or even a, Law that could make music a 'placing together' of sounds that formed a preordained Whole – even though it was a man (Igor Stravinsky) who had decided on the conditions of preordainment. Stravinsky's very late serial pieces sometimes sound startlingly like the most 'grotesque' manifestations of Ars Nova counterpoint: though still more they sound like himself, wrung dry and purged as he approached death. It cannot be fortuitous that the most moving of them should be the *Requiem Canticles*, a setting of fairly brief passages from the Latin Missa pro Defunctis for two soloists, chorus, and an orchestra exiguously employed – in six vocal sections and a purely instrumental prelude, interlude, and postlude.

The nine sections of the *Requiem Canticles* last in toto only just over fourteen minutes. Although they were written for a specific occasion (the exequies and in memory of Helen Buchanan Seeger), it seems probable that Stravinsky, who was in the early 1960s in poor health, thought of them as an elegy for himself, and in so doing, consciously introduced references to music he'd composed over a long life – especially *Les Noces* and *Le Sacre du Printemps* from his 'primitive' phase, and *Oedipus Rex* and the *Symphonies of Wind Instruments* from his neo-classical middle years. Significantly, although the *Requiem Canticles* are strictly serial and chromatic, they don't eschew repeated notes. Indeed the Prelude opens with an ostinato of repeated semiquavers at a tempo of semiquaver = 250. The reiterated Fs establish a modal centre if not exactly a tonality, but what is evoked is not so much a rite of spring as a bleak and remotely disembodied rite of winter in which the melodic string parts (never more than three of them) wispily rotate in cross rhythms of threes against twos, frequently through the ambiguous interval of a diminished third. The ostinato notes swell from single pitches to chords derived from sequential notes of the row, but synchronization between the ostinato notes and the melodic parts is seldom exact. Reminiscences of *Les Noces* and *Le Sacre* sound purged, even crystallized – especially when the Prelude is succeeded by the first choral movement, in which the row is introduced in two six-note segments, the first six linearly on harp and flute, the second as a wide-spread chord. Our awareness of history depends on memory; Stravinsky relives the past in mathematical lucidity, combining skeletonic linear textures with block chords of typically tingling acidity.

The succeeding 'Dies Irae' extracts an astonishing ferocity from dissonant repeated chords for the chorus interspersed with wildly scurrying arabesques from the orchestra. Never before had a Day of Wrath been so wrathfully disruptive in so brief a time and space; and when the bass solo chants the 'Tuba mirum' with intermittent fanfares on trumpets and bassoons, the *wounded grandeur* of the vocal line recalls the spiritually maimed and ultimately blinded King Oedipus of thirty years earlier. The succeeding Interlude for flutes, bassoons, horns, and timpani also reinvokes the world of King Oedipus, pared to the bare bone, in a slow $\frac{3}{8}$ with block chords in cross rhythms. Mostly at a dynamic of *mf*, the Interlude expires more with a whimper than a bang.

The 'Rex tremendae' is indeed tremendous in $\frac{2}{2}$, with the row disposed linearly in the four-part chorus, and the orchestra potent in row-derived block chords involving *almost*-emotive dominant sevenths and whole-tone progressions. When the contralto solo chants the 'Lacrimosa' her vocal line, ringing through the orchestra's sustained chords, reminds us of the agony of Oedipus's wife Jocasta, weirdly fusing the High Baroque with peasant-folk lamentation:

Here the scoring is for flutes, strings, and trombones; but the final choral movement, the 'Libera me', returns to Stravinsky's Russian roots, with some choral voices declaiming the text in row-derived block-chords in a hollow, organum-like texture, while other choric voices urgently *speak* the appeals for liberation. The music both looks and sounds more like Stravinsky's most primitive ritual music or his music for the Russian Orthodox Church than like the fragmented serialism of Viennese Webern; and the veering between the 'whiteness' of ionian C major and the high sharpness into which the voices gravitate culminates in a pun when B sharp 'stands for' the original C naturals.

This may be a reconciliation of opposites rather than an ultimate dubiety; certainly it is capped by a Postlude that is directly related to one of the 'central' and most severely ritualistic of Stravinsky's works, the *Symphonies of Wind Instruments*, a piece which exploits the natural overtone series of bells and in so doing to a degree hands back musical com-position to God. The ghostly quality of the sharply glinting, luminously shining final sonorities, beginning with a chord that incorporates all the chromatic semitones, makes for a threnody on himself as dying-composer that is also an elegy for *us*. Miraculously it works: which is indeed testimony to the magnitude of Stravinsky's achievement.

27

God and Gospel

Arvo Pärt's *Passio Domini nostri Jesu Christi secundum Joannem* (1982), John Tavener's *Fall and Resurrection* (2000), and works by Górecki, Macmillan, and Finnissy

At the time this is written in his sixties, Arvo Pärt, an Estonian, came from a remote country whose traditions were rooted in an ancestrally religious past while being at the same time a part of the Soviet republic. Perhaps it was not therefore surprising that Pärt needed time in which to discover what his direction must be. He began by composing music roughly in Western traditions, with some kinship with the solitudinous inner drama of Sibelius. For a while he tried himself out in the then fashionable technique of chromatic serialism; then dabbled in serialism's polar opposite, totally unpreordained aleatoricism. Satisfied with neither, Pärt submitted himself to a self-imposed silence of several years. When he began to compose again he discovered that he had been *born* again – not of course in the crude evangelical sense, but in that all his music was now concerned with Christian ritual and with the numinous. Even purely instrumental pieces seek the 'eternal silence' at the heart of sound, as is indicated by the title – *Tabula rasa* – of the work that made his name familiar.

Here, hardly less than in his liturgical vocal music, Pärt is creating music that suggests that his technical conversion was a spiritual experience. From the late 1960s onwards his music displays a debt to monodic religious incantation, to medieval organum and heterophony, and to the austerely mathematical polyphony of Machaut and his early Renaissance successors, Ockeghem and Obrecht, whose work Pärt studied during his 'silent' years. If one wants points of reference to the nature of Pärt's music beyond these sources, one might mention the music Stravinsky wrote for the Russian

Orthodox Church, the festive music of central European Janáček, the children's music of Orff, and Satie's *Socrate*. One might mention too the music of Britten, since Pärt composed a five-minute threnody on his death in 1976 – a piece which, scored for a single bell and strings, starts from God's or Nature's bell-like overtone series and swells, bell-like, into multiple intertwining canons that palliate the finality of death in seeming to 'go on' inexhaustibly. The effect has that 'purity of spirit' that Pärt greatly admires in Britten's music: though this doesn't mean that Pärt's *Threnody* was directly influenced by the British composer, any more than by the other composers mentioned above.

Pärt is remarkable because he found it necessary, and possible, to pare away so much, leaving the residue the more meaningful the more exiguous it had become. One might have expected that the doctrinally and allegorically religious nature of Pärt's music would render it remote from most people in an age of unfaith. Such is not the case, for Pärt's innocence seems, if more 'metaphysical' than Britten's, no less pertinent to what the Prayer Book calls 'men of good will'. Magic occurs in *Summa*, a setting for four unaccompanied voices of the Latin version of the Creed. In not attempting to illustrate or express the words the setting resembles medieval music and is distinct from a late Renaissance composer such as Byrd. There is no modulation, and hardly any shift in modality. The magic lies in the memorability of the tune, undulating between stepwise movement and wide-eyed arpeggiated figures in a hypnotic rhythm that bears us on its gentle current, as it was in the beginning, is now, and ever shall be. In the scale and the arpeggio lie the fountain of melody; and when the piece ends on an 'empty' fifth it really does sound like the voice of God – of which in the Middle Ages the fifth, as the most 'absolute' of consonances, had been a prime symbol. Moreover, a comparable effect may be created in a work of Pärt that has no ostensibly religious connotation, for in setting a lyric by the German romantic poet Clemens Brentano, 'Es sang von langen Jahren', Pärt makes, for alto voice, violin, and viola, music that counterpoints the human lover's yearning with the super- (or sub-) human song of a nightingale. At once wistful and consolatory, this music hints now at folk-song, now at devotional incantation, now at a troubadour aubade, now at a child's ditty. This music, like much of Britten's, is Edenic.

Even so, Pärt, as a twentieth-century European rooted in Estonia and Russia and affiliated with Germany where he now lives, cannot but be aware of the bestialities that man may now inflict on his kind, compared with which those of Germany's horrendous Thirty Years War pale: so it is appropriate that Pärt's biggest work should be a retelling of the Passion story, using techniques comparable with those of Heinrich Schütz. But whereas Schütz told the tale in vernacular German, stressing the reality of Christ as a man alive in the then-present world, Pärt uses the traditional

Latin, and calls on clearly defined 'allegorical' technique that impart to the story an epic abstraction. In so doing he reminds us that Mircea Eliade, in *The Myth of the Eternal Return*, has told us that

> primitive peoples do all they can to abolish Time, to conceive of life as a paradise of archetypes wherein Time does not exist if we refuse to notice it. Suffering takes the place of history. In *Illo tempore*, patterns are repeated cyclically; dreams are fulfilled, or calamities occur,

but nothing can be done about them by individual volition. Monotheism, however – especially of the Christian varieties – being based on a direct revelation of divinity, necessarily entails 'the salvation of Time'. The Old Testament victory over the forces of darkness no longer recurs seasonally each spring, but is projected into the future of a messianic 'illus tempus'. The New Testament Christ-King lives out his agon, being in one sense eternally recurrent (like spring) but in another sense, having risen from the dead, 'fixed and finite'. In this sense Christianity is 'the religion of fallen man; and this to the extent to which modern man is irremediably identified with history and progress, and to which history and progress are a fall'.

Pärt's St John Passion is a *demonstratio* of this relation between time and eternity, between the story of a man's life and the death of a god. In a very specific sense the work is *crucial*, remembering that the Christian Cross is a symbol that breaks, with its diagonals, the circularity of the archetypes. It is a history that purports to be the tale of a real man, yet in so far as it is a sacred history this man's tale is outside Time. This conditions the Passion's elaborately codified techniques and structure. The heart of the matter is human speech through which the Word became flesh; for this Word is metamorphosed into act. Whereas Schütz's Passions, dating from the Thirty Years War of the seventeenth century, record the moment at which HOMO FACTUS EST, Pärt's Passion, inverting the process, records the moment when flesh returns to spirit, 'and man became a living soul'.

So Pärt's Passion starts from the Sacred Word that tells a human story, albeit in the Latin Vulgate that evades a particularized time and place. Even the Evangelist – traditionally since the Middle Ages the narrator of the divine legend – is impersonated not realistically by a single voice but by four voices (SATB), suggesting that the tale-teller is potentially any man, woman, or child. Momently, one of the Evangelists becomes Peter, a fallible creature like ourselves; but the only characters from the Gospel who are personified by soloists are Jesus (who in accord with tradition is a manly baritone) and Pilate (who is a light-weight tenor, to indicate the superficiality of even a Very Important Person who teeters between the Kingdom of God and that of Caesar). A small mixed chorus represents the people, or *turba*, usually actively involved in the events but occasionally functioning as comment- ators. Unlike Schütz, Pärt employs instrumental support, though, compared with Bach's scoring, Pärt's is minimal. An organ always accompanies the words of Christ, much as Bach haloes Christ's utterances with strings. In addition, Pärt uses solo violin, oboe, cello, and bassoon: a string-and-woodwind quartet from which he wrests remarkable richness and variety of sonority.

The chorus opens with an apostrophe in the form of a sequence of homophonic chords in six parts, each word separated from its sequel by a comma, imparting a hieratic gravity. All the parts are in the aeolian mode and the organ doubles the voices' chords whilst holding an octave pedal on E. The basic pulse is the minim, though changes of time signature reflect the stresses one may give to words so momentous. Despite the plain diatonicism, passing dissonances abound, so the total effect is pain-ridden:

When the narration proper begins the words (from John 18: 1–40) describe the Agony in the Garden. At first only the bass of the four Evangelists tells the tale, in a plainchant-like line in the aeolian mode. The norm of movement is the crotchet with a metronome mark of 144: which is around normal speaking-pace, and which makes the minim, at 72, the basic speed of the human pulse. The number of crotchets a bar varies semantically in that the grouping of tones corresponds to their spoken stresses, though they are sometimes submitted to doublings and triplings that have allegorical import. Unimportant conjunctive words (such as 'et' or 'cum') are allotted bars of $\frac{1}{4}$, with no accentual meaning. As the recited phrases approach cadence they are underpinned by an instrumental bass, with the cello, oscillating between the tones of an A minor triad, stressing the fourth A to E. The last cadential phrase ('et discipulis eius') is accompanied by oboe, playing an inversion of the voice part as the text refers to Judas the betrayer. This is the first 'conjunctio oppositorum' of many throughout the Passion and it is to the point that Judas should introduce duality into unity. At the words 'quia frequenter' the tenor Evangelist joins the bass in duet; but whereas the bass remains plainchant-like in syllabic movement by step, the tenor oscillates between the tones of an A minor triad. As in *Summa*, the two fundamental melodic sources – scale and arpeggio – are always in mirror-inversion between soprano and tenor, and alto and bass. Pärt's St John Passion affirms faith in a Credo of ultimate melodic verities.

Further evidence of God's inscrutable purpose is offered when the clauses of the narration are echoed by pairs of instruments that reduce the motives to their barest bones, one uttering a rising or falling fourth or third, the other undulating between adjacent tones. If more than two instruments are used, they too involve mirror-inversions; even at the reference to the priests and Pharisees brandishing their weapons there is no disturbance of the devotional mood and mode. The pauses in the declamation are metrically notated in silent bars; and although the instrumental parts grow slightly more animated, their mirror-inversions still suspend us outside time. When the oboe arpeggios leap in sixths instead of fourths or fifths their enhanced vivacity serves not to portray events theatrically, but to introduce a shift in numerical proportions appropriate to Christ's first utterance. For when he asks 'Whom seek ye?' in a descending minor third C to A and a rising scale through A B C his note-values are neither in the basic narrative crotchet nor in the rhetorical minims of the apostrophe, but in sustained semibreves. The mirror-inversions persist.

Up to this point the music has been narrative, as the Word becomes Flesh and the *turba*–chorus seeks its scapegoat. In four homophonic parts the *turba* yell Jesus's name, with soprano and tenor, and alto and bass, now echoing the mirror-inversions previously sung by the Evangelists. But there are two crucial differences: first, the scale figure now gravitates around E instead of A, while the arpeggio has become a triad of (heavenly) E *major* instead of A minor; and secondly, the syllabic declamation has become rhetorical, with a pulse of four times $\frac{6}{4}$. The dramatic effect of this is disproportionate to the simplicity of means; and still more remarkably the effect is enhanced, rather than enfeebled, as the same dramatic crisis recurs throughout the Passion. The near-identity of these E major 'explosions' is palpable; they happen again and again, 'according to the Scriptures'. Even so, subtle variations within the chords ensure that each outburst sounds pristine, thereby offering further evidence as to how the piece exists both within and outside time. Christ's response to the hurly-burly – 'Ego sum' – is as usual accompanied by organ over a deep pedal E. The gravity of his habitual dotted minims and semibreve is evidence that *His* living is 'larger than Life'.

Pärt's conventions remain rigidly stylized as the next narrative section is sung by all four Evangelists in the same crotchet-syllabic metre and the same aeolian mode. Again in mirror-inversion, soprano and tenor, alto and bass, adhere to their stepwise or arpeggiated figures, and again the cadential points are emphasized in instrumental echoes of either or both. The instruments range rather more widely, the violin leaping to the heights in its arpeggio while the bassoon hums its scale in its lowest octave. When the *turba* again yells for Christ to be delivered to them they do so with the same lurch to dominant E major, instead of to an A minor triad. This time the latent false relations and other dissonances are, though still mirror-inverted, more physically painful, being harbingers of Crucifixion, whereby flesh will return to spirit: which is why 'celestial' E major is associated with such dire events.

Christ sings his first consecutive sentence when he appeals to his arraigners to let his friends go free, since he has admitted to his identity. Although his declamation is syllabic like that of the narrators, his note values are three times longer, in dotted minims: so the movement by step preserves a link with human speech while the expanded durations render the declamation heroic, and potentially holy. A fusion of the human with the divine is overt in the first episode of violent activity – Peter's impetuous assault on the priest's servant's ear. Christ's remonstrance to Peter – 'mitte gladium tuum in vaginum' – in solemn long notes, restores the balance; but the profound depths of Peter's human fallibility are explored in his three denials of Christ. Although much ground has been covered in these narrative sections, Pärt adheres to his exiguously 'allegorical' conventions. The Evangelists tell the story in the same syllabic crotchet metre, with the pauses scrupulously notated; the thematic substance barely departs from the mirror-inverted aeolian undulation by step or in variously disposed arpeggios. The instrumental cadences also recur, if less frequently, and at the moment of Peter's ultimate denial the familiar shift to an E major triad occurs in still terser form, for oboe and tenor merely pivot in inversion between A and C.

When Peter warms himself at the fire of coals ('for it was cold') there's a slight hint of expressivity perhaps prompted by Peter's heart-warming fallibility. This triggers Christ's longest arioso thus far, in which he defends the truth of his message; his recitative is again by step, which relates it to human speech, though its basic pulse is again heroically in minims or dotted minims. The cadential phrase broadens to four times $\frac{4}{4}$ on an aspiring scale. The pedal E pervades this section, a rock that Peter may hopefully cling to; but when the narrators resume the story of Peter's denials they return to their tale-telling crotchet movement. The *turba*'s yell at Peter's third denial releases another explosive E major triad. In his betrayal of Christ – a milder version of Judas's – he becomes one of the *turba*–crowd himself, the dissonant false relations being a pun both musically and theologically. But there is no audible representation of the crowing cock, unless the A minor arpeggios are cawed raucously, as they could but probably shouldn't be.

So far the Passion has been a narration of the Word that intermittently turns into action, especially in reference to all-too-human Peter. Another dimension emerges with the appearance of Pilate, the only character apart from Christ who has an independent part distinct from the Evangelist's. Christ's dialogue with Pilate displays both an increase in physicality, Pilate being a well-meaning man who acts awry because he is unaware of the numinous; and also in metaphysical content in that the dialogue concerns the nature of Jewry and of kingship and, more deeply, the relationship between this world and Christ's Kingdom which is not 'of it'. The dialogue ends with Pilate's eternal conundrum 'What is truth?': which is the climax of the argument though not of the action. In this long section there are three 'beats' simultaneously in action: the narrators' basic crotchets; Pilate's minim pulse that places him as a human leader 'above' the narrators but 'below' Christ's dotted minims which are a trinity of crotchets. So Pilate's converse with Jesus generates drama without effacing the quasi-eternal recurrence of the basic motives. The essence of Pärt's Passion is that it unfolds within the old 'paradise of archetypes and repetition' while manifesting the Cross's release from that deception. In this sense Pilate's music is intermediary. It looks, and often sounds, like the broken arpeggios and undulating scales of the Evangelist's archetypes, but tends to transmute aeolian into lydian modality, with a bass on F rather than E, and with increasingly intrusive, devilishly sharp tritones because the Fall was a necessary harbinger of divine grace. When Pilate chants his million-dollar question 'Quid est verum?' his tones are an inversion of Christ's first utterance when he enquired 'Whom do you seek?' They are, however, a tone higher (B D C B) and are accompanied by mirror inversions of an F major, not A minor, triad. Pilate, being a Great Man, even if only materially speaking, ought to be God-like; though he does not know the answer to his famous question, he wishes he did, and so attests to man's potentiality.

The climax to the Gospel story occurs when the *turba* choose Christ as sacrificial victim, rather than Barabas the malefactor; and when Pilate, notwithstanding his unanswered question and his blundering good intentions, washes his hands of the matter. This washing is no purgation but on abrogation of human responsibility because divinity is beyond 'great' Pilate's reach – perhaps further beyond it than that of the meek who are said to inherit the earth. Here Pilate's high-registered, F major-triad-centred arioso threatens desperation ('Ecco adduco vobis eum foras'); and the turba's next explosion on an E major triad becomes, in relation to Pilate's F majorish line, acutely dissonant. When Pilate reminds Jesus that his fate is in his (Pilate's) hands and suggests that it might help if he acted less cussedly, his minim-moving line is not only in the lydian mode on F but is over a pedal note that has shifted from the quasi-eternal E to F also. Traditionally F major is a pastoral, and therefore potentially earthy, key: which makes the effect of the next E major triad 'explosion' the more cataclysmic. Even so, the dissonance-content of this explosion is exceeded by that occurring when Christ has the 'parody-inscription' *Rex Judaeorum* affixed to him, while the 'licentious soldiery' rend his garments. During this outburst the organ droops down the scale to F natural, as though heaven and earth are grinding against one another. Henceforth, the pathos of the final scene is not so much presented in doctrinal allegory as 'incarnate' in the music, for Jesus's humanity is affirmed when he meets the three Marys and sings 'Ecce mater tua' to the familiar undulation before falling and fading, on the words 'ecce filius tuus', from F to E.

But the Evangelists intermittently remind us of the cyclical nature of these events which happen in order that the Scriptures may be fulfilled. After several bars of empty but 'pregnant' silence Christ cries 'Consummatum est' on a scale declining to low A, in his trinitarian dotted minims but ending with a breve worth *four* crotchets. The organ re-establishes the cavernous E as pedal note, but dissonantly inveigles Pilate's F naturals into its four-part texture. After a very long pause the Evangelists intone the words 'Et inclinato capite tradidit spiritus' in unison octaves on the tonic A, in the basic crotchet pulse, slowing to semibreves. This slackening of the pulse and freezing of the blood recalls the end of Satie's *Socrate*, a work that Pärt admires, though the probity of his vision ensures that this passage is in no way parasitic.

And what happens after that deathly music is remote indeed from Satie's purged chastity, 'all passion spent'. For Christ's Passion is just about to reveal its majesty, in the largo coda that balances the initial apostrophe, sung to the words 'qui passus est quo nobis, miserere nobis, Amen'. At the end of the work's seventy-minute duration – in which there has been virtually no 'development' in a story that exists in time in so far as it is human yet outside time in so far as it is divine – there is a moment of sudden illumination: dark death is alchemized into lustrous light which may be momently realizable in this life, whatever may or may not happen 'beyond'. After all that plain diatonic modality a key-signature of two sharps appears. The very slow pulse veers between Christ's Trinitarian dotted minims and Pilate's human but grand minims; the organ pedal treads majestically down an octave from low to lower D. The choric voices are all divided à 2, rising in monumental eight-part homophony from D major consonance to powerful dissonance, swelling from *pp* to *mf*. The voices are silent while the organ pauses on the subdominant G before descending to F sharp: above which the chorus chant D major triads in first inversion, then grind into dissonant suspensions for the word 'miserere'. The pedal note subsides to E, from which tone the human–divine story had originally emerged. For eight slow beats it stays in suspension; only then does it resolve on to octave Ds while the chorus cries AMEN triple-forte in high-spaced, blazing triads:

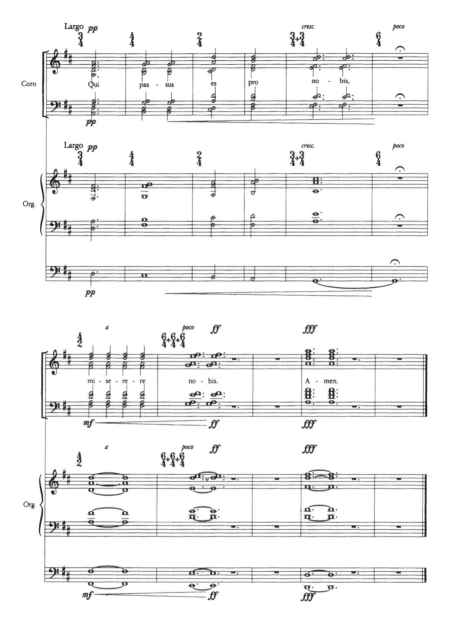

Throughout the seventy-minute duration of Pärt's St John Passion there has been no previous music unambiguously in glorious D major; when it occurs, it sounds both inevitable and irresistible. The narrative Word has indeed become Flesh in which Spirit is now incarnate; and it is the death of the flesh of God that has made the miracle possible. This is why Pärt is no minimalist; far from relaxing into the savage paradise of archetypes and repetition, he is poised on the verge between Being and Becoming, or rather between Becoming and Being, since time is, 'for the time being', transfigured: as are we in what is surely a sublime moment in late twentieth-century music. That Britten's *War Requiem* also ends poised between D major and E is fascinating, if almost certainly co-incidence.

This coda's D major blaze of light is a miracle in its psychic as well as psychological effects, for it enacts the famously mysterious statement about *logos* at the beginning of St John's Gospel:

> In the beginning was the Word, and the Word was with God, and the Word was God. The same was in the beginning with God. All things were made by him; and without him was not anything made that was made. In him was life; and the life was the light of men. And the light shineth in darkness; and the darkness comprehended it not.

Few passages in biblical or any other literature have attracted as much exegesis as this, in which the word 'logos' has meanings even more multiple than those attached to the word Passio(n), of which the root is in passive suffering, while it has undertones of anger and overtones of sexual desire, and is associated, by way of the Greek pathos, with pity and terror. In the plainest sense *logos* is simply the words spoken by Jesus. It may mean a statement, testament, saying, or discourse; collectively, it became the whole of what Jesus said, until the ultimate *logos* denotes the eternal truth presumed to be revealed to man by God, through his Son descended to earth. The Word is thus rational thought mirroring the ultimate reality of the universe: which amounts to an account of how art, and especially music which is the most abstract of the arts, functions. The end of Pärt's St John Passion is a *revelation* of this; only the severity of its abnegation and the strict discipline of its allegory makes it possible that, through it, we may have life 'abundantly'. Clearly Pärt's Passion is the most theologically precise, and in that sense the most 'religious', work discussed in this book. Equally clearly, that doesn't make its 'allegory' as great as Bach's B minor Mass or Beethoven's *Missa Solemnis*. Still, a dose of theological precision may be salutory at a time when spiritual values are in peril.

Pärt's *Passio Domini nostri Jesu Christi secundum Johannem* is the most extreme point so far in what might be a return in European music from an aesthetic of expression-and-communication to narrative allegory designed to promote praise and worship. Whether this means that history is a circular process, wherein humankind's story is unwinding itself to start afresh, is a moot point; but we ought to note that although Pärt is exceptional in the rigour of his re-created gospel, he is not unique. If no other composer has followed his path so scrupulously, at least two others have reverted to a notion of music as a kind of celestial allegory and in so doing have attracted, if not the respect that Pärt has won from a variety of musicians, a popular success that probably exceeds his. These two composers are Henryk Górecki, a Pole who, born in 1933, is around the same age as Pärt, and John Tavener, an Englishman who, born in 1944, is eleven years Pärt's junior.

Górecki's cultural and racial origins are not far removed from Pärt's, for he comes from Poland, being a third member of his beleaguered country's avant-garde *troika*, a contemporary of Penderecki, and twenty years younger than Lutoslawski. During the 1950s he made music, such as his First Symphony of 1959, more or less in their tradition; but in the sixties he hinted at *renouvellement* in the title of his *Three Pieces in the Old Style*, since for him, as for Pärt, to be new was to be old. This music is purged of harmonic, rhythmic, and textural sophistications in re-cognizing the plain modalism of Polish folk song and of liturgical incantation harking back to the Middle Ages. A zealous Roman Catholic and a passionate lover of his native culture, Górecki lives in an ugly industrial city but composes in a remote rural hermitage. Many of his later works are specifically liturgical, or at least devotional, mostly with Latin texts. But his world changed when, in 1976, he composed his Third Symphony for an Orff-like orchestra of multiply divided strings, woodwind, horns, trombones, and piano, plus a soprano soloist: a work that achieved a tremendous, and world-wide, success – in a populist manner that amazed and appalled the modest composer – though his dismay must have been palliated by the pecuniary rewards entailed.

The work consists of three movements, all slow, all laments or 'sorrowful songs', to exiguous Polish texts with deep spiritual and humane connotations. The first movement, which extends to about 25 of the total 55 minutes, opens with double basses whispering a quasi-liturgical theme in unremitting $\frac{2}{4}$ time, strictly in the aeolian mode on E. Fugal entries at the orthodox fifth insinuate themselves on strings which, being divided à 2, attain ten voices in all. As the parts accumulate, from bottom to top, a massive crescendo accrues, the pulse being unbroken, the polyphony seamless. Without break, the fugato unwinds as the parts coalesce and then drop out, leaving only unison Es. The obsession with this traditionally heavenly pitch parallels that in Pärt's St John Passion and, as in that work, most of the 'technical' devices have liturgically symbolic significance.

Long delayed, the soprano soloist enters to chant a fifteenth-century Polish lament of the Virgin Mary adapted from a traditional source: a stepwise-moving cantillation with something of the radiance of Orff's settings of religious texts for children. The voice is depersonalized in being echoed by gong-like harp and piano, enveloped in a dense but concordant halo of string and wind homophony; there is a parallel with Stravinsky's (if not with Rachmaninov's) music for the Russian Orthodox Church. Momentarily, the string-clusters undulate before reaching not the original E major but a luminous D major triad, whereby the 'holy' D–E complex we've commented on in both Pärt's Passion and in late works of Stravinsky is repeated, and Górecki's music returns to its initial $\frac{2}{4}$ incantation, still in or on aeolian E.

The relatively short but still slower second movement brings the soprano solo to the centre of the inaction, the text being near-contemporary: an appeal for the Virgin's pity inscribed by an eighteen-year-old Polish girl on the walls of a Gestapo prison in the Tatra Mountains. The invocation of the Virgin is (predictably) a fifth, A to E, the upper tone lifting to G sharp, then drooping to F sharp. Against this tingling sonority the voice's melody (composed by Górecki in 'traditional' style) and tenebrously declaimed in long, slow notes, seems the more awe-ful. The basic modality becomes B flat minor, a 'dark' key much favoured by Russian nationalist composers in their frequent gloomy moments – and 'symbolically' distinguished in being a devilish tritone away from the heavenly aeolian E. Although the soprano soars in arches, there is no climax; voice and orchestra fade into tolling bells, the exaltation being, like the suffering, as it was, is now, and ever shall be.

Bell-overtones have here much the same import as they have in Pärt's music, and they increasingly dominate Górecki's third and last movement. The text is again historical, yet near-contemporary: the lament of a mother for her son slain in the First World War. The tune has folk origins in nineteenth-century Poland, and Górecki underlines historicity by incorporating a remarkable, folk-inflected chord sequence from Chopin's Mazurka opus 17 no. 4, reinforced by an allusion to the famous dissonance at the climax to the first movement of Beethoven's Eroica Symphony. These references hardly register as quotations but combine with the verbal text to suggest a universality somewhere between folk-song and liturgy, and the terrors inherent in historical time and in the world-as-it-is. Gradually, real events that turn out to be also mythical create something that, though not conventional symphonic development, is growth and evolution: for the last stanza of the verses is set in unsullied diatonic A major, that key of youthful vernality, as against death-haunted B flat minor. The crotchet pulse is continuous as the Mother asks Nature (rather than God?) to bless the earth in the spring of the year. We recall Janáček's comparable apotheosis, though Górecki's is closer to the child-like Second Simplicity of Orff. Even so, the music's incandescence persuades us not only to accept, but to rejoice in, its infantilism.

We may suspect that Górecki's Third Symphony, though a genuine creation, owed its 'fabulous' success in part to its being 'about' tragic, near-contemporary events, musicked in terms both technically and 'symbolically' luminous: so that the music seemed to matter to and to inspire people who had themselves lived through some of those events. This may be why its prodigious success doesn't seem to have lasted. Although there are now a fair number of rival recordings, live performances are declining in frequency. We shouldn't, however, assume that the initial triumph of Górecki's Third was undeserved, and there may be a parallel to the case of Górecki's Third near at home, in the no less legendary success of our own Holy Minimalist, John Tavener – said to be a remote descendant of the great Tudor composer with the same Christian name and almost the same surname, except for an additional r. The sixteenth-century John Taverner was something of an outside in that he was (erroneously) thought to have engaged, during the volatile shifts in creed that dominated the century, in the persecution of Roman Catholics; the current John Tavener is an outsider in that his music, in today's aggressively secular age, is all dedicated to a return to the Christian faith as expressed in the ancient rites of the Greek Orthodox Church – of which he is a practising member and one well-versed in Russian and Byzantine Orthodoxies. The fervour of his religious conviction is indubitable, and the potent accessibility of his music has given him an audience probably as large and certainly as committed as the public that sent Górecki's Third Symphony to the Top of the Pops. Clearly, a lot of people need what he has to offer, or think they do. Tavener himself was, like Górecki, astonished by his first populist successes, especially that of the genuinely aspirational cello chant he called *The Protecting Veil*. The sustained unfolding of melodic line justifies, and validates, the powerful appeal of this piece, though some 'clever' folk, resenting its success, have even attributed it to base motivations. That is unfair; and Tavener needs defending, though I cannot accept what he does as the obvious and only Future of Music.

Like most very successful composers, Tavener is highly prolific, and almost all his music has direct links with liturgy, worship, or ritual theatre. His relationship to 'conventional' music will be revealed if we start with a work that is in effect an opera, though he terms it 'an icon in music and dance'. *Mary of Egypt* was written between 1986 and 1992; and the Mary of Egypt who is the heroine was also known as the Whore of Alexandria, being one of the holy sinners beloved of Tavener. The theme of the 'aural icon' is the mutual reciprocity of the Whore and the Holy Man, and the 'story' follows a purgatorial pilgrimage whereby Alexandria the Whore and Zossima the Holy Man meet, as lovers, in the desert. The techniques of the piece are rooted in monodic cantillations both oriental and occidental, the first three acts being initiated in a Prologue in 'unearthly stillness'.

The writing for the Sinner–Woman and the Saint–Monk is melismatically ornate and microtonally expressive, though both composer and librettist (Mother Tekla, Tavener's nun-friend) wished to present the characters 'impersonally': Mary being accompanied by a 'symbolic' solo flute, an instrument of human sexual love that may be potentially transcendent, whilst Zossima is accompanied by a heroic trombone, hierarchically solemn and possibly inhuman as well as superhuman. Many of the satisfactions we look for from opera cannot occur in this piece, though the scene in which Alexandria and Zossima remeet, after forty-seven years, in the desert, genuinely attains transcendence, culminating in a 'Blessed Duet' in which the two lovers musically chase one another in liquidly uprising scales echoed by their attendant flute and trombone, over eternity's endless drone. This effects a catharsis relatable to that of Greek tragedy. By Act V Mary has died and the monk–lover returns to bury her with the help of the desert animals – a rare moment of worldly vivacity in the iconic stillness. The opera–icon doesn't, however, attain the 'eternal moments' that are captured in short pieces such as *The Protecting Veil* and *The Penitent Thief*, and perhaps again in the large-scale work, *Fall and Resurrection* that was commissioned for, and performed in, St Paul's Cathedral, in celebration of the New Millennium we have recently entered.

Fall and Resurrection unblushingly attempts, in the composer's words, to encompass 'all that has taken place since the beginning of time, and before time'. The text was assembled, if not exactly written, by Tavener's nun-friend and spiritual adviser: who produced, after five or six trials, a text of the iconic nature the composer wanted, replacing the Aristotelian character of Western Christianity with the Platonism of Eastern Orthodoxy, encouraging the use of simple primary colours and of geometric and mathematical symbols similar to those employed by Pärt, if less meticulously worked out. In general the text restores the aesthetic and ideological unity favoured by the Desert Fathers and the Sufi.

This text inspires in Tavener musical imagery of startlingly primitive simplicity – at least as compared with Beethoven's titanic assault on first and last things in his *Missa Solemnis*. Tavener wouldn't (I hope and think) dispute Beethoven's pre-eminence, but he might justifiably claim that his own simple but not simple-minded innocence is precisely what is needed at this millennial juncture in history. Certainly his innocence involves considerable courage, beyond the mere effrontery of tackling so vast a subject on so grand a scale. Tavener wrote for specific artists – soprano, counter-tenor, tenor, and bass soloists; a large mixed chorus; a cathedral choir with boy trebles and altos; and an orchestra rich in violins and double-basses, but with only two cellos and no violas: Fall and Resurrection call for the heights and the depths! The woodwind and brass embrace two each of piccolos and recorders (but no flutes); two oboes, bassoons, and a contrabassoon; four trumpets (in D) and four trombones; two horns and two saxophones, one of which impersonates the Serpent, possibly with recollections of the sleazy saxophones in Vaughan Williams's Sixth Symphony. Extras include a number of 'ethnic' instruments such as a ram's horn and a kaval; an extensive percussion section; an electric guitar; and a large organ (initially that of St Paul's).

These forces are deployed in ways having little resemblance to their normal use in oratorio, though this is the genre to which Tavener assigns his piece. Part I describes, in vividly physical sound-images, the Fall, preluded by an evocation of the silence and darkness 'before time'; followed by an amorphous twittering and tittering signifying chaos, and a vision of

Paradise which, being about five times as long as the section devoted to time-before-time, would seem to be even more miraculously 'beyond time' than timelessness'. The sound-images that project these cosmic events could hardly be simpler – booming double basses and bumbling drums for pre-time; twirling melodic arabesques over endless drones for chaos and vacancy; innocuously wandering recorders for frail Adam and Eve against the vastness of the universe; woodwind swirls for animate nature and fallen man, with the hissing trills of the Serpent as the link between unconscious but animate nature and man in his fallen state. The Fall itself is heralded by a fright-ful blast on the ram's horn, an instrument taken from Nature and at once sub- and super-human. Tavener's iconic musical images are always symbolic as well as physical; even the inarticulate noises of Chaos are derived from a single Byzantine chant (about the Cross) that pervades the whole work. No tune or theme can be recognized as such in chaos's rapidly proliferating hurly-burly, which is pre-human. Against that chaos, human Adam and Eve immediately address one another in monodic chant that is almost song, with microtonally expressive pitch-inflexions in a style between ancient liturgical incantation and even more ancient folk-lament. After the Fall, these laments become heart-rending in their exposed vulnerability, leading into the Psalmist's aspiration, sung by countertenor solo, towards the hills, whence cometh our help. Melismatic recorder over drums and an ostinato on harp define a turning-point, since the Lord responds to our cry, promising that the prophets will help us since, like Stravinsky's Tiresias, they are blind but can see in the dark.

In the following section, Prediction, the countertenor solo carries the narrative burden, quoting bits from the Prophets, interspersed with dance music piped melismatically by a folk flute called a kaval. The kaval tune is monophonic and multi-metred, based on music from the Greek world where Tavener now partly lives. Between the clauses of this Greek peasant-music, prancing over long-sustained drones, the choir interjects the Passion story in telescoped form, with blood-thirsty yells for crucifixion distantly echoing those in Bach's Passions, while the Psalmist intermittently reiterates the Byzantine chant of crucifixion. According to Tavener, the Crucifixion was 'an unwitting attempt by humanity to destroy order': an attempt that failed since it is impossible to expunge the divine. So the third part of the oratorio describes how even an imperfect harmony with God may 'process' to the perfect harmony which is achieved 'when the personal *logos* and the *sophia* of each created being is the effective and determining subject of that being'. This is why it is the 'sinful' Mary Magdalene who redeems Eve when, recognizing Christ, she falls prostrate before him, leading us into a 'Cosmic Dance of the Resurrection'. If sin, like crucifixion, is an essential gateway to bliss, we may understand why, in a work always monodically or hetero-phonically conceived, several redemptive moments are scored for dulcetly harmonic parallel thirds on strings. Maybe they give the Devil his due: as happens too when the Great Organ – a man-made contraption – enters to set the seal on God's victory. 'All is transfigured', says the hopeful composer; certainly the music, which has been *primordial* throughout the work, finally dissolves into God's music of the bells' overtones, pealing in a real building (St Paul's Cathedral) in the real world. This is an admittedly theatrical device which Pärt would never 'descend' to. Still, vision and theatricality are near allied. I find it impressive that Tavener has the courage of his grand conviction; what some people think of as his simplemindedness may be single-mindedness and simple-heartedness. Though one may not believe in the truth of the tale he tells, one respects the faith with which he holds to it.

Although 'holy minimalists' like Pärt and Tavener are exceptional among composers of their generation, there are a few composers here in Britain who have holy aspects without being in any sense minimal. In particular two of the most palpably 'progressive' among British composers who count as young – though one of them has just turned forty, the other fifty – are also Roman Catholic converts whose faith has to a degree conditioned their music. The Scot James Macmillan composed, between 1996 and 1998, a trinity of works that may count as religious testaments. The first, *The World's Ransoming*, a concertante piece for cor anglais and orchestra, pays homage to Maundy Thursday; the second, a Concerto for cello and orchestra, is inspired by the Christian crisis of Good Friday; while the third is a symphony entitled *Vigil*, which awaits the comfort of the Resurrection on Easter Day. While Macmillan's music is densely textured and has sometimes been allied with what has been called the New Complexity (in distinction from minimalism's New Simplicity) Macmillan's musical images share with Tavener's a forceful immediacy: for which reason his music is not difficult to listen to, though it is often demanding of singers and players. The concept of these three pieces is far more dramatic and even theatrical than is Pärt's music, with the solo cor anglais acting as a 'character' defined by the instrument's tone colour; and with the solo cello in the Concerto being an heroic protagonist (Christ?) who is triumphant (but only just) through the murderous events of the Friday called Good. In both works the quasi-operatic soloists 'speak' as readily as do the characters of a born opera composer such as Britten; while in the symphony the recognizable and memorable quotations from plainchant and from a Bach chorale help us to chart our bearings. The virtuosity of Macmillan's orchestration is another bonus for his listeners; everything 'sounds' superbly, and each gesture makes its point, without being specifically liturgical. The dramas Macmillan unfolds profit from the 'universal' Christian themes he deals in, but they are not dependent on an ecclesiastical context, as Tavener's tend to be. Indeed, in the width and breadth of his references to the 'real' world Macmillan may count as a pluralist; the Cello Concerto directly involves the 1996 Massacre of the Innocents by a presumably mad gunman in the Scottish city of Dunblane, during the time when Macmillan was working on this score. The symbolism of the scoring – emulating, for instance, the hammered nails of crucifixion – is sometimes even more overt than Tavener's; the final movement, entitled 'Dearest Wood and dearest Iron', borrows that superscripture from the plainchant Crux Fidelis, and climaxes in a long and difficult cadenza for the soloist, harassed by the pounding of metal bar, bass drum, and the plywood cube borrowed from the Russian mystical composer Ustvolskaya. The cello, in its cadenza, whimpers and howls in scary emulation of the slaughtered infants at Dunblane: a Tavener-like explicitness that may affect the work's durability, though it hasn't done so yet.

The other composer of this duo, Michael Finnissy, is my most unexpected candidate for admission to a book on 'religious' music. He was born in 1947 when American Abstract Expressionist painters were forging the most radically innovatory styles of the battered twentieth century. If there can be a visual equivalent to (much or most) of Finnissy's music it is in the paintings of Jackson Pollock, waggishly known as Jack the Dripper partly for his iconoclasm, but also because he dripped, splashed, and sprayed paint with a random precision that amounted to genius. Finnissy's music, especially that for his own instrument the piano, has an instinctual dexterity reminiscent of Pollock's spontaneity: which amounts to a triumph for the pluralism that has tended to displace concepts like tradition and value. Since anything goes, an artist young in heart may borrow from a multiplicity of global village sources, while from his own world he may deploy 'materials' regardless of distinctions between genres and categories. If that makes for bewilderment, that is because our world is itself bewildered, and bewilderment may stimulate and enliven, as well as deconstruct.

This is evident in the large-scale piano work called *English Country Tunes*, dating from 1977. If the title arouses expectations of benign English pastoralism we are in for a 'rude' shock, since the second word in the title is said to be a pun on the first syllable of the word 'country'. The Old Folk wouldn't have objected to that, and might even have recognized in the ferocious bangings and bashings of Finnissy's Loud Music an industrialized version of the percussive hubbub they'd employed, in 'olden' times, to scare away evil. That may be part of Finnissy's motivation, though the more patent point of his raucous racket brings in political issues that have served savagely to demolish the presumptive innocence of the old songs. Politically, Finnissy says he is an old-fashioned but unregenerate leftie; socially, he thinks he is still marginalized because he is gay. This was probably true once, and although it's less true now one can understand why some of his music comes across as explosively angry, laceratingly nostalgic, and strongly moving in the very violence of its disparities. The long stretches of immensely loud 'New Complexity' music sound as though they are being improvised in the heat of the moment, as they probably were, originally. But even the most rebarbative passages are now notated and we're told that the pianist Ian Pace, if not the composer himself, can play them accurately. Accuracy is hardly the point, for it doesn't make much difference to the effect. But I can hear that Finnissy's keyboard escapades, triggered by his admiration for the pianism of the New World's great Charles Ives, take the listener's, as well as the performer's, breath away. Finnissy sees his art partly as a reanimation of what the past may do to a world in flux: the 'past' including Verdi (whom Finnissy has rehashed), along with blues and boogie, and the intentional chaos of John Cage's indeterminacy. The music emerges as pluralistically polyphonic, polytonal, polyharmonic, and polymetrical, as well as polyethnic, since it draws, not entirely impartially, on the ragbag of 'material' that a multicultural metropolis, such as Finnissy's native London, may spew up.

A Jack the Dripper-style random precision calls not only for precision but for genius, if it is to convince. Unsurprisingly, there are occasions when Finnissy's startlements, persisting a shade too long, cease to startle. What matters, however, is that there are also, in the *English Country Tunes*, moments of stillness through which old tunes of the Folk, who were folk long before industrial technocracies were invented, glimmer in pathetic fragmentation through the hurly-burly, distilling a bloom redolent if not of worlds old and lost, at least of their spiritual values, which may still resuscitate us human creatures. If we listen to the first of Finnissy's tattered tunes, appropriately called 'Midsummer morn'; then to the frenzied babel of tongues he discovers in 'Lies and marvels' and even in the heart-rending 'Seeds of love'; and lastly to the least fragmented of his reconstructed old tunes 'My bonny boy': we understand why Finnissy is on the side of the angels. The momentary quietude of this music tells us, from the hazardous heart of our world, that while there is life there is hope and, no less, that while there is hope there is life. 'My bonny boy' is a love-song: in this case presumably, though not exclusively, homosexual.

So perhaps we can see why Finnissy, springing from the bewildered heart of our pluralistic world, belongs in this book, and does so the more his 'spiritual' values entail no retreat from the mundane world's more obnoxious aspects. In this light it proves to be no surprise that the radical Finnissy has over the last decade composed a fair measure of devotional music, some of which he thinks of in liturgical contexts. Particularly remarkable, and indeed beautiful, are the *Seven Sacred Motets* of 1993, written for unaccompanied voices to traditional Latin texts, some of them from liturgical contexts, others from the Bible, set in a variety of styles, some rooted in plainchant, other in medieval organum or heterophony, or in Ars Antiqua or Ars Nova. This is not in principle different from the practice of British composers of Vaughan Williams's generation, except that the 'old' sources are a few hundred years further back. The relative remoteness of the models means that quasi-oriental grace-notes, long sustained drones shifting between the parts, pure modal melodies usually stemming from pentatonic figurations, and rhythms of considerable metrical complexity sometimes strictly notated, sometimes scored in 'open' durations, combine to generate a spiritually orientated music that is at once very old and very new. The harshness and occasional wildness of thirteenth- and fourteenth-century liturgical music may lend itself more readily to adaptation into terms meaningful to us than do the more blandly harmonic processes of sixteenth-century polyphony; certainly in a piece like his motet on the *Salve Regina* Finnissy extracts from wide-soaring lines over sustained drones of eternity an *ecstasis* that, as the soprano wafts to a high C, is indeed *out of this world*, yet devoid of the theatricality that may creep into Tavener's music when he is less than 'inspired'. Equally remarkable is the end of Finnissy's fourth motet, with words from St Luke: for when Mary 'ponders these words in her heart' the mode shifts up a semitone, irradiating, by so simple a procedure, her heart and ours. We may recall that Holst, in his setting of the medieval carol 'I sing of a maiden', used exactly the same device, with comparably startling effect. It is interesting too that Finnissy's vocal writing, alarming though it often looks, is surprisingly tractable in performance. Can it be that he generates faith in the act of per-form-ance, because spiritual truths may per-sist (live through) the lives in which we sub-sist? I suspect the answer to that question is No. It seems to me improbable that the wheel is coming full circle, though this doesn't mean that phenomena like Arvo Pärt and John Tavener are insignificant in relation to the future of music. In any case a man like myself, who does not KNOW, feels more comfortable in ending this book not back at its starting point, but with an epilogue about a chapter of the New World, a Plain Man called Aaron Copland, a Brooklyner from New York City who in 1950 wrote a song cycle to poems of Emily Dickinson, a Private Woman who lived in nineteenth-century New England. Neither Dickinson's poetry nor Copland's music is Religious Music in the same sense as is most of the music discussed in this book; but their words and music deal in first and last things, speaking direct into the ears of those who nurture 'a Taste for the Infinite'.

28

A Plain Man, a Private Woman, and First and Last Things

Aaron Copland's *12 Poems of Emily Dickinson* for voice and piano (1950)

Aaron Copland was an urban American Jew of Russian extraction born, as he memorably remarked,

> on November 14 1900 on a street in Brooklyn that can only be described as drab. It had none of the garish colour of the ghetto, none of the charm of an old New England thoroughfare, or even a pioneer street. It fills me with mild wonder every time I realize that a musician was born on that street. Music was the last thing anyone would ever have connected with that street. In fact, noone ever had connected music with my family or that street. *The idea was entirely original with me.* [my italics]

Such aboriginality was the heart of Copland's American identity, on the premise of which he became the prime mover and shaker who made American music 'tick' – not because (as his friend and disciple Leonard Bernstein put it) he had 'been around so long but simply because he was the strongest and the best'. Bernstein also remarked that Copland's greatest virtue was that he was 'plain'; after this book's range over many centuries, exploring the (almost) innumerable varieties of 'religions' functions man has discovered in music, it is appropriate that we should end with Copland's plain unpretentiousness. His religions testament is rock-bottom; he wrote only one work – the choral *In the Beginning* – which has a quasi-biblical text and is directly influenced by Gospel musics both black and white, and by Jewish synagogue music. This work requires too many performers, and is too difficult, to be likely to be sung in a church service. None the less Copland did write, in 1950, at the height of his powers, a work which, in setting poems of Emily Dickinson for voice and piano, indubitably confronted first and last things, though neither poet nor composer was Christian.

Apparently a polar opposite to Big City Copland, the poet Emily Dickinson was born in what Thoreau called 'a New England everlasting and unfallen, with dew on the grass', in the early nineteenth century, in the provincial township of Amherst where her family had long been associated with the Calvinistically inclined Church, and her father was President of Amherst College. Although she was not, despite the white clothing she favoured in later life, strictly speaking a recluse, she was no conformist to local *moeurs*; and confessed, in one of her remarkable letters to Thomas Higgenson, a clergyman for whom she appears to have harboured a passion of some sexual avidity, that 'I had a Terror since September that I could tell to none; and so I sing as the Boy does at the Burial-Ground, because I am afraid.' Her family, she adds, 'are Religious, except me, and address an Eclipse, every morning, whom they call their Father'. She herself was independent of man or God; 'you ask of my Companions. Hills, sir, and the Sundown, and a Dog as large as myself, that my Father bought me. They are better than Beings, because they Know, but do not tell; and the Noise in the Pool at Noon excels my piano.'

So Emily Dickinson, in the middle years of the nineteenth century, wrote innumerable small poems which, though indebted to the evangelical hymnody of the time, amounted to gnomic, aphoristic, un- or anti-evangelical statements that viewed men, women, children, and animate creatures in the context of eternity. A hundred or so years later, during his student days in Paris and then in metropolitan New York, Copland created – climacterically in the magnificent *Piano Variations* of 1930 – a music hard and skeletonic in texture and rigidly geometrical in structure, yet also instinct with human tenderness, mirth, and grace. If this music has the starkness of the New York skyline, it is also aware of skyline vistas, proffering a tentatively affirmative answer to the Biblical question: can these bones live? From this aboriginal music Copland went on to explore, in his theatre-music for dance and his remarkably intelligent film-scores, a Russo-Hebraic, Negro-Cowboy American mythology mirroring the country's polyethnicity – especially in the ballets *Billy the Kid* (1938) and *Appalachian Spring* (1943–4) – and creating an American musical vernacular vastly influential on two generations of lesser composers.

It was only to be expected that, as Copland grew to maturity, the 'difficult' idiom of his early works would coalesce with the manners of his 'functional' music for theatre and cinema; and it was also possible, even probable, that this fusion might trigger the superficially improbable marriage of the twentieth-century urban composer with the nineteenth-century provincial–agrarian poet. This happened when, in his fiftieth year, Copland's set twelve of Dickinson's poems for solo voices and piano. They were the first solo-vocal work he had written since 1928; twenty years later, the mere presence of a human voice implied a shift away from the Big City 'machine' towards a fallible humanity, in forms involving the 'lonesomeness', perhaps the innocence, and certainly the formidable intelligence that accrued from the 'terrifying honesty' of this extraordinary, in some ways Blake-like, poet. Emily Dickinson wrote of 'myself and Silence, some strange race / Wrecked Solitary here'; of the fascination and the contagion of the world; of the necessity for, and the impossibility of, merely human love; and of the backcloth to our solitariness provided by Nature and Eternity. With only a single if wide-ranging human voice (the songs were written for the operatic mezzo, Jennie Tourel) and a piano employed with characteristic exiguity, Copland created a sonic world that elides nineteenth-century provincial New England with twentieth-century New York City, making an art that parallels the words of Thoreau: 'I wish to see the world through the medium of much air or heaven, for there is no paint like the air.'

No music could fulfil this prescription more consummately than does Copland's setting of the first poem in the cycle: which is the longest number, and among the most beautiful. It offers a continuum of Nature within which the aspects of human experience embraced by the songs live, move, and have their being. Here is the text, in Dickinson's eccentric punctuation which is not meant to be grammatical, but to tell one how to read, and still more to recite:

> Nature – the Gentlest Mother is,
> Impatient of No Child –
> The feeblest – or the waywardest –
> Her Admonitions mild –
>
> In Forest – and the Hill –
> By Traveller – be heard –
> Restraining Rampant Squirrel –
> Or too impetuous Bird –
>
> How fair her Conversation –
> A Summer Afternoon –
> Her Household – Her Assembly –
> And when the Sun goes down –
>
> Her voice among the Aisles
> Incite the timid prayer
> Of the minutest Cricket –
> The most unworthy Flower –
>
> When all the children sleep
> She turns as long away
> As will suffice to light Her Lamps –
> Then bending from the Sky –
>
> With infinite Affection
> And infiniter Care –
> Her Golden Finger on Her lip –
> Wills Silence – Everywhere –

This poem, written around 1863 during Dickinson's vintage years, seems to view Nature as beneficent while at the same time distilling impersonal emotions of mystery and awe. The slightly asymmetrical hymn-book movement, the half-rhymes, and the hesitancies – as though to catch the breath – invoke a pristine wonder, bearing us through Nature's fecundity, whether or no 'she' can be said to 'care'. Certainly, Nature won't tell, for the backcloth to her is Silence within which the activity of animate creatures is apparently self-willed. Rampant squirrels or impetuous birds would seem to be as contrariously divisive as are we human beings. Peace comes to them, and to us, only if created nature accepts creating Nature's seasonal process, asking no questions that are of their 'nature' unanswerable. The wonder of it must, and may, suffice.

Copland's music to this poem creates precisely the open-eared and wide-eyed wonder of the poem, wherein nature and human love are counter-pointed with death and eternity. The song has a key-signature of three flats, though the tonality is ambiguously between E flat major and the mixolydian mode on B flat. The 'crystalline' piano writing (so designated by the composer) emulates bird and beast noises in empty space, the thin textures and precisely double-dotted rhythms making for a luminosity typical of Copland's piano sonorities, now radiant rather than (as in the *Piano Variations*) sharply metallic. When the voice enters its phrases are declamatory, veering between major thirds and stepwise movement in 'speaking' rhythms, distantly recalling Hebraic incantation:

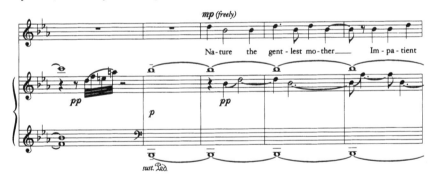

The piano part is mostly in two voices, one for each hand, over a slow-moving, ostinato-like bass. The consistency of the figuration, despite the spasmodic squawks of birds, grunts of beasts, and buzzing of insects, validates the continuum wherein life persists, occasionally shifting in tonal gravity but seldom modulating to a new 'home' since the earth is a totality. For the third stanza there is a change of key-signature to one flat and more than a hint of pastoral F major; the interweaving of arpeggiated thirds in the right hand and of scalewise figures in the left grows more animated, glittering as the words describe Nature's infinite variety: until, at the reference to that 'minutest Cricket' and 'most unworthy Flower', pentatonic chitterings blossom into multiple trills that may – like those in late Beethoven – be seraphic. Then, within double pedal notes on B flats high and low, we return to humanity as Nature offers her benediction to the sleeping children. The song ends, like Copland's great Piano Sonata of a decade earlier, with a gradual slowing down of life's momentum, as Nature 'wills silence everywhere'. The expansion of the vocal line, both in time-values and in range of pitch, equates emptiness with peace.

The second poem in the cycle is late in date (1883) and the musical setting lives up to the first line in being fast and furious:

> There came a Wind like a Bugle –
> It quivered through the Grass
> And a Green Chill upon the Heat
> So ominous did pass
> We barred the Windows, and the Doors
> As from an Emerald Ghost –
> The Doom's electric Moccasin
> That very instant passed –
> On a strange Mob of panting Trees
> And Fences fled away
> And Rivers where the Houses ran
> Those looked that lived – that Day –
> The Bell within the steeple wild
> The flying tidings told –
> So much has come
> And much can go,
> And yet abide the World.

Here the capitalizations are peculiarly crafty, elevating Nature's Green Chill and that alarming Emerald Ghost over some of mankind's most treasured contrivances, including the heaven-aspiring steeple: though the final line allows the World desperately to survive. Copland's setting has a key-signature of three sharps, its tonality being ambiguous between A major and the lydian mode on D – the former admitting to Nature's 'innocence', the latter (more dubiously) to her 'care'. The vocal line is grand as well as fierce, often in 'primitive' pentatonics; and the piano part at first acts out Nature's unbridled racket – revealing, in ironic contrast to the first song's calm, what Nature is 'really' like. Chattering semiquavers around A in the right hand buffet against G minor quavers in the left: from which bitonality that Emerald Ghost makes a dramatic appearance by leaping through a devilish tritone from B to E sharp, capped by a savagely declamatory electric Moccasin. As floods and uprooted trees make for chaos, the piano texture turns into 'blurred' fourths and seconds in a triple, replacing the duple, metre. Back in $\frac{2}{4}$, The World's survival is grandly in the lydian mode on A, with telescoped dominant-tonic dissonances on piano:

After so much outgoing fury the next song, 'Why do they shut me out of Heaven?', is in Dickinson's vein of wry whimsy, for of course it is not 'they' but Emily herself who eschews Paradise. The style is that of Gospel music, perhaps more white than black, with an arresting opening phrase pivoting on godly fourths and fifths:

The phrase ends with an angry leap up to high G flat: after which Emily pricks bubbles of pretension by singing 'a little minor', modulating from a possible F minor to a probable E flat minor, 'timid as a bird'. With a key-signature of four flats but with added flat sevenths, the song appeals, again in falling fourths, to the angels to leave Heaven's door slightly ajar: though sad-sighing seventh chords sound more comic-pathetic than dolorous, presumably because Dickinson doesn't believe that the Doorkeeper really exists and suspects that, if he did, he wouldn't be a Gentleman. At the *da capo*, however, anger returns in more exasperated form, since her question ('Did I sing too loud?') now leaps through a fraught sixth, to A flat, instead of through a fifth to G flat. Comic pathos, or pathetic comedy, seems to be replaced by sorrowful regret since the sighing seventh-chords this time close on a 'lugubrious' triad of F minor, the key traditionally associated with the infernal regions since in the baroque era it was the lowest minor key in common use, as 'heavenly' E major was the 'highest' major key.

If this Gospel song is seriously playful, the fourth number, 'The World feels Dusty', is peculiarly cryptic in text:

> The World – feels Dusty
> When we stop to Die –
> We want the Dew – then –
> Honors – taste dry –

> Flags – vex a Dying Face –
> But the least Fan
> Stirr'd by a Friend's Hand –
> Cools – like the Rain –
>
> Mine be the Ministry
> When thy Thirst comes –
> And Hybla Balms –
> Dews of Thessaly – to Fetch –

Characteristically, Dickinson pays homage to human compassion as distinct from Flags and public Honours that may be incidental, even accidental, to one's life and death. The poem's corporeal gait – with pause-mark dashes in almost every line and sometimes more than one per line – is even more tentative than usual: which is hardly surprising if the verse reflects specific moments of expiration. In two (admittedly 'very slow') pages the song mirrors this in phrases at once valedictory and aspirational: the valediction being in the piano's dissonantly sighing thirds and fifths, the aspiration in the voice's nobly uplifting contours, both in the physically literal and in a metaphoric sense. The key-signature has two sharps, but the song is in neither D major nor B minor but in a dorian mode on B that compromises between the two. It's a moment of holy-seeming magic when the Friend's Hand 'Cools – like the Rain' and the piano's weeping intervals become minor thirds, possibly in B *major*:

Although the final vocal phrase would seem to be in B minor with sharpened cadential seventh the piano enharmonically translates the A sharp into B flat, and the accompaniment trails off over a first inversion E flat major triad as though the ultimate mystery of the moment of death were incomprehensible, or perhaps inapprehensible: as of course it is.

It is probably not fortuitous that the death-song of 'The World feels Dusty' should be followed by the cycle's only 'straight' love-song – though since one suspects it must be addressed to Thomas Higgenson, it is more a song about love's impossibility:

> Heart, we will forget him!
> You and I – tonight!
> You may forget the warmth he gave –
> I will forget the light!
>
> When you have done, pray tell me
> That I my thoughts may dim;
> Haste! lest while you're lagging
> I remember him!

The plethora of exclamation marks, the tremors in the swaying rhythm, render the words relatively conventional, at least for Dickinson; and the music might be a peculiarly refined parlour song, overtly in E flat major and with clearly defined, if not always orthodox, modulations to B minor, C sharp minor and B major. The tempo is 'very slow', the crotchet pulse regular, with piano part in two 'real' parts, the spacing typically wide. The 'louder and faster' expansion of the vocal line as she tries to dim and dumb down her thoughts, makes for a deeply expressive climax, while the final phrase, prompted by her fear of remembering, creates a reverberating sonority to support the voice's painfully semitonic appoggiatura on the final, most crucial, word 'Him'.

This autobiographical climax is capped by a fair-sized scherzo on a nature-poem ('Dear March, come in') in which the month of March, personified, is entrapped in human duologue with the poet, though any replies March utters are not verbal, but presumably in her own ('natural') terms. Here Emily confronts Nature, posing as a Heroine in the seasonal drama of Spring; she survives sportive tussles with Nature's 'indifference' but not the hurts – on the evidence of the previous song – that other human beings can and do inflict. On the whole, this March-scherzo in a rapid $\frac{6}{8}$ and in F sharp major's six glittering sharps is a merry song, with the conversational vocal line skittish but with 'open' intervals often floating around the jazzy chord of the 'added sixth'. Adherence to speech rhythms as Emily dialogues with Nature makes for an interaction of quaver triplets and duplets in the vocal part; as usual, there is much empty space (or air) in the wind-blown piano part. Free modulations – to B minor and F minor and sundry modal permutations of them – enact Nature's exuberant unpredictability: though the sweetly seductive chord of the added sixth in F sharp is a beacon to lure us home. The song ends – after reiterated, wide-spaced F sharp major chords with added seconds explicitly marked 'indifferent' – with a delicately spread chord of the added sixth itself: wiping away, perhaps, a tear over Nature's volatility:

The cycle's climax comes in the next number, marking the halfway house. 'Sleep is supposed to be' is an alarmingly grand poem unusually in three-lined, one-rhymed stanzas:

> Sleep is supposed to be
> By Souls of sanity
> The shutting of the Eye.
>
> Sleep is the station grand
> Down which on either hand
> The hosts of witness stand!
>
> Morning has not occurred!
> That shall Aurora be –
> East of Eternity –
>
> One with the banner gay –
> One in the red array –
> That is the break of Day!

In this poem, written in 1848, before Dickinson had evolved her personalized pause-mark dashes and capitalizations, our everyday or every night sleep is contrasted with our Last Sleep on the brink of eternity. For

Dickinson, this carries no specifically Christian connotations though the grandeur of the concept is palpable, and Copland's music catches not only its majesty, but also its awe and terror. The key-signature is that of B flat minor, though since the sixths are usually sharpened, the mode is probably dorian on B flat. Peremptory dotted and double-dotted rhythms again hint at Jewish liturgical incantation; the spacing of the wide-arpeggiated vocal phrases makes them echo into empty space and endless time. The voice part, riddled with leaps of seventh, ninth, tenth, and even eleventh, is more congenial to a Jewish cantor or Negro Gospel-singer than to an academy-trained concert singer, and nowadays one might think that only a Jessye Norman could produce a vocal line fully adequate to the piano part's thunderous sonorities, which at first are consonant, though in the last two stanzas their dissonance-quota soars in violent false relations no less abrasive than those of the *Piano Variations*. At the end the voice is startlingly wrenched up a semitone to blaze fortissimo, and unaccompanied, in E major – traditionally, if here only in wish-fulfilment, the key of Heaven! The piano sonorities, held on the pedal, rumblingly reverberate through the singer's sustained E natural:

No wonder Copland asks for a 'long pause' before the cycle returns to relative normality in the next song, about Spring's seasonal renewal.

This song, after the assault of the previous number, seems bemusedly indeterminate:

> When they come back – if Blossoms do –
> I always feel a doubt
> If Blossoms can be born again
> When once the Art is out –
>
> When they begin, if Robins may,
> I always had a fear
> I did not tell, it was their Last Experiment
> Last Year.
>
> When it is May, if May return,
> Has nobody a pang

Lest at a face so beautiful
He might not look again;

If I am there – one does not know
What Party – One may be
Tomorrow, but if I *am* there
I take back all I say –

Doubting seasonal process is perhaps the ultimate unfaith, more radical than wobbly belief in a Named God. Copland expresses this by taking his cue from the verse's wavery rhythm and circular argument, beginning his setting in 'quietly expressive' vein in an unassuming, undulating movement that reflects the uncertainties of the words. The key-signature has two flats, but a third (A flat) appears in the first two bars, only for the fourth bar to cadence in F major (with one flat *less* than the signature). Gently flowing arpeggios are bandied between the hands, and their up and down arches combine with the fluctuating tempo to create doubt's Essence. Anxiety about the robins' Last Experiment makes for a small but clangorous climax elevated to or around F sharp major; but flatwards modulations return us to tempo and to a coda murmuring the F major figure of rising fifth and falling third, with an oddly disturbing final cadence from a first inverted triad of E minor to F major with added sharp seventh. The poet's bemusement is subtly captured, though this interludial song can reveal its full significance only in the context of the whole cycle.

And the answer to dubiety seems to be, on the evidence of the next song, despair, for the number is unequivocally deathly:

I felt a Funeral in my Brain,
And Mourners to and fro
Kept treading – treading – till it seemed
That Sense was breaking through –

And when they all were seated
A service, like a Drum, –
Kept beating – beating – till I thought
My Mind was going numb –

And then I heard them lift a Box
And creak across my Soul
With those same Boots of Lead again, –
Then Space – began to toll,

As all the Heavens were a Bell,
And Being, but an Ear,
And I, and Silence, some strange Race –
Wrecked, Solitary, here –

And then a Plank in Reason, broke
And I dropped down, and down –
And hit a world, at every plunge –
And Finished knowing – then –

In this fearsome and fearful poem almost all the rhymes are imperfect and, in the last stanza, completely disappear. The imagery, however, is as vivid as a nightmare, which perhaps the poem originally was. In the first two stanzas the repetitions of treading and beating are horridly constrictive of the natural pulse; in the penultimate verse the punctuation's separation of the words 'Silence' and 'Solitary', and in the last verse the break in Reason's unequivocally lifeless 'Plank', are trenchantly acted out, while in the last line the capital F for Finished, followed by the lower case for 'knowing', make their remorseless point, the more so because the poem, like so many of Dickinson's, ceases on a dash and Silence. We never learn whatever it was she didn't know!

Copland's music tends to be 'openly' American in texture but here the textures are muddily constricted. Although marked 'rather fast', the pulse is grimly funereal, with a procession of thick triads of A flat major and minor, often telescoped in false relations played by the right hand, while the left hand grinds and groans in chromatic semitones:

The figuration change for the second stanza's 'Service', with piano imitating the thudding Drum and the vocal line chromatically anguished. In the last three stanzas the textures clarify a little, at first with (Last?) trumpets in double-dotted rhythms in parallel fifths, and in C major at that. But for the piece's scary end there is a return to the A flattish tonality of the opening, expiring on the tritone D flat to G natural:

The last three songs deal in what William James called Varieties of Religious Experience, in terms that are more psychological than religious, let alone theological. In 'I've heard an Organ talk sometimes' the variety would seem to be Bostonian, though Emily may be implying that any little old New England chapel may, at the right moment, work like a Cathedral. Though the words deny any suggestion of mystical experience – or at least of any direct apprehension of it – Copland sets them with a grandeur appropriate to a cathedral, in processions of plain diatonic concords not grammatically related yet palpably churchy and organ-like in sonority. Occasionally, the rhythms and harmonies overlap in ways that Charles Ives had been wont to use to emulate the *rightness*, in lovingly amateur performance, of wrong notes, caused by fallible synchronicity. Both vocal line and piano part are marked 'simply', for Dickinson approached holy awe in humility; when she confesses that she 'understood no word' the organ uttered, Copland rewards her with peculiarly expressive false relations:

That the end achieves a triumph for B flat major over its minor in an immense sweeping arpeggio attests to the power of wish-fulfilment, which may seem truer than truth. The direction 'Grandioso', beloved of popular nineteenth-century American composers such as MacDowell and Gottschalk – and of course of tub-thumping hymn-pounders dubious about the worth of their wares! – springs irresistibly and unironically to mind.

Although the next song is called 'Going to Heaven' it too is basically in 'earthy' B flat, a fifth lower than 'pastoral' F major. The idiom is modelled this time not on New England hymnody but on Gospel music black rather than white.

Going to Heaven!
I don't know when –
Pray do not ask me how!
Indeed I'm too astonished
To think of answering you!

Going to Heaven!
How dim it sounds

And yet it will be done
As sure as flocks go home at night
Unto the Shepherd's arm!

Perhaps you're going too!
Who knows?
If you should get there first
Save just a little space for me
Close to the two I lost –

The smallest 'Robe' will fit me
And just a bit of 'Crown' –
For you know we do not mind our dress
When we are going home –

I'm glad I don't believe it
For it would stop my breath –
And I'd like to look a little more
At such a curious Earth.

I'm glad *they* did believe it
Whom I have never found
Since the mighty Autumn afternoon
I left them in the ground.

This is another wistfully playful poem dismissing a Heaven in which Emily can't 'believe', though qualifying disbelief slightly by admitting that she is 'glad' her parents did believe. Copland's music is playful too, setting the words 'Going to Heaven' to a sprightly ascent through a sixth for the voice, imitated by the piano in vestigial canons, with the pianist's two hands slightly unsynchronized, since these child-like heaven-seekers are a shade out of step. But the jolly dance rhythm of $\frac{6}{8}$ against $\frac{3}{4}$ and the voice part's mingle of quaver triplets and duplets combine with the prevailing pentatonics to counter doubt in somewhat 'black' innocence. When Emily pleads for a little place to be reserved for her 'close to the two I lost' the music modulates freely and remotely – to what might be lydian G major (a mode of healing), but returns *da capo* to B flat major, with the piano's canons even more gauchely out of synchronicity. She pipes the words 'I'm glad I don't believe it' unaccompanied, standing on her own, and rather slow; but admits that she is glad they *did* believe it, still slower and more musingly, by modulating sharpwards to heavenly E major. A major triad of this key occur as the final cadence, held by the piano's sustaining pedal, whilst high in treble register the pianist tinkles the original 'Going to Heaven' ascent at the original tempo, and still in B flat, a devil's tritone away from the celestial E major chord:

The epilogic song 'Because I could not stop for Death' is one of Dickinson's tragic masterpieces, countering her tremulous jokes, written again in the crucial year of 1863.

> Because I could not stop for Death –
> He kindly stopped for me –
> The Carriage held but just ourselves
> And Immortality.
>
> We slowly drove – He knew no haste
> And I had put away
> My labour and my leisure too,
> For His Civility –
>
> We passed the School, where Children strove
> At Recess – in the Ring –
> We passed the Fields of Gazing Grain –
> We passed the Setting Sun –
>
> Or rather – He passed Us –
> The Dews grew quivering and chill –
> For only Gossamer, my Gown –
> My Tippett, only Tulle –
>
> We paused before a House that seemed
> A Swelling of the Ground –
> The Roof was scarcely visible –
> The Cornice – in the Ground –

303

Since then – 'tis Centuries – and yet
Feels shorter than a Day
I first surmised the Horses' Heads
Were toward Eternity –

Copland's setting of this great poem ties up with the tremendous declamatory setting of the seventh poem, 'Sleep is supposed to be' which, forming the cycle's climax, had concerned the mysterious relationship between sleep and death. Copland's suspended boogie rhythm, his widely arpeggiated vocal lines and false-related, bell-clanging piano sonorities, had admitted that, although Dickinson couldn't comprehend what the difference between sleep and eternity was, such a distinction might, just possibly, exist. It may even be possible that there are affinities between the vast American Emptiness that Copland discovered in the finale of his Piano Sonata of 1940 and Emily Dickinson's no less empty Eternity. The grandeur of the seventh song may be a kind of rhetoric complementary to the American Innocence; in the final song, however, the same sublimated boogie rhythm acquires a tragic dignity, or what Copland calls 'a quiet grace'. Here the bluesy boogie rhythm (which for old barrelhouse pianists had signified the dusty bustle of the World) becomes the ambling of Death's horse-and-carriage, making him a Gentleman of sorts, if we're willing to be on speaking terms. Both poet and composer respond to Death with courteous familiarity and see, over those Empty Fields of Gazing Grain, the gambolling school-children of the future who, in playing, also *strive* to learn life's lessons, alongside a 'Swelling of the Ground' that is at once a tomb and a pregnant womb.

The key-signature has three sharps, but the basic tonality is dorian on B, with its sharpened sixths. The opening figuration of the piano part is identical with, but a semitone higher than, that of the seventh song's dorian mode on B flat; and possibly for the first time in the cycle the rhythm attains a gently regular pulse more appropriate to 'old' New England than to brash New York. Here the gentle pulse flowers into lyrical melody in which the leaps now suggest not strain, but a freedom allied to that of the Air and of those Fields of Gazing Grain. Consider, for instance, the ceremonious phrase in which Death 'kindly stopped' for me:

A Chariot that can ride so equably may at least give the illusion of *going somewhere*; and while we're alive, illusion may suffice. Neither Dickinson nor Copland felt capable of commenting on what happens when we're dead; though it's appropriate and moving that Copland asks his singer to come to *rest* on a high, long F sharp if she can make it, but also provides her with a humbler alternative an octave lower, if she can't. Through the singer's sustained F sharp, in either octave, the piano's boogie-rhythmed Chariot achieves consummation on the major triad of a tierce de Picardie:

The peculiarly American moment of sublimity that Dickinson and Copland here achieve – she from her mid-nineteenth-century provinciality, he from his mid-twentieth-century urban metropolis – are now a precious part of our heritage too, given the pace at which the whole world, for better and for worse, is being Americanized. Out of the denial of spontaneous lyricism that was a consequence of the mechanized world he grew up in, Copland won through to a kind of serenity which is in no sense religious – as is the peace that is sometimes born of the polymorphous textures of the music of Charles Ives – but is rather a dissolution and suspension of movement: a running-down of Western Time's clock, as the pulse slackens with the energetic harmonies statically interlocked and the melodies cadencing in Copland's 'quiet grace'.

Verbally, this peculiarly American experience – which increasingly pertains to industrial civilization in general, and has something to do with America's geographical immensity – has been described in a famous passage from Scott Fitzgerald's *The Last Tycoon* (who hasn't of course arrived yet):

> I looked back as we crossed the crest of the foothills – with the air so clear that you could see the leaves on the Sunset Mountains two miles away. It's startling to you sometimes – just air, unobstructed, uncomplicated air.

This is a precise description of the end of Copland's great Piano Sonata or of the last song in his Emily Dickinson cycle. A hundred years earlier the same vision was discernible here and there in Emily Dickinson's poetry – certainly in those Fields of Gazing Grain beside which Death's Chariot unperturbedly, and perhaps even benignly, trundled. I type these words on the hundredth anniversary of Copland's birth, and feel that no apology is necessary for treating his piece in greater depth than any other discussed in this book, even those of Stravinsky who was Copland's Russian mentor. Of course this doesn't mean that I consider Copland a greater composer than Stravinsky, let alone than Bach and Beethoven, and the many other old or fairly old masters whose contribution to 'religious' music has been assessed. It does mean that I think Copland's view of those 'first and last things' is sensitively in tune with our assessment of them or at least, not to beg any questions, with mine. I agree with Bernstein that Copland's 'plainness' makes him an artist who may stand, generously and nobly, for most of us, if not for all.

Epilogue

We have seen in this book how for coming up for over a thousand years people have made music in praise of a God they profess to believe in while at the same time inflicting in His name appalling brutalities and indignities on other people whose gods don't accord with their own. It would seem that religions are wish-fulfilments that are supposed to bind us together but usually don't. Yet if religions generate ghastly evils, their wish-fulfilments embrace the heights of our aspirations along with the depths of our depravity: as we have noted in surveying the musics man has created over the centuries. In the final chapter we were able to detect, if not a credible creed, at least a 'taste for the infinite' in the music of Aaron Copland, an American Plain Man who was an outsider in being Jewish, yet was also a plain representative of urban democracy in the most materially prosperous industrial technocracy of the modern world. This suggests that I and the multitudes like me who, being ag-nostic, do not *know*, should also admit that things unknown are not necessarily unknowable. This does not mean that we ought, like Pärt or Tavener, to go back to the beginning, to start again; but it does mean that we should keep minds open and senses alert, recognizing that the most efficacious aid towards having life more 'abundantly' may lie in the varied and often contradictory wish-fulfilments from which great and less than great composers have made worshipful music.

If we view music in the widest historical context, we realize that it is a language that functions on its own terms. Its meanings are more basic than those of the other arts, in that its language is semiological; its imitative properties, in so far as they exist in (say) the henniness of Rameau's *poule* or the cuckoldry of Beethoven's cuckoo, are superficial, even trivial. Its essence lies in its relation to the science of number: which is why our progressive Western world, though it has tended to forget that all art is revelation as well as incarnation, has never totally denied the religious implications of music, as a means of 'binding', if not as an ultimate repository of truth. In classical – Greek and Roman – eras philosophy embraced concepts fundamental to the Western musical mind, from Plato's creation myth, through the description of musical harmony in relation to embryology offered in Corpus Hermeticus, to Plotinus's notion of Universal Harmony. Pythagoras's complementary accounts of music as a revelation of divine order (scientifically in the Harmonic Series, religiously in the Eleusian Mysteries), and as guide to and moulder of human conduct, recur in sundry guises across the centuries; nor is there a radical change of front when, with Boethius, the Classical merges into the medieval Christian world. Though we would understand this better if Boethius had completed the musical sections of his immense treatise on the mathematical sciences, enough survives to illuminate the distinctions and the interlinkings between *musica mundana* (the Music of the Spheres), *musica humana* (music uttered by human voices), and *musica instrumentalis* (music made through man-constructed *instruments*, using dead matter in the interests of spiritual life). The status of *musica instrumentalis* is precarious, since matter always threatens to be material.

This view pervades Judaic and Islamic musical thought also, overlapping with Christian Europe. Although the writings of Philo, Isaac ben Solomon and the Brethren of Purity are often too strictly metaphysical to be apprehensible in Western terms, it would seem that angels, in or above whatever culture they spread their wings, sing in comparably dulcet tones and with the same respect for geometric principles. There is no disparity between, on the one hand, a Sufi description of heavenly music or Rumi's Song of the Reed Flute or his Remembrancer of the Melodies of Paradise and, on the other hand, the Christian accounts of angelic music presented by Dionysus the Areopagite, not to mention individualized audible angels, recounted by the likes of Richard Rolle and Henry Suso.

By the time of Europe's Renaissance and post-Renaissance – conveniently to use a term now discredited because considered politically incorrect in demeaning previous cultures that lacked the Renaissance's advantages – the modern world was painfully in labour, and soon to be triumphantly delivered. Music as a science of number then merged into a science of mind and understanding in the modern sense; or at least the new science became a means whereby supernatural elements in human experience might seem to be under man's conscious control. In the treatises of Ficino, Agrippa, and Zarlino the equilibrium between magic and mind, spiritual understanding and intellectual comprehension, intuitive improvization and literate harmonic and tonal proportion is exact: all musical intervals have precise relationships to our human intellect and senses, and even to the autonomous functions of habit, so that the irrational and the rational elements of experience may and do co-operate. Half a century later Johannes Kepler had defined 'the metaphysics of harmony' with a profundity still unrivalled. Most later theorists of music, such as Kirchner and Werckmeister, owe much to Kepler in discussing the interlacing of music's human with its cosmological and astrological dimensions.

Significantly, it was at this time (broadly speaking the seventeenth century) that great composers most consorted with musical philosophers. Early in the century Dowland's Christianized Platonism found direct material expression through his Orphic lute; a century or more later Bach's audibly numerical theology was intimately indebted to the mathematical and tonal speculations of Werckmeister. A few composers, such as John Bull (1562–1628), an intrepid experimenter on keyboards, had close affinities with ambitious cosmologists such as the Rosicrucian Robert Fludd, whose non-sense is far from being a denial of experiential probity. Though Bull and Fludd may sometimes seem to us lunatic, they have a basic sanity that looks back to Dowland and Zarlino, forward to Bach and Kepler. Here music is simultaneously revelation and incarnation.

During the Enlightenment and the age of Romanticism the divine aspects of music became near allied to madness. True, Mozart as *wunderkind* would seem to have operated in instantaneous 'moments' of magic, whereby he became a musical humanist who had no need to make overt reference to the Music of the Spheres, except in so far as Tamino's flute and Papageno's bells are Masonic metamorphoses of it. Yet even for less enlightened early romanticists like Chateaubriand and Novalis the Music of the Spheres, if no longer part of an accredited faith, is still a relevant notion – though to attain its transcendence the stimulation of drink or drugs may be necessary, as it was, for that matter, for the ancient shamen. In this context, it is astonishing, and deeply moving, that the greatest of nineteenth-century composers, Beethoven, should speak, in his famous conversations with Bettina, of his *raptus* in terms exactly comparable with those of Kepler, using the scientific terminology of his day ('I am electrical by nature') in a manner we now know to be accurate, though by normal mortals it was in his day imperfectly understood. Beethoven is giving what we would call a psychological and physiological reinterpretation to ancient truths.

I suggested, in the chapter on Beethoven's *Missa Solemnis*, that the mathematical–psychological integration of the work's vast structure 'passeth understanding' in being 'out of this world', albeit apprehensible only within it. Beethoven, in discovering or even inventing a 'faith', remains unique; lesser men of the early nineteenth century, such as Schumann, went mad under the pressures of self-reliance, metamorphosing the Music of the Spheres into a remorsely reiterated tone (A) hammered through the brain, while seeking desperate alleviation in synthetically mathematical contrivances like cyphers and cryptograms. Wagner alone maintained, and justified, Beethovenian Inspiration, though his Schopenhauerian Will seems, relative to Beethoven's, curiously *self*-conscious in its rediscovery of the unconscious. This, if a limitation, is also a part of Wagner's status as 'the beginning of modern music'. Modern man, drunk on the pride of self-reliance and trusting nothing beyond the self, has sometimes threatened to end up as demonstrably idiotic.

The cosmology of twentieth-century and twenty-first-century music is still problematical, partly because 'new-age' philosophers such as Rudolf Steiner,

Pierre-Jean Jouve and George Gurdjieff tend to be obfuscatingly verbose in proportion to their mistrust of rationality. Still, we may still regard Stockhausen – as he certainly regards himself – as a musician–scientist–priest in the ancient succession and as a shaman preoccupied with 'music the Centre of Man'; electrophonics now bolster a 'new' religious music that is also as old as the hills. We no longer hear so much about Stockhausen as a Leader as we used to, either through performances of his music or from his own proselytizing; but he is certainly not discountable, and may still offer an answer to the Holy Fool John Cage, that musician–saint–scientist–priest of the New as distinct from the Old World, whose notorious 'silent piece' (called 4′ 33″ because that's how long it lasts) fulfils the kabbalistic prognosis that the ultimate end of music is silence. The philosophical backcloth to Cage's piece is far from nonsensical, the point being that in the unexpected silence we may all create our own music from the random sounds we randomly hear. If this is an ultimate fulfilment of democracy, it is also 'the end of music as we have known it': for most of us a consummation on the whole to be deplored, rather than devoutly to be wished.

So I hang on to that 'taste for the infinite' that the Finnish composer Einojuhani Rautavaara (born in 1928) says he inherited from his ambivalent culture – 'a crossing of the Hellene with Moses'. This central if dual evolution was tinged with 'archprotestant Lutheran pietism, somewhat grey and black with not much colour', though bleakness was countered by momentary glimpses of the numinous such as almost all children experience. His series of works based on angel-figures as mantras culminated in the Seventh Symphony of 1994, which, entitled 'Angel of Light', is a four-movement symphony recalling the 'pure water' of the later symphonic Sibelius, irradiated with modal light reflected from angelic wings! Perhaps we all carry memories of the numinous from our however distant childhoods, and so might say, with Rautavaara, that, although not men of faith, we are teased with that 'taste for the infinite'. This may be true of the majority of people today, even those living in heavily industrialized technocracies. This is why 'religious music' is likely to remain our aural bread and wine: whether it be a Gregorian chant which is the rudimentary language of Christian prayer; or a Mass of Byrd which is a humanized (and harmonized) ritual; or Bach's Mass in B minor, which both abstractly *and* operatically *enacts* an incarnation; or Beethoven's *Missa Solemnis* which confronts the unknowable in anxious pride or angry exultation; or Stravinsky's *Symphony of Psalms* which transforms art back into rite; or Copland's Emily Dickinson songs that tell us that a plain man in New York City may still discover a Taste for the Infinite in Old New England. Though paradox cannot be evaded, it is life-enhancing.

York, England: 1 December 2000

310

Index